Kankanaey
A Role and Reference Grammar Analysis

SIL International®

Publications in Linguistics
152

Publications in Linguistics are published by SIL International®. The series is a venue for works covering a broad range of topics in linguistics, especially the analytical treatment of minority languages from all parts of the world. While most volumes are authored by members of SIL, suitable works by others will also form part of the series.

Series Editors

Mike Cahill

Volume Editor

Mary Huttar

Production Staff

Bonnie Brown, Managing Editor
Lois Gourley, Composition Supervisor
Judy Benjamin, Compositor
Barbara Alber, Cover Design

Kankanaey
A Role and Reference Grammar Analysis

Janet L. Allen

SIL International®
Dallas, Texas

© 2014 by SIL International®
Library of Congress Catalog No: 2014939156
ISBN: 978-1-55671-296-8
ISSN: 1040-0850

Printed in the United States of America

All rights reserved.

No part of this publication may be reproduced, stored in a retrieval system, or transmitted in any form or by any means—electronic, mechanical, photocopy, recording, or otherwise—without the express permission of SIL International®. However, short passages, generally understood to be within the limits of fair use, may be quoted without permission.

Copies of this and other publications of SIL International® may be obtained from

SIL International Publications
7500 W. Camp Wisdom Road
Dallas, TX 75236-5629

Voice: 972-708-7404
Fax: 972-708-7363
publications_intl@sil.org
www.sil.org/resources/publications

Contents

Acknowledgements ix
List of Figures xi
List of Tables xv
Maps xvii
Preface xxi
Abbreviations xxiii

1 Introduction to Kankanaey and to Role and Reference Grammar 1
   1.1 The Kankanaey language in its context 1
      1.1.1 Austronesian and Philippine-type languages 2
      1.1.2 Tagalog, a meso-Philippine language 7
      1.1.3 Iloko, a northern Philippine Cordilleran language 10
      1.1.4 Other Cordilleran languages 13
      1.1.5 Conventions used in this book 14
   1.2 Role and Reference Grammar—a practical model 15
      1.2.1 Introduction 15
      1.2.2 Constituent projections 16
      1.2.3 Semantic structure 20
      1.2.4 Operator projection 23
      1.2.5 Information structure 25
   1.3 Conclusion 26

2 The Lexicon and Predicate Formation 29
   2.1 The Kankanaey lexicon 29

2.1.1 Roots 29
2.1.2 Word-building processes 33
2.2 Predicate formation.. 36
2.2.1 *Aktionsart* logical structures 37
2.2.2 Tests for *Aktionsart* classes 38
2.2.3 Identificational and attribute state predicates 41
2.2.4 Other state predicates 43
2.2.5 Process predicates 48
2.2.6 Achievement and accomplishment predicates 49
2.2.7 Activity predicates 53
2.2.8 Semelfactive predicates 61
2.2.9 Active accomplishment predicates 62
2.2.10 Causative predicates 65
2.3 Derived predicates 68
2.3.1 Potential predicates 68
2.3.2 Predicates with temporal immediacy 71
2.3.3 Passive states with *ma-* 72
2.3.4 Derived predicates with *i-* and *i...an* 74
2.3.5 Derived activity predicates with *maki-* 76
2.3.6 Derived causative predicates with *pa-* 76
2.3.7 Predicates with the possession root *oka* 81
2.3.8 Class roots with predicating affixes—argument incorporation . 81
2.4 Predicates built with numbers 83
2.4.1 Predicating affixation 83
2.4.2 Unique affixation 85
2.4.3 Glottal infix with numbers 86
2.5 Existential predicates 87
2.6 Conclusion 88

3 Reference Phrases 91
3.1 Reference Phrase structure 92
3.1.1 Reference Phrase markers 92
3.1.2 Reference Phrase nucleus 96
3.1.3 Arguments of the Reference Phrase nucleus 103
3.1.4 Peripheries in the Reference Phrase 106
3.2 Operators in the Reference Phrase 110
3.2.1 Reference Phrase operators 112
3.2.2 Core$_R$ operators 116
3.2.3 Nuclear$_R$ operator: nominal aspect 120
3.3 Complex Reference Phrase constructions 122
3.3.1 Phrasal juncture 122
3.3.2 Nuclear or core juncture 124

Contents

- 3.4 Affixed roots in the Reference Phrase nucleus 126
  - 3.4.1 Roots with nominalizing affixation 126
  - 3.4.2 Existentials in the nucleus of a reference expression 128
  - 3.4.3 Roots with predicating affixation 129
- 3.5 Reference Phrase as predicate 132
- 3.6 The anaphor *siya* 134

4 Simple Clauses 139
- 4.1 Simple clause structure 139
  - 4.1.1 The nucleus 140
  - 4.1.2 Core arguments 141
  - 4.1.3 Non-verbal predicates in the clause nucleus 149
  - 4.1.4 Peripheries in the clause 156
  - 4.1.5 A pre-core slot? 165
  - 4.1.6 Clitic pronoun displacement 167
- 4.2 Modifiers in the clause 169
  - 4.2.1 Nuclear operators 171
  - 4.2.2 Core-level operators 184
  - 4.2.3 Clause-level operators 194
  - 4.2.4 Other modification 199

5 Complex Clauses and Sentences 209
- 5.1 Clausal juncture in the sentence 210
- 5.2 Detached positions 212
  - 5.2.1 Left-detached position 213
  - 5.2.2 Right-detached position 222
- 5.3 Clause peripheries 223
  - 5.3.1 Clauses that modify in the right clause periphery 224
  - 5.3.2 Clarifying restatement clauses 227
- 5.4 Complex clauses 228
  - 5.4.1 Non-subordinate core junctures 229
  - 5.4.2 Core subordination 235
  - 5.4.3 Quotation complement subordination 236
  - 5.4.4 Other clausal complements 239
- 5.5 The sentence complex 244
  - 5.5.1 Reasoning sequences 245
  - 5.5.2 Action sequences 247
- 5.6 Relative clauses 250

6 Privileged Syntactic Arguments 255
- 6.1 The Privileged Syntactic Argument of the clause 255
  - 6.1.1 Assigning macrorole status and the Privileged Syntactic Argument of the clause 256

6.1.2 Privileged Syntactic Argument case coding 257
  6.1.3 Ordering in basic clauses 259
  6.1.4 Privileged Syntactic Argument indexing on the predicate 261
 6.2 Privileged Syntactic Arguments of other constructions 294
  6.2.1 Control of reflexive antecedence 294
  6.2.2 Pivot with left-displaced pronominal arguments 295
  6.2.3 Controller and pivot interpretation in core junctures 296
  6.2.4 Pivot in nominalization 299
  6.2.5 Pivot interpretation in relativization 305
  6.2.6 Summary of Privileged Syntactic Argument coding and
         behaviors in Kankanaey 306
 6.3 Non-Privileged Syntactic Argument functions 308
  6.3.1 Co-reference across clause boundaries 308
  6.3.2 Flagging non-Privileged Syntactic Argument arguments
         in a clause 310
 6.4 Conclusion 313

7 Information Structure 315
 7.1 Information structure 315
  7.1.1 Morphosyntactic variables in marking information 316
  7.1.2 Clauses with no focus domain 317
 7.2 New information—the focus domain 319
  7.2.1 Clause focus 320
  7.2.2 Predicate focus 321
  7.2.3 Narrow focus 326
 7.3 Outside the focus domain 335
  7.3.1 Detached Reference Phrases with basic clauses 336
  7.3.2 Detached Reference Phrases with equative clauses 339
 7.4 Conclusion 341

8 Conclusion 345

Appendix A Phonology and Morphophonology of Kankanaey 347

Appendix B Reference Phrase Markers, Pronouns, and Affixes 365

Appendix C Sample Kankanaey Texts 371

References 387

Index 397

Acknowledgements

I am deeply grateful to:
 - Dr. Robert D. Van Valin, Jr. for his unflagging encouragement of my endeavors in applying RRG to the analysis of the Kankanaey language that has fascinated me for the past thirty-seven years. His insightful comments and suggestions have informed this work from its beginning.
 - my colleagues and administrators at GIAL, who have supported my efforts in every way.
 - my life partner, Lawrence Allen, who has been my cheerleader, back-up and consultant for every step. Without his wholehearted support this project could never have been started or finished. As my style editor he patiently figured out what I was trying to say and helped me make it readable.
 - my editor, Mary Huttar.
 - my Christian friends, who have specifically prayed for me and encouraged me in this endeavor.
 - our many friends for whom Kankanaey is their mother tongue, as much a part of their lives as breathing. They have allowed me to share their lives and language, and it is our interactions that form the basis for this work. They have authored, transcribed, or edited the texts from which the examples in this book are taken. These include: Betty Alilao, Linda Alumno, Jovita Atayoc, Juanito Basalong, Atayoc Bay-an, Bernard Bugsit, Abdon Butag, Bilia Cayad-an, Martha Cayad-an, Esther Danio, Albert Donato, Suelio Fianza, Robert Gallaw, Rafael Guerzon, Lydia Langdeo, Benjamin Lasegan, James Leganio, Sexta Menci, Robert Mensi, Adeline Molitas, Espirita Monte, Hencio Monte, John Pacito, Catalino Pasking, James Palangyos, Laureen Sabado Powell,

Esther Tatpiec, Julio Tatpiec, Adela Wance, Emilio Wance, Pancho Wance, and Rosa Wance.

I retain full responsibility for all technical inconsistencies, misunderstandings, errors in expression and ignorance of existing work or further data.

List of Figures

Figure 1.1 Constituent projection (basic) 16
Figure 1.2 Core constituents 17
Figure 1.3 Clause constituents 17
Figure 1.4 Sentence complex and sentence constituents 18
Figure 1.5 Kankanaey clause constituent projection example 19
Figure 1.6 Kankanaey RP constituent structure example 20
Figure 1.7 Kankanaey predicate logical structure with macroroles
  and PSA assigned.. 23
Figure 1.8 Kankanaey clause with operator projection 24
Figure 1.9 Kankanaey example with information structure
  projection 25
Figure 1.10 Constituent and information structure narrow-focus
  example 26
Figure 3.1 Constituent projection of a Kankanaey RP 92
Figure 3.2 Kankanaey RP with direct argument 104
Figure 3.3 Pronominal RP with core arguments...................................... 105
Figure 3.4 Kankanaey RP structure with operator projection................... 111
Figure 3.5 Example of RP constituent and operator projections.............. 116
Figure 3.6 Kankanaey RP constituent projection with affixed-
  root nucleus.. 131
Figure 3.7 Kankanaey RPs: another constituent projection with
  affixed-root nucleus... 132
Figure 4.1 Components of the layered structure of the clause.................. 139
Figure 4.2 Kankanaey clause structure constituent projection 140
Figure 4.3 Clause with class-word predicate 149

List of Figures

Figure 4.4 Focal equative clause 150
Figure 4.5 Existential clause with peripheral modifier 162
Figure 4.6 Kankanaey clause structure constituent projection #2 169
Figure 4.7 Constituent and operator projections for Kankanaey 170
Figure 4.8 Aspect, modality, and negation operators in a Kankanaey clause 194
Figure 4.9 Clause with epistemic modality operator 196
Figure 5.1 Kankanaey sentence display 209
Figure 5.2 Pre-core slot in a subordinate clause 226
Figure 5.3 Direct quotation sentence 237
Figure 5.4 Indirect quotation sentence 239
Figure 5.5 Recursive clausal complements 243
Figure 6.1 Actor-Undergoer hierarchy and assignment principles 256
Figure 6.2 Macrorole assignment and affixation with a state predicate 262
Figure 6.3 Macrorole assignment and affix indexing for two Actor roles 264
Figure 6.4 Macrorole assignment and affix linking with a one-macrorole activity predicate 266
Figure 6.5 Macrorole assignment and affix linking with a two-argument state predicate 268
Figure 6.6 Macrorole assignment and affix linking with a perception-state predicate 269
Figure 6.7 Macrorole assignment and affixation with a causative option 270
Figure 6.8 Macrorole status and affixation with no PATIENT in the Logical Structure 271
Figure 6.9 Macrorole assignment and affixation with a three-place predicate of transfer 273
Figure 6.10 Macrorole assignment and affixation with self-affecting movement 274
Figure 6.11 Macrorole assignment and applicative affixation 275
Figure 6.12 Macroroles and affixation with overt causative prefix 276
Figure 6.13 Macrorole assignment and *kaCV*-indexing for state-causing predicates 280
Figure 6.14 Reciprocal macrorole assignment and indexing 280
Figure 6.15 Macrorole assignment and affixation related to the Lexical Content Hierarchy 286
Figure 7.1 Clause structure with basic functions 316
Figure 7.2 Kankanaey sentence with potential and one actual focus domain 320

Figure 7.3 Equative clause structure in Kankanaey with focus domains 327
Figure 7.4 Kankanaey clause structure with focal RP in post-core slot 334
Figure 7.5 Recursive left-detachment 341

List of Tables

Table 1.1 Iloko and Kankanaey pronoun patterns 11
Table 1.2 Lexical representations for *Aktionsart* classes 21
Table 1.3 The Actor-Undergoer hierarchy 22
Table 1.4 Operators in the layered structure of the clause 24
Table 2.1 Predicate types in Kankanaey 37
Table 2.2 Kankanaey tests for *Aktionsart* classes 38
Table 2.3 Basic predicating affixes in Kankanaey perfective aspect 41
Table 2.4 Kankanaey existential forms 87
Table 3.1 Kankanaey common RMs 93
Table 3.2 Kankanaey proper RMs 94
Table 3.3 Kankanaey demonstrative pronouns as RPs 97
Table 3.4 Demonstrative-related RP markers 98
Table 3.5 Kankanaey personal pronouns 99
Table 3.6 Operators in the layered structure of the RP 111
Table 3.7 Kankanaey demonstrative modifiers 112
Table 3.8 Kankanaey deictic RP markers with corresponding demonstrative pronouns 114
Table 3.9 Some nominalizing affixes in Kankanaey 126
Table 3.10 Personal pronouns (class III) as predicates 133
Table 3.11 Demonstrative pronouns as predicates and oblique phrases 134
Table 4.1 Kankanaey common RP markers 142
Table 4.2 Kankanaey proper RP markers 143
Table 4.3 Kankanaey demonstrative pronouns as direct arguments 144
Table 4.4 Kankanaey personal pronouns 145

Table 4.5 Oblique argument markers and pronouns 146
Table 4.6 Kankanaey existentials.. 151
Table 4.7 Layers of the clause with operators 170
Table 4.8 Evidential particles 198
Table 4.9 Timing and extent adverbs 200
Table 4.10 Kankanaey confidence particles.. 205
Table 4.11 Kankanaey request particles 206
Table 4.12 Kankanaey surprise particles 206
Table 4.13 Kankanaey exclamations... 206
Table 4.14 Kankanaey interactive particles... 207
Table 4.15 Miscellaneous particles.. 207
Table 5.1 Reasons and results... 227
Table 6.1 Personal pronoun patterns.. 258
Table 6.2 Actor-indexing affixation... 263
Table 6.3 Undergoer-indexing affixation.. 267
Table 6.4 Personal pronoun displacement patterns............................... 296
Table 6.5 PSA properties for Kankanaey constructions 307

Maps

Map 1. The location of the Philippines in Southeast Asia.

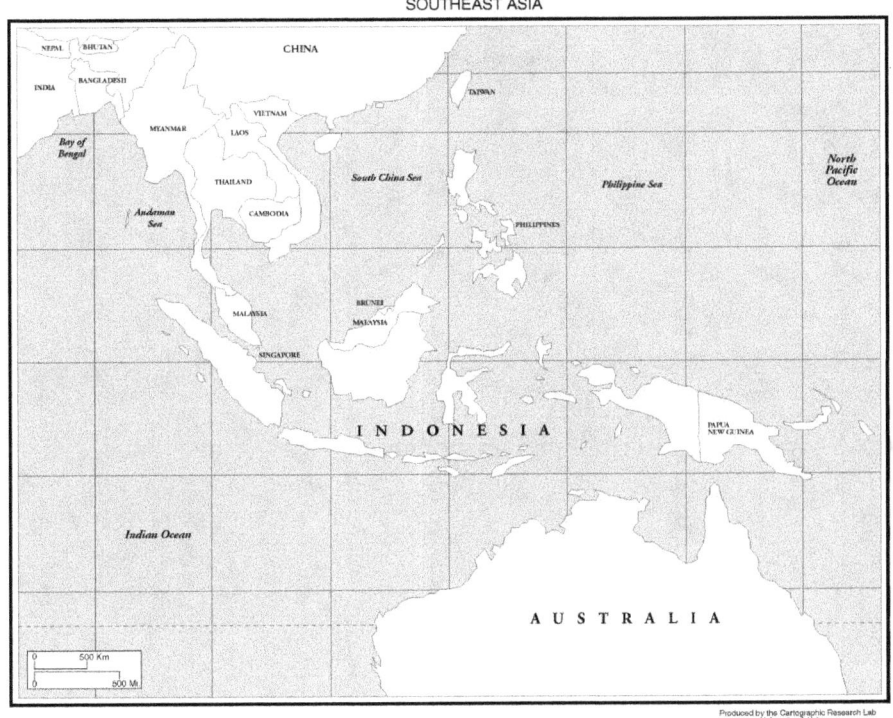

http://alabamamaps.ua.edu/contemporarymaps/world/asia/seasia2.jpg

Map 2. Luzon, the northern island of the Philippines, with the mountains of the Cordillera visible in the northern half of the island.

http://www.sil.org/asia/philippines/philippine_language_map.html

Maps xix

Map 3. Language map of northern Luzon indicates the boundaries of the languages spoken there. Kankanaey is spoken in language area 23 at lower left side. Tagalog is spoken in area 52 around Manila, and Iloko is spoken in area 2 surrounding the Cordilleran region. Central Bontok is in area 67 in the inset and Tuwali Ifugao in area 27.

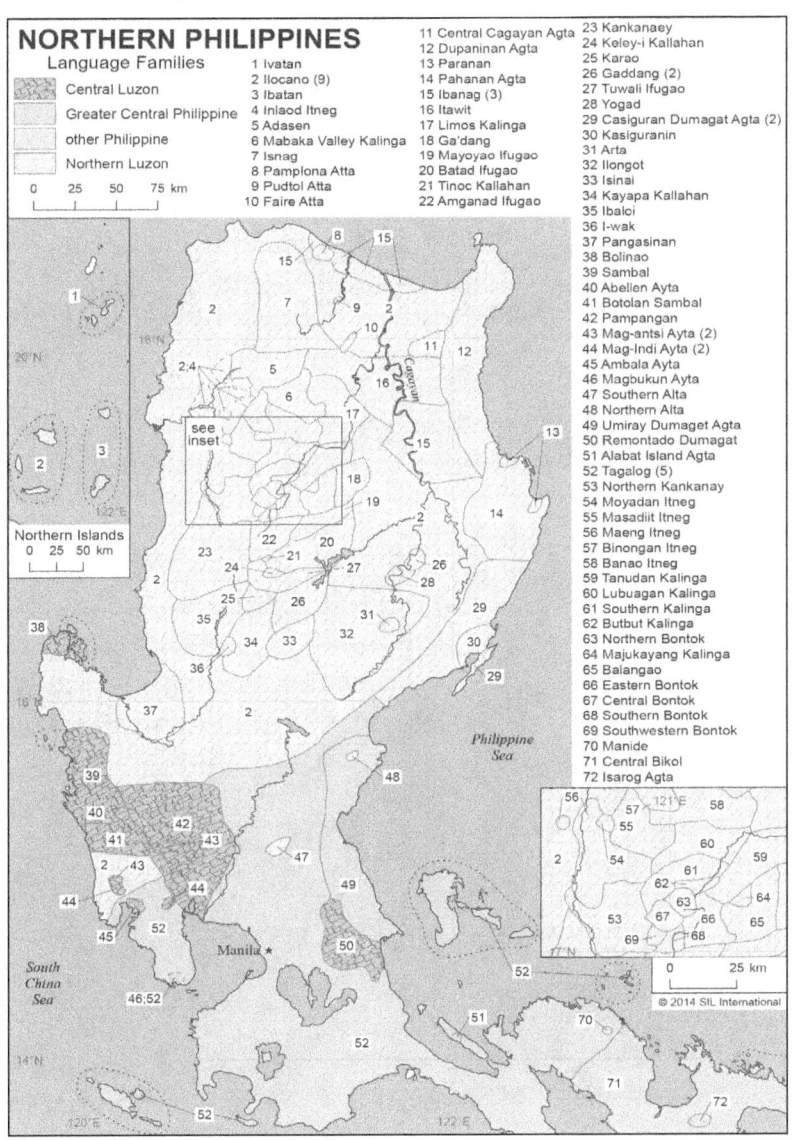

http://www.ethnologue.com

Kankanaey – land and people

Preface

This book presents Kankanaey, a language of the Philippines, in its linguistic setting. Chapter 1 gives an overview of the theoretical model used in this analysis, Role and Reference Grammar, as presented in Van Valin and LaPolla (1997) and Van Valin (2005). Chapter 2 begins the description of the Kankanaey language by examining the lexicon and predicate formation. Chapters 3 and 4 present reference phrases and simple clauses. Chapter 5 explores the details of complex constructions. Chapter 6 puts together the evidence for grammatical relations, while chapter 7 lays out the resources of this language to express information flow in context.

The research behind this study was carried out by the author and her husband, Lawrence Allen, under the auspices of SIL Philippines from 1975 to the present, but primarily up to 1997 in intermittent but extended residence in the municipalities of Kibungan, Atok and Kapangan in Benguet Province.

A diverse corpus of written texts and transcribed oral texts authored by Kankanaey speakers formed the data base from which the examples were drawn. This corpus included oral tradition narratives, poetry, extemporaneous lyrics, personal-experience and historical narratives, recipes and explanatory texts, formal hortatory discourses, and personal letters. Personal details such as names of people and places have been changed in examples quoted in this work; gender and plurality were at times also changed to obscure any personal reference. A 5000-root Kankanaey-English dictionary with many spontaneously-generated example sentences was also consulted for corroboration of the description and analysis. Some examples, particularly in the earlier chapters, were simplified from the original texts. A few examples came from texts translated from English to Kankanaey by a Kankanaey speaker, but they were not used as the basis for analysis unless other original material also evidenced the construction in question. Because we lived in three different dialect areas of the Kankanaey-speaking region, some dialect differences in syntax were observed, but this sketch reflects most closely the dialect spoken in Kibungan, Benguet, home of most of the native authors.

Abbreviations

-	prefix or suffix
<...>	infix
>	goes with following morpheme
<	goes with earlier discontinuous morpheme
=	enclitic morpheme
◊	potentiality
1	first person/near or in relation to speaker
1 + 2	first and second person
2	second person/near or in relation to hearer
3	third person/far from speaker and hearer
4	impersonal
I, II, III, IV, V	class
ABIL	abilitative
ACT	actor macrorole index
ADJ	adjective
ANTI	antipassive
ARG(S)	argument(s)
ASSOC	associate index
ATT	attributant index
B	bound
BRMi	indefinite bound reference phrase marker
c	CAUSEE role
C	(subscript) core
C	consonant
CAUS	causative

CHANGE	changed-state operator/index
CLM	clause-linkage marker
COLL	collective
COMP	comparative
d	definite (noun phrase marker)
d	DIRECTIONAL role (verb marker)
DEM	demonstrative pronoun
DRM	demonstrative-related RM
DISP	displacement marker
DUR	durative aspect
EVID	evidential particle
EXCL	exclamation
EXIS	existential
FUT	future particle
HSY	hearsay evidential particle
i	indefinite
IMM	precipitate-actor index
INGR	ingressive
INTS	intensive aspect
IRR	irrealis particle
l	LOCUS role
LDP	left-detached position
LH	lexical (content) hierarchy
LK	linker
LOC	locative marker or demonstrative
LS	logical structure
m	middle
N	(subscript) nuclear
NEG	negative
NEGEXIS	negative existential
NOM	nominalizer, nominal
NUC	nucleus
O	oblique
ORMd	definite oblique reference phrase marker
P	perfective aspect
p, pl	plural
PART	particle
PRED	predicate
PRM	personal reference phrase marker
PRO	pronoun
PROC	process
PROG	progressive aspect

Abbreviations

PSA	privileged syntactic argument
Q	question marker
QT	quote-marker
R	(subscript) reference
RDP	right-detached position
RECENT	recent
RECIP	reciprocal
REF	referential word
RelCl	relative clause
RM	reference phrase marker
RP	reference phrase
RRG	Role and Reference Grammar
S	single argument
s	singular
s	state
SEML	semelfactive
SR	semantic representation
T	transitive
t	THEME role
Th	non-PSA THEME role
U, UND	undergoer macrorole index
UNIT	reciprocal unit
V	vowel
VOC	vocative particle
VVLP	Van Valin and LaPolla (1997)

1

Introduction to Kankanaey and to Role and Reference Grammar

1.1 The Kankanaey language in its context

Kankanaey[1] (ISO: kne) is spoken by some 150,000 people living in the provinces of Benguet, Nueva Vizcaya, Ilocos Sur, La Union, and Mountain Province on the island of Luzon, the Philippines. *Ethnologue* (Lewis 2009) classifies Kankanaey as Austronesian, Malayo-Polynesian, Northern Philippine, Northern Luzon, South-Central Cordilleran, Central Cordilleran, Nuclear Cordilleran, Bontok-Kankanay. Kankanaey is the southernmost of the Nuclear Cordilleran languages, and its range abuts the large Iloko-speaking coastal plain on the west. South and southeast is the Ibaloi language, of the Southern Cordilleran group. To the east the Kankanaey area shares a boundary with Tuwali Ifugao and Amganad Ifugao, and to the north are the Northern Kankanay and Central Bontok languages. See maps 2 and 3 of the Austronesian language family region and a language map of the Cordilleran region of the Philippines.

---

[1] "Kankanaey" is pronounced [kɜnkɜˈnaʔɨj].

Typological studies of Austronesian languages, notably Himmelmann (2005a), as well as more specific studies and surveys of Philippine languages, such as Reid (1974, 2002) and Reid and Liao (2004), have provided a wealth of information with which to compare and contrast the Kankanaey data. This section will first highlight some of the general characteristics of Austronesian languages, and show how these characteristics are exemplified in typical Philippine languages, including Kankanaey. Well-documented languages in the wider area include Bahasa Indonesia in the neighboring country to the south, Cebuano in the central Philippines, and Sama in the southern Philippines. The focus will then narrow to compare the features of Kankanaey with Tagalog, which has long been studied as representative of Philippine-type languages, and with Iloko. As the lingua franca of the Cordillera, Iloko has exerted a significant influence on other languages in the area. Finally, Kankanaey will be compared to two languages with which it is closely related, Bontok to the north and Tuwali Ifugao to the east.

Very little has been published on the Kankanaey language. This author has written five short studies on various aspects of the language, and Lawrence Allen has published three phonological studies as well as editing and contributing to many publications in the Kankanaey language itself. Patterson (2007) reanalyzes the morphophonemics of reduplication in Kankanaey.

1.1.1 Austronesian and Philippine-type languages

Austronesian is one of the largest language families in the world. *Ethnologue* (Lewis 2009) lists 1257 languages in that category. In the Austronesian family, the Malayo Polynesian group contains a further subgroup of 179 Philippine languages, of which fifty-two are in northern Luzon and eight share the Nuclear Cordilleran grouping with Kankanaey. Among others, Blust (1999) and Malcolm Ross (2002:17–20) have used various criteria, both phonological and lexical, to trace the history of these languages and to subdivide Austronesian into typological groups, without perfect consensus. Himmelmann (2005a:111) suggests geographical criteria to group the Austronesian languages, defining Western Austronesian as non-Oceanic Austronesian languages, and Philippine languages as those in the Republic of the Philippines. Adelaar (2005) gives a historical account and perspective with new groupings. Not surprisingly, with these differing approaches, the category "Philippine" or "Philippine-type" is not always clearly defined, nor is Northern Philippine a subgroup at the same level in all taxonomies.

1.1.1.1 Morphology

This study touches on the morphophonemics of Kankanaey only when necessary to separate morphemes in order to understand examples. The complex morphophonemics are very typical of Philippine-type languages. For example, its homorganic nasal, which is realized as a velar nasal before vowels but assimilates in various ways before consonants, is common throughout the Austronesian family (Himmelmann 2005a:118). Another widespread morpheme is the infix <um> (<om> in the Kankanaey orthography). The form is shared, but the functions in Kankanaey cover a different set than in many other languages.

Reduplication is a morphological process that is productive in all Western Austronesian languages (Himmelmann 2005a:121). Kankanaey uses a subset of all the types of reduplication that are possible, mostly to express aspectual concepts. Many Kankanaey roots have repeated syllables, probably fossilized forms of historical root formation. See appendix A for discussion of Kankanaey morphophonology.

1.1.1.2 Lexicon

Many Austronesian languages tend to have lexical bases that are underdetermined as to word class (Himmelmann 2005a:128). The Kankanaey lexicon is made up of roots which may be used in their base form or with affixation. The word class is determined by the affixation and the function of the word in a clause, either to predicate or to refer. Himmelmann refers to this type of lexicon as having morphologically and syntactically subcategorized roots.

Reid (2002) gives a comprehensive listing of the wide variety of labels that have been used for Philippine-language nominal markers. In this study they are labeled "Reference Phrase Markers." Reid and Liao (2004) note that Bontok has three distinct "case" markers for nominal phrases; Iloko to the west of the Kankanaey has only two, while Kabayan Inibaloi, abutting the Kankanaey area to the south and east, has five.

Kankanaey does not have many prepositions, but the oblique marker *si* can often be translated into English with a preposition, based on the semantics of the nuclear word. This oblique marker precedes adjuncts and is an obligatory concomitant of what few prepositions there are.

Many Austronesian languages have more than one negator. Kambera of eastern Indonesia (Klamer 2005:723), for example, has five forms, including a 'not yet' negator. Kankanaey has two simple negators, one that modifies states, nominals and whole propositions, and the other that modifies dynamic predicates. Like Kambera, it also has a 'not yet' negator.

Discourse particles, "small, uninflected words that are only loosely integrated into the sentence structure" (Fischer 2006:4), expressing speaker attitude toward the truth or relevance of an utterance, are common in Indonesian (Ewing 2005:254) and many Philippine languages, including Kankanaey.

1.1.1.3 Predicates

Linguists working in the Philippines have yet to agree on how to describe and characterize the complex systems of predicate formation in the over one hundred languages of the country. Reid and Liao (2004) in their survey found that certain predicating affixes have common forms throughout the Philippines. Thus, they posit three typical Actor-referencing affixes: MAG-, -UM-, and MANG-. Dynamic Undergoer-referencing affixes are typically similar to -EN, -AN, I-, and I...AN. Prefixes typically similar to MA- mark Statives. Other affixes may be used for other types of predicates in the different languages, but these eight are nearly universal in the Philippine languages surveyed, and have close counterparts in Kankanaey.

Himmelmann (2005a:112ff.) has proposed a category that he calls "symmetrical voice languages" as a subset of Austronesian languages that includes Philippine-type languages. Not all of the characteristics that he lists fit the Kankanaey data. He describes symmetrical voices as independent from each other (one not derived from another) with a syntactically equivalent Actor voice and Undergoer voice. The alternative analysis, in Himmelmann's view, is an ergative analysis in which the Actor-voice is analyzed as an antipassive (Himmelmann 2002:14). Neither analysis[2] fits

---

[2] It is beyond the scope of this study to present arguments against certain analyses. Definitions of key terms such as "syntactic transitivity" would clarify some of

1.1 The Kankanaey language in its context

the Kankanaey data satisfactorily. Himmelmann's defining features for Philippine-type languages (2005a:113) do include Kankanaey characteristics—at least two different Undergoer voices, clitic phrase markers, and pronominal second-position clitics. Kankanaey, like many other languages in the area, also shows split-intransitivity based on semantic differences and affixation differences between intransitive predicates that index an Actor vs. an Undergoer.

Wolff (2002:439) suggests that verbs in Philippine-type languages have at least four different possible role-indexations: actor, patient, local, and some other (such as instrumental, benefactive, etc.) An analysis proposed by Walter Spitz (2001) for Hiligaynon names ten voices, constrained by event phase—inception for Actor voices, exhaustion for Undergoer. The analysis of Kankanaey proposed in this volume is based on the concept that Actor and Undergoer are best understood as "macroroles"; in Kankanaey an Undergoer voice is the default expression of verbs with both Actor and Undergoer roles. Within the Actor and Undergoer voices there are thematic-role indexing variations.

Givón (1994:8–9) notes that a major component of transitivity is the relative topicality of the Actor and Patient in a semantic event; an "inverse" voice may encode a P argument that is more highly topical than the A argument. Some Philippine linguists have found an "inverse" pattern in argument ordering, for example, in Cebuano (Payne 1994) and Obo Manobo (Brainard and VanderMolen 2006). Kankanaey handles the situation of a more-topical patient by dropping the agent of dynamic Undergoer voices or by using the passive state voice.

Existentials in many Western Austronesian languages are clearly differentiated from verbs; in Kankanaey the existentials generally occur unaffixed, but may also take some predicating affixation. Many other languages have a locative predicate, such as the Tagalog *nasa* 'is in/at'; in Kankanaey the existential serves as the predicate with locative phrases.

Talmy (1991, 2000) suggests a division between what he calls verb-framed languages and satellite-framed languages. Verb-framing involves encoding the path or trajectory of motion within the predicate rather than

---

the apparent contradictions. This analysis of Kankanaey uses the Role and Reference Grammar model, with its concept of a clause core that holds both direct and oblique arguments. Syntactically, transitive clauses have two direct arguments, while intransitive clauses have only one.

expressing it in a "satellite" expression. Huang and Tanangkingsing (2005) in their study of motion verbs found that in the six Western Austronesian languages they studied, greater attention is typically given to path rather than manner information in motion events. Motion roots exhibit very high path salience in Kankanaey as well, eliminating the need for specific prepositions. An oblique referent is most often sufficient to identify the direction or location of motion.

1.1.1.4 Grammatical relations

An ergative pattern of noun phrase (NP) distribution is "very rare" in Austronesian languages, according to Himmelman (2005a:158). Kankanaey reference phrases have a clearly ergative pattern of distribution, in that the single argument of an intransitive clause takes the same case marking as the Undergoer argument in a transitive clause. An ergative analysis of NP distribution presupposes that core arguments are clearly distinguished from obliques, which is indeed the case in Kankanaey. Reference phrase markers and pronouns have distinct oblique forms. An ergative analysis also suggests that a transitive absolutive Actor would be a marked construction, which is also the case in Kankanaey, with its intransitive Actor voice and marked Antipassive voice.

In many western Austronesian languages, core (clitic) pronouns are displaced to a clause-second position, sometimes called the *Wackernagel*[3] position. Kankanaey clitic pronouns follow this rule, and often take a different case form in their displaced position. Other Austronesian languages, such as Makassar in south Sulawesi (Jukes 2005:664), have a similar case-shifting phenomenon with displaced clitic pronouns.

Woollams (2005:541) finds "identificational" clauses in Karo Batak to have a subject-predicate order except when the first NP is clearly focal (as in *wh-* questions or with focal marker). Nias, related to the Batak languages of Sumatra, is also analyzed as having an NP in the predicate-initial position with a case-marked headless relative clause as its argument (Brown 2005:569). Zeitoun (2005) notes this same construction in Tsoa of Taiwan, considering the first NP to be the predicating constituent, and uses the term "nominal clauses" for the second NP. Indonesian (Ewing 2005:235) has a

---

[3] This phenomenon was first discussed by Jacob Wackernagel (1892).

cleft construction in which a headless relative clause serves as subject of a specific-nominal predicate. Kankanaey has an equative clause structure similar to these, although the labels used in Role and Reference Grammar are different.

The issue of "subjecthood" has been explored and debated in many Philippine-type languages, as summarized in Himmelmann (2005a:152–159). This study of Kankanaey does not look for a "subject." Instead it uses the RRG concept of a "privileged syntactic argument," which is defined by its properties for each separate construction.

1.1.2 Tagalog, a meso-Philippine language

Several linguists have offered analyses of Tagalog, a major language in the Philippines, including Foley and Van Valin (1984), Kroeger (1993), Halpern (1998) and Himmelman (2005b). Kankanaey shares many features with Tagalog, but differs in important ways as well.

1.1.2.1 Clitics

Clitic pronouns and clitic particles in Tagalog contrast with their Kankanaey counterparts in several ways. Tagalog, as well as other Philippine languages, moves pronouns in clusters, but Kankanaey is much more constrained in that only the transitive Actor or the single-argument pronouns are clitics and available for displacement. Tagalog clitic pronouns and particles show complex placement and ordering patterns while Kankanaey simply orders the single clitic pronoun before any clitic particles. Anderson (2008), using an Optimality Theory-based analysis, found that phonology, morphology and syntax all affect the clitics in Tagalog. Halpern (1998:105) proposed that verbal clitics are "associated with an ordered set of slots" defined by grammatical and phonological factors, noting that Tagalog orders monosyllabic pronouns before particles, which in turn precede bisyllabic pronouns, all following the clause-initial element. Another definition of clitic placement is suggested by Kroeger (1993:121), who notes that in Tagalog "clitics occur immediately after the first daughter of the smallest maximal projection which contains them." Kankanaey clitic pronouns are displaced from the predicate with which they are associated to the position immediately following clause-initial words such as negators and some conjunctions.

1.1.2.2 Negation

Himmelmann (2005a:140–141) notes that in Tagalog "there are no particles, negators or other kinds of grammatical markers which would clearly distinguish between a verbal and an equational clause type." By contrast, many Austronesian languages have a choice of negators (e.g., Malay, and Kimaragang Dusun, a language closely related in syntax and morphology to Tagalog (Kroeger 2005:397)). In both these languages the negator for predicates formed by adjectives and verbs is different from the negator used with NP predicates in equative clauses. In Kankanaey there are also two negators, but their distribution as noted above is defined by dynamic vs. non-dynamic predicates, clearly distinguishing between verbal and equative clause types.

1.1.2.3 Existential constructions

Examining the existential in Tagalog, Sabbagh (2009) found four distinct types. He analyzes the Tagalog existential as an impersonal clause with no subject. Kroeger (1993) also notes the lack of any nominative argument with existential predicates. Himmelmann (2005b), however, notes that a nominative phrase (*ang*-marked phrase or nominative pronoun) in an existential clause expresses a possessor. In contrast, Kankanaey existentials function as predicates, taking the same kind of single argument as intransitive predicates. Possession is expressed on the single argument of existentials as on any other phrase, i.e., with the genitive/ergative case.

1.1.2.4 Noun phrase construction

Many who have analyzed Tagalog include nominals without phrase markers as indefinite noun phrases (e.g., Sabbagh 2009, Kroeger 1993). Kankanaey distinguishes definite and indefinite reference by an indicator on the phrase markers (determiners). Kankanaey nominals without phrase markers function as predicates in Kankanaey.

1.1 The Kankanaey language in its context

The case-marking functions of Philippine noun phrase markers differ from language to language. In Tagalog, *ang* assigns nominative case to the "subject" or "privileged argument" of a clause. The marker *sa* is used to mark "dative case" (Kroeger 1993:13) for goals, recipients, locations, and definite objects; all other non-nominative arguments take *ng*. In contrast, Cebuano *sa* covers actors in Undergoer voice and undergoers in Actor voice (Himmelmann 2005a:144). Kankanaey reference phrase markers divide the roles differently—absolutive vs. ergative vs. oblique—and as noted above can specify definiteness on each marker.

1.1.2.5 Clause structure

Both Tagalog and Kankanaey have a default predicate-initial clause order. Direct arguments have a more free order in Tagalog than Kankanaey's rigid VSO order. Tagalog has an inverted SVO order, in which the initial S is followed by *ay*. Kankanaey does not have a similar construction, although both languages displace clitic pronouns to a pre-predicate position when there is a displacing element preceding the predicate.

Tagalog and Kankanaey share a similar equative construction, where two NPs with the same case marking (*ang* in Tagalog, *di(n)* in Kankanaey) are juxtaposed and interpreted to be coreferential. Himmelmann (2005b:356) analyzes the first NP as the predicate, the analysis taken in this study of Kankanaey as well. Kroeger (2009:819, 822–823) views the second NP as the predicating element, a headless relative clause in a pseudocleft construction, although there is no overt relative marker (present in headed relative clauses).

1.1.2.6 Complex constructions

Tagalog has been analyzed as having modal verbs (Kroeger 1993:68), or "pseudo verbs" (Schachter and Otanes 1972:262). These words do not have verbal marking, but they can take arguments. Kankanaey has equivalents to many of the Philippine-type pseudo verbs; they precede the clause core and take no predicate affixation. However, while argument pronouns do attach to them, they do not exhibit a predicate-argument relationship with the pronouns. Instead, Kankanaey "pseudo verbs" are analyzed by their grammatical function as modals or adverbials and by the level within the clause which they modify.

In linked clauses, both Tagalog and Kankanaey have restrictions on the affixation that may be used in the linked clause and the function of the gapped argument. Nominalized clauses are also common in both languages, but they are difficult to compare, being analyzed from varying theoretical presuppositions.

1.1.3 Iloko, a northern Philippine Cordilleran language

Iloko (Ilocano/Ilokano) is spoken by nearly seven million people (nine million by some sources) in the broad lowland areas of the northern Philippines (see map 3). Of the major languages of the Philippines, Iloko is the one most closely related to Kankanaey. A "pidginized form" (Lewis 2009) of Iloko is the trade language throughout the Luzon Cordillera, and is used by many Kankanaey speakers in their business and other contacts with the larger community. Some points of similarity and difference with Iloko are of interest.

1.1.3.1 Pronouns

Iloko personal pronouns are phonologically very similar to Kankanaey, and have three sets for the clause core, but not along the same functional lines as Kankanaey. Iloko has Actor/possessor pronouns, absolutive pronouns that cover S and U functions, and an independent set that serves predicatively (Rubino 2005:333, table 11.5). In Kankanaey there are Actor/possessor pronouns, absolutive pronouns that express the S relation, and independent predicative pronouns that also serve the absolutive U function. Table 1.1 compares the patterning of the personal pronouns in both languages, giving just one example in each group.

1.1 The Kankanaey language in its context

Table 1.1. Iloko and Kankanaey pronoun patterns

Person/number	Transitive Actor/ possessor	Single-Subject	Transitive Undergoer	Independent/ Predicative
ILOKO				
ERGATIVE:1s (and 1p, 2s, 2p, 3s)	=k(o)	=ak		siak
UNDIFFERENTIATED 1+2 (and 1+2p, 3p)	=ta			data
KANKANAEY				
DIFFERENTIATED:1s (and 1p, 2s, 2p)	=k(o)	=ak		sak?en
ACCUSATIVE: 1+2 (and 1+2p, 3p)	=ta			daita
ERGATIVE: 3s	=na	Ø/sisya		sisya

Iloko pronouns have some similarities in their split system to Kankanaey, in that the speaker and addressee pronouns take a more differentiated pattern (Iloko is ergative while Kankanaey is completely differentiated), but combinations of speaker and addressee and third person plural group together in taking another pattern (accusative in Kankanaey and undifferentiated in Iloko). The third person singular pronoun in both languages follows an ergative pattern.

Demonstrative pronouns in Iloko express a five-way range of visible and temporal distance, while Kankanaey has only three. Iloko and Kankanaey clitic pronouns are displaced to the *Wackernagel* (clause-second) position, but Kankanaey displays no agent neutralization, and less pronoun portmanteau than Iloko.

1.1.3.2 Noun phrases

Iloko noun phrase markers distinguish singular from plural, and proper from common; there is also a demonstrative-based marker that specifies definiteness. As case markers they differentiate only between core and oblique status, unlike Kankanaey markers that assign ergative and absolutive case, with separate oblique marking.

Iloko uses six reduplication patterns (Rubino 2005:329) to express various types of aspectual information in nominal and verbal morphology, only three of which are productive in Kankanaey, with somewhat overlapping functions.

Iloko has extensive nominalizing affixation, including complete sets for manner gerunds, instruments, and locatives that correlate to the predicating affixation. Kankanaey has a much smaller inventory of nominalization, but shares the feature of nominalizing an Actor with the *maN-* prefix.

1.1.3.3 Predicates

Predicate affixes in Iloko mirror the Kankanaey affixes almost exactly, with very similar distinctions based on the semantics of the absolutive argument. Actor and Undergoer voices are distinguished as well as "potentive"-mood variations (Rubino 2005:340), which in this book are analyzed for Kankanaey as passive voice affixation in Undergoer voice.

Iloko has two negators, *saan* for general negation and *di*, which is the preferred form with verbs (Rubino 2005:332). The distinction between stative and non-stative negation that Kankanaey exhibits is not as sharp in Iloko.

1.1.3.4 Clause

As outlined by Rubino (2005:331–332) Iloko clauses have the same canonical constituent order as Kankanaey:

VERB (+ERG) + ABS (+ adjunct)

Equational clauses are defined for Iloko as those that take a noun phrase or prepositional phrase as the predicate. Equational clauses with nominal-phrase predicates are used to contrast or identify referents, as in Kankanaey.

Existentials in both languages are used to express existence, location and possession. In Iloko, the argument of the existential is not case-marked, unlike Kankanaey. The negative existential is a single word, and takes a case-marked argument.

1.1.4 Other Cordilleran languages

The minority languages of the Philippines have been studied for many years. Numerous articles, dictionaries, and text collections have been published by linguists associated with SIL Philippines, the Linguistic Society of the Philippines and other organizations. The minority languages in the Kankanaey area have been classified as noted above; Kankanaey is included in the Nuclear Cordilleran group. Reid and Liao's (2004) overview of typical structures and processes in Philippine languages includes those in the Nuclear Cordilleran group. This group is comprised of Kankanaey, Bontok, Northern Kankanay, Finallig, Balangao, and four Ifugao languages, as noted on map 3. This analysis will be limited to just a few of the many parallels between Kankanaey, Bontok, and Tuwali Ifugao.

1.1.4.1 Bontok

Kankanaey shares a large percentage of its lexical inventory with Bontok to its north. Some phonological differences, for example, some fricatives where Kankanaey has plosives give a first impression of unintelligibility that is easily resolved in a short time of conversational interaction.

Kankanaey follows the Bontok pattern with a reference phrase marker that is bound when ergative and free-standing when absolutive. Furthermore, Kankanaey is similar to Bontok in using demonstrative-related markers. Kankanaey has a set of three (speaker-associated, addressee-associated, remote) where Bontok has but two. These demonstrative-related markers have a very weak deictic function.

Bontok allows independent pronouns to follow displaced clitic pronouns, like Tagalog. Kankanaey does not allow that pattern. In most syntactic patterns, though, Bontok and Kankanaey show themselves to be very closely related.

1.1.4.2 Tuwali Ifugao

Tuwali Ifugao, one of the Ifugao dialects in the Nuclear Cordilleran group, is spoken to the east of the Kankanaey area. Other than Reid's areal work (e.g., Reid 1974, Reid and Liao 2004), the main research on this language has been done by Richard and Lou Hohulin (See Hohulin 2012).

Like Bontok, Tuwali Ifugao (hereafter T. Ifugao) differs from Kankanaey phonologically, making mutual comprehension difficult at first. The lexicon is substantially different from Kankanaey as well, placing T. Ifugao further from Kankanaey than its northern neighbors like Bontok. The system of noun phrase markers is more complex in T. Ifugao than Kankanaey, although several forms are nearly homophonous.

Like Kankanaey, T. Ifugao has different negators for stative and non-stative predicates, and a separate negative-existential form. With verbs, T. Ifugao further differentiates negative past from negative non-past.

The basic predicating affixation of both Bontok and T. Ifugao follows Reid and Liao's prototypical list. Syntactic constructions show many similarities between Kankanaey and T. Ifugao such as the equative clause construction. Nominalization (topicalization in Hohulins' terms) is used in both languages for WH-questions and contrastive focus. Both languages share the special form for nominalized transitive agents *(maN-)* noted in section 1.1.3.2 regarding Iloko.

1.1.5 Conventions used in this book

Examples are presented with the dash (-) indicating morpheme breaks in both the Kankanaey (italics) and the gloss lines. The equal sign (=) indicates clitic elements. Chevrons <…> indicate an infix. The gloss of a discontinuous morpheme may have a single chevron pointing toward its other half, and the tilde ~ follows a reduplicative prefix. The period (.) indicates multiple-word morpheme glosses.

The symbol [ʔ] represents glottal stop following a consonant; glottal stop is also required intervocalically and word initial before a vowel but is not written unless necessary for a particular example. The digraph *ng* represents the velar nasal; the letter *e* represents a close central unrounded vowel. Morphophonemic processes distort some of the affixed words, especially segment deletion, vowel harmony and nasal assimilation. These are given a fuller display or the underlying vowel used when it is helpful.

Pronouns are identified by person, number, and class; demonstratives by proximity to person, and class. Affixes are tagged to reflect their indexing function, but may not be separately glossed when irrelevant to the example. Tables of affixes and pronoun classes are located when introduced, as well as in appendix B.

1.2 Role and Reference Grammar—a practical model

1.2.1 Introduction

To describe a language, one needs a framework within which to work. Describing a language in a theory-neutral manner is difficult and may lead to *ad hoc* definitions and labels. RRG has proven to be a very practical framework for the description of Kankanaey, and the author hopes by this work to demonstrate the usefulness of RRG as a tool for field linguists.

RRG looks at language structure from four perspectives—the surface forms, the underlying semantic structure, the modifying grammatical elements, and the pragmatic information structure—and provides mechanisms for discovering, describing and integrating them all.

The surface forms are the basis for the morphosyntactic representation. The constituents occur in their actual order in the "constituent projection" diagrams. Nodes in these tree diagrams identify levels of constituent grouping. A separate but similar constituent projection is used for noun phrase analysis.

The second perspective, the underlying semantic structure, provides a clear system of lexical decomposition. For predicates, this system is an *Aktionsart*-based method of representing the semantics of predicates with their arguments, proposed originally in Vendler (1967). The semantic representation is linked to the syntactic structure by means of an algorithm, or set of steps. The semantic roles of arguments are correlated with macroroles called Actor and Undergoer. Syntactic rules are based on the macrorole assignment and status of the arguments that appear in the surface forms. General and construction-specific rules comprise the syntax-semantics linking algorithm.

Thirdly, grammatical modifiers are described in a separate representation—the "operator projection"—that correlates grammatical information with the morphosyntactic representation. These modifiers are ordered according to the levels that are identified in the "constituent projection" mentioned above, both for clauses and for noun phrases.

Lastly, RRG addresses the functional issue of information flow by using a "focus projection." This simple diagram indicates the actual extent of focus (new information) in a construction, compared with the possible extent of the "focus domain" of the construction.

The following discussion expands this overview to give the reader a fuller introduction to the RRG model. It also provides a preview of the specific application and adaptation of the model to the analysis of Kankanaey.

1.2.2 Constituent projections

Role and Reference Grammar proposes a linear, layered conception of syntactic organization, without positing any underlying forms or movement rules. The layers in this organization are represented as nodes in a constituent projection display in figure 1.1.

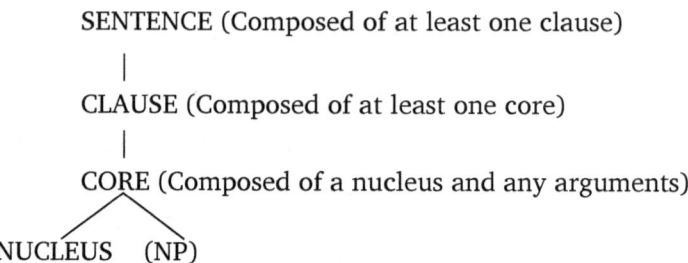

Figure 1.1. Constituent projection (basic).

1.2.2.1 Core constituents

As seen in figure 1.1, a sentence is composed of at least one clause, which in turn is composed of at least one core. Figure 1.2 displays the constituent projection of a Kankanaey core. Within the clause core are the nuclear predicating element and its arguments, expressed traditionally as noun phrases. In RRG noun phrases are termed "reference phrases" (RP). This term is especially appropriate for Kankanaey due to the high percentage of reference phrases that are nominalized clauses. The order in which the constituents of the core occur is language-specific. Kankanaey is a predicate-initial language and can take up to three arguments.

Adverbs that modify the nucleus are not core elements, but are found in positions preceding or following the nucleus. These positions are called nuclear peripheries. Peripheries are connected by arrows to the node at the appropriate level. The full constituent projection of a core is shown in figure 1.2.

1.2 Role and Reference Grammar—a practical model

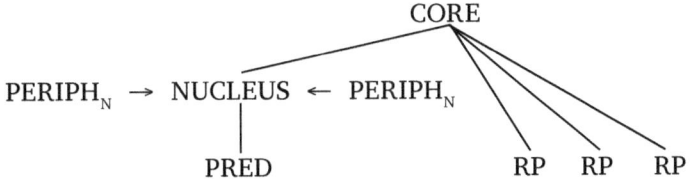

Figure 1.2. Core constituents.

1.2.2.2 Clause constituents

Within a clause, core-level modifiers such as adverbial phrases are placed in peripheral positions either preceding or following the core. There are also optional peripheral positions that precede and follow the clause level. In this way, modifying information is represented at the appropriate level but is kept separate from the essential structure. See figure 1.3.

Two other positions are represented in figure 1.3—a Pre-core Slot (PrCS) and a Post-core Slot (PoCS) for core information that occurs outside the core but inside the clause. In many languages, new information that comprises the actual focus domain is found in one of these positions. Kankanaey makes very limited use of these slots. Note in figure 1.3 that the peripheries for clause and core levels are labeled as such.

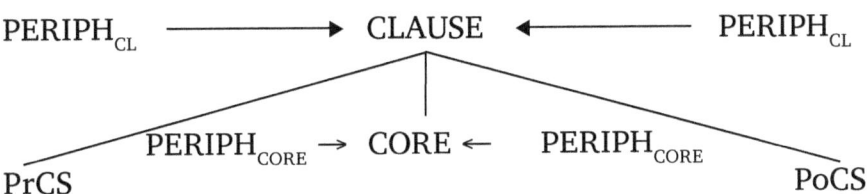

Figure 1.3. Clause constituents.

1.2.2.3 Sentence constituents

As a sentence grammar, the highest level addressed by RRG is a TEXT node to accommodate multiple-sentence constructions (Van Valin 2005:192). For Kankanaey, this node is labeled "Sentence Complex."

As displayed above in figure 1.1, a sentence consists of at least one independent clause.

Furthermore, a sentence may have information in detached positions. These are labeled the left-detached position (tagged 'LDP') and right-detached position ('RDP'). Detached positions are identified by an overt detachment marker. In Kankanaey, either an intonational pause or a detachment particle separates the information in the detached positions from the main clause. The detached positions may hold words, phrases, or clauses. The pragmatic function of the left-detached position is to orient the hearer in some way to the central clause that follows, whether time/space orientation, participant orientation, or logical orientation. The right-detached position tends to carry explanatory information related to the central clause. Figure 1.4 displays the constituent projection of the upper levels of syntactic structure.

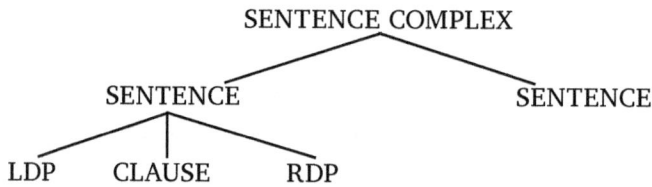

Figure 1.4. Sentence complex and sentence constituents.

An example of the constituent structure of a Kankanaey clause is displayed in figure 1.5. Note that only the predicate, arguments, and peripheral phrase are represented as constituents.[4]

---

[4] Abbreviations for figure 1.5: RP Reference Phrase, PRED predicating word, = bound morpheme, Q question word, NEG negator, P perfective, HSY hearsay, an evidential, BPRM bound personal reference phrase marker, RMd reference phrase marker definite, LOC marker for temporal/spatial location.

1.2 Role and Reference Grammar—a practical model

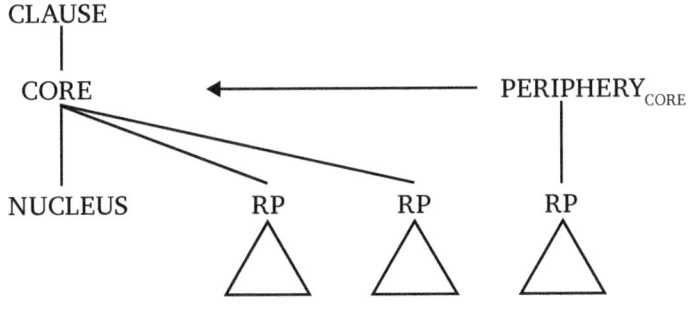

Ay	adi	p<in>no	=n Elsa	din batya	ed agsapa?
Q	NEG	fill.P	BPRM Elsa	RMd tub	LOC morning

'Did Elsa not fill the laundry-tub this morning?'

Figure 1.5. Kankanaey clause constituent projection example

1.2.2.4 Reference phrases

Role and Reference Grammar analyzes reference phrases (RP) as having a layered structure similar to the clause. RP constituent projections, like clauses, have nodes for core and nucleus. The RP has an argument position for possessive or other genitive-type phrases. Peripheral positions for adjectives and relative clauses are also part of the constituent projection for RPs. The openness of the theory to acknowledging any type of word as the nucleus of an RP is very appropriate for Kankanaey, where a reference phrase may be identified as a reference phrase marker followed by a core whose nucleus holds an affixed or un-affixed lexical root.

Figure 1.6 shows an example of an RP constituent projection display for Kankanaey.

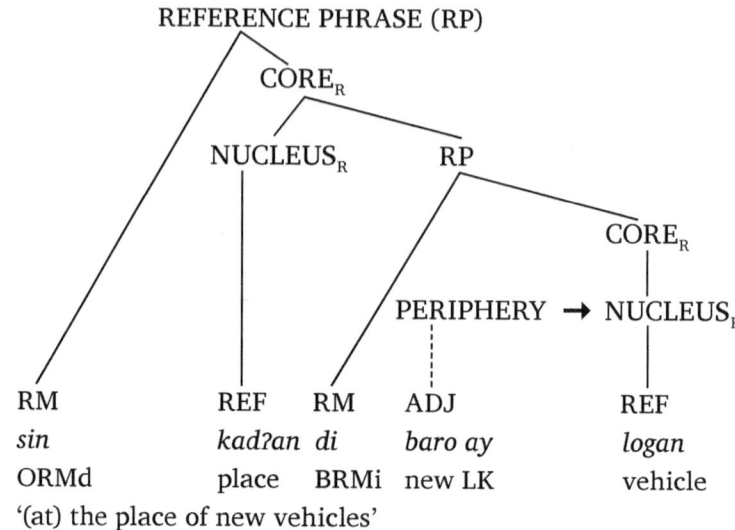

Figure 1.6. Kankanaey RP constituent structure example.

1.2.3 Semantic structure

1.2.3.1 Logical structures

RRG proposes that the Logical Structure (LS) of a predication, with its argument positions, forms the basis for syntactic representation. The LS theory expands on Dowty's (1979) representational scheme based on Vendler's (1967) *Aktionsart* classification. A predicate's *Aktionsart* classification is identified by reliable grammatical tests that have been established for English and other languages. As one example, Test 3 (Van Valin 2005:35–36) presents the criterion "occurs with adverbs like *quickly* or *slowly*," effectively assigning the feature [–punctual] to activities, accomplishments, and active accomplishments. A modified set of tests adapted for Kankanaey enables the same classifications to be identified for this language.

Each *Aktionsart* predicate type has its own semantic representation based on the distinction between states and activities. Predicates are shown in Logical Structure representations as constants marked with a prime accent ('). State and activity predicates are differentiated by the absence or presence of **do'**. Thus, a state is represented as **predicate'** (x) or (x, y) while an activity is represented as **do'** (x, [**predicate'** (x) or (x, y)]). (The variables represent arguments of the

1.2 Role and Reference Grammar—a practical model

predicates.) A very small set of modifiers such as CAUSE and BECOME build the other *Aktionsart* types from these two predicates. The lexical representations for *Aktionsart* classes from Van Valin (2005:45) are given in table 1.2.[5]

Table 1.2. Lexical representations for *Aktionsart* classes

Class	Logical structure
STATE	**predicate'** (x) or (x, y)
ACTIVITY	**do'** (x, [**predicate'** (x) or (x, y)])
ACHIEVEMENT	INGR **predicate'** (x) or (x,y) INGR **do'** (x, [**predicate'** (x) or (x, y)])
SEMELFACTIVE	SEML **predicate'** (x) or (x, y) SEML **do'** (x, [**predicate'** (x) or (x, y)])
ACCOMPLISHMENT	BECOME **predicate'** (x) or (x, y) BECOME **do'** (x, [**predicate'** (x) or (x y)])
ACTIVE ACCOMPLISHMENT	**do'** (x, [**predicate'** (x) or (x, y)]) & INGR **predicate'** (z, x) or (y)
CAUSATIVE	[α] CAUSE [β], where α, β are logical structures of any type

The modifier BECOME has traditionally been used to express an accomplishment, although technically an accomplishment is a process leading to an achievement (thus PROC + INGR). Because Kankanaey has a contrast between processes that have a specified end result and those that do not, this description includes the operator PROC in its lexical decomposition of Kankanaey process predicates.

1.2.3.2 Macroroles and privileged syntactic argument

Argument positions for each predicate type in this system of lexical representation are represented by variables (x, y), regardless of the specific semantic role each argument may fill. The various semantic role relationships of arguments to their predicate are generalized in RRG into

---

[5] Abbreviations for table 1.2: INGR ingressive (expresses punctual changes of state or activity), SEML semelfactive (Smith 1997) (punctual events with no result state), PROC process.

two macroroles, Actor and Undergoer. An argument may be assigned macrorole status, based on its position in the *Aktionsart* logical structure. The Actor-Undergoer hierarchy, shown in table 1.3 from Van Valin (2005:126), orders the argument positions in relation to their availability for macrorole assignment. (A further predicate DO indicates explicit agency.) The principles for macrorole assignment are listed below the hierarchy in table 1.3. As argued in Guerrero-Valenzuela and Van Valin (2004), most languages tend to present a mixed system for undergoer selection and thus need both principles A and B to adequately account for all the patterns.

Table 1.3. The Actor-Undergoer hierarchy

ACTOR   UNDERGOER
Arg. of   >   1ˢᵗ arg. of   >   1ˢᵗ arg. of   >   2ⁿᵈ arg. of   >   Arg. of
DO   **do′** (x,…)   **pred′** (x,y)   **pred′** (x,y)   **pred′** (x)

<u>Actor</u>: assign to highest (left-most) ranking argument in LS
<u>Undergoer</u>:
    Principle A: assign to lowest ranking argument in LS (default)
                        -or
    Principle B: assign to second highest ranking argument in LS

Syntax and verbal morphology interact with macrorole assignment. For example, if an argument in the logical structure is blocked from macrorole assignment, this will be reflected in the form of the verb and the structure of the clause. However, semantic transitivity in terms of two macroroles will not necessarily map into syntactic transitivity in terms of the clause structure. One important result of macrorole assignment is that one of the macrorole-assigned arguments will be chosen to hold a privileged syntactic role in clause structure, often as the "subject." This privileged syntactic argument (PSA) may have unique coding and behavioral properties. Language-specific linking algorithms must be established for assigning PSA status to an argument, delineating the privileges of that argument, and providing for the marking and positioning of other constituents.

For Kankanaey, the *Aktionsart* classification and macrorole assignment fit the data very well. Variable pragmatic assignment to Undergoer (Principles A and B) in Kankanaey is especially useful. Included in the

1.2 Role and Reference Grammar—a practical model

Kankanaey linking algorithm is the ergative pattern of PSA assignment in the clause.

Figure 1.7 illustrates part of the analysis of the clause from figure 1.5. It shows the logical structure of the predicate, macrorole assignment and PSA selection. In the logical structure, 'fill' is shown to be a causative accomplishment predicate, in that the predicate does not denote the specific action, only the effect produced. As the left-most argument in the logical structure, *Elsa* is assigned the Actor macrorole. The right-most argument, *batya*, is assigned the Undergoer macrorole in accordance with principle A in table 1.3. In Kankanaey, the Undergoer is the default choice for PSA. This choice then influences the affix on the verb, the order of the arguments, and the type of reference phrase markers on the arguments.

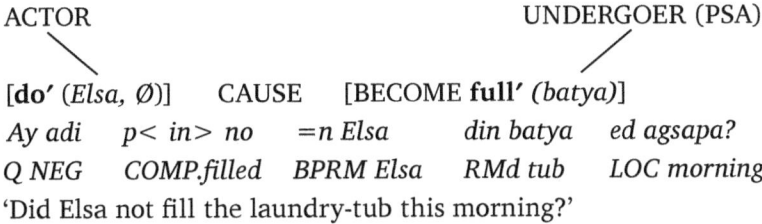

[do' (Elsa, Ø)]   CAUSE   [BECOME **full'** *(batya)*]
Ay adi   p< in> no   =n Elsa   din batya   ed agsapa?
Q NEG   COMP.filled   BPRM Elsa   RMd tub   LOC morning
'Did Elsa not fill the laundry-tub this morning?'

Figure 1.7. Kankanaey predicate logical structure with macroroles and PSA assigned.

1.2.4 Operator projection

Grammatical categories such as tense, aspect, negation, and illocutionary force are termed "operators" in RRG. Operators occur at the clause, core, and nuclear levels in a sentence and are analyzed separately from the clause constituents. Operators that occur in reference phrases, such as number and definiteness, are also analyzed separately. The "Operator Projection" identifies the layer of the structure that each operator modifies. This is important when analyzing complex constructions. The operators in a clause are shown in table 1.4, from Van Valin (2005:9).

Table 1.4. Operators in the layered structure of the clause

Nucleus: Aspect
          Negation
          Directionals (only those modifying orientation of action or event without reference to participants)

Core: Directionals (only those expressing the orientation or motion of one participant with reference to another participant or to the speaker)
          Event quantification
          Modality (root modals, e.g., ability, permission, obligation)
          Internal (narrow scope) negation

Clausal: Status (epistemic modals, external negation)
          Tense
          Evidentials
          Illocutionary force

Kankanaey follows these norms in almost every case. One notable exception is the absence of tense. Perfective aspect (a nuclear level modifier expressed by affixation on the predicate) indicates completion and thus realis.

In figure 1.8 operators are shown for the Kankanaey example sentence. They are represented in the Operator Projection using arrows to identify the level being modified. Note that the negation in this clause is not limited to one constituent but applies at the core level, and that perfective aspect (the infix <in>, tagged P) is a nuclear operator. The yes-no question word *ay* 'Q' indicates the illocutionary force, a clause-level operator.

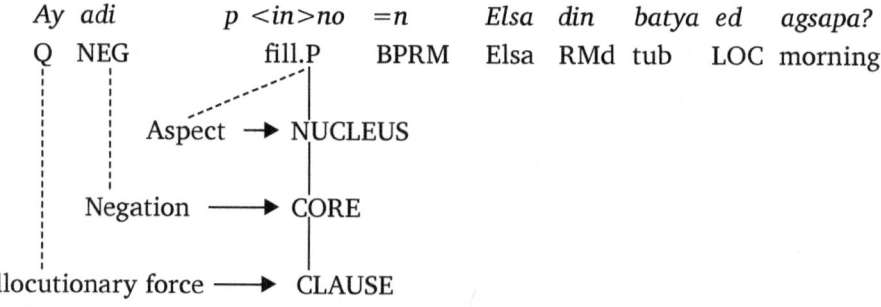

'Did Elsa not fill the laundry-tub this morning?'

Figure 1.8. Kankanaey clause with operator projection.

1.2.5 Information structure

The fourth perspective in the RRG framework examines the pragmatic flow of information. It recognizes the influence of the larger context in a syntactic analysis of any sentence. Constituents of a sentence may express information that is new to the hearer, or that refers to information already known or presupposed. RRG builds upon Lambrecht's theory of information structure (e.g., Lambrecht 1994), in which topical information is presupposed while "focus" refers to information that is new. It draws a distinction between the possible domain of focus information in a given structure and the actual focus of a given clause. An entire clause could potentially be new information. However, in the Kankanaey clause that we are using as an example, the information units =n Elsa and din batya 'the tub' and ed agsapa 'this morning' are presented as definite, known entities. This leaves only the modified nucleus adi pinno 'didn't fill' as the focus information. The focus structure projection is shown in figure 1.9.

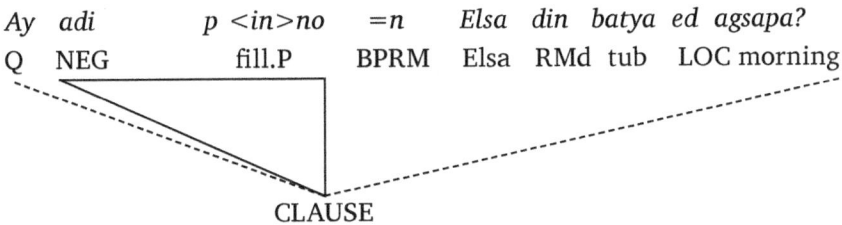

Actual focus domain ———
Potential focus domain ----
'Did Elsa not fill the laundry-tub this morning?'

Figure 1.9. Kankanaey example with information structure projection.

The predicate-first structure of Kankanaey fits with its focus-first tendency, a tendency common to many languages. The information structure analysis explains the syntactic phenomenon in Kankanaey of a narrow-focus RP being placed in the clause-nuclear position. Figure 1.10 represents the constituent structure and the information structure when the example sentence is reconfigured to express narrow focus on the constituent Elsa.[6]

---

[6] Abbreviations for figure 1.10: PRM Personal Reference Phrase Marker, RMi indefinite Reference Phrase Marker, ORMd oblique Reference Phrase Marker.

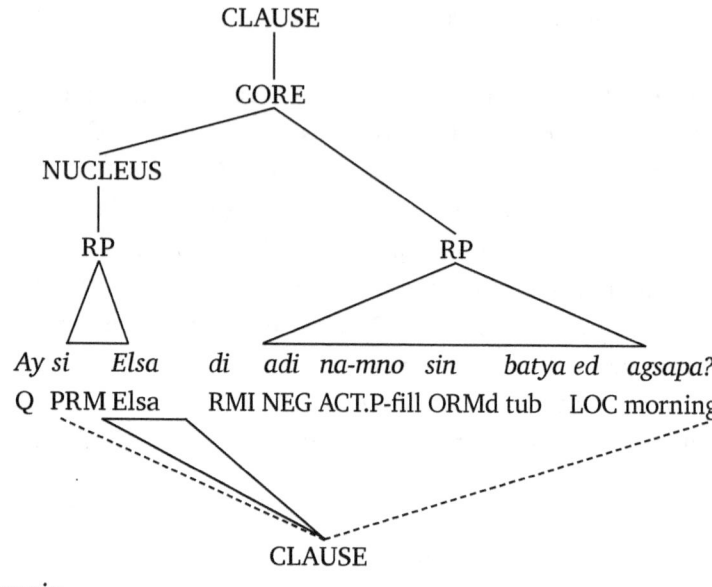

Actual focus domain ———
Potential focus domain ---------

'Is Elsa the (one who) did not fill the laundry-tub this morning?'

Figure 1.10. Constituent and information structure narrow-focus example.

1.3 Conclusion

This introductory chapter has provided an introduction to the Kankanaey language, and an overview of Role and Reference Grammar as it has been used to analyze and describe this beautiful language. The "layered structure of the clause" with its several positions gives a clear explanation of how the constituents of a clause are ordered and, more satisfying, an explanation of the hierarchical relationships between them. RRG's separation of "operators" from the other clause constituents has proved to be helpful in sorting out many confusing details. The analysis of the logical structure of predicates is most helpful in understanding the relationships that arguments have with their predicates. The complicated affixation and voice alternations in Kankanaey lose their mystery when the logical structure is used as the starting point for "macrorole" assignment and syntactic relations. And finally, understanding the pragmatic "focus

1.3 Conclusion

structure" of clauses has provided a tool that aids linguistic research from clause analysis to whole discourse analysis.

The following chapters will describe the Kankanaey language in detail, using the tools and strategies of RRG. Chapter 2 deals with morphology, especially predicate formation using lexical decomposition. Chapters 3 and 4 deal with the constituents and operators of reference phrases and simple clauses, respectively. Chapter 5 looks at complex constructions, while chapter 6 analyzes those complexities in terms of their privileged syntactic arguments. Chapter 7 deals with the flow of information as it is managed through Kankanaey grammar. Appendices and references follow the conclusion in chapter 8.

2

The Lexicon and Predicate Formation

2.1 The Kankanaey lexicon

Kankanaey lexical items[1] may be syntactically categorized as content or function lexemes. Content lexemes include roots in both open and closed categories. The first section of this chapter deals with open classes of content roots. Small closed classes of independent syntactic standing, comprised of adverbs, modals and semantic particles, are discussed elsewhere, as are function lexemes, including conjunctions, determiners, interrogative markers, and a wide array of inflectional and derivational affixes.

2.1.1 Roots

As in other Philippine languages, many Kankanaey content roots allow both referring and predicating usages, depending on the affixation. This

---

[1] Glottal stops are not orthographically represented when intervocalic or word initial, and cannot occur syllable final. In this study, they are written only word medially after another consonant, or when relevant to the discussion.

study considers the roots to be pre-categorical as far as syntactic category or "part of speech" is concerned. Content roots are divided into broad categories—classes, properties, statives (including perception statives), actions and physicals. Erstwhile 'nouns' are termed 'classes' to reflect the fact that when they function as predicates they indicate a classification rather than an object instantiating that classification. Physicals are given a separate classification because they involve their participant in self-affecting ways. They also take unique predicating affixes, as will be seen in section 2.2 on predicate formation. The Kankanaey lexical content categories are as follows.

>Class
>Property
>Stative
>Perception-stative
>Physical
>Action

2.1.1.1 Class roots

Following Reid's label (2004:436) class roots indicate a class of entities by physical or other sensory characteristics. Typical examples are seen in examples (2.1) to (2.3).

(2.1) *babai*
       'female, especially human'
(2.2) *beey*
       'house, home of person or animal; container where something is usually kept'
(2.3) *begas*
       'hulled rice'

2.1.1.2 Property roots

Property roots indicate an essential characteristic, such as size, color, texture etc.

2.1 The Kankanaey lexicon

(2.4) *em?ek*
'soft (easily cut)'
(2.5) *emis*
'sweet, tasty'
(2.6) *ando*
'tall, long'

2.1.1.3 Stative roots

Stative roots indicate a changeable physical condition, not necessarily permanent. States that specifically follow a change induced by an outside effector are termed result-stative roots in the discussion.

(2.7) *tey*
'dead'
(2.8) *gadgad*
'mangy'
(2.9) *kemi*
'dented in, partially crushed'
(2.10) *beteng*
'drunk'

2.1.1.4 Perception-stative roots

Perception roots indicate a perception by an animate being, including physical, emotional and mental perception-states. Because animate beings are able to actively perceive, with control, intent and cognition, these roots may form predicates of a wider range than those based on simple stative roots.

(2.11) *ila*
'see, look at'
(2.12) *bongot*
'angry'
(2.13) *kibtot*
'startled'

(2.14) *kiyapot*
'rushed, stressed'

2.1.1.5 Physical roots

Physical roots indicate movement and position—natural movements as well as body movements and positions. (They do not include body functions.) These roots may denote a location or direction as in (2.15) to (2.18) or indicate manner of movement, as in (2.19) and (2.20).

(2.15) *tedted*
'drip'
(2.16) *ali*
'move toward speaker, come'
(2.17) *saa*
'go home'
(2.18) *balalong*
'move downwards, descend'
(2.19) *sekad*
'stamp, stomp'
(2.20) *tagtag*
'run'

2.1.1.6 Action roots

Action roots indicate activity by an animate, usually intentional participant. Some action roots denote the trajectory of that action to a second participant; some specify a participant as an entity involved in the action but not as the end-point. Rather than using a generic type of action root modified by phrases, Kankanaey uses roots that are highly specific as to manner of action. Many roots specify properties of the target of the action, giving an undergoer-orientation that fits well with the ergative syntactic alignment. The specificity of Kankanaey roots may be noticed in many of the examples that follow.

(2.21) *togda*
'eat lunch'

2.1 The Kankanaey lexicon

(2.22) *tilid*
'carry something on one shoulder'
(2.23) *tobʔong*
'put a relatively small amount of something into a relatively large amount of water'
(2.24) *todyok*
'jab or poke upwards at something'

2.1.2 Word-building processes

2.1.2.1 Reduplication

Several types of reduplication are used to build words in Kankanaey.[2] McCarthy and Prince (1998:286) state that reduplication is not syllable copying but rather a "templatic target which is affixed to the base and is satisfied by copying elements of the base." Reduplication may be applied to unaffixed or affixed roots,[3] and copies either the first CV, CVC, or CV(C)CV of the base form, with different functions fulfilled by each type. These functions will be explained in section 2.2 and chapter 4; the examples in (2.25) to (2.27) are not exhaustive. Intervocalic glottal stops have been shown where relevant.

(2.25) *beey* 'house' + CV- → *bebeey* 'houses'
(2.26) *padas* 'try' + CVC- → *padpadas* 'experiences'
(2.27) *saʔig* 'stack in rows' + CVC(C)V- → *saʔisaʔig* 'stacking more and more rows'

---

[2] Kankanaey has numerous roots whose canonical shape contains apparent reduplication. Some of these irreducible roots consist of two identical syllables, as in *taktak* and *baba*. Other roots, such as *togingging* and *wagawag*, have two identical syllables with an apparent prefix or infix. These roots do not exemplify reduplication as a word-building process.

[3] The fascinating interaction of reduplication and phonology in Kankanaey is covered in appendix A, Phonology and Morphophonology of Kankanaey.

2.1.2.2 Prefixes

Many predicating and nominalizing affixes are prefixes, attaching directly to the front of the root as in (2.28). Most reduplicative affixation applies before prefixation, as seen in the derivation in (2.29), but some functions of CVC reduplication are applied to already-prefixed stems, as seen in the derivation in (2.30). (See appendix A and Paterson (2007) for fuller analyses.) Some roots drop their first vowel when prefixed, as in (2.31), where the glottal then metathesizes with the second consonant under phonological constraints. With one-syllable or vowel-reduced roots, reduplication is applied after the predicative affixation, as in (2.32).

(2.28) tokdo 'sit' + ka- → katokdo 'seat-mate'
(2.29) beteng 'drunk' + CV- + na- → nabebeteng 'was drunk'
(2.30) geyek 'tickle' + ma- + CVC- → magmageyek 'ticklish'
(2.31) ʔemis 'sweet, tasty' + ma- → mamʔis 'sweet, tasty'
(2.32) tey 'dead' + ma- + CVC- → matmatey 'dying'

2.1.2.3 Suffixes

Two predicating affixes are suffixes, -en and -an. Some roots drop their last vowel when suffixed, as in (2.33).

(2.33) dateng 'arrive' + -an → datngan 'come upon, find'

2.1.2.4 Infixes

One predicating affix, <om> and a perfective affix <in> are infixed following the first consonant of the root. Two examples are seen in (2.34).

(2.34) ʔayos 'flow down' + <om> → ʔ<om>ayos 'flows down'
      kaan 'remove' + <in> → k<in>aan 'removed'

Reduplication generally precedes the predicating infixation, which precedes the aspect infixation, as seen in (2.35) the step-by-step construction of the word *pinmanapanakpak*. (Vowel reduction occurs when the two infixes co-occur before a vowel, thus <in> + <om> → <inm>.) In (2.36), the reducible vowel in the root re-orders the reduplication to follow predicating affixation.

(2.35) panakpak 'hit with slapping sound'
       + CVCV- → panapanakpak
       + <om> → pomanapanakpak
       + <in> → pinmanapanakpak 'was repeatedly hitting/slapping'

(2.36) betak 'explode'
       + <om> → bomtak
       + CVC- → bombomtak
       + <in> → binombomtak 'were exploding'

A few highly marked affixes include an infixed glottal stop before the second vowel, as in (2.37).

(2.37) banga 'pot' + CVC- <ʔ> → bangbangʔa 'little old pots, toy pots'

2.1.2.5 Circumfixes

A number of affixes have two parts, a prefix or infix and a suffix (most often -an). The functions of these circumfixes are unique, not a sum of the functions of the two parts. They are tagged by glossing the prefix or infix, and using a left-pointing chevron (<) for the suffix. Two examples are seen in (2.38).

(2.38) ila 'see'   + ka-...-an → ka-ila-an   'appearance'
                                           NOM-see<
       oto 'cook' + i-...-an → i-oto-an   'cook for someone'
                                            UNDd-cook<

2.1.2.6 Co-occurring affixes

A few prefixes can occur in combination with other prefixes or infixes at the front of the root. One of these, the prefix i-, has several functions, one of which is to indicate the presence of a second argument as in (2.39). Other more specialized prefixes include those underlined in (2.40).

(2.39) *payag* 'set down' + *ka-* + *i-* → *kaipayag* 'set it down suddenly'

(2.40) *ila* 'see' + *man-* + *asi-* → *man?asiila*
                                                          'see each other'

   ila 'see' + *man-* + *pa-* → *manpaila*
                                                          'appear, show oneself'

   esa 'one' + CVC- + *mang-* + *i-* + *pan-* → *mangipan?es?esa*
                                                          'concentrate on it'

As has been shown, the mechanics of word formation in Kankankaey is complex and multi-functional. The semantics and subsequent syntactic constructions utilizing these complex words will be covered in section 2.2 and in the following chapters.

2.2 Predicate formation

Van Valin and LaPolla (1997:154) note that "the information contained in lexical entries is very important, as it consists of the crucial semantic, morphosyntactic and other properties which determine how a lexical item will behave grammatically. The logical structure of the verb is the heart of its lexical entry." As detailed in section 2.1.1, the lexicon of Kankanaey is arranged by root morphemes, and indicates the crucial semantic properties of each root. This section looks at how affixation is used to create predicates and to indicate their logical structures.

Kankanaey roots depend on affixation to license their function in a phrase or clause. Section 2.2 deals with predicate formation, the process that creates a word that is able to function grammatically in its context, although it does not specify what that function is. Predicating affixes abound in Kankanaey and may license a word to either predicate or refer, depending on the construction in which it appears. The predicates that each may form are a function of the interaction of affixation with the properties of the root that are relevant in each specific context.

One system of classifying predicates in terms of event semantics is *Aktionsart,* proposed by Vendler (1967), which categorizes states of affairs by whether they are "happenings" or static situations, and distinguishes the happenings by their temporal properties and the dynamicity of the event. VVLP (1997) and Van Valin (2005) expanded the list of categories to reflect resultant situations, adding semelfactives and complex predicates—active accomplishments and causatives. To accommodate the full range of predicates, this study includes classification and attribute predicates as subtypes of states.

2.2.1 *Aktionsart* logical structures

Aktionsart predicate classes are shown in table 2.1. Their labels have been adapted for Kankanaey to account for morphosyntactically consequential generalizations and distinctions. *Aktionsart* predicates are described in terms of their "logical structures" (LS) which include the minimum number of semantic arguments that each predicate may require. The following discussion includes the representation of these logical structures. The conventions of LS representation include predicates in boldface with a prime (in Kankanaey these are root categories), predicate modifiers in all caps, arguments as x, y, z, etc., and parentheses and brackets enclosing arguments of the predicate(s). See section 1.2.3.1 for a fuller explanation of the Logical Structures used for *Aktionsart* classes.

Table 2.1. Predicate types in Kankanaey

Aktionsart class	Logical structure
CLASS/ATTRIBUTE	**be'** (x, [**root'**])
EXPERIENCE-STATE	**feel'** (x, [**root'**])
STATE	**root'** (x, (y))
PROCESS	PROC **root'** (x)
ACHIEVEMENT	INGR **root'** (x)\
ACCOMPLISHMENT	PROC+ INGR **root'** (x)
SEMELFACTIVE	SEML **root'** (x, (y)) SEML **do'** (x, [**root'** (x, (y))])
ACTIVITY	**do'** (x, [**root'** (x, (y))])
ACTIVE ACCOMPLISHMENT	**do'** (x, [**root'** (x, (y))]) & INGR **root'** (z, x,) or (y)
CAUSATIVE	α CAUSE [**root'** (x, (y))] where α is an unspecified predicate

2.2.2 Tests for *Aktionsart* classes

The *Aktionsart* classes may be determined in any given language by tests that isolate relevant semantic features of each class. The tests in table 2.2 and used for Kankanaey are adapted from Van Valin (2005:35–40).

Table 2.2. Kankanaey tests for *Aktionsart* classes

Criterion	State	Achiev	Seml	Process	Activity	Act-Accomp	Causative
1. CVC interpretation	-	plural	iterative	progress	progress	progress	+/-
2. CV	+	-	-	-	-	+	+/-
3. Pace modifier	-	-	-	+	+	+	+/-
4. Time designation	FOR	AFTER	FOR	FOR	FOR	AFTER	+/-
5. Stative modifier	+	+	-	-	-	+	+/-
6. 'Cause' paraphrase	-	-	-	-	-	-	+
7. Negator	*baken*	*adi*	*adi*	*adi*	*adi*	*adi*	*adi*

Tests 1 and 2 ask whether the predicate occurs with temporal aspect marking. In Kankanaey, CVC reduplication serves several functions, among them indicating progressive aspect. The availability and function of CVC reduplication is crucial to answering Test 1, as it must read iteratively for semelfactives, as an ongoing situation for activities and changes of state, and indicate plurality for achievements. Test 2, unique to Kankanaey, asks whether the predicate occurs with CV reduplication, which generally indicates duration of a temporary static situation, including the relevant effect of actions, providing evidence for the presence of a state predicate in the semantic structure. Temporal aspect is covered in detail in chapter 4.

Test 3 asks whether expressions of pace can co-occur with the predicate. Such 'pace' designations exclude stative and punctual predicates. Kankanaey has very few adverbs, none regarding pace; modifying pace verbs such as 'do quickly' however can be used for Test 3. The tests suggested for English (Van

2.2 Predicate formation

Valin 2005) include "manner" adverbs such as 'vigorously'. but no general verbs of manner such as 'do vigorously' have been attested in Kankanaey. A reduplicative 'intensive' affix (CVC(C)V) can intensify either vigor or repetition. This affix may differentiate predicates with an activity component but is not crucial, as other tests also provide sufficient contrasts.

A time word with the indefinite oblique marker *si* can indicate duration if the predicate allows duration. If the predicate is punctual, it indicates the time span before the event. Test 4 asks how time designations interact with the predicate in question—whether the time phrase will indicate duration ('FOR x minutes') or end-point ('AFTER x minutes') in relation to the predicate. Kankanaey does not have prepositions parallel to the English 'for,' 'in', or 'after,' so this test only asks for the interpretation. Time duration of a state of affairs that culminates in an end-point is not expressed as a phrase within the clause.

Natural modes of expression are exemplified by the following sentences:

(2.41) a. *At?atik di maobla mon enggay piga ay*
little RMi work but even how.many LK

agew asi ma-kdeng.
day and.then UNDs-finish
'There is only a little work to be done, but still it will be several days before it's finished.'

b. *Man-balin na ay tapey ma-pa-labas*
ACT-turn.into DEM1I LK wine UNDs-CAUS-pass

di esa=y bowan.
RMi one=LK month
'This will turn into wine (when) one month has been allowed to pass.'

Thus, no test is available in Kankanaey to identify predicates that involve both duration and an end-point.

Test 5 asks whether a predicate can be used as a stative modifier. It identifies process, semelfactives and activities as those that cannot be so used. Relative clauses formed with passive constructions are ideal for examining this criterion; section 2.3.3.1 includes examples of stative modification.

Test 6 asks whether the predicate can be paraphrased with "cause." Although Kankanaey has an overt cause prefix that easily identifies many causative predicates, causative predicates that are not morphologically marked may be identified by this test.

Test 7, also unique to this study, asks for the form of negator that is used with the predicate, since Kankanaey has two forms, *adi* and *baken*, that modify different predicate types. This test uncovers state predicates in the logical structure.

Sections 2.2.3 and following look at each type of predicate with its logical structure and examine how Kankanaey builds such predicates.

A note is in order here for understanding the glossing. One syntactic function of predicating affixation is to index one argument of the predication. This function depends not only on the predicate type but also on factors that range from phrase and clause formation to discourse-level considerations. The tags for the affixes reflect this indexing function, as will be clarified in later chapters. The examples will include tags to identify the relevant affix. Affixation that is irrelevant to a given example may not be separately identified.

Table 2.3 lists the basic predicating affixes of Kankanaey and indicates the number of arguments they allow. This number will not be greater than the number of arguments in the logical structure. (A few exceptions such as weather predicates will be noted as needed.) The table also includes a second form for each affix that includes perfective aspect. Some morphophonemic processes create alternate forms.[4]

---

[4] In table 2.3 *N*- represents a nasal consonant that replaces the first consonant of the following morpheme and assimilates to its place of articulation: bilabial, alveolar, or velar (includes ʔ).

2.2 Predicate formation

Table 2.3. Basic predicating affixes in Kankanaey
(second form includes perfective aspect)

1 argument	2–3 arguments
man-, nan-	*i-, in-*
maN-, naN-	*-en, <in>*
ma-, na-	*-an, <in>...-an*
<om>, <in(o)m>	*i-...-an, in-...-an*

2.2.3 Identificational and attribute state predicates

State predicates depict states of affairs that are static and atelic. This section covers identificational and attributive state predicates that are unaffixed. They are subtypes of *Aktionsart* states.

2.2.3.1 Identificational states

Identificational states have the logical structure: **be′** (x, [**class′**]).

The single argument is an entity being identified by the predicate. These states are formed with class roots and no affixation. The class root indicates a classification and does not refer to any particular instance of that class, as in (2.42) and (2.43). Overt plurality is not normally expressed in identificational state predicates.

(2.42) *Babai   din   anak=da.*
      female/girl RMd child=3pII
      'Their child is a girl.'

(2.43) *Anak=mi   si   Martin.*
      child=1pII PRM   Martin
      'Martin is (one of) our child(ren).'

2.2.3.2 Attribute states

Attribute states have the logical structure: **be′** (x, [**property′**]).

The single argument is an entity bearing the specific individual-level property denoted in the root. Attribute states do not occur with time phrases or with reduplication that indicates time duration. These predicates are formed with two classes of property roots—a small group that takes no affixation to form attribute state predicates, and those that take predicating affixes. Many in the first group of unaffixed state predicates begin with the letter a, leading to a speculation of an historical aspect-neutral prefix. The resistance of some of these forms to affixation may be due to the fact that they express very common attributes, as in (2.44).

(2.44)   *addawi* 'near' and *asag?en* 'far'
        ad?ado 'many' and *at?atik* 'few'
        aptik 'short' and *ando* 'tall' and *annawa* 'wide'
        as?asi 'dirty' and *ay?ayyo* 'still good'

2.2.3.2.1 Attribute-state affixation

Most property roots form attribute state predicates with affixation that is arbitrarily specified by the property root. The three affixes *ma-, na-,* and *man-* (tagged ATT) may form these state predicates, as in (2.45) to (2.47). Consistent with the logical structure that specifies only one argument, these affixes indicate an intransitive predicate. When these affixes occur with property roots, they are identical to each other in function, and do not indicate aspect.[5]

(2.45)   *Na-kayang din dontog.*
        ATT-high RMd mountain
        'The mountain is tall.'

---

[5] When prefixed to other roots, these affixes indicate aspect and differ significantly in function.

2.2 Predicate formation

(2.46) *Ma-ngetit   din   bistida.*
       ATT-black   RMd   dress
       'The dress is black.'

(2.47) *Man-kilat   din   sabsabong.*
       ATT-white   RMd   flower
       'The flower is white.'

For some unaffixed attribute predicates, an initial CVC reduplication has frozen into a required form, as may be noticed in (2.44) and in (2.48).

(2.48) *Dakdake   din   aso   ya   kitkitoy   din   oken=na.*
       large   RMd   dog   and   small   RMd   puppy=3sII
       'The dog is big and its puppy is small.'

2.2.4 Other state predicates

2.2.4.1 Experience states

Physical, emotional or mental experiences are temporary, stage-level states that have come about for an EXPERIENCER argument. State experiences do not denote cognitive attention or direction, the EXPERIENCER having no control over that state of affairs. Experience states may be used as stative modifiers in a reference phrase.

Experience states have the logical structure: **feel′** (x, [**root′**]).

Formed with stative roots of non-directable experience, they are formed with the affix *ma-*, tagged UND(ergoer)s(tate) which can take perfective marking (P) as *na-*. The EXPERIENCERs of these predicates are animate beings, most often human, as in (2.49) and in the second clause of (2.50). Examples (2.51) and (2.52) show other experience states.

(2.49)   Nasdaaw(na-sedaaw)=ak   sin   kaad?ado   =n di
         UNDs.P-amazed=1sI   ORMd   large.quantity =BRMi

   pilak=na.
   money=3sII
   'I was amazed at how much money he had (lit. the large quantity of his money).'

(2.50)   Istay=ak   en maitapi   tan   anggay   ay
         almost=1sI   go join   because already LK

   ma-skaw=ak.
   UNDs-chilled=1sI
   'I almost went[6] to join (them at the fire) because I was really cold.'

(2.51)   Masnit(ma-sinit)/Nasnit   si   Aden   sin   songbat=mo.
         UNDs/UNDs.P-offended   PRM   Aden   ORMd   answer=2sII
   'Aden is/was offended by your answer.'

(2.52)   Na-sngang=ak   isonga   adi=ak   makakali.
         UNDs.P-mental.block=1sI   therefore NEG=1sI   able.speak
   'I had a mental block, therefore I couldn't speak.'

2.2.4.2 Physical states

"Physical" roots in this study are those that denote movement generally in or through space, and those that denote physical positions. Physical position predicates may express static situations, especially with CV reduplication.

Physical states have the simple logical structure: **physical'** (x).

Physical states of body position may be formed with a variety of affixes: *ma-* is used when no intentionality is possible, *man-* and <*om*> are more ambiguous.

---

[6] Completion of a state of affairs in Kankanaey (usually translated with past tense in English) is often set by perfective aspect marking on one clause, and the following clauses may be interpreted within that time frame, even though, as in this example, they are not marked with perfective aspect.

2.2 Predicate formation

The latter two affixes can also form change-of-state predicates such as process or accomplishment. CV reduplication specifies durative aspect, ensuring a stative interpretation. Note the various affixes in (2.53) to (2.56).

(2.53) Nan-do~dodlon=da   ay   pasya.
       ACT-CV-positioned.close=3pI LK   extreme
       'They are stacked/lined up too close together.'

(2.54) Ma-bo~bokʔong=ak   tan   mansakit gitang=ko.
       UNDs-DUR-arched=1sI   because hurt   lower.back=1sII
       'I am hunched over because my lower back hurts.'

(2.55) T<om>o~tokdo=kami   sin   baliwang.
       UNDm-CV-sit=1pI   ORMd   front.yard
       'We were sitting (for a long time) in front of the building.'

(2.56) Siga-a(n)=k   ay   pag   ʔ<om>alagey.
       dislike-UND=1sII   LK   PART   UNDm-stand
       'I hate to just stand.' (e.g., in line)

2.2.4.3 Perception states

Perception states have a PERCEIVER and a STIMULUS corresponding to the two arguments in the logical structure:

perception-stative′ (x, y).

In Kankanaey these predicates are built with the suffix -en (perfective <in>). Perception states are usually unambiguously non-volitional, as in (2.57) to (2.59).

(2.57) Dengng-e(n)=m   di   palato ay   mankilis.
       hear-UND=2sII   RMi   plate   LK   clink
       'You will hear some plates clinking.'

(2.58) <In>ila=k   si   Mrs. Mantad   sin   bas.
        UND.P-see=1sII   PRM   Mrs. Mantad   ORMd   bus
        'I saw/*looked at Mrs. Mantad on the bus.'

(2.59) Ay   d<in>law=mo   din   yegyeg?
        Q   UND.P-feel=2sII   RMd   earthquake
        'Did you feel the earthquake?'

2.2.4.4 Result states

Result state predicates have the logical structure: **stative′** (x).

Result states are non-inherent situations that come about by some process and are stage-level states. Because they follow a change of state, they are often morphologically ambiguous with achievement predicates, especially when given perfective affixation. The pragmatic context usually disambiguates the two. Result-states take as their argument an entity such as a THEME or PATIENT that has come to be in that state, generally due to a change in location or condition. The affix tag reflects the argument role. Another type of non-inherent state is an effect upon an entity that does not involve a total change. This section will look at wholly-affected states and partially-affected states. Result states are freely used as stative modifiers.

2.2.4.4.1 Result-state affixation

Kankanaey result-state predicates are formed with stative roots and the affix *ma-* (*na-* perfective). Examples (2.60) and (2.61) demonstrate this alternation. In isolation some result-state predicates with perfective marking are ambiguous as to telicity and punctuality, as in (2.62) where it could be an achievement predicate. Example (2.63) shows the result-state predicate used as a stative modifier (bracketed).

(2.60) *Mo inomem (inomen=mo)   sa,   ma-beteng=ka.*
        if   drink =2sII   DEM2I   UNDs-drunk=2sI
        'If you drink that, you'll be/get drunk.'

2.2 Predicate formation

(2.61) *Na-beteng   si   Sefin.*
        UNDs.P-drunk PRM   Sefin
        'Sefin is/was drunk.'

(2.62) *Na-p?es   din   goma=na.*
        UNDs.P-deflate RMd   innertube=3sII
        'Its innertube went/was flat.'

(2.63) *Inila=k   din   [na-p?es   ay]   goma=na.*
        saw=1s   RMd   UNDsP-deflate   LK   innertube=3sII
        'I saw its flat tire.'

Result states may just happen, or be caused deliberately. With *ma-/na-* the predicate does not imply any causer, as in (2.64). The denotation is only the resultant state. To specify deliberate cause, a causative state predicate is used, as detailed in section 2.2.10.

(2.64) *Na-kilot   din   sakdoan.*
        UNDs.P-dirty   RMd   water-fetching-place
        'The place to get water is dirty.'

Some roots denote an effect that is partial, temporary, or external. The affix used to form these state predicates is analyzed in this study as a circumfix *(ma-...-an)*. The PATIENT is basically unchanged by the effect, being presented as the locus of the state. The tag UNDls (for locus state) will indicate the circumfix and the left-chevron < will indicate that the final *-an* is part of the affix. Example (2.65) indicates a partial effect, (2.66) illustrates a surface effect, and (2.67) exemplifies a temporary effect.

(2.65) *Mo man?emes=ka sin   kaagawan, ma-kolang-an   dada=m.*
        if bathe=2sI   ORMd daytime   UNDls-insufficient< blood=2sII
        'If you bathe in the daytime, your blood will be reduced/lessened.'

(2.66) *En=ka   mansidom   tan   sana   ay ma-koning-an=ka.*
        go=2sI take.shelter because DEM2V LK UNDls-sunburn<=2sI
        'Go take shelter because there you are getting sunburned.'

(2.67) *Ma-loya-an=ak   sin   inoto=da   ay bagoong.*
UNDls -dirty<=1sI ORMd cooked=3pII LK anchovy.paste
'I am repulsed/lose appetite by the anchovy paste they cooked.'

When a predicate indicates that something or someone is the locus of an effect, it is often in an adversative sense with an unwelcome effect. Examples (2.68) to (2.70) illustrate adversative states with a variety of roots.

(2.68) *Na-abos-an=kami=s   gasol   ed   na-sdem.*
UNDls.P-used.up<1pI=ORMi   gas   LOC   UNDs.P-afternoon
'We ran out of bottled-gas yesterday.'

(2.69) *Wat=ak na-aga~agag-an   ay nan-(t)agta~tagtag ed   agsapa.*
only=1sI UNDls.P-CVCCV-rush< LK ACT.P-CVCCV-run LOC morning
'I was just terribly rushed racing about this morning.'

(2.70) *Na-labi-an=kami   sin   danan.*
UNDls.P-night<=1pI   ORMd path
'We were be-nighted (i.e., overtaken by nightfall) on the trail.'

2.2.5 Process predicates

A process predicate in Kankanaey has the logical structure: PROC **root'** (x) .

Processes are changes of state that begin, but do not have an inherent telicity or endpoint. They are spontaneous events without an external cause, so the participant may be seen as both initiator and affected entity, a "middle" situation (see Kemmer 1993:16–19). The tag indicates an Undergoer index with state changes. Process predicates indicate atelic progression in a particular direction, and are most often formed with property roots. The entity is asserted to exhibit more of that property, but the predicate does not specify how far in that direction the process will progress. Example (2.71) illustrates a Process predicate. The infix <*om*> indicates change of state, and it is the denotation of the property root that specifies whether the change is necessarily complete.

2.2 Predicate formation

(2.71) Ng\<om\>etit   din   lokto   mo ibilag= mo   Ø.
       UNDm-black   RMd   yam   if put.in.sun=2sII 4III
       'The yams will darken (but not necessarily turn black) if you put them out in the sun.'

2.2.6 Achievement and accomplishment predicates

Achievement predicates assert an instantaneous change of state while accomplishment predicates involve a process leading to the achievement of a state. The operators in the logical structures of these predicates reflect this difference. Achievements have an INGRessive operator (instantaneous change) while accomplishments have a BECOME (process + ingressive) operator.

The logical structure for achievements is INGR **root'** (x).
The logical structure for accomplishments is BECOME **root'** (x).

Kankanaey achievements and accomplishments are based on result-stative roots, property roots, physical roots and experience-stative roots that have a single participant. Kankanaey uses two methods of creating achievement and accomplishment predicates: \<om\> affixation with most roots and *na-* affixation with result-state roots.

2.2.6.1 *Achievement and accomplishment predicates with* \<om\>

As with Process predicates, many changes of state in Kankanaey are indicated by the infix \<om\>. The instantaneous or gradual time factor is part of the semantic content of each stative root, so this use of \<om\> (there are several) may be seen to indicate the change of state, while the root specifies the appropriate value for duration and telicity. The affix is thus tagged UNDm for all state-change predicates that are formed with \<om\>. With physical roots (section 2.2.6.1.2) indicating change of position or movement, the indexed participant is both effector and affected. The affix with these roots is tagged ACTm to reflect the role of effector as perhaps more primary.

2.2.6.1.1 With result-state, property and experience-stative roots

Achievement and accomplishment predicates with result-stative roots and experience-stative roots are exemplified in (2.72) and (2.73).

(2.72) B<in-om>tak   din   goma=na.
        UNDm.P-burst RMd   innertube=3sII
        'Its innertube popped.'

Example (2.73) has perfective marking to set the event in the real past, but the change to the depressed state *sadot* probably was not instantaneous. Thus, it may be categorized as an accomplishment predicate.

(2.73) S<inm>adot   sin   nateyan   ama=na.
        UNDm.P-sad   ORMd   death   father=3sII
        'He became sad/unmotivated at his father's death.'

2.2.6.1.2 With physical roots

"Physical" roots in this study are those that denote movement generally in or through space, and those that denote physical positions of animate entities. When a predicate indicates that a person or animal changes position, it may be an achievement predicate with the affix <*om*>, as in examples (2.74) and (2.75) where the Actor index reflects the intentionality or sentience of the participant.

(2.74) Basta   t<om>okdo=ka   sin   doy   kad?an di   bato.
        simply   ACTm-sit=2sI   ORMd   DEM3V   place   BRMi rock
        'Just sit down there by the rock.'

(2.75) ?<om>alagey=ka.
        ACTm-stand=2sI
        'Stand up!'

In the second clause of (2.76), the affix indicates the onset of the change of the direction of movement but does not indicate that any end-point is

2.2 Predicate formation

reached, unlike the first predicate in this example, an active accomplishment with the root 'climb uphill'.

(2.76) Tinikid=mi   din   dontog   asi=kami   pay
        climb.uphill=1pII   RMd   mountain then=1pI   furthermore

       b<om>alalong.
       ACTm-descend
       'We scaled the mountain, then we began going downhill.'

The time phrases included in (2.77) and (2.78) are interpreted as time elapsed before the change of position. Many changes of positional or physical movement are intentional or directed; these are covered in section 2.2.7.

(2.77) Kaanen=da   din   inbalod=da   et   doy
        remove=3pII   RMd   binding=3pII   and   DEM3V

       ninina   yan   t<om>okdo.
       little.while   and   ACTm-sit
       'They removed what they had bound her with and there in a little bit she sat up.'

(2.78) Maga   di   na-bayag,   b<inm>aba   din   talipyano.
        NEGEXIS   RMi   UNDs.P-long.time   ACTm-descend   RMd   airplane
        'It wasn't very long, the airplane came down lower.'

2.2.6.2 Achievement and accomplishment predicates with na- (perfective)

As mentioned earlier, result-state predicates often take on an accomplishment or achievement interpretation when marked as completed, as in (2.79), repeated from (2.62), which is ambiguous. With the inflected prefix *na-*, the predicate may indicate an event, the completion of the change of state as in (2.80). Ambiguity as to achievement or state predication can be dispelled with a time frame in context as in (2.81). Negation also disambiguates, as a state reading is negated by *baken* while an achievement reading is negated by *adi* as in (2.82).

(2.79) *Na-pʔes din goma=na.*
UNDs.P-deflate RMd innertube=3sII
'Its innertube went/was flat.'

(2.80) *Na-tdok di danom sin bagan.*
UNDs.P-dry.up RMi water ORMd spring
'The water in the spring (has) dried up.'

(2.81) *Na-tey si ama=na ed tawen.*
UNDs.P-die PRM father=3sII past.time year
'His father *was dead/ died last year.'

(2.82) *Adi na- pʔes din goma=na. Baken*
NEG UNDs.P-deflate RMd innertube=3sII NEG

na- pʔes din goma=na.
UNDs.P-deflate RMd innertube=3sII
'Its innertube didn't go flat (i.e., it didn't happen).' 'Its innertube isn't flat (i.e., it's fine).'

Some result-stative roots indicate a position or relative location. As an achievement or accomplishment, a predicate based on such roots indicates a change of location or position. While there may be an element of intention in some movements, the denotation of the roots is that of a direction or goal or particular position, as in (2.83) and the perfective affix indicates an achievement reading of the stative. In the flow of a narrative, perfective marking regularly indicates an achievement as an event, as in (2.84).

(2.83) *Na-gʔas din nowang Biti.*
UNDs.P-fall RMd water.buffalo Biti
'Biti's water buffalo fell (over a drop-off).'

2.2 Predicate formation

(2.84)   *Pag*   *et*   *na-tokang*   Ø   *yan inila=k*   *ay*
then   PART   UNDs.P-tip.over   3sI   and saw=1sII   LK

ma-anod   Ø.
UNDs-wash.downstream   3sI
'Then he suddenly fell over (*was in horizontal position) and I saw that he would be swept away by the water.'

2.2.6.3 Time/pace phrases with achievements and accomplishments

Oblique time phrases do not indicate duration with achievement predicates but rather the time span before the change, as in (2.85). Time and pace indicators with accomplishment predicates modify the PROCESS element, as in (2.86).

(2.85)   *Awni*   *ta*   *asi=tako*   *b<om>ala*   *sin*   *maika-dwa*
later   so.that   next=1pI   ACTm-emerge   ORMd   ordinal-two

ay bowan.
LK month
'Wait and then we'll go out in the second month.'

(2.86)   ...*insigon*   *sin*   *ka-dalas*   *di*   *sanglay*   *ay*
depending   ORMd   NOM-quick   BRMi   roots   LK

k<om>ompitay.
UNDm-soft
'...depending on the quickness of the roots to soften.'

2.2.7 Activity predicates

Activity predicates indicate dynamic events, "happenings" with no inherent temporal end-point. Activities have Actor arguments that do the activity. In the logical structure, the constant **do'** with an Actor argument (x) is the indicator of an activity predicate, thus **do'** (x, [**root'** (x/x, y)]). The root specifies whether the (x) argument is an inanimate EFFECTOR, such as a MOVER, or EMITTER, or an animate, potentially deliberate Actor such as a

PERFORMER, CONSUMER, USER, PERCEIVER, etc. Three different types of roots form activity predicates in Kankanaey: physical actions, actions that affect another entity, and perceptions. Sections 2.2.7.1 to 2.2.7.3 will cover the various roots and affixes that form activity predicates.

2.2.7.1 Physical actions

Some activity predicates denote physical motion, emission or positioning. In Kankanaey, these activity predicates are formed with the prefix *man-* (in a few arbitrary cases, *maN-*). The logical structure for these predicates is **do'** (x, [**root'** (x)]). Examples (2.87) and (2.88) illustrate motion and emission activities. Although as noted in section 2.2.6.1.2 a physical position may be interpreted as an accomplishment, it is more common to assume that there is a degree of intentionality to an entity being in a physical position, and thus the participant is viewed as an Actor, as in (2.89). Note that in (2.90) the speaker is not crying uncontrolledly like an infant.

(2.87)   *Man-dan*   *si*   *Romy*   *ya*   *managtag (maN-+tagtag)*
        ACT-walk   PRM   Romy   and   ACT-run

        si   *Lydia.*
        PRM   Lydia
        'Romy walks and Lydia runs.'

(2.88)   *Palalo*   *ay*   *man-ngisangis*   *di*   *segit.*
        too.much   LK   ACT-shine.brightly   RMi   sunlight
        'The sunshine is too bright.'

(2.89)   *Man-salikaot*   Ø   *sin*   *ed*   *baeg.*
        ACT-crouch   3sI   ORMd   LOC   rafter-rack
        'She was crouching up in the drying rack.'

(2.90)   *Pag=ak*   *man-ʔoga*   *tan*   *mansakit*   *nemnem=ko.*
        then=1sI   ACT-cry   because   hurt   thought=1sII
        'Then I cried, because I felt sad.' (idiom: 'thoughts were sick/painful')

2.2 Predicate formation

Movement activity predicates without any specification of being deliberate, intentional, controlled or animate can be formed with the middle-situation infix <om>. The intentionality of the argument of **do'** in activities formed with this infix is blocked. Examples (2.91) and (2.92) exemplify activities effected by natural forces while the human EFFECTOR of the predicate in (2.93) is presented as mindlessly playing.

(2.91)   *?<om>aloyas   din   dada=na.*
        ACTm-flow   RMd   blood=3sII
        'His blood flows down.'

(2.92)   *S<om>aliktoto   din   innapoy.*
        ACTm-boil   RMd   cooked.rice
        'The rice boils.'

(2.93)   *G<om>oy~goyang   si   Baby.*
        ACTm-PROG-play.aimlessly   PRM Baby
        'Baby is playing (not with objects).'

The nuance of intentionality may be seen in the comparison of two predicates built with *onod* 'follow.' Example (2.94) shows overt intention while in (2.95), the path taken only happens to be the same as the brother. There is no intent to overtake or deliberately trace his steps. In fact, the 'following' is temporal as well as spatial. Example (2.96) is a commonly heard response to an invitation to go somewhere.

(2.94)   *Man-lisi=ak   koma   ta   asi=ak*
        ACT-move.to.side=1sI PART so.that then=1sI

        on~onod-en   sisya.
        CVC-follow-UND   3sIII
        'I was going to pull over (and let his vehicle overtake mine) so that I would then be following him.'

(2.95) ?<om>onod=ak   en   agi=k.
        ACTm-follow=1sI OPRM   brother=1sII
        'I will follow along after my brother.'

(2.96) Asi=ak   ?<om>onod!
        then=1sI   ACTm-follow
        'I'll come along later (you go ahead)!'

2.2.7.1.1 Onset of Activity predicates

Onset of activity is often indicated in Kankanaey by a predicate like 'begin', but some roots may express onset with <om> as a change involving self-affecting movement. The "middle" designation indicates that initiation as well as affectedness are within the same participant. Because these include an Activity predicate, the indexing is with the participant as Actor.

The Logical Structure for onset of Activities is INGR **do'** (x, [**root'** (x)]).

One example, from a story of a talking bird, is in (2.97) with a root that is usually prefixed with *man-* to express the activity of birds in the sky. The root used in example (2.98) is also usually affixed with *man-* to express the sun's light emission, but with <om> the predicate specifically indicates the onset, such as when coming out from behind a cloud or after a storm.

(2.97) "Witdokit,"   kanana(kanaen=na)   yan   pag   t<om>ayaw.
        witdokit   say=3sII   and   PART   ACTm-fly
        '"Witdokit," it said, and then flew away.'

(2.98) Awni=t   s<om>git.
        later=PART   ACTm-sunshine
        'In a little bit the sun will come out.'

2.2.7.2 Actions affecting a second participant

Some activity predicates are based on roots that denote actions by an animate entity which affect other participants. As noted in Van Valin and LaPolla (1997:122–123), the second argument of many activity predicates differs from other arguments in logical structures, in that they are often non-referential and tend to be inherent in the meaning of the predicate, characterizing the nature or locus of the action. This may be because the atelic nature of activity predicates precludes a full effect upon a second participant from being specified. (This study has simplified the classifications of Kankanaey roots; it may be shown, as Latrouite (2011) did for Tagalog, that some roots favor the formation of activity predicates because the denotation of the root primarily carries information about the ACTOR's role. Other roots may disfavor the formation of activity predicates because the root denotes salient information about the affected second participant.) The logical structure of these activity predicates is represented as:

do' (x, [**root'** (x, y)]).

The affix used to form most activities in Kankanaey is *man-*. Roots of consumption, and creation can form the basis of an activity predicate, so long as the second argument is not specific, as in (2.99) and (2.100). In (2.101) there is no referential entity that is pinched by the scissors.

(2.99) *Man-sibo   din   anak   si   digo.*
       ACT-sip   RMd   child   ORM   broth
       'The child sips (some) broth.'

(2.100) *Man-solat=ak   koma   ay   dagos.*
        ACT-write=1sI   PART   LK   immediately
        'I should have written (a letter?) right back.'

(2.101) *Man-ipit   di   kaltib   mo   i-pokis   Ø.*
        ACT-pinch   RMi   scissors   if   UNDt-cut.hair   4III
        'A scissors pinches if (one) uses them for haircutting.'

When the effect of an activity upon a specific second participant is explicitly partial, the infix <om_2> (not the middle situation operator) expresses this situation. For example, in (2.102) the activity is atelic in that it is not known how many of the eggs will be taken, but it is certain that some will be left behind.

(2.102) K<om_2>awet=ka   sin   itlog sin   kobongan.
         ACT-reach.in&get=2sI   ORMd   egg   ORMd   nest
         'Reach in and get some of the eggs in the nest.'

Some activity predicates do affect a definite second participant, but with no change of state or lasting effect on it that could delimit the activity. Definite second participants may be the locus of the activity, as in predicates of physical interaction such as 'hold' in (2.103) and (2.104). With a definite activity locus, Kankanaey uses one of the Undergoer voices.

(2.103) I-g?en=mo   Ø   sin   siki=na.
         UNDt-hold=2sII   3sIII   ORMd   leg=3sII
         'Hold it by its legs.'

(2.104) Kawe-e(n)=m   si   Lola.
         hug-UND=2sII   PRM   grannie
         'Hug Grannie!'

2.2.7.3 Activities of experience

The third group of activity predicates is formed with state roots of inner experience, including emotion and perception. When the EXPERIENCER of a situation is presented as exhibiting or expressing the experience with intention or cognitive involvement, a **do'** component is included in the LS, represented as:

> feelings: **do'** (x, [**feel'** (x, [**pred'**])]).
> perceptions: **do'** (x, [**perceive'** (x, (y))]).

2.2 Predicate formation

Activity predicates with one participant are formed using the affix *man-*. Example (2.105) illustrates this affixation with the feeling root *bongot* 'anger'—a predicate that indicates the anger is outwardly expressed, as is the 'happiness' of example (2.106). In (2.107) the root *sakit* 'pain/illness' with *man-* affixation can only mean 'sick' in this context, while in (2.108) the sufferer is cognizant of the pain exhibited by the affected body part.

(2.105) *Man-bongot si Akod.*
ACT-angry PRM Akod
'Akod is angry.'

(2.106) *Man-layad din poso=k si dakdake.*
ACT-happy RMd heart=1pII ORM big
'My heart is very happy (lit. hugely happy).'

(2.107) *Man-sakit din manok Pabling.*
ACT-sick/hurt RMd chicken Pabling
'Pabling's chickens are sick/*hurting.'

(2.108) *Man-sakit din tengnged=ko.*
ACT-sick/hurt RMd neck.back=1sII
'The back of my neck is hurting/*sick.'

With the prefix *man-*, perception predicates allow for intentionality of the Actor, who directs his perception toward a nonreferential STIMULUS, as in (2.109).

(2.109) *Man-ila=ka=s asawa=m.*
ACT-see=2sI=OPRM spouse=2sII
'Keep an eye out/Look for a wife (for yourself)!'

When the STIMULUS of a perception root is referential, the Kankanaey activity predicate is formed with the suffix *-en* (tagged UND). These perception predicates are most often interpreted as cognizant, but not volitional, experience. In (2.110) conscious directed perception of the definite STIMULUS is indicated. In (2.111), the CONTENT of the mental perception is stated, but conscious awareness, not volition, is indicated in perception activities. Example (2.112) shows this distinction as well, with the activity an expected event, but not a planned event.

(2.110) Deng~dengek(denge-en=ko)   din   bogaw   di   mangan?anap
       CVC-hear-UND=1sII   RMd   shout   BRMi   searching

       en   sak?en.
       OPRM   1sIII
       'I was listening to the shouts of those searching for me (he was hiding).'

(2.111) Pag =dan   ammo-en   ay   wada   baw   di
       then=3pII know-UND   LK   EXIS   EVID   RMi

       mantabtabon   ay   guerrilla.
       hiding   LK   guerrilla
       'Then they knew that aha, there were guerrillas who were hiding.'

(2.112) Ila-e(n)=k   si   Mrs. Mantad   si   bigat.
        see-UND1sII   PRM   Mrs. Mantad   ORM   next-day
        'I'll see/*look for Mrs. Mantad tomorrow.'

Imperative perception predicates necessarily imply directed perception as in (2.113). In (2.114) the omitted STIMULUS is the referential situation in general, yielding a cautionary imperative.

(2.113) Adi=kayo   deng~dengngen(denge-en)   din   lawlawa   ay   ibagbaga
        NEG=2pI   CVC-hear-UND   RMd   bad   LK   saying

        =n di   odom
        =BRMi   other
        'Don't listen to/pay attention to the bad things that others are saying!'

(2.114) *Ila-em(-en=mo)*   *tan*   *maitok?o= ka.*
see-UND=2sII   because   hit.head=2sI
'Watch out lest you hit your head.'

2.2.8 Semelfactive predicates

Aktionsart semelfactives are punctual activities that do not affect any second participant in the action. The punctuality is denoted by the action root, differentiating them from the activity predicates described in section 2.2.7.

The logical structure is represented as: SEML **do'** (x, [**action'** (x, (y))]).

Semelfactives in Kankanaey are expressed like activities with the affixes *man-* or suffixes *-en* or *-an*, as in (2.115) and (2.116). A few roots take <*om*>, such as a group denoting light-emission, which is perhaps a type of punctual physical action. Example (2.117) is representative.

(2.115) Nan-akbis   si   Tonia.
ACT-sneeze   PRM   Tonia
'Tonia sneezed.'

(2.116) *Teg~tegteg-en=da*   *din*   *pappait.*
CVC-pound.on-UND=3pII   RMd   wild.sunflower
'They repeatedly pound on the sunflowers.'

(2.117) *B<om>on~boniing*   *din*   *komkomti.*
ACTm-CVC-glow   RMd   firefly.
'The firefly/ies are blinking.'

CVC reduplication on a semelfactive must be interpreted as iterative or plural rather than indicating time duration of one event. Examples (2.116) and (2.117) above show the iterative interpretation of CVC.

Many punctual action roots are onomatopoetic and imply repetition as semelfactive predicates. A few example roots are listed in (2.118). In (2.119) the pragmatic intent is probably more than one blow on the door.

(2.118) pagpag   palakpak   pikpik   tegteg
         'strike or tap' 'clap, applaud' 'pat gently' 'pound with a blunt object'

(2.119) Togtog-em(-en=mo)   din   tangeb.
         strike-UND=2sII   RMd   door
         'Knock (on) the door.'

2.2.9 Active accomplishment predicates

Active accomplishment predicates are formed with action roots that indicate movement, consumption and creation, where the specified action entails a resulting change of state or location for the Actor or for another entity. As pointed out by Van Valin (2005:44–45), these might be "more accurately characterized as 'active achievements'."

2.2.9.1 Active accomplishments with self-affecting motions

Linear spatial movements with specific locative end-points have the logical structure:

$$\textbf{do}'\ (x,\ [\textbf{motion}'\ (x)])\ \&\ \textbf{INGR}\ \textbf{be-at}'\ (y,\ x)$$

The locative state structure included in this logical structure cannot occur as an independent state predicate structure, but its presence influences and licences state-related phenomena. Very few self-affecting motion roots in Kankanaey can form active accomplishments. In the data gathered, only five roots are used to form predicates that can be followed by an end-point. The root *saa* 'go home' lexicalizes the end-point. Locative phrases occurring with the general roots *ey* 'go', *ali* 'come' and *dateng* 'arrive' always indicate the endpoint. Not surprisingly, given the rugged terrain occupied by the Kankanaey people, the roots *tikid* 'go uphill' and *balalong* 'go downhill' can also imply reaching the inherent end-point (hilltop or valley). Example (2.120) shows two active accomplishment predicates. In (2.121) the destination of a means of public transportation is mentioned. Time phrases, as in (2.122), indicate time before reaching the destination, not time spent in traveling, since the root denotes the punctual arrival at home.

2.2 Predicate formation

(2.120) *Ay ʔ<om>ali=ka   sina   ono s<om>aa=ka?*
       Q   ACTm-come=2sI DEM1IV   or   ACTm-go.home=2sI
       'Will you come here or go home?'

(2.121) *Emey(ʔ<om>ey)   din   dyipni   ay   nay   ed   UBC.*
       ACTm-go   RMd   jeepney   LK   DEM1V   LOC   UBC
       'This jeepney will go to U.B.C.'

(2.122) *Nay   enggay   piga   ay agew   yan asi=da*
       DEM1V   already   how.many   LK day   and then=3pI

       s<om>aa.
       ACTm-go.home
       'Here it is still how many days before (lit. and then) they come home.'

In (2.123) and (2.124), it may be seen that the verb specifying the mode of 'going' cannot specify the destination by itself alone. In (2.123) the active accomplishment predicate *emey* (with morphophonemic changes) with a place name indicates arrival, while in (2.124) the place name with only the 'walk' predicate can not indicate endpoint.

(2.123) *Kabigatana, nankoyog=kami   ay   nan-dadʔan(CVC-dan)   ay*
       Next.day   accompany=1pI LK   ACT-PROG-walk   LK

       <om>ey   ed   Ambagan.
       ACT-go   LOC   Ambagan
       'The next day, we went together walking to Ambagan.'

(2.124) *Man-dan   di   bas   ed   Balakbak.*
       ACT-walk   RMi   bus   LOC   Balakbak
       'The bus goes through/*to Balakbak.'

With the suffix *-en*, the root *dateng* 'arrive' can form an active accomplishment with the meaning of 'come to' or 'find'. It cannot denote control over the situation, as seen in (2.125) and (2.126). In (2.127) the 'sudden' particle and the lack of the definiteness operator on the reference phrase marker attest to the markedness of this construction. With other motion verbs, the predicate created by *-en* is not an active accomplishment, as in (2.128).

(2.125) *Datng-ek(-en=ko)   din   ketang asi=ak   pag   songen.*
arrive-UND=1sII   RMd   brook   then=1sI   next   go.upstream
'I came to the brook, then I followed it upstream.'

(2.126) *Atikawkawe(n) =na   Ø,   datng-e(n)=na   din   eten*
sort.through=3sII   4III   arrive-UND=3sII   RMd   skirt

Dania.
Dania
'Sorting through it, he found Dania's skirt.'

(2.127) *Idi   inmaddawi=ak, d<in>teng=ko=et   di*
when   go.far=1sI   UND.P-arrive=1sII=PART   RMi

ginawang.
river.
'When I had gone a fair way, I suddenly arrived at a river.'

(2.128) *Adi=ka   dan-en   din   danom ay   sana.*
NEG=2sI   walk-UND RMd   water LK   DEM2V
'Don't walk in that water!'

The suffix *-an* with *dateng* also creates an active accomplishment predicate that specifies a person as locus (l), 'come upon', as in (2.129).

(2.129) *Idi=et   d<om>ateng=ak   ed   Badiw,*
when=sudden   ACT-arrive=1sI   LOC   Badiw

d<in>teng-ak(-an=ko)   si   manong
UND1.P-arrive<=1sII   PRM   brother
'Well, when I got to Badiw, I came across (my) older-brother.'

2.2 Predicate formation

2.2.9.2 Active accomplishments with other-affecting actions

Active accomplishment predicates can denote a specified action by one participant that results in some change of state for a second participant. (These predicates must be distinguished from causative achievements in which an *unspecified* action precedes an effect.) Action roots can specify manner, direction and other semantic particulars. The logical structure as suggested by Van Valin (2005:45) is as follows:

$$\textbf{do}' \ (x, [\textbf{pred}_1' \ (x, y)]) \ \& \ \text{INGR} \ \textbf{pred}_2' \ (y)$$

Predicates of consumption and creation, formed with the suffix *-en*, should be understood as active accomplishments because the entity consumed or created is specific and fully affected. In example (2.130), the plan is to consume the entire quantity of beer, and in (2.131) the buildings were built from scratch, not fixed or enlarged.

(2.130) *Inom-en=tako   din   nay   Stateside.*
        drink-UND=1+2P   RMd   DEM1V   stateside
        'Let's drink this imported beer!'

(2.131) *?<in>amag   di   gobilno   di   Pidinsiya   ya*
        UND.P-make   BRMi   government   RMi   gov't-center   and

        iskowilaan   sina.
        school   DEM1IV
        'The government built a municipal center and school here.'

2.2.10 Causative predicates

Kankanaey has a prefix *pa-* which derives overt causative predicates from a wide variety of roots, see section 2.3.6. Many causative predicates, however, may be constructed from stative roots by the use of transitive *-en*, which requires an Actor argument. In Kankanaey, the action is unspecified (**do'** (x, Ø)) and causes a change of state of the affected participant, as seen in the logical structure of these predicates.

2.2.10.1 Causative change-of-state predicates

With result-stative roots, the suffix *-en* creates causative achievement predicates with this logical structure:

[**do′** (x, Ø)] CAUSE [INGR **stative′** (y)].

The activity part of the predicate is unspecified, as such predicates do not indicate what action causes the resultant change of state. They only assert that such a change is caused by some effector. For example, in (2.132), 'break' does not indicate the action by which the person would cause the jar to be broken.

(2.132) *Mo gopak-e(n)=m   san   bogsit, bayad-a(n)=m   Ø.*
if   break-UND=2sII RM   jar   pay-UNDl=2sII 4III
'If you break that jar, you'll pay for it.'

In (2.133) and (2.134) a fuzzy semantic line may have been crossed—the action involved in 'drop/let fall' is very nearly unspecified. The semantic particulars relate to the effect on the second participant, which is total but due to natural causes. With this root, the prefix *i-* (*in-* perfective) connotes more intention than with the suffix *-en*; either may be used to form the predicate.

(2.133) *In-tekdag=da   din   armas   sin   talipyano.*
UNDt.P-fall.distance=3pII RMd   weapons   ORMd   airplane
'They dropped the weapons from the airplane.'

(2.134) *Adi=ka   eg~ʔegas-en   Ø   tan*
NEG=2sI   CVC-fall.short.distance-UND   4III   because

  ma-gopak   Ø.
  UNDs-break   4I
  'Don't let it fall it because it will break.'

2.2.10.2 Three-argument predicates

Three-argument predicates such as 'put', 'sell', 'give', and 'tell' are causative achievement predicates in Kankanaey. They all involve a locative state predicate (e.g., **be-at'**), which as noted in section 2.2.9.1, can only be part of complex predicates in Kankanaey. (It will be noted in section 2.5 that simple location is expressed not with a locative predicate but with the existential.) Again, the activity causes the achievement of a change-of-location state, but is not otherwise specified. One possible logical structure follows, where (y) is a location and (z) is a theme argument:

[**do'** (x, Ø)] CAUSE [INGR **be-at'** (y, z)].

The affixes *i-*, *-an* and *i-...-an* are used to form causative achievements. Example (2.135) has two causative achievement predicates indicated by *i-*, while (2.136) shows an *i-...-an* marked predicate. Chapter 6 explains the variable assignment of affixes to predicates.

(2.135) *Mabalin   ay i-paw?it=ko   Ø   en   Jery   ono*
       possible   LK UNDt-send=1sII   4III OPRM   Jery   or

       i-gto=k   Ø   pay.laeng   isna.
       UNDt-store=1sII   4III   PART   DEM1IV
       'It's possible for me to send it to Jery or to still store it here.'

(2.136) *Asi=na   i-dawt-an   dakami   si   pala   kanen.*
       then=3sII   UNDd-give<   1pIII   ORMi   for   food
       'Then he gave us (something, i.e., money) for (getting) food.'

The resulting location may be inherent, as in (2.137), where a recipient is implied.

(2.137) Asi=ak   i-dawat   Ø   mo   <om>ey=ak
       and.then=1sI   UNDt-give   4III   if/when   ACT-go=1sI

   issa.
   DEM2IV
   'I'll give it to (to you) when I go to your place (lit. there).'

2.3 Derived predicates

Some predicates are derived from non-canonical roots, such as causatives from attribute roots, and activities from property roots. Other predicates are derived by increasing or decreasing the participants from the default norm specified by the root, or by expanding the possible roles a participant could fill. The affixes used for these predicates may add semantic content or license a participant to hold a specific role. Types of derived predicates that are covered in this section are: potential predicates, derived attributives, predicates with temporal immediacy, passive statives, complex predicates with extra licensed participants and derived causatives.

2.3.1 Potential predicates

A predicate expressing the potentiality of a state of affairs lacks agentivity and has a potentiality operator as part of the predicate. With EFFECTORS and EXPERIENCERS, especially humans, it indicates ability. With ATTRIBUTANTS it indicates propensity. The symbol ◊ indicates potentiality.

2.3.1.1 Potential activities with **maka-**

Potential activities may be derived with experience and action roots using the prefix *maka-*, tagged ABIL(itative), which blocks the agency implicature of **do'** with these roots. This derivation yields predicates that express the ability of the EFFECTOR in relation to the root. The semantic representation (SR) for the derivation of *maka-anges* 'able to breathe' is shown in (2.138) and exemplified in (2.139). An example with EXPERIENCERS is (2.140).

2.3 Derived predicates 69

(2.138) *man-anges si Mims*   SR: **do'** (Mims, [**breathe'** (Mims)])
'Mims breathes/takes a breath.'
maka-anges si Mims   SR: ◊ **do'** (Mims, [**breathe'** (Mims)])
'Mims can breathe.'

(2.139) *Mang-i-pa-kayabkab   tet?ewa   Ø   mo   adi=ka*
ACT-Th-CAUS-heart.pound   true   4I   if/when   NEG=2sI

maka-anges.
ABIL-breathe
'It really is frightening (makes the heart pound) when you can't breathe.'

(2.140) *Olay   sin   mabolinget,   maka-ila=ka   pay   dedan.*
even   ORMd   darkness   ABIL-see=2sI   PART   PART
'Even in the dark, you are nevertheless able to see.'

With perfective marking, the lack of agency implicature yields a 'fortuitous' reading, as in (2.141). This derived form is often used with the negative to deflect responsibility for one's lack of success, as in (2.142). The negator for the potential activities is *adi*, as in (2.142).

(2.141) *Enggay   naka-a=ak   si   esa   ay   reference=ko*
already ABIL-get=1sI   ORMi   one   LK   reference=1sII

en   da Danlo.
OPRM   pl Danlo
'I was already able to get one reference from Danlo (and someone with him.)'

(2.142) *Adi=ak   naka-solat   ay dagos   tan*
       NEG=1sI   ABIL.P-write   LK immediately   because

   na-sangaw=ak   sin   pitsa.
   UNDs.P-distract=1sI   ORMd   date
   'I wasn't able to write (you) immediately because I got confused about the date.'

2.3.1.2 Potential attributives with maka-

With certain roots, potentiality tends to be interpreted as propensity, as in (2.143), and these predicates fall into the attributive class, describing their ATTRIBUTANT as an individual-level stative, and taking *baken* as the negator, as in (2.144).

(2.143) *Ma-lastog   ono   maka-etek=da.*
       ATT-lie   or   ABIL-deceive=3pI
       'They are liars, deceivers.'

(2.144) *Baken   maka-apal   si   ka-dwa=k.*
       NEG   ABIL-envy   PRM   companion-two=1sII
       'My husband is not (an) envious (person).'

2.3.1.3 Potential causative states with kaCV-

When the ability to trigger emotions or mental states can be attributed to something or someone, an abilitative-attributive predicate is formed with *ka-* followed by CV reduplication of the state root. Like attribute predicates, it does not inflect for aspect, and thus cannot assert that a participant actually caused the state, although pragmatically this is generally the assumption. (The symbol ◊ indicates potentiality.) The EXPERIENCER is unspecified in the Stative LS (compare to Van Valin and LaPolla, 402):

$$[\mathbf{be'}\ (...x...)]\ \Diamond\ \text{CAUSE}\ [\mathbf{feel'}\ (\emptyset,\ \mathbf{pred'})].$$

2.3 Derived predicates

Thus, in (2.145) the 'words' had the potential to offend, while in (2.146) the 'path' is characterized by its potential for causing 'fear'. Like attributive predicates, this derived predicate is negated with *baken*, as in (2.147).

(2.145) *Kasi-sinit   tomet   din   kali=m.*
       ATT.ABIL-offended PART   RMd   word=2sII
       'Your words were certainly offensive.'

(2.146) *Kae-egyat   ay danan Ø   tan   deppas   Ø.*
       ATT.ABIL-fear LK path   4I because precipice 4I
       'It's a scary/dangerous path because it's precipitous.'

(2.147) *Baken koma   kae-egyat   di   pese.*
       NEG   should   ATT.ABIL-fear RMi   death
       'Death should not be frightening (to anyone).'

2.3.2 Predicates with temporal immediacy

The prefix *ka-* can indicate temporal immediacy—a suddenly beginning event, or a just-completed event.

2.3.2.1 Inchoative predicates with ka-

Actions that are not inherently precipitous may be prefixed by *ka-*, tagged IMM(ediate), to indicate that the event is suddenly beginning, as in (2.138) and (2.149). This affix forms an achievement predicate with this logical structure:

$$\text{INGR do' } (x, [\text{root'} (x, (y))]).$$

(2.148) *ngem   ka-posipos=ak   et   adi ...*
       but   IMM-twist/turn=1sI   PART   PART
       'but I just quickly twisted really...(and escaped!)'

(2.149) Et   doy   etay   ka-sigbo   Ø,   en=(n)a   pay   kano=n
       and DEM3V PART   IMM-dive   3sI   go=3sII   PART HSY=DISP

ila-(e)n   Ø.
see-UND   3sIII
'And there wow! he dove right in, he went to see him (upon realizing his friend was stuck underwater).'

2.3.2.2 Recently completed predicates with ka-CVC

The combination of CVC reduplication with the prefix *ka-* indicates recently completed activities or changes of state. Examples (2.150) and (2.151) show this predicate.

(2.150) Sa=y   address=na   tan   doy
       DEM2I=RMi   address=3sII   because   DEM3IV

kakal~kali=k.
RECENT-speak=1sII
'That's his address (I know) because I just now spoke (with him).'

(2.151) Kadat~dateng=mi=d   labi   en   da   Pedring.
       RECENT-arrive=1pII=LOC night OPRM   pl Pedring
'We just arrived last night—Pedring and others and I.'

2.3.3 Passive states with *ma-*

Previous examples have shown that the prefix *ma-* can form several different kinds of predicate, and passive states are yet another use of this prefix. Any two-argument predicate with a state **pred′** in its logical structure may be passivized by a process (see section 1.2.5.3 of chapter 6) in which *ma-* replaces *-en* or co-occurs with *i-*, *-an*, or *i...an*. (Perfective aspect is marked on *ma-* yielding *na-*.)

Passive states have only one direct argument, the affected entity. Examples of passive states are shown in (2.152) to (2.154).

2.3 Derived predicates

(2.152) *Na-galabgab-an   din   takkay Malisay.*
UNDls.P-scratch<   RMd   hand   Malisay
'Malisay's hand was scratched.'

(2.153) *Na-sawad=ak   sin   tolo   ay   pewek.*
UNDs.P-block=1sI ORMd three LK   typhoon
'I was blocked (from my plans) by the three typhoons.'

(2.154) *Nakdeng   ay   nai-galot=kami   amin...*
done   LK   UNDts.P-tie=1plI   all
'(When) all of us were fastened (by seatbelts)...

Imperfective marking on passive predicates (*ma-* as opposed to perfective *na-*) creates an open-ended proposition that may easily imply potentiality rather than assurance of its fulfillment. A passive derivation from a directed-perception activity is shown in (2.155) by the semantic representations built on *ila* + 2s 'see you', and in (2.156).

(2.155) *Ila-en=mi sikʔa.* SR: **do'** (we [**see'** (we, you)]) 'We are looking at/see you.'
Ma-ila=ka.   SR: ◊ (**see'** (∅, you))   'You are able to be seen/ visible.'

(2.156) *Ma-lako-an   amin.*
UNDls -buy<   all
'Everything can be bought (it's all for sale).'

2.3.3.1 Passives as stative modifiers

Passive predicates can be used as stative modifiers. For example, in (2.157) the reference phrase *din itlog* 'the eggs' has a linked modifier, the passive predicate *na-i-do~dolin* 'were stored'. This passive was derived from the causative achievement predicate *i-dolin*. CV reduplication was added to indicate that the resulting state had duration in time.

(2.157) *Na-boyok   din   itlog   ay nai-do~dolin.*
UNDs-rot   RMd   egg   LK   UNDts.P-CV-store
'The stored eggs/eggs that were stored are rotten.'

Test 5 (see table 2.2) above predicts that semelfactive, activity and process predicates cannot serve as stative modifiers. This is borne out by examples (2.158) to (2.160), which attempt to passivize semelfactive, activity, and process predicates by adding a co-occuring *ma-*, all of which are ungrammatical.

(2.158) **Na-ek   din   anak   ay   na-pikpik(-en).*
UNDs-sleep   RMd   child   LK   UNDs-pat
*'The patted child/child who was patted slept.'

(2.159) **Na-ek   din   anak   ay   na-man-dan.*
UNDs-sleep   RMd   child   LK   UNDs-ACT-walk
*'The walked child/child who walked slept.'

(2.160) **Ay   in-dolin=mo   din   lokto   ay*
Q   UNDt.P-store=2sII   RMd   yams   LK

na-ng\<om\>etit?
UNDs-UNDm-black
*'Did you store the darkened yams/yams that darkened?'

2.3.4 Derived predicates with *i-* and *i...an*

Many predicates formed from any root class may express a situation not entailed by the root denotation, such as an entity being used or moved in the course of the main event. Such predicates take the affix *i-* as an applicative to license the participant introduced by such a state of affairs, such as an INSTRUMENT, CONCOMITANT, or other THEMES that are moved or used. The Actor of these activity predicates is generally interpreted as agentive, even causative, depending on the root. In (2.161), which exemplifies a causative semelfactive predicate, the item that 'knocks' is brandished by an agent. In (2.162), the prefix *i-* with

2.3 Derived predicates

'take to sleep' has licensed the 'doll' as a concomitant THEME and with 'pillow' it has licensed the 'towel' as an instrument THEME.

(2.161) *I-togtog=na   din   payong   sin   tangeb.*
UNDt-knock   RMd   umbrella   ORMd   door
'She knocked (with) the umbrella on the door.'

(2.162) *I-ek=na   din   daldali=na;   i-pongan=(n)a*
UNDt-sleep=3sII   RMd   doll=3sII   UNDt-pillow=3sII

din   towalya.
RMd   towel
'She takes her doll to sleep with her; she uses the towel as a pillow.'

Many actions and movements may be specified in terms of direction vis-à-vis some entity, whether literally 'toward' or 'away from' the entity, or more metaphorically, as in the case of a BENEFICIARY or other RECIPIENT. The *i...an* circumfix, tagged UNDd(irectional), is used as an applicative to form the predicate and to license such entities when they are specified as relevant to the activity. Example (2.163) compares three predicates based on *tagtag* 'run.' Examples (2.164 to (2.167) exemplify various interpretations of directional specification.

(2.163) *managtag   i-tagtag*
maN-tagtag
'to run'   'to run off with something'

i-tagtag-an
i...an-tagtag
'to run from something or someone'

(2.164) *I-tneng-a(n)=m   kod   mo   sino   san*
UNDd-hear<=2sII   please   if   what   DRM

i-bog~bogaw=da.
UNDt-PROG-shout=3pII
'Please listen (attentively) to (hear) whatever it is they are shouting about.'

(2.165) *I-tep?a-a(n)=m   pay   din   manok   si*
        UNDd-toss<=2sII   PART   RMd   chicken   ORMi

   kane(n)=na.
   food=3sII
   'Toss the chicken some food.'

(2.166) *Iandoanas   tatang=na.*
        i-ando-a(n)=na=s(i)
        UNDd-tall<=3sII=PRM   father=3sII
        'He passes his father in height.'

(2.167) *I-lako-a(n)=m   kod   sak?en   si   arina.*
        UNDd-buy<=2sII   please   1sIII   ORMi   flour
        'Please buy me some flour.'

2.3.5 Derived activity predicates with *maki-*

The prefix *maki-* (ASSOC for 'associate') indicates that a participant joins others in an activity. The time phrase indicates duration of the activity with no inherent telic point, as in (2.168). A more detailed look at this predicate is found in chapter 6.

(2.168) *Siyat=ta=n   maki-line   si   piga   ay   oras.*
        must=1+2I=DISP   ASSOC-line ORMi   how.many   LK   hour
        'We have to stand in line for how many hours.' (e.g., at the post office)

2.3.6 Derived causative predicates with *pa-*

The prefix *pa-* (CAUS) on the root adds an agentive CAUSER participant to the logical structure of a predicate, often in addition to other affixation that specifies the presence of affected participants. The causing activity is unspecified, and β represents another Logical Structure:

$$[\text{DO} (x, [\textbf{do}', \varnothing)] \text{ CAUSE } [\beta].$$

2.3 Derived predicates

2.3.6.1 With the prefix man-

Man-+pa- forms causative predicates such as the causative activities in (2.169) and (2.170) and the causative perception-state in (2.171). Often these predicates take a reflexive function, as may be seen in examples (2.170) through (2.173). With place names, as in (2.174), *man-pa-* creates a causative locative state, indicating 'to head toward' that place.

(2.169) *Man-beey   kano   di   kabonyan   sidi   ay*
       ACT-house   HSY   RMi   god   DEM3IV   LK

       man-pa-kan   si   ma-dagaang-an.
       ACT-CAUS-eat   ORMi   UNDls -hunger<
       'Gods live there, they say, who feed hungry (people).'

(2.170) *Asi=ak   man-pa-amag   si   baro   ay   beey=ko.*
       then=1sI   ACT-CAUS-make   ORMi   new   LK   house=1sII
       'Then I'll have a new house built for me.'

(2.171) *Na-bayang-an   Ø   et   man-pa-ligat   Ø   tan*
       UNDls.P-wound<   3sI   and   ACT-CAUS-suffer   3sI   because

       man-ga~gate   Ø.
       ACT-CV-itchy   4I
       'He got a wound and he's having a hard time (causing himself to suffer) because it is always itchy.'

(2.172) *Man-pa-pokis=ak   kod.*
       ACT-CAUS-cut.hair=1sI   please
       'I'd like to get a haircut please.'

(2.173) *Man-pa-ila=ak   si   doktor.*
       ACT-CAUS-see=1sI   ORMi   doctor
       'I'm going to see a doctor (lit. cause myself to be seen by a doctor).'

(2.174) Nan-logan=kami   en   Mrs. Mayos   ay
       ACT.P-vehicle=1pI OPRM   Mrs. Mayos   LK

   man-pa-Bagyo.
   ACT-CAUS-Bagyo
   'Mrs. Mayos and I got on a vehicle to go to Baguio.'

2.3.6.2 With i-, -en and -an

With *i-*, *pa-* forms causative active accomplishments, causative perception-states or causative activities, as in (2.175) to (2.177) respectively.

(2.175) I-pa-kan=mo   din   sakati   sin   baka.
        CAUS.ACT-eat=2sII   RMd   grass   ORMd   cow
        'Feed the grass to the cow.'

(2.176) Asi=na   i-pa-dnge   Ø   sin   soldados=na.
        then=3sII   UNDt-CAUS-hear   4I   ORMd   soldiers=3sII
        'Then he told it to his soldiers. (lit. caused to hear it)'

(2.177) Olay   i-pa-chekup=yo   agan?o   Ø   ta.say
        OK   UNDt-CAUS-check=2pII   before   4III   so.that

   ma-pnek   di   bayer=yo.
   UNDs-satisfy   RMi   buyer=2pII
   'It's OK to have it checked out first so your buyer will be satisfied.'

With *-en*, *pa-* also forms causative activities and causative states, with action roots in (2.178) to (2.180), stative roots as exemplified in (2.181) and (2.182) and even a class root in (2.183). Time expressions, as in (2.179), indicate duration of the action.

(2.178) Pa-kan-en=da   si   Doligen.
        CAUS-eat-UND=3pII   PRM   Doligen
        'They fed Doligen.'

2.3 Derived predicates

(2.179) P<in>a-kan   di   man-ili   di   soldados   si
       CAUS-UND.P-eat   BRMi   ACT-town   RMi   soldiers   ORMi

       dowa   ay   agew.
       two   LK   day
       'The townspeople fed soldiers for two days.'

(2.180) En=ak pa-lobwat-en   dakayo   ed   Bagyo.
       go=1sI CAUS-depart-UND   2pIII   LOC   Bagyo
       'I am going to see you off (lit. cause to depart) in Baguio.'

(2.181) Masapol   ay   pa-pigsa-e(n)=m   din   nemnem=mo
       necessary LK   CAUS-strong-UND=2sII   RMd   mind=2sII

       ya   t<om>oled=ka.
       and   UNDm-brave=2sI
       'It's necessary that you strengthen your mind and become brave.'

(2.182) Pa-sadot-e(n)=na=s   Ana   gapo   sin
       CAUS-sad-UND=3sII=PRM   Ana   due.to   ORMd

       ka-iwed   di   anak=na.
       NOM-NEGEXIS   RMi   child=3sII
       'He made Ana sad because of her not having children.'

(2.183) Si   sak?en   koma   di   mang-onod   sin   papilis
       PRM   1sIII1   IRR   RMi   ACT-follow   ORMd   papers

       ngem   pa-bigat-e(n)=k   Ø.
       but   CAUS-morrow-UND=1sII   4III
       'I should be the one to follow-up on the paperwork but I put it off.'

There are very few instances of *pa...an* in Kankanaey. One of these is with the general movement root *ey* 'to go'. The *pa-* prefix triggers morphophonemic assimilation with this root in both the *i-pa-* and *pa...an* affixations when forming the predicate 'put', as seen in (2.184).

This may indicate a process of lexicalization underway as a new action root.

(2.184) *Pay?am*　　　　　　Ø　si　　　danom　asi=ka
　　　　pa-?ey-an=mo
　　　　CAUS.ACT-go<=2sII　4III　ORMi　water　then=2sII

　　　　ipe?ey　　　　Ø　sin　ref.
　　　　i-pa-?ey
　　　　CAUS.ACT-go　4III　ORMd　ref
　　　　'Put water in/on it and then put it in the refrigerator.'

2.3.6.3 With ka-

Causative *pa-* can co-occur with *ka-* as in (2.185), where the second (oblique) participant must be acknowledged by the *i-* 'Theme' prefix.

(2.185) *Doy*　　*ka-i-pa-kaan*　　　si　　　*ama=na;*
　　　　DEM3V　IMM-Th-CAUS-leave　PRM　father=3sII

　　　　ka-i-pa-sardeng　　　Ø　　en　　　Henli.
　　　　IMM-Th-CAUS-stop　　3sI　OPRM　Henli
　　　　'There, his father immediately made (him) leave; he made Henli stop (going to school).'

2.3.6.4 With no other affixation

At times, *pa-* occurs alone, perhaps as a shortcut, and creates idiosyncratic predicates, depending on the denotation and lexical type of the root. For example, in (2.186) *pa-* combines with a physical-position root to create a causative-state predicate, while in (2.187), *pa-* combines with an action root to create an ambiguous causative predicate.

(2.186) *Pa-alodos=mo*　　　Ø　sin　　dingding.
　　　　CAUS-in.line=2sII　4III　ORMd　wall
　　　　'Place it along the base of the wall.'

2.3 Derived predicates

(2.187) *Ma-baew-an   Ø,   asi   pa-soso   Ø.*
       UNDls-cool.off<   4I   then   CAUS-suck   3sI/4I?
       '(When the bottle of milk) has been cooled down, then have (the baby) drink (it).'

2.3.7 Predicates with the possession root *oka*

The root *oka* denotes simple possession in its unaffixed form, as in (2.188). With predicating affixation, the meaning includes change of possession, as in (2.189) and (2.190).

(2.188) *Oka   =n di anak=ko   din   sapatos ay doy.*
        belong.to   BRMi child=1sII RMd shoes   LK DEM3V
        'Those shoes belong to my child.'

(2.189) *Oka-en   Pidlo   din   bingay=na   ay   daga.*
        belong-UND   Pidlo   RMd   share=3sII   LK   land
        'Pidlo will take possession of his share of land.'

(2.190) *Oka-an=da   din   pedis   di   nangon?ona   ay*
        belong-UNDl=3pII   RMd   bile   BRMi   preceded   LK

napalti.
butchered
'They will offer up (in ritual) the bile of the preceding (animal) that was butchered.'

2.3.8 Class roots with predicating affixes—argument incorporation

Predicate affixes are typically used with action or stative roots. When a class root takes predicating affixes, the resulting predicate denotes a typical activity or state involving entities of the denoted class. A special case in point is the affixation possible on number words. Section 2.4 details this intriguing set of affixes.

2.3.8.1 Natural phenomena

One analysis of predicates of natural phenomena is that they incorporate their only argument. Dynamic natural events are activity predicates with *man-*, while states that come about by natural means are affixed with *ma-*. Thus, in (2.191) rain is expressed as an activity predicate while nightfall is a state predicate. In (2.192) both earthquakes and typhoons are expressed as activities with *man-*. (The modifier 'strong' is an adverbial adjunct.)

(2.191) *Man-ʔodan dowan ma-labi.*
ACT-rain while UNDs-night
'It was raining as night came on.'

(2.192) *Nan-yegyeg si na-pigsa~pigsa, ya nan-pewek*
ACT-earthquake LK ATT-CVCCV-strong and ACT-typhoon

si na-pi~pigsa et linibo di nat~na-tey.
LK ATT-CV-strong and thousands RMi CVC-UNDs-die
'It earthquaked extremely strongly, and it typhooned strongly over time and those who died were (numbered in the) thousands.'

2.3.8.2 Class roots as nonreferential participants

With other class roots, an activity predicate indicates that the root is a nonreferential undergoer. Examples of such activities would include many predicates about gathering things, as in (2.193). When a state predicate is formed with *ma-* or *ma...an*, as in (2.194) and (2.195), the root denotes a state affecting the participant.

(2.193) *Mang-owang=tako!*
maN-kowang
ACT-worm=1+2pI
'Let's dig worms!'

(2.194) *Na-kowang=da.*
    UNDs.P-worm=3pI
    'They are infested with worms.'

(2.195) *Na-dalangki-an   din   moyang   ay   nay.*
    UNDls-cradle.cap< RMd   baby   LK   DEM1V
    'This baby has cradle-cap (a scalp condition).'

2.4 Predicates built with numbers

Predicates built with numbers show more variety than those built with other types of roots. Common affixes build predicates with numbers but there is other affixation unique to numerical predicates.

2.4.1 Predicating affixation

Numbers can be affixed with almost any predicating affix to indicate activities or states having to do with that number. Examples (2.196) to (2.202) show numbers with the most common affixes including reduplication.

(2.196) *Man-tolo   din   balat   mo   pit?ing-e(n)=m   Ø.*
    ACT-three   RMd   banana   if   break.in.hands-UND=2sII   4III
    'The banana will split into three parts if you break it in your hands.'

(2.197) *Opat-e(n)=m   din   lokto.*
    four-UND=2sII   RMd   yams
    '(Divide/cut) the yam into four.'

(2.198) *Opat-e(n)=m   di   lako-a(n)=m.*
    four-UND=2sII   RMi   buy-UNDl=2sII
    'Buy four.'

(2.199) *Ma-opat   din   mangga   =s di.*
    UNDs-four   RMd   mango   =DEM3IV
    'Mangoes cost four pesos there.'

(2.200) *Pan-tolo-en=da   din   tawid=na.*
UND.CAUS-three=3pII   RMd   inheritance=3sII
'They will divide his estate into three.'

(2.201) *Man-taoli   Ø   sin   ka-tlo=na.*
ACT-return   3sI   ORMd   ordinal-three=4II
'He will return day after tomorrow (in 3 days).'

(2.202) *Sino   san   ka-dwa=m?*
who   DRM   NOM-two=2sII
'Who is your companion?'

CV reduplication with numbers is common when the number is the nuclear element in the clause core, as in (2.203).

(2.203) *To~tolo   din   bisita=mi.*
CV-three   RMd   visitor=1pII
'We have three visitors.'

When an unaffixed property root is being used as a predicate, reduplication of the initial CVC may occur as a predicating affix without adding any semantic information. CVC reduplication is evident with numerals and a few other instances. See (2.204) and (2.205).

(2.204) *Doddowa(dow~dowa)   da.*
CVC-two   3pI
'There are two of them (lit. they are two).'

(2.205) *Law~lawa din   aso ay   nay.*
CVC-bad   RMd   dog LK   this
'This dog is bad.'

CVC reduplication is an idiomatic way of estimating, used most commonly with the numbers three, five, and seven, as in (2.206).

2.4 Predicates built with numbers   85

(2.206) *Tol~tolo   di   anak=mi.*
       CVC-three   RMi   child=1pII
       'We have just a few kids.'

2.4.2 Unique affixation

Several unique affixes have developed in Kankanaey to express fine points regarding mathematical concepts. Examples (2.207) to (2.214) have affixes observed only with numbers, and include some metaphorical extensions. Vowel deletion and other morphophonemic processes are clarified in the following examples.

(2.207) *Mamin-dowa=ka   ay   manakdo (maN-sakdo).*
       times-two=2sI   LK   ANTI-fetch.water
       'Fetch water twice.'

(2.208) *<Inm>ey=ak   sidi   si   namin-tolo.*
       ACTm-go=1sI DEM3IV   ORMi   times-three
       'I went there three times.'

(2.209) *Ay   sa=y   maika-pito   ay   anak=yo?*
       Q   DEM2I=RMi   sequence-seven   LK   child=2pII
       'Is that your seventh child?'

(2.210) *Sag-o~opat   di   ala-en=yo.*
       each-CV-four   RMi   take-UND=2pII
       'Take four apiece.'

(2.211) *Sag-do~dowa-e(n)=m   di   i-watwat=mo   sin*
       each-CV-two-UND=2sII   RMi   UNDt-distribute=2sII   ORMd

       anan?ak.
       children
       'What you distribute to the children, make it two apiece.'

(2.212) *Kap?atam (ka-?opat-an=m)*   kod   sa.
?-four<=2sII   please   DEM2I
'Please bring that up to four (as when vendor offers 3 for a certain price).'

(2.213) *I-pi-dwa=m*   kod   ∅.
UNDt-?-two=2sII   please   4III
'Please say/do it again (repeat).'

(2.214) *I-pingsan*   *...ma-mingsan*   *...pingsan*
UNDt-once   ...UNDs-once   ...first.cousin
'do once'   '...next/sometime' '...first cousin'

2.4.3 Glottal infix with numbers

A glottal stop [?] infixed before the second vowel of the root indicates a limitation, 'only'. This combines with reduplicative affixation and predicating affixation in unique ways with number roots, as seen in (2.215) to (2.218).

(2.215) *Tol~tol<?>o*   din   *anak=mi.*
CVC-?-three   RMd   child=1pII
'Our kids are only three (i.e., we have just three kids).'

(2.216) *Tol~tol<?>o*   din   *book=na.*
CVC-?-three   RMd   hair=3sII
'He is balding.'

(2.217) *Pit~pit<?>o-e(n)=m*   di   *lako-a(n)=m.*
CVC-?-seven-UND=2sII   RMi   buy-UNDl=2sII
'Just buy seven.'

(2.218) *Mat?olo (ma<?>tolo)*   di   *na-bay?an.*
UNDs-?-three   RMi   UNDs.P-left.over
'There are only a few left.'

2.5 Existential predicates

Existentials are the final type of predicate that will be introduced in this chapter. Existentials occur in their base form to express simple existence or physical presence. With a locative phrase, they express location. With a possessive phrase, they express possession. Kankanaey has three existentials—one positive, *wada*, and two interchangeable negatives, *maga* and *iwed*, which vary by geographical dialect. *Wada* may be shortened to *wa* when the following reference-marker is shortened and cliticized. Table 2.4 shows the existential forms.

Table 2.4. Kankanaey existential forms
Positive	*wada/wa*
Negative	*maga*
	iwed

With an indefinite argument, the existential indicates simple existence, as in (2.219). With a definite argument, the existential indicates physical presence, as in (2.220).

(2.219) *Iwed di danan.*
   NEGEXIS RMi path
   'There wasn't any path/road.'

(2.220) *Ay wada=s Mrs. Mayano? Iwed Ø.*
   Q EXIS=PRM Mrs. Mayano NEGEXIS 3sI
   'Is Mrs. Mayano here?' 'No/she's not.'

Location is shown by locative phrases following the existential, as in (2.221) and (2.222). When an indefinite argument has a possessor, as in (2.223), the existential indicates that possession.

(2.221) *Wa=y balat sin apis gowab=da.*
   EXIS=RMi banana ORM area below=3pII
   'There are banana trees just below their place.'

(2.222) Wada=da=s   di.
EXIS=3pI=>   DEM3IV
'They are there.'

(2.223) Maga=y   sapatos=na.
NEGEXIS-RMi   shoes=3sII
'He doesn't have any shoes.'

Existential predicates can take some of the predicating affixation introduced in previous sections, as in (2.224) and (2.225). A euphemistic expression using ma-...-an is seen in (2.226).

(2.224) Emey=et   di   piga   ay minoto,
go=PART   RMi   how.many   LK minute

ka-wada=et   di   logan.
IMM-EXIS=PART   RMi   vehicle
'A few minutes went by, (and) suddenly there was a vehicle.'

(2.225) Aket   ma-iwed   din   anak=ko   mo?
why   UNDs-NEGEXIS   RMd   child=1sII   why
'Why has my child disappeared?'

(2.226) Mo ma-wad?-an=ka,   man-tee=ka   sin   beey.
if UNDls-EXIS<=2sI   ACT-stay=2sI ORM   house
'If you get pregnant (lit. become locus of existence), stay at home.'

Existentials may be used in many constructions—in clauses, in reference phrases, and with predicating and nominalizing affixes. Chapter 4 will show the existential as it functions in various constructions. Chapter 7 will include the role of existentials in its study of information flow in Kankanaey discourse.

2.6 Conclusion

This chapter has introduced the Kankanaey lexicon, with its roots and affixes. A complex variety of basic predicates are formed by the combination

2.6 Conclusion

of affixes with different types of roots. Other derived predicates are built with more affixes and combinations of affixes. Numbers and existentials form yet other types of predicates. Chapter 3 will turn to reference phrases in Kankanaey, and then chapter 4 will put predicates and their reference phrase arguments together in the clause structures of Kankanaey.

3

Reference Phrases

Reference phrases were introduced in chapter 1, where the concept of the layered structure was explained. This chapter will explore Kankanaey reference phrases in more detail. In section 3.1 the various constituents are explained; in section 3.2 the modifiers at each level are examined. Complex reference phrases and those with affixed roots in the nucleus are examined in sections 3.3 and 3.4. Reference phrases placed in the predicate position of a clause are introduced in 3.5. The chapter ends with a look at an interesting anaphor, the multi-use *siya*.

Figure 3.1 displays an example of a Kankanaey reference phrase in its constituent structure projection, repeated from figure 1.6 in chapter 1.

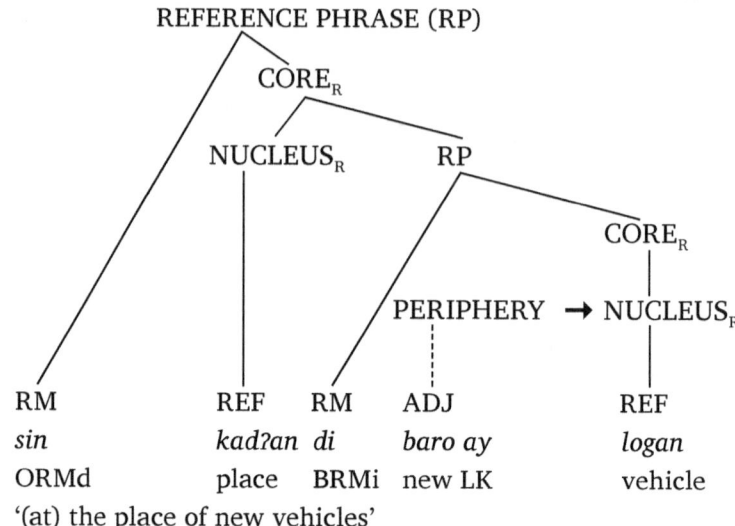

Figure 3.1. Constituent projection of a Kankanaey RP (Reference Phrase).

3.1 Reference Phrase structure

3.1.1 Reference Phrase markers

Reference phrases (RP) in Kankanaey are preceded by a reference phrase marker, except in the case of most pronouns. This marker identifies the phrase as having the semantic function of reference, and licenses it to function as an argument or adjunct in a syntactic construction. Reference phrase markers (hereafter RM) occur in the initial position of an RP. With the exception of most pronouns, every reference phrase must be marked as such by a RM.

3.1.1.1 Markers for common reference phrases

The common RP (as opposed to proper names and pronominals) uses the markers displayed in table 3.1. These markers identify the syntactic relationship of the RP to the predicate, a system that will be explained fully in chapter 4. Note that the Undergoer argument of a transitive predicate takes the same RM as the single argument of an intransitive predicate,

3.1 Reference Phrase structure

while a transitive Actor argument takes the Bound reference phrase marker (BRM). Optional contractions of RMs that cliticize to a preceding vowel-final word are shown in the table.

The tags 'd' and 'i' mark definite and indefinite RPs, respectively. The grammatical category of definiteness is covered in section 3.2.1.2.

Table 3.1. Kankanaey common RMs

Relation to predicate:	Single argument or transitive Undergoer	Transitive Actor	Oblique
definite	din (RMd)/=n	=n din (BRMd)	sin (ORMd)
indefinite	di (RMi)/=y	=n di (BRMi)	si (ORMi)/=s

Example (3.1) shows the full and contracted forms of the definite RM with a single argument. Examples (3.2) and (3.3) show transitive predicates with two arguments. In many examples, such as (3.2) the marker *din* appears to be the same for both direct arguments, because the clitic =*n* preceding the bound reference phrase marker only appears following a vowel-final word, as in (3.3). A three-argument clause (grammatical but pragmatically unlikely) is given in (3.4). The third argument takes oblique marking.

(3.1)   *Man-ʔoga   din   anak.*   or   *Man-ʔoga=n   anak.*
       ACT-cry   RMd   child   ACT-cry=RMd   child
       'The child cries.'

(3.2)   *I-pigpig   din   anak   din   onas.*
       UNDt-fling   BRMd   child   RMd   sugarcane
       'The child flings the sugarcane.'

(3.3)   *I-tanga   =n din   anak   din   onas.*
       UNDt-hold.in.mouth   =BRMd   child   RMd   sugarcane
       'The child holds the sugarcane in his mouth.'

(3.4)   *In-adawa   =n din   anak   din   onas   sin   moyang.*
       UND.P-hand   BRMd   child   RMd   cane   ORMd   baby
       'The child handed the sugarcane to the baby.'

The BRM marker =n din that marks a transitive Actor argument in basic clauses is a required clitic if the preceding word ends in a vowel; the clitic is not a contraction or an 'ergative' suffix on the predicate. This can be seen in (3.5) where a vowel-final particle intervenes between the predicate and the BRMd.

(3.5) Gel?ad-an kano =n din anak din onas.
 peel-UNDl HSY =BRMd child RMd sugarcane
 'They say the child peels the sugarcane.'

3.1.1.2 Markers for proper-name reference phrases

Reference phrases that specify a proper name or kin term use a set of RMs different from common RPs. Table 3.2 displays the markers that precede proper names and kin terms. The tags for these markers include P for proper/personal. Like common RPs, the same marker is used for the single argument of an intransitive predicate and the Undergoer argument of a transitive predicate.

Table 3.2. Kankanaey proper RMs

	Single argument or Transitive Undergoer	Transitive Actor	Oblique
proper and kin names singular	si / =s (PRM)	=n ∅ (BPRM)	en (OPRM)
proper and kin names plural	da (PRM.pl)	=n da (BPRM pl)	en da (OPRM pl)
place or time	--	--	ed (LOC)

The PRM for proper names that function as single arguments of a predicate is si, optionally contracted to =s after vowel-final words as in (3.6).

(3.6) Man-?oga si Langdew. or Man-?oga=s Langdew.
 ACT-cry PRM Langdew
 'Langdew cries.'

3.1 Reference Phrase structure

Although the PRM *si* is homophonous with the marker for an indefinite oblique common RP (ORMi, cf. table 3.1), word order and the common vs. proper distinction disambiguate them, as in (3.7).

(3.7) *Man-sibo   si   Rony   si   digo.*
       ACT-sip   PRM   Rony   ORMi   broth
       'Rony sips (some) broth.'

The BPRM is manifested only by the clitic =*n* after a vowel, as in (3.8). Otherwise it is null for proper names, as in (3.9). Examples (3.10) and (3.11) exemplify the plural proper marking. Third arguments are oblique, as seen in the last RP in (3.11).

(3.8) *I-tanga=n   Langdew   din   onas.*
       UND-hold.in.mouth=BPRM Langdew   RMd   sugarcane
       'Langdew holds the sugarcane in his mouth.'

(3.9) *I-agadang   Langdew   si   ama=na   ed   Balang.*
       UNDt-cross.river Langdew   PRM   father=3sII LOC   Balang
       'Langdew takes his father across the river at Balang.'

(3.10) *Adi   ammo   =n   da tatang din   istorya.*
       NEG   know.UND   =BPRM   pl father   RMd   story
       'Father and the others don't know the story.'

(3.11) *In-dawat   Langdew   din   onas   en   da Margita.*
       UND.P-give Langdew   RMd   cane   OPRM   pl Margita
       'Langdew gave the sugarcane to Margita and the others.'

3.1.1.3 Combinations of Reference Phrase Markers

PRMs mark reference phrases as referential and identifiable. In cases where a participant known to the speaker but new to the hearer is referred to by name, the indefinite common nominal marker *di* /=*y* may precede the personal marker *si* to yield "a certain person named..." as in (3.12). Another combination, shown in (3.13), combines the definite common marker and the personal marker. In texts dealing with historical events, this combination is often used to refer to someone who is deceased. Here it may imply a more impersonal reference to the woman as the child's mother than if the personal marker *si* were used alone.

(3.12) *Wada=y   si   Nabulay   ed   nabbaon   ed   Abas.*
         EXIS=RMi   PRM   Nabulay   LOC   long.ago   LOC   Abas
         'There was a (certain woman named) Nabulay long ago in Abas.'

(3.13) *Din   anak   ya   din   si   ina=na   di*
         RMd   child   and   RMd   PRM   mother=3sII   RMi

  na-bay?an.
  UNDs-left
  '(Those) left behind were the child and her mother (lit. the mother of her).'

3.1.2 Reference Phrase nucleus

3.1.2.1 Pronouns

A reference phrase in Kankanaey may consist of simply a demonstrative or personal pronoun.

3.1.2.1.1 Demonstrative pronouns

Demonstrative pronouns (DEM) in Kankanaey are divided into five classes, three of which may be used as reference phrases. Table 3.3 displays these pronouns, with some alternate forms that may reflect local dialect differences. Note that like the RMs discussed above, single arguments and transitive Undergoer arguments take the same form, DEM class I, while transitive Actors are expressed by DEM class II. Demonstrative pronouns indicate referents that are near the speaker (tagged by 1), near the hearer (tagged 2), or not near to either (tagged 3), as seen in table 3.3. Two of the oblique demonstratives have clitic contractions which are possible following vowel-final words. Demonstratives I and II also have a plural form.

3.1 Reference Phrase structure

Table 3.3. Kankanaey demonstrative pronouns as reference phrases

Pronoun Class / TAG	Single and Trans. Undergoer	Trans.actor	Oblique
	I	II	IV
DEM1	na	nina	sina/isna
	da na (pl)		=s na
DEM2	sa	nisa/nasa	issa
	da sa (pl)		=s sa
DEM3	di	nidi/nadi	sidi/isdi
	da di (pl)		=s di

Example (3.14) illustrates a demonstrative pronoun as the Undergoer argument of a transitive verb. The contracted form of the oblique DEM1IV appears in example (3.15).

(3.14) *I-pigpig   din   anak   di.*
       UNDt-fling BRMd   child   DEM3I
       'The child flings that.'

(3.15) *din   opisina=s na...*
       RMd   office=DEM1IV
       'the office here...'

3.1.2.1.2 Demonstrative-related Reference Phrase Markers

The common RM *din* introduced in section 3.1.1.1 above is probably historically related to the 3I demonstrative pronoun *di*. The other class I and the class IV demonstratives 1 and 2 also have related RMs as shown in table 3.4. These demonstrative-related RMs have a very weak deictic function, explained in section 3.2.1.2.

Table 3.4. Demonstrative-related RMs

Function:	Single or transitive Actor argument	Oblique
DEM-related RM	*nan* (1) *san* (2)	*isnan* (1) *issan* (2)
Tag:	DRM	ODRM

3.1.2.1.3 Personal pronouns

Kankanaey personal pronouns identify person and number. They are assigned to classes I to III, which indicate syntactic relationships. The person distinctions are first, first with second, second, and third. Each of these may be pluralized. Another (less elegant) way to group these pronouns is by positing dual, inclusive and exclusive forms of the first person plural. A set of impersonal pronouns is tagged as fourth 'person'; these do not allow plural marking.

The Kankanaey pronouns present a very mixed pattern of marking the relations within a clause. The three patterns that personal pronouns exhibit can be seen in table 3.5. Chapter 6 explores the significance of the pronoun patterns more fully. Rather than reflect the various patterns, the pronoun class numbers indicate the relationship to the predicate, which is sufficient for purposes of describing clause constructions. Thus, single arguments of a predicate are expressed by Class I pronouns, transitive Actor arguments by Class II pronouns, and Undergoer arguments in transitive clauses by Class III pronouns. Note that classes I and II are clitic, while III are free-standing. The pronouns I and III with an ergative pattern are not clitic. Further uses of these classes, such as II for possessive pronouns and III for focal pronouns, are discussed in sections 3.1.3.1 and 3.5.

3.1 Reference Phrase structure

Table 3.5. Kankanaey personal pronouns

pronoun class	I	II	III
	Single	Trans.Actor	Trans. Undergoer
Tripartite split:			
1s	=ak	=ko/=k	(PRM +) sak?en
2s	=ka	=mo/=m	(PRM +) sik?a
1p	=kami	=mi	PRM + dakami
2p	=kayo	=yo	PRM + dakayo
Accusative split:			
3p	=da	=da	PRM + daida
1+2	=ta	=ta	PRM + daita
1+2p	=tako	=tako	PRM + datako
Ergative split:			
3s	Ø/sisya	=na	Ø/(PRM +) sisya
4 (impersonal s/p)	Ø	=na	Ø/siya

Examples (3.16) and (3.17) illustrate clauses with pronoun arguments. In (3.16) 3p is the single argument and is expressed by Class I. In (3.17) 3s is the Actor and 1p the Undergoer: the Actor is a Class II pronoun, while the Undergoer is expressed by Class III.

(3.16) *Man-?oga=da.*
ACT-cry=3pI
'They cry.'

(3.17) *Liw?-an=na=s   dakami.*
forget-UND=3sII=PRM   1pIII
'He/she forgets us.'

In section 3.1.1.1 above it was noted that the reference marker for the transitive Undergoer is realized as *din* while for the Actor argument it is *din* as well, except that it is bound to the predicate with =*n* when the predicate is vowel-final. The only structural difference is the clitic bond. A similar distinction holds with pronouns. Transitive Actor pronouns (Class II) and single argument pronouns (Class I) are clitics, bound to the predicate or other preceding word, but the binding of class II is tighter, involving morphophonemic changes with the singular forms, as seen with 1sII =*ko* which follows consonants but shortens to =*k* after vowels. In (3.18) further morphophonemic reduction is seen with *asog-ak* where the suffix -*an* combines with the 1s pronoun =*ko* 'to yield' -*ak* (not to be confused with =*ak*, which is 1s in Class I). With *mo* it would yield -*am,* and with *na,* -*ana*.

(3.18) *Asog-ak*   *si*   *Fianzo.*
       asog-an=ko
       persuade-UND.1sII   PRM   Fianzo
       'I (will) persuade Fianzo.'

3.1.2.2 Lexical roots in the Reference Phrase nucleus

The nucleus in simple RPs is an unaffixed lexical root. The major root classifications in Kankanaey are described in chapter 2. Class roots normally occur without affixation to function as the nucleus of a reference phrase, referring to an instance of that class. Examples (3.19) and (3.20), repeated from (3.7) and (3.8) above, have class roots in the bracketed RP nucleus.

(3.19) *Man-sibo*   *si*   *Rony*   *si*   [*digo*].
       ACT-sip   PRM   Rony   ORMi   broth
       'Rony sips (some) broth.'

(3.20) *I-tanga=n*   *Langdew*   *din*   [*onas*].
       UND-hold.in.mouth=BPRM   Langdew   RMd   sugarcane
       'Langdew holds the sugarcane in his mouth.'

Unaffixed roots other than class roots in the nucleus of an RP may refer to an abstraction of the denotation of the root, as with property and experience-stative roots such as *gasto* 'expense', *teg?in* 'cold (weather)', *beteng* 'drunkenness', and *iliw* 'homesickness'. Example (3.21) shows a property word as an unaffixed root.

3.1 Reference Phrase structure 101

(3.21) Maga=y lawa sidi.
NEGEXIS=RMi bad DEM3IV
'There's nothing bad there.'

Action roots also can refer to an abstraction of the event, such as *ponpon* 'burial'. Examples (3.22) to (3.24) exemplify action roots in the RP nucleus.

(3.22) D<in>nge=k din [bogaw]=na.
UND.P-hear=1sII RMd shout=3sII
'I heard his shout.'

(3.23) Adi=ka kaigeb?at si [yamyam].
NEG=2sI do.w/o.provocation ORMi scold
'Don't light into (him) with scolding.'

(3.24) Wadwada din [obla]=k sin opisina.
priority RMd work=1sII ORMd office
'My work at the office is deemed more important.'

With action roots involving transfer of an entity, such as *abang* 'rent' and *otang* 'debt,' the unaffixed root can refer to the money to be transferred, as in (3.25), but is dependent on the context, as in (3.26).

(3.25) Mo din [lako] =n di diblo asi=yo kod
as.for RMd sell BRMi book then=2pII please

alaen mo omali=kayo.
get if/when come=2pI
'As for (the money from) the sale of the books, please just get it when you come here.'

(3.26) Man?anos=kayo   kod   tan   ad?ado   di   [otang]=mi
       be.patient=2sI   please   'cuz   many   RMi   debt=1pII

   ay   daan   mabayadan.
   LK   not.yet   paid
   'Please be patient, because we have a lot of debts that (we) haven't been able to pay yet.'

With action roots of communication, the unaffixed root most often refers to the product of the communication, as *kalalag* 'prayer', *iitaw* 'dream', and *kali* 'word, language'. Example (3.27) shows an inner state *iyaman* 'gratitude' and a communication product *solat* 'letter' as referential terms.

(3.27) Peteg   di   iyaman=ko   sin   [solat]=mo.
       great   RMi   thankful=1sII   ORMd   write=2sII
       'I'm very grateful for your letter.'

A few result-state roots occur unaffixed, referencing the inanimate cause of the result-state, thus *sangaw* 'distraction' from the stative root 'distracted'. Contextual clarification differentiates the readings 'viewpoint' or 'appearance' for the perception-state root *ila* 'see' in (3.28) and (3.29).

(3.28) Baken   rumbeng   ay   isin?eng=ko=s   daida   si
       NEG   right   LK   gaze=1sII=PRM   3pIII   ORMi

   kaman   nadi   ay   [ila].
   like   DEM3II   LK   see
   'It wasn't right that I was looking at them from a viewpoint like that (superior attitude).'

(3.29) Din   beey,   owat   kaman   ay?ayam   di   [ila]=na.
       RMd   house   just   like   toys   RMi   see=3sII
       'The houses, just like toys was their appearance (from an airplane).'

3.1 Reference Phrase structure

Section 3.4.1 below covers nominalizing affixation, such as *kina-* in (3.30), which is more common than unaffixed root nominalization and more specific, as table 3.9 there attests.

(3.30)   Mo   <om>ituray   din   aklong   si   [kina-baknang]...
         if   ACT-govern   RMd   desire   ORM   NOM-rich
         'When/If the desire for wealth drives (a person)....'

3.1.3 Arguments of the Reference Phrase nucleus

A reference phrase nucleus can take one direct argument. Section 3.1.3.1 details the bound direct argument within an RP core. Pronominal RPs may take a clarifying oblique RP argument, explained in 3.1.3.2.

3.1.3.1 The direct argument of an Reference Phrase nucleus

The RP nucleus can take one direct argument, itself a full reference phrase. A direct argument immediately follows the nucleus and is bound to it, using the same markers or pronoun class as transitive actors in a clause. The direct argument (bracketed) may stand in a possessive or other genitive-type relationship to the nucleus, as in (3.31) to (3.33).

(3.31)   din   aso=[yo]
         RMd   dog=2pII
         'your (pl) dog'

(3.32)   din   aso   [=n   Langdew]
         RMd   dog   BPRM   Langdew
         'Langdew's dog'

(3.33)   din   silbi   [=n di   manok]
         RMd   purpose   BRMi   chicken
         'the purpose of chickens'

Figure 3.2 shows an oblique RP with a genitive argument.

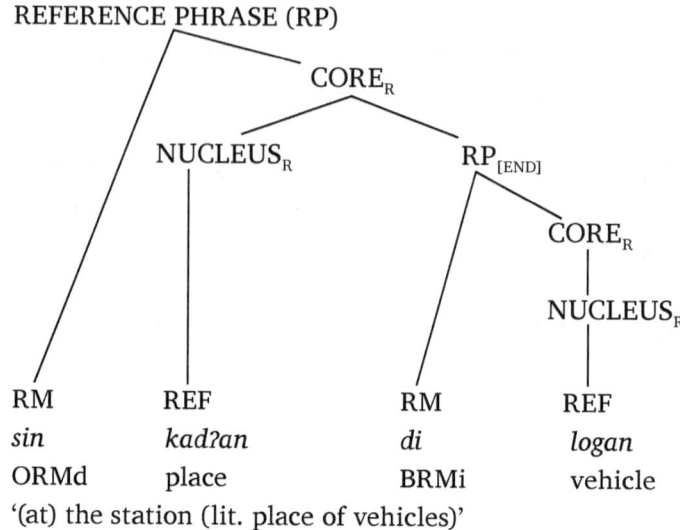

Figure 3.2. Kankanaey RP with direct argument.

When the nucleus of the RP is not a pronoun or root, i.e., when it is an affixed word, the relationship of the direct argument is constrained by the type of root and the affixation on it. Further discussion of the ramifications of affixed roots in RP nuclei is in section 3.4 below.

3.1.3.2 Oblique core arguments of pronominal Reference Phrases

A plural pronominal expression is often ambiguous as to the exact referents. An oblique RP (bracketed in the following examples) can follow a plural pronoun or other plural RP to specify the other referent(s), as seen in (3.34) to (3.36). This construction is more natural than a coordinate construction, such as those found in the English translations. Another construction to handle ambiguity is shown in section 3.1.4.1 below.

(3.34) kami   [sin   among=ko]; kayo [sin   pamilya=m]
        1pI   ORMd boss=1sII   2pI   ORMd family=2sII
        'my employer and I; you and your family'

3.1 Reference Phrase structure

(3.35) Nan-logan   kami   [en   Mrs.   Mayadno]   ay
        ACT.P-vehicle 1pI   OPRM   Mrs.   M   LK

  man-pa-Bagyo.
  ACT-CAUS-Bagyo
  'Mrs. Mayadno and I rode (took a bus) going to Baguio.'

(3.36) Nan-adawag   da   ina=na   [en   ama=na].
        ACT-plead   PRM.pl   mother=3sII   OPRM   father=3sII
        'His mother and father pled.'

Figure 3.3 shows the first RP from example (3.34). It has a pronominal nucleus with an oblique argument in the core of the RP. Within that oblique RP is a direct argument, the possessive pronoun.

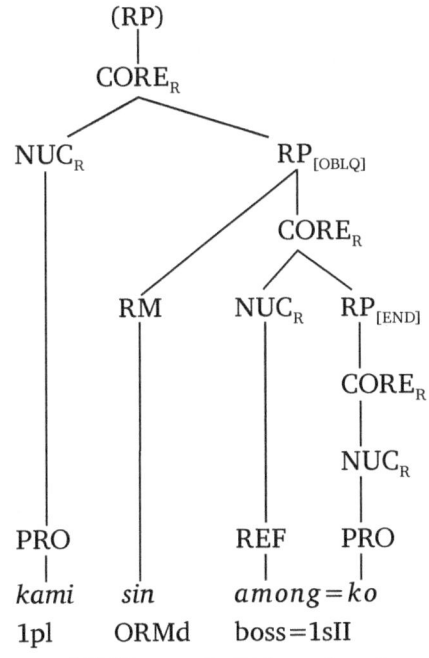

Figure 3.3. Pronominal RP with core arguments.

3.1.4 Peripheries in the Reference Phrase

Like a clause, a reference phrase can be modified at each level of its structure. For Kankanaey, peripheries are posited to the right of the RP level, and on either side of the RP core (Core$_R$) and RP nucleus (Nucleus$_R$). The peripheries are used to incorporate lexical modifiers into the structure. These modifiers are words, phrases or clauses that often require overt linkage, usually the linker *ay*.

3.1.4.1 Reference Phrase periphery

Nominal coreferents, appositives that clarify the referent, are in the RP periphery, linked with *ay*. Examples (3.37) and (3.38) show these clarifying, non-restrictive modifiers.

(3.37) nan   mayor   [ay Felimon Rido]   ed   Binggal
       DRM   mayor   LK Felimon Rido   LOC   Binggal
       'the mayor, Felimon Rido, of/in Binggal'

(3.38) si   bigat   [ay agew di   ponpon]
       ORM   next.day   LK   day   BRM   burial
       'the next day, the day of the burial'

Ambiguous pronouns, including demonstratives and question words, may also be clarified by a modifying *ay*-linked nominal, as shown in the bracketed RPs in (3.39) to (3.42).

(3.39) Sa.pay.koma.ta mayat   di   kasasaad =[yo   ay
       (wish)   good   RMi   situation=2pII   LK

   sin-pamilya]
   UNIT-family
   'May the situation of you (who are) a family unit be good.'

3.1 Reference Phrase structure

(3.40) Layd-en   [nina   ay   nakay]...
        want-UND   DEM1II   LK   old.man
        'This-one old man wants ...'

(3.41) i-gink-a(n)=[m   ay   lalaki]
        UNDd-quiet<=2sII   LK   man
        'You keep it quiet, (man)' (not a vocative, but to differentiate the addressee from the woman of the couple.)

(3.42) [Sino   ay agew]   di   <om>ali-an=da?
        what   LK day   RMi   NOM-come<=3pII
        'What day is the time of their coming?'

Indefinite RPs, such as those that introduce new participants, can take non-restrictive, attributive modifiers in the left RP periphery, as in (3.43). With a definite RP, an attributive modifier would be interpreted as restrictive, as in section 3.1.4.3.2.

(3.43) Wada=y   [nakayang   ay]   dontog   ed   Baknon.
        EXIS=RMi   high   LK   mountain   LOC   Baknon
        'There is a high mountain at Baknon.'

3.1.4.2 Core$_R$ peripheries

RPs with pronouns or lexical roots in their nuclei do not use the core$_R$ periphery. When the RP is a nominalized clause, its core peripheral adjuncts are in the RP-core periphery. Nominalized clauses are described in section 3.4.3.

3.1.4.3 Nuclear$_R$ peripheries

Left and right nuclear peripheries in Kankanaey hold restrictive modifiers. Attributive modifiers and relative clauses may be placed on either side of the nucleus. No nominal nuclear modifiers have been observed in Kankanaey that correspond to English nominals such as 'brick wall' or 'bamboo floor'. Such expressions are rendered in Kankanaey by relative clauses.

3.1.4.3.1 Relative clauses

Relative clauses, bracketed in the next six examples, are linked most commonly from the right nuclear periphery, but may also freely occur in the left as in (3.49). Relative clauses do not necessarily embed, and are usually found in the final position in the phrase. They may modify the nucleus regardless of other elements that may follow the nucleus.[1] Thus, in (3.44) the relative clause modifies *gomot*, not *dapan=ko*. In (3.45) both relative clauses modify the nuclear word *begas* 'rice'. In (3.46) however, the second bracketed relative clause is embedded within the first. Context and pragmatics influence the interpretation. Examples (3.47) and (3.48) exemplify the range of possible relativizations. Chapter 5 explores relative clauses and their internal structure more fully than is relevant to reference phrases, which are in focus here.

(3.44) *Din gomot di dapan= ko [ay napotoan...]*
RMd digit BRMi foot=1sII LK UNDls.cut
'My toe (lit. digit of my foot) that had a piece cut off it.'

(3.45) *si begas [ay kan-en di mantonod] [ay*
ORMi rice LK eat-UND BRMi harvesters LK

i-balalong=mi]
UNDt-descend=1pII
'with rice that the harvesters will eat that we will carry down'

(3.46) *Man-beey kano di kabonyan sidi [ay manpakan*
ACT-house HSY RMi gods DEM3IV LK ACT.CAUS.eat

si madagaangan [ay man?illeng sin isdi]].
ORM UNDls.hunger LK ACT-rest ORMd DEM3IV
'They say that gods live there who feed hungry (people) who rest there.'

---

[1] In many Philippine languages, a relative clause refers back to noun in the main clause, not to the closest preceding noun (as in English). Sherri Brainard, p.c.

3.1 Reference Phrase structure

(3.47)   *sin*   *timpo*   *[ay*   *naki-asawa-an=mi]*
         ORMd   time   LK   ACTa.P-spouse-NOM=1pII
         'at the time when we got married'

(3.48)   *din*   *logan*   *[ay*   *in-baga=da*   *din*   *numero=na]*
         RMd   vehicle   LK   UNDt.P-tell=3pII   RMd   number=3sII
         'the vehicle whose number they had told (me)'

(3.49)   *din*   *[in-dawat=yo*   *en*   *sak?en*   *ay]*   *Biblia*
         RMd   UNDt.P-give=2pII   OPRM   1sIII   LK   Bible
         'the Bible that you gave to me'

3.1.4.3.2 Attributive modifiers

When an RP is definite, descriptive modifiers are generally interpreted as restrictive. Attributive words are in the nuclear periphery. They require overt linkage with *ay,* as in (3.50). Restrictive attributives may occur in the right nuclear periphery, as in (3.51). (Unlike English, Kankanaey age relation is lexically specified for kin terms while gender is optional.)

(3.50)   *din*   *[kitkitoy*   *ay]*   *anak=ko.*
         RMd   small   LK   child=1sII
         'my little child' (as distinct from the older ones)

(3.51)   *din*   *pangpangoan=ko*   *[ay*   *lalaki]*
         RMd   older.sibling=1sII   LK   male
         'my elder brother'

The comparative phrase *kaman* + DEMII are attributive and restrictive in function. This phrase is linked from the left nuclear periphery, as in (3.52).

(3.52) Baken   rumbeng   ay   isinʔeng=ko=s   daida   si
        NEG   right   LK   gaze=1sII=PRM   3pIII   ORMi

   [kaman   nadi   ay]   ila.
   like   DEM3II   LK   see
   'It wasn't right for me to be looking at them from that point of view (superior attitude).'

3.1.4.3.3 Adjunct modifiers

RPs that bear a locative relationship to the nucleus are restrictive modifiers, and are in the right nuclear periphery. They immediately follow the nucleus and any direct argument. Locative RPs are marked with an Oblique RM, either the proper place-name oblique *ed*, as in (3.53), or *sin*, as in (3.54) and (3.55). Note that the locative phrase in (3.53) locates the 'place', not the 'vehicle,' in Tiblak. The Oblique demonstrative pronoun (DEMIV) may also occur in this position.

(3.53) sin   kadʔan   di   logan   [ed   Tiblak]
        ORMd   place   BRMi vehicle   LOC   Tiblak
        '(at) the station (lit. place of vehicles) in Tiblak'

(3.54) din   bayang=na   [sin   lopa=na]
        RMd   wound=3sII   ORMd   face=3sII
        'his wound on his face'

(3.55) Wadwada   din   obla=k   [sin   opisina.]
        priority   RMd   work=1sII   ORMd   office
        'My work at the office is deemed more important.'

3.2 Operators in the Reference Phrase

In chapter 1 the concept of grammatical modifiers, termed "operators" in RRG, was introduced. Reference phrases have these operators at each level. Table 3.6 (adapted for Kankanaey from Van Valin 2005:24) lists the RP operators and shows the levels that they modify.

3.2 Operators in the Reference Phrase　　　　　　　　　　　　　　　111

Table 3.6. Operators in the layered structure of the RP

Nuclear$_R$ operator:

　　Nominal aspect

Core$_R$ operators:

　　Number

　　Quantification

RP operators:

　　Definiteness

　　Deixis

Operators in the RP may be expressed by reduplication, affixes or separate words. They are represented below the constituent projection in a mirror-image "operator projection" that indicates the type of modification at each level.

Figure 3.4 adds these positions to the abstract structure of the Kankanaey RP. Arrows in the operator projection indicate the level that each operator modifies.

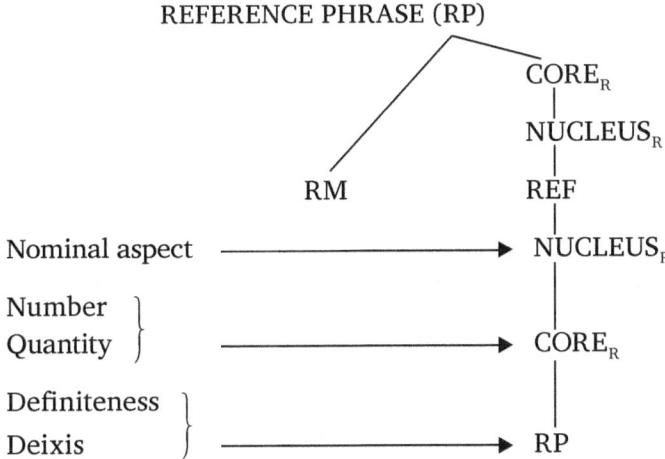

Figure 3.4. Kankanaey RP structure with operator projection.

3.2.1 Reference Phrase operators

3.2.1.1 Deixis

Deixis is shown by modifying demonstratives. Demonstrative pronouns class V (table 3.7 below) are atibutive. As modifiers of an RP, they usually specify spatial or figurative proximity to the participants. They may be in the right RP-periphery, as exemplified in (3.56) to (3.58); they follow the core and are linked by *ay*.

Table 3.7. Kankanaey demonstrative modifiers

		Attributive
	TAG:	V
1 (near to speaker)		*nay*
2 (near to hearer)		*sana*
3 (not near to either)		*doy*

(3.56) Din   istorya   [ay   nay]
       RMd   story   LK   DEM1V
       'This story (author is about to tell)'

(3.57) din   anak=da   [ay   sana]
       RMd   child=3pII   LK   DEM2V
       'that (previously-mentioned) child of theirs'

(3.58) Itoltoloy=yo   din   obla=yo   [ay   sana].
       continue=2pII   RMd   work=2pII   LK   DEM2V
       'Keep on with that work of yours.'

Demonstratives may precede the core in the left RP periphery, as in (3.59) to (3.61). The unstressed linker *ay* may be dropped after the *y*-final demonstratives *nay* and *doy*, as in (3.60).

3.2 Operators in the Reference Phrase   113

(3.59) Ka-dama   sin   sana   ay   banig   Nabulay.
        ACT.IMM-fight   ORMd   DEM2V   LK   ghost   Nabulay
        '(He) attacked that (aforementioned) ghost of Nabulay.'

(3.60) sin   doy   kad?an   di   bato
        ORMd   DEM3V   place   BRMi   rock
        'at that (well-known) place of the rock'

(3.61) Ibagak   [sin   nay   panteeeak   sina].
        tell=1sII   ORMd   DEM1V   NOM.stay.1sII   DEM1IV
        'I will tell (it to) these (people) I am staying with here.'

Deictic operators precede any relative clauses, as seen in (3.62) and (3.63).

(3.62) sin   timpo   [ay nay]   ay   kolang   am?in   di
        ORM   time   LK DEM1V   LK   lack   every   BRM

        ka-sapol-an
        NOM-need-NOM
        'at this time when there is a shortage of every needed thing'

(3.63) Na-labi   din   alas   sinko   [ay doy]   ay
        ATT-night   RM   time   five   LK DEM3V   LK

        s<om>aa-a(n)=k.
        NOM-go.home<=1sII
        'It's dark at that five o'clock my go-home time.'

3.2.1.2 Definiteness

Table 3.4 above noted that some reference phrase markers are related to the demonstrative pronouns. Demonstrative-related RMs (DRM) with deixis 1 and 2 (near speaker, near hearer) are not strongly deictic and are used more frequently in the northern parts of the Kankanaey-speaking area. The default RMs 3 are not deictic at all. Table 3.8

displays the full set with the corresponding demonstrative pronouns for comparison.

Table 3.8. Kankanaey deictic RP markers with corresponding demonstrative pronouns

	Direct Argument DRM	DEM I	Oblique Argument DRM	DEM IV
1	nan	na	isnan	sina/isna
2	san	sa	issan	issa
3	di(n)	di	si(n)	sidi/isdi

The final -*n* of the reference phrase markers correlates with referentiality and identifiability of the whole reference phrase. This final -*n* functions as a definiteness operator for the RP, especially for the non-bound forms. The "indefinite" RMs are not specifically marked as such; they may be more accurately described as neutral as regards definiteness.

In many contexts where RPs (bracketed) are non-referential as in (3.64), hypothetical as in (3.65), or not known to the hearer, the lack of the definiteness marker fills an important semantic function. In (3.66) a brand-new participant is introduced by name using a combination of indefinite marker and personal marker.

(3.64) Si   Maria   [di   Pa   ya   Ma]   ed   nowani.
        PRM   Maria   RMi   pa   and   ma   LOC   present-time
        'Maria is the father and mother at this time (since parents have passed away).'

(3.65) Siyat   wa[=y   mapa]   si   e~egen-an.
        must   EXIS=RMi   map   ORMi   CV-hold-UND1
        '(You'd) have to be holding a map (lit. there must be a map to hold) (or you'd get lost).'

3.2 Operators in the Reference Phrase

(3.66) ngem   idi   wada[=y   si   Doligen]   ay
       but   when   EXIS=RMi   PRM   Doligen   LK

p<in>a-kan=da...
UND.P-CAUS-eat=3pII
'but (once) there was a (certain) Doligen whom they fed...'

3.2.1.3 Negation

Kankanaey does not have argument negation as such. Negation of an argument RP is handled by the negative existential construction, as in (3.67). When an RP is functioning as the predicate in an RP-RP equative clause, it may be negated with *baken* preceding the entire RP, as in (3.68), with the predicative RP in brackets. This, however, is predicate negation rather than argument negation.

(3.67) Iwed   di   begas=na.
       NEGEXIS   RMi   rice=3sII
       'He has no rice (lit. his rice does not exist).'

(3.68) [Baken   din   begas]   di   bayo-e(n)=na.
       NEG   RMd   rice   RMi   pound-UND =3sII
       'What he will pound is [not the rice].'

Figure 3.5 shows an example of both constituent and operator projections for a reference phrase in Kankanaey.

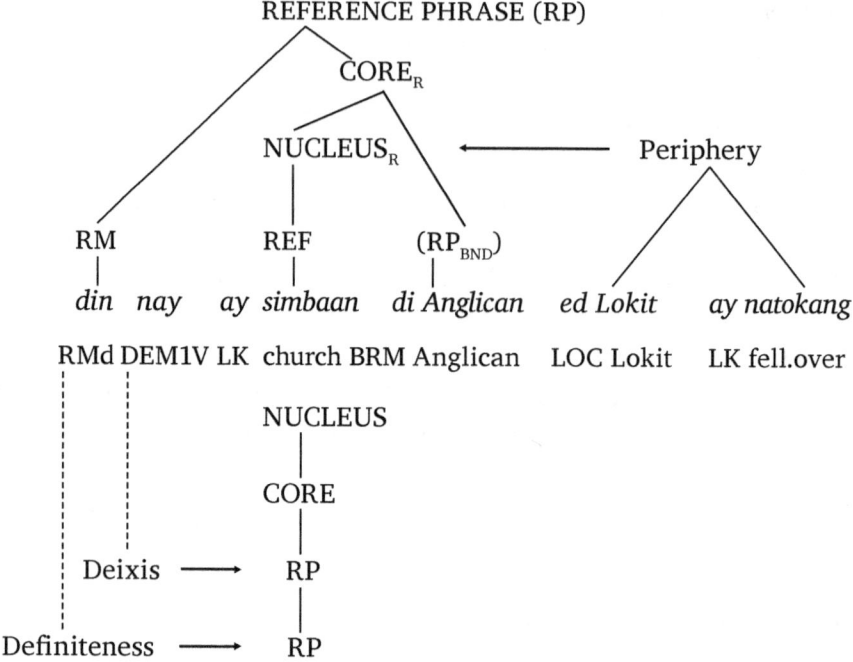

'this Anglican church in Lokit that fell over'

Figure 3.5. Example of RP constituent and operator projections.

3.2.2 Core_R operators

Operators that modify the core of a reference phrase core are mostly concerned with number—plurality and quantifiers, as discussed in 3.2.2.1 and 3.2.2.2. Negation is usually considered a core operator, but in Kankanaey there is no RP-internal negation. The negator *baken* before a class root negates it as a class, not an RP referring to an instance of that class. A concept such as 'no rice' is expressed with the negative existential.

3.2.2.1 Plurality

Kankanaey uses two strategies to express plurality: reduplicative affixation and an overt plural marker. Plurality is usually determined by context, but

3.2 Operators in the Reference Phrase 117

countable objects in the RP nucleus can take plural marking if necessary for clarity or emphasis.

3.2.2.1.1 Reduplication

Plurality may be indicated on countable RPs by *CV* or *CVC* reduplication (note the symbol ~), as in (3.69) and (3.70). The form of reduplication seems to be arbitrarily assigned to the lexical root. There is no other distinction between count and mass nouns.

(3.69)   *In-kosokos=na*   *din*   *be~beey*   *sin*   *il~ili.*
        UNDt.P-collapse=3sII   RMd   pl-house   ORMd   pl-town
        'It (the earthquake) collapsed (all/many of) the houses in (all) the towns.'

(3.70)   *Bayʔa(n)=m*   *si*   *ag~agi=mi.*
        leave. UNDl=2sII   PRM   pl-relative=1pII
        'Leave our relatives alone.'

3.2.2.1.2 Plural marker da

As noted in table 3.2 and table 3.3 above, plurality of demonstratives and proper names is obligatorily marked with *da*, as in (3.71) and (3.72).

(3.71)   *<om>ali*   [*da*   *Alicia*].
        ACTm-come   pl   Alicia
        'Alicia (and others) will come.'

(3.72)   *Adi=ak*   *<in>ila*   [*da*   *di]*   *ay*   *nankakay.*
        NEG=1sI   UND.P-see   pl   DEM3I   LK   elders
        'I didn't see those elders.'

The plural marker can also precede the RM as an alternative to reduplication. Often the context of a sentence makes overt plural marking unnecessary, but when a speaker wishes to specify that there are more than one, the plural *da* can precede the RM, as in (3.73) and (3.74).

(3.73) Il?ila(en)=k   [da   nan]   litrato.
        looking=1sII   pl   DRM   picture
        'I was looking at these pictures (in an album).'

(3.74) In-kosokos=na   din   be~beey   ya   [da   din]
        UNDt.P-collapse=3s   RMd   pl-house   and   pl   RMd

        siged   ay   danan.
        good   LK   road
        'It collapsed the houses and (all) the good roads.'

When the nucleus is a word derived from an action or stative root (see section 3.4.3), reduplication cannot be applied to the nucleus for overt plurality marking. In such cases overt plurality must use the plural marker *da* preceding the RM, as in (3.75).

(3.75) Man-golo   [da   din]   man-bonong.
        ACT-disrupt   pl   RMd   ACT-pray
        'The (ones who) pray (i.e., the traditional priests) will make a fuss.'

3.2.2.2 Quantity

RPs may be quantified by overt numbers or by general quantifiers, the most common of which is *amin* 'all'.

3.2.2.2.1 Numbers

Numbers are linked from the left with *ay*. The linker can be shortened to =y after vowel-final quantifiers and numbers, the only instances of *ay* being contracted, as in (3.76). Attributive modifiers in the nuclear periphery are ordered closer to the nucleus than numbers, as seen in (3.77). General quantifiers such as 'many' or 'few' are also linked from the left, as in (3.78).

(3.76) I-tapos=mi   di   tolo=y   bowan.
        UNDt-finish=1pII   RMi   three=LK   month
        'We will finish three months (doing something).'

3.2 Operators in the Reference Phrase

(3.77) din   dowa=y   pasado   ay   mayor=yo
RMd   two=LK   past   LK   mayor=2pII
'your last two mayors'

(3.78) Isdi   <in>aspo=k   di   ad?ado   ay   ga-gait.
DEM3IV   UND-meet=1sII   RMi   many   LK   pl~friend
'There I met up with many friends.'

3.2.2.2.2 Inclusive quantifiers

The quantifiers *kaadoan* 'most' and *amin* 'all' (with variants *am?in* and *nam?in*) can function as the nucleus of an RP, as in (3.79) and (3.80).

(3.79) Adi   ma-dlaw   di   kaadoan.
NEG   UNDs-notice   RMi   most
'Most (of the mistakes) can't be noticed.'

(3.80) Sa=y   pangitaltalka(n)=k   si   amin.
DEM2I=RMi   NOM-trust=1sII   ORMi   all
'That's who I am relying on for everything.'

The quantifier *amin* can also modify the core of the RP. When quantifying pronouns, it follows the pronoun with no connector, as in (3.81) and (3.82). When quantifying other RP nuclei, the quantifier precedes the nucleus and is linked with *ay*, as in (3.83).

(3.81) Tamang-en=[yo   amin]   ed   demang.
look-UND=2pII   all   LOC   other.side
'All of you look over there.'

(3.82) [Piga   amin]   di   daan?
how.much   all   RMi   not.yet
'How much in all is still remaining?'

(3.83) Si   dakayo   di   maka-ammo   si   [amin   ay]
       PRM   2pIII   RMi   ACT.ABIL-know   ORMi   all   LK

   kasapolan=yo.
   needs=2pII
   'You are responsible for all your needs.'

The general quantifier can also precede the entire RP, yielding the possibility that the quantifier is in the nucleus of an RP with the second RP as its bound argument, as in (3.84).

(3.84) Ma-agom   am?in   din   M   company
       UNDs-gather   all   BRMd   M   company
       'All of the M Company gathered together.'

Finally, the inclusive quantifier does not take a RM in a left-detached phrase expressing a general inclusiveness, as in (3.85) and (3.86), where both quantifiers appear.

(3.85) [Am?in   ay   ipogaw]   et   matey=da.
       all   LK   person   PART   die=3pI
       'All people, they will die.'

(3.86) [Kaadoan,   mo   baken   nam?in],   et   laydena   ay
       most   if   NEG   all   PART   want.4II   LK

   man-i-dawat.
   ACT-Th-give
   'Most, if not all, they wanted to give something.' (after an earthquake)

3.2.3 Nuclear$_R$ operator: nominal aspect

Nominal aspect in Kankanaey indicates specification of a set of individuals denoted by the root, or a special kind of instance of that object. Kankanaey has affixes that indicate a paired unit, a single measured unit, a large group of individuals, or a diminuative kind of referent.

3.2 Operators in the Reference Phrase

The prefix *sin-* with kin terms indicates a matched pair, such as mother-child, siblings, or spouses, as in example (3.87).

(3.87)   Ed   nabayag   kano   wada   di   sin-asawa.
         LOC   P.long.time   HSY   EXIS   RMi   unit-spouse
         'Once upon a time there was a married couple.'

The prefix *sinka-* with a container or specified span indicates one such measured unit. For example, *sinka-* + *palanggana* 'basin' means a basinful, *sinka-* + *gamet* 'pick up in hand' means 'a handful', while *sinka-* + *basa* 'read' means 'one read-through'.

A large group, such as a crowd or herd, is indicated by the affix (*ka-+CVC(C)V~*) on a class root, as in (3.88).

(3.88)   *kabisa~bisaang*
         kaCVCV-pig
         'herd of pigs'

Three affixes indicate the referent as different in kind from the normal denotation of the root. The prefix *sinan-* (sometimes with *CV~*) indicates imitation or representation, such as the 'statue' in (3.89). Another affixation, *CVC* +<*in*> as in (3.90), indicates the same diminution, namely representation, such as a carving. Because this affixation is identical to verbal aspect affixation, there is some doubt as to its classification as a nominal aspect marker. Falseness may denote pretense or denigration, as with the *CVC* reduplication and an infixed glottal stop, as in (3.91).

(3.89)   *Wada=y*   *sinan-i~ipogaw*   *sin*   *sango.*
         EXIS=RMi   false-CV~person   ORMd   front
         'There is a statue (of someone) at the front.'

(3.90)   *t<in>ol~toldo*
         CVC<in>-eagle
         'eagle figure'

(3.91) bang~bang<ʔ>a=k
        CVC<ʔ>pot(banga)=1sII
        'My toy pots/ my little old pots'

3.3 Complex Reference Phrase constructions

Three levels of juncture are possible in the referring phrase: RP phrase level as well as core$_R$, and nucleus$_R$ levels. RRG posits three types of relationships cross-linguistically between units that join at any level—coordinate, subordinate, and cosubordinate. Kankanaey RPs use mostly coordinate relationships, with only the relative clause in a subordinate relationship to the nucleus$_R$. These will be exemplified and explained in the following sections. No evidence of cosubordinate relationships involving shared operators in the RP has been found in Kankanaey.

3.3.1 Phrasal juncture

Sometimes two RPs are joined in a coordinate construction with the conjunctions *ya* 'and' or *ono* 'or'. The two RPs share the same syntactic function in a clause, such as a direct argument or an oblique adjunct. The first RM carries the syntactic case-marking function for both cores, and the second RP is given a 'dummy' RM—always unbound *din,* or *si* with personal names. Coordinate RPs appear in the clause, as in (3.92).

(3.92) Kumusta   baw   abe   [en   kadwa=m]   ya   [din
        greet   EVID   also   OPRM   spouse=2sII   and   RMd

        anʔak=yo].
        kids=2pII
        'Oh yeah, greetings also to your wife and your (pl) kids.'

In (3.93) both RPs express a referent for which thanks is being expressed (oblique relationship to the predicate), but the relative clause is not shared with the first referent. In (3.94) the second RP has a deictic modifier.

3.3 Complex Reference Phrase constructions

(3.93) [sin   solat=mo]   ya   [din   tikit   ya   libro   ay
       ORMd   letter=2sII and   RMd   tickets and   book   LK

in-paw?it=mo]
UNDit.P-send=2sII
(Thanks) 'for your letter and the tickets and book that you sent.'

(3.94) Marowam=ka   [sin   sine]   ono   [din   doy
       accustomed=2sI   ORMd   cinema   or   RMd   DEM3V

beliard].
billiard
'You are used to the movies or those billiard games.'

In (3.95) the bound Actor function is filled by a coordinate set of RPs—'you man or you woman.' The bound pronoun cannot be repeated as such in the second RP, where it appears as the free-standing form of the pronoun.

(3.95) Iginka(n)[=m   ∅   ay   lalaki]   ono   [sik?a   ay
       UNDd-quiet<=2sII   4III   LK   man   or   2sIII   LK

babai]
woman
'You man or you woman be quiet about it.' (from wedding advice regarding critical thoughts)

When the first of two coordinate RPs is marked by *din*, as in (3.96) and (3.97), the second RP core will take the same marking. In such a case, it is not possible to know whether the second RM is a "dummy" or not. Not every junction between RPs follows the dummy-RP convention: a few instances with a repeated oblique RM, as in (3.98), have been noted.

(3.96) | *Sino* | *di* | *banolen=tako,* | *[din* | *siping]* | *ono* | *[din*
 | what | RMi | value.UND=1+2p | RMd | money | or | RMd

awak Narding]?
body Narding
'What is it we value (more), the money or Narding's body (health)?'

(3.97) | *Inawat=ko* | *[din* | *solat=yo]* | *ya* | *[din*
 | UND.P.receive=1sII | RMd | letter=2pII | and | RMd

intatapi=yo].
UNDt. included=2pII
'I received your letter and what you had enclosed.'

(3.98) | *Man-ʔiyaman=ak* | *[en Diyos]* | *ya* | *[en dakayo].*
 | ACT-thank=1sI | OPRM God | and OPRM | 2pIII
'I give thanks to God and to you...'

3.3.2 Nuclear or core juncture

A reference phrase can have two nuclei joined in a coordinate relationship by the conjunctions *ya* 'and' or *ono* 'or'. Coordinate RP nuclei are exemplified in (3.99). In this example the nuclei share a possessor argument. In example (3.100) coordinate cores are shown, as each nucleus has its own possessor argument.

(3.99) | *Ammo=tako* | *din* | *mayat* | *ay* | *[panggep* | *ono*
 | know.UNDp=1+2pII | RMd | good | LK | intention | or

plano]=na.
plan=3sII
'We know his good intentions or plans.'

(3.100) | *din* | *[anak=ko]* | *ya* | *[apo=k]*
 | RMd | child=1sII | and | grandchild=1sII
'my children and my grandchildren'

3.3 Complex Reference Phrase constructions 125

Another example of nuclear coordination is given in (3.101), where the two nuclei share the bracketed non-restrictive relative clause in the RP periphery. Coordinate nuclei can also share restrictive modifiers, such as the bracketed modifier in (3.102).

(3.101) di   lokto   ya   onas   [ay   l<in>a~lagba=na]
        RMi   yams   and   s.cane   LK   UND.P-DUR-basket=3sII
        'some yams and sugarcane that she had basketed'

(3.102) din   [odom   ay]   kenggit   ya   okook
        RMd   other   LK   large.trap   and   small.trap
        'the other (i.e., remaining) large traps and small traps'

Each nucleus in a coordinate construction can have its own periphery, however, as the bracketed modifiers show in (3.103) and (3.104). Pragmatics determines the scope of such restrictive modifiers. Descriptive words that are joined by *ya* will both modify the RP nuclear nominal, as in (3.105).

(3.103) Man- i-lak~lako=da   si   [bogos   ay]   balitok
        ACT-Th-PROG-sell=3pI   ORMi   bogus   LK   gold

        ya   paltog.
        and   gun
        'They were selling fake gold and (real) guns.'

(3.104) sin   [nassawaan   ay]   kenggit   ya   [nassawaan
        ORMd   ten   LK   large.trap   and   ten

        abe   ay]   okook
        also   LK   small.trap
        'the ten large traps and also-ten small traps'

(3.105) din   [na-ka~kayang   ya   kinittoy]   ay   be~beey
        RMd   ATT-pl-tall   and   pl.little   LK   pl-house
        '(both) the tall and small houses'

3.4 Affixed roots in the Reference Phrase nucleus

To this point we have examined RPs with pronouns and unaffixed roots in the nucleus. However, affixed roots may also occur as the nuclear reference entity in an RP. Not at all uncommon in Kankanaey, affixed nuclei comprised forty-two percent of the *di(n)*-marked RPs in an analysis of nearly three thousand RPs in natural texts. Of RPs with the oblique marker *si(n)*, 29 percent had affixed nuclei. The affixation may be nominalizing. This will be discussed in section 3.4.1. Predicative affixation, as discussed in chapter 2, may also occur on RP nuclei. Section 3.4.3 looks at RP nuclei with predicative affixation.

3.4.1 Roots with nominalizing affixation

Table 3.9 lists a few nominalizing affixes of Kankanaey (a full table is found in appendix B). Attached to specific root types, they may express reference to an entity related to the root in some way, such as the possessor, companion, instrument, or means. They may refer to an attribute as an abstract entity, or to the spatial or temporal locus of a state or event. Examples (3.106) to (3.113) show a variety of phrases with nominalized nuclei.

Table 3.9. Some nominalizing affixes in Kankanaey

Affix	Root type	Denotation
akin-	class	owner
ka-	action	companion
kina-	attribute	quality
maN-	action	actor
paN-, pan-	various	instrument used
-an with some other affixes	any	time or place or event

(3.106) din   ka-tolong=ko
        RMd NOM-help=1sII
        'my helper (usually househelper)'

3.4 Affixed roots in the Reference Phrase nucleus

(3.107) *gapo   sin   kina-ngina=na*
  due.to   ORMd   NOM-expensive=3sII
  'due to its expensiveness'

(3.108) *sin   panganan*
            paN-kan-an
  ORMd   NOM-eat<
  'at the restaurant/on the plates'

(3.109) *sin   na-tey-an   tatang=na*
  ORMd   NOM-die<   daddy=3sII
  'at the time/place/event of his dad's death'

(3.110) *Natken   di   inglis=da,   kaman   sin   pang-i-ngadan*
                                                            paN-i-ngadan
  different   RMi   English=3pII   like   ORMd   NOM-Th-name

  si   badbado.
  ORMi   clothing
  'Their (Australian) English is different, like what they use to name (various pieces of) clothing.

(3.111) *di   panlaydak   sin   nakikalkaliak*
              pan-layad-an=ko   *naki-kal~kali-an=ko*
  RMi   NOM-happy<=1sII   ORMd   NOM.P-CVC-speak<=1sII

  sin   nankakay
  ORMd   old.men
  'what made me happy about my conversation with the old men'

(3.112) *pan-logan=ko   ay   emey   ed   singbaan*
  NOM-vehicle=1sII   LK   go   LOC   church
  'what I will use for a ride to go to church (fare money)'

(3.113) din   ka-i-basal-an   di   pan-asi-ka-awat-an
       RMd   NOM-Th-base<   RMi   NOM-RECIP-NOM-receive<
       'the memorandum of agreement (lit. basis of mutual understanding)'

3.4.2 Existentials in the nucleus of a reference expression

Existentials can be used in the nucleus of a reference phrase in two ways: with nominalizing affixes or unaffixed. The prefix *ka-* and circumfix *ka...an* refer to the existence or presence of an entity, as in (3.114) and (3.115). Note that in (3.116), the much-shortened *kad?an* (probably from *ka-wada-an*) indicates current location.

(3.114) Mon   gapo   sin   ka-iwed   di
        but   reason   ORMd   NOM-NEGEXIS   BRMi

        padpadas=ko, ...
        experience=1sII
        'But due to my not having any experience...(lit. absence of)'

(3.115) Siya   di   gapo   si   ka-wada-an   di   kaag
        4III   RMi   reason   ORMi   NOM-EXIS<   BRMi   monkey

        sinan   daga   ay   nay.
        DEM1VI   earth   LK   DEM1V
        'That is the reason for the existence/presence of monkeys here on this earth.'

(3.116) Into=y   kad?a=m?
                            ka-wada-a(n)=m
        where=RMi   place=2s
        'Where are you?'

Unaffixed existentials in the reference phrase nucleus may refer to either located entities or possessors. If there is a locative phrase, the existential will refer to the entity that is present in that location. In (3.117), the argument of the existential predicate is the entity which is located by the

3.4 Affixed roots in the Reference Phrase nucleus

oblique phase. In (3.118) that existential fills the nucleus, referring to the omitted entity that is located as noted.

(3.117) *Wa=y   balat   sin   apis   gowab=da.*
       EXIS=RMi banana ORM area   below=3pII
       'There are banana trees just below their place.'

(3.118) *Daan   maom   din   wada   sin   apis   gowab=da.*
       not-yet   ripe   RMd   EXIS   ORM   area   below=3pII
       'The ones below their place aren't ripe yet.'

When possessive predicates formed by unaffixed existentials are functioning as reference expression nuclei, they cannot omit any arguments. In such cases, the pronominal possessor is the referent while the whole clause fills the nucleus slot, as in (3.119).

(3.119) *S<inm>aa   din   wada   di   anak=na   ay   babai.*
        ACT.P=go.home   RMd   EXIS   RMi   child=3sII   LK   female
        'The one who had the daughter went home.'

3.4.3 Roots with predicating affixation

Chapter 2 presented details of predicate formation, with the introduction of predicate affixes. As was mentioned in that chapter, predicating affixation performs multiple functions. One of those functions is to index or cross-reference one participant RP. In the case of predicates built from action or state roots, the predicating affixes give a cross-reference in terms of macrorole (ACT(or) or UND(ergoer)) and in terms of generalized thematic sub-roles such as PATIENT and LOCUS. With attribute roots, the affix indexes the ATTRIBUTANT.

Any affixed predicate can occur as the nucleus of a reference phrase. With such an affixed nucleus, the RP refers to an entity that would fill the semantic role indicated by its affixation. Thus, an affixed attribute root such as *na-pintas* 'pretty' denotes 'the pretty one' when preceded by a RM, as in (3.120).

(3.120) *Idawat=mo   Ø   [sin   na-pintas].*
　　　　give.Th=2sII   4III   ORMd   ATT-pretty
　　　　'Give it to the pretty one.'

Other examples of RPs with affixed nuclei follow in examples (3.121) to (3.123).

(3.121) *din   nan-akbis*
　　　　RMd   ACT.P-sneeze
　　　　'the one who sneezed'

(3.122) *di   <inm>ali*
　　　　RMi   ACTm.P-come
　　　　'those who came'

(3.123) *Dengdengek   din   bogaw   [di   mang-an~anap*
　　　　　　　　　　　　　　　　　　　　　　　maN-an~anap
　　　　hear.1sII   RMd   shout   BRmi   NOM-PROG-search

　　　　en   sak?en].
　　　　OPRM   1sIII
　　　　'I was listening to the shouts of those looking for me.'

As with other referential nuclei, direct arguments are allowed. With affixed roots they will not be possessors but ergative Actors, as in (3.124). With the special RECENT affixation that marks its single argument with class II pronouns or the bound RM, the direct argument is indicated in the same way, as in (3.125).

(3.124) *din   oto-en=da,   din   i-oto-an=da*
　　　　RMd   cook-UND=3pII   RMd   UNDd-cook<=3pII
　　　　'what they will cook, who they will cook for'

3.4 *Affixed roots in the Reference Phrase nucleus* 131

(3.125) din kat~ka-tey=na ay doy
    ka+CVC-tey=na
  RMd RECENT-dead=3sII LK DEM3V
  'that one who just died

If an entire clause core is included within the RP, with peripheral phrases and other modifiers, it begins to look like a "headless relative clause." In this description the presence of a RM rather than the linker *ay* that precedes relative clauses leads to an analysis of an expanded RP. This avoids an embedding analysis of every affixed root in an RP nucleus. Figure 3.6 expands the template for RPs, increasing the constituent nodes with both direct and oblique arguments and an adjunct phrase. Figure 3.7 shows two oblique arguments.

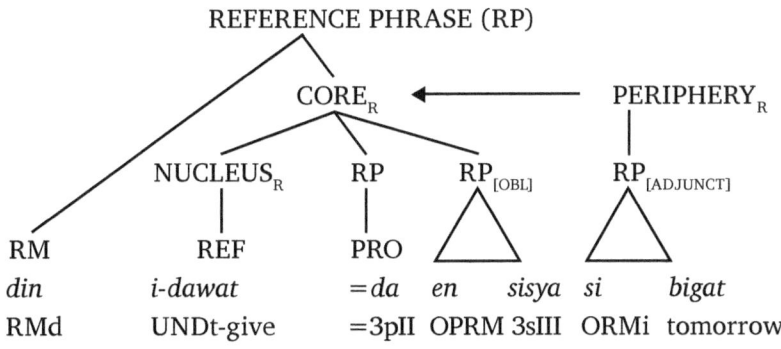

Figure 3.6. Kankanaey RP constituent projection with affixed-root nucleus.

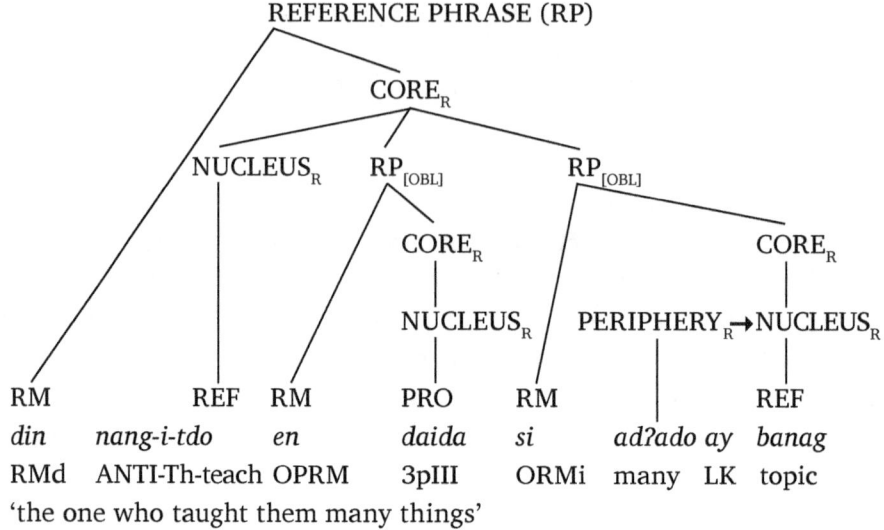

Figure 3.7. Kankanaey RPs: another constituent projection with affixed-root nucleus.

3.5 Reference Phrase as predicate

A reference phrase can function as the predicate of an equative clause. Matthews (1997:116) defines "equational predication" as an assertion "that two referents are identical." An equative clause in Kankanaey consists of two juxtaposed RPs; there is no copula. The first RP is always definite; the second RP may not be. The semantic force of this type of clause is to assert that the first RP is coreferential with the second. In example (3.126) the pragmatic function may be to correct a misperception about what someone took along with him. The first RP (bracketed) serves as the predicating element of the clause. This construction is detailed in chapter 4, and its function is fully explored in chapter 7. Section 3.5 will address the forms that an RP takes when it is functioning as a predicate. Common RPs with the predicating function in equative clauses are marked with *din* (RMd).

(3.126) [*Din lokto*] *di i-takin=na*.
    RMd yams RMi UNDt-take.along=3sII
    '(It's) the yams (that) he will take with him.'

3.5 Reference Phrase as predicate

Proper name RPs with the predicate function are marked with *si* (PRM) for singular, *da* (PRM.pl) for plural, as in (3.127).

(3.127) [Da   Elsa]   di   i-takin=na.
         PRM.pl Elsa   RMi   UNDt-take.along=3sII
         '(It's) Elsa's group (that) he will take with him.'

Table 3.10 displays the marking of personal pronouns when they are used as predicates. Note that the PRM *si* is optional with some of the pronouns. Example (3.128) uses a personal pronoun in the predicate position.

Table 3.10. Personal pronouns (class III) as predicates

1s	(PRM +) *sak?en*	1p	PRM + *dakami*
2s	(PRM +) *sik?a*	2p	PRM + *dakayo*
1+2	PRM + *daita*	1+2p	PRM + *datako*
3s	*sisya*	3p	PRM + *daida*
4	*sa*		

(3.128) [Sak?en] di   i-takin=na.
         1sIII   RMi   UNDt-take.along=3sII
         '(It's) me (that) he will take with him.'

Table 3.11 displays the unique forms (class III) and marking of demonstrative pronouns in predicate position. An example is given in (3.129). Oblique-marked class III demonstratives are found in complex constructions where a class II or class IV demonstrative, which might otherwise be acceptable, would be ambiguous or less specific. They are included in this table and an example given in (3.130).

Table 3.11. Demonstrative pronouns as predicates and oblique phrases

			(sing.)	(pl.)
PRM	+	DEM1III	(si) naey	da naey
PRM	+	DEM2III	(si) sana	da sana
PRM	+	DEM3III	(si) dooy	da dooy
OPRM	+	DEM1III	en naey	en da naey
OPRM	+	DEM2III	en sana	en da sana
OPRM	+	DEM3III	en dooy	en da doy

(3.129) *[Si   sana]   di   i-takin=na.*
       PRM   DEM2III   RMi   UNDt-take.along=3sII
       '(It's) that one (by you) that he will take with him.'

(3.130) *Sin   nangititdoan   di   padi   [en   da   naey*
        ORMd NOM.P.teach   BRMi priest   OPRM pl   DEM1III

   ay   banag]...
   LK   topic
   'When the priest was teaching these topics (lit. the teaching-time of the priest)...'

3.6 The anaphor *siya*

Personal pronouns and demonstrative pronouns have already been explored in this chapter. Another kind of pronoun that has not yet been discussed is *siya*. It is interesting that *siya* is cognate with the Tagalog third person singular specific pronoun (Himmelmann 2005b:358). The Kankanaey third person singular absolutive/predicate pronoun *sisya* is suspiciously similar to the personal reference phrase marker *si* +*siya*. This multifunctional word might be more accurately termed a "pro-form," because it can represent not only an RP, but can also function as an adjective, a predicate, and a conjunction, and give anaphoric reference to a predicate, a clause, and even a paragraph!

As a pronoun, *siya* is forth person (impersonal) and often functions as the first RP in RP-RP clauses, more or less interchangeably with the absolutive

3.6 The anaphor siya

near-hearer demonstrative *sa*. This function is shown in example (3.131), where the intervening particle would not be possible with *sa*. When a person is the antecedent, *sisya* '3sIII' can sometimes be interchanged with *siya*, as in (3.132). The second RP in the clause is bracketed to clarify these examples.

(3.131) …*tan   siya   met laeng   [di   os~osal-en=da].*
        because   4III   PART   RMi   CVC-use-UND=3pII
        'because that's what they are using anyway.'

(3.132) *Din   an?anak   ay   nay   et   siya   [din*
        RMd   child   LK   DEM1V   PART   4III   RMd

    mang-ay~ayoan   sin   man-sakit].
    ANTI-CVC-care.for   ORMd   ACT-sick
    'This kid, that's who was taking care of the sick person.'

As an adjective, *siya* means 'like, thus' and can modify the DEMI in the function of first RP in the equative clause structure, as seen in (3.133) and (3.134).

(3.133) *Layde~layd-e(n)=k   ay   mang-ila=d   Bingga   ngem*
        CVCCV-enjoy-UND=1sII   LK   ANTI-see=LOC   Bingga   but

    siya   na[=y   pasamak].
    like   DEM1I=RMi   event
    'I really want to visit (lit. see) Bingga (town) but like this is what has happened.'

(3.134) *Aw,   siya   sa   [din   eg~egen-a(n)=k].*
        yes   like   DEM1I   RMd   CVC-carry-UNDl=1sII
        'Yes, what I am carrying is like that (the same amount).'

As a predicate, *siya* means '(It is) like, it is the same' as in example (3.135). Followed by DEMI, it means 'It is like this/that'. Examples (3.136) and (3.137) illustrate this function. The brackets enclose the predicate *siya* in these examples.

(3.135) *Ban~bantay-a(n)=na   abe   si   manang=na   tan*
CVC-watch-UND1=3sII also PRM   sister=3sII   because

[siya   abe]   ay   na-ataki   Ø.
same   also   LK   UNDs-attack3sI   3sI
'He is taking care of his older sister because [it's the same situation again (as a previously mentioned person)], she had a heart attack.'

(3.136) *Na-biteg=da.   [Siya   ngin]   di   tan*
UNDs-poor=3pI   like   PART   DEM3I   because

adi=da   man-obla.
NEG=3pI   ACT-work
'They are poor. [It's probably like] that because they don't work.'

(3.137) *Bol~bolod-e(n)=k   kali=yo   ngem   olay   a,*
CVC-borrow-UND=1sII   word=2pII   but   OK   PART

[siya   pay]   di   sin   ngalat.
like   PART   DEM3I   ORMd   conversation
'I'm borrowing your words (i.e., English) but never mind, [it's like] that in conversation.'

Standing alone, *siya* is a general deictic, meaning 'that's it, that's right, that's so, yeah' with positive connotations. *Siya* can be used as a tag question, as in (3.138), or to ask for confirmation of the following *ay*-linked clause, as in (3.139).

(3.138) *Pag =yon   <om>ey   ed   States,   ay   baken   siya?*
then=2pII   ACTm-go   LOC   States   Q   NEG   so
'Then you go to (i.e., leave for) the States, isn't that so?'

3.6 The anaphor siya

(3.139)   Wada   baw   di   dama-ge(n)=k   mo   siya   ay
            EXIS   EVID   RMi   news-UND=1sII   if   it's.so   LK

            tet?ewa   din   in-baga=m   en   Lin.
            true   RMd   UNDt.P-tell=2sII   OPRM   Lin
            'Oh yeah, I have a question as to whether what you told Lin is true.'

Standing alone, *siya* often functions as a summary concession clause 'that may be so, even so' before contrary information, as in (3.140) and (3.141).

(3.140)   Et   siya,   mon   adi=kami   baw   ammo.
            and   it's.so   but   NEG=1pI   EVID   know.UND
            'And that was so, but it turned out that we didn't know. (The situation was not as it had seemed!)'

(3.141)   Adi   na-kaan   din   bokol   di   bayang=ko   ngem   siya
            NEG   UNDs-remove   RMd   lump   RMi   wound=1sII   but   it's.so

            ay baken   kaman   din   rik~rikna-e(n)=k   ed   idi.
            LK NEG   like   RMd   CVC-feel-UND=1sII   LOC   past.time
            'The lump in my wound didn't go away, but even so it isn't like what I was feeling before.'

Siya can be followed by an oblique RP and translates 'It's the same for/the same goes for'. Interestingly, this use of *siya* is interchangeable with *isona* which is cognate with the 3s independent pronoun in Iloko (Rubino 2005:333). Both expressions are shown in (3.142) and (3.143).

(3.142)   [Siya   met   abe]   en   sik?a   ay   babai.
            same   PART   PART   OPRM   2sIII   LK   female
            'The same goes for you, woman.'

(3.143)   Et   [isona   abe]   en   sik?a   ay   babai.
            and   same   also   OPRM   2sIIi   LK   female
            'And the same goes for you, woman.'

Another use of *siya* is in the left-detached formulaic subordinate clause *(idi) siya di* 'when thus that' (bracketed). This clause wraps up the preceding clause, sentence, or even paragraph: 'that being the case, at that point'. Any clause that follows this introduction is an important clause on the discourse level that indicates a change of scene or action, as in (3.144), where the whole preceding conversation is summed up and dismissed.

(3.144) [*Idi*   *siya*   *di]*   *et*   *man-ayag*   *da*   *din*
when   like   DEM3I   PART   ACT-invite   pl   RMd

man-ot~oto   *ay*   *mang-(k)an.*
ACT-CVC-cook   LK   ACT-eat
'At that point, the ones cooking called us to come eat.' (and thus ended that discussion)

Finally, *siya* is part of the conjunction *(et) siyadin*. This is followed by full clauses, and the CLM indicates a logical connection to the larger previous discourse context '(and) so, therefore, that's why, etc.', as in (3.145). This has been taken over in many areas by the weaker Iloko CLM *isonga* 'therefore'.

(3.145) *Nai-potipot*   *din*   *book*   *sin*   *bab?a*   *=n di*   *dalit*   *et*
UNDts-twist   RMd   hair   ORMd   tooth   BRMi   eel   and

siyadin   *adi*   *ka-balin*   *ay*   *adi*   *ka-lokmos*   Ø.
therefore   NEG   UNDs-able   LK   NEG   UNDs-slip.off   4I
'The hair was twisted around the eel's teeth and that's why it was impossible, it could not slip off.'

4

Simple Clauses

4.1 Simple clause structure

Following the Role and Reference Grammar model of a layered structure as it is presented in VanValin (2005), a clause includes a core and optional peripheral or modifying information. As seen in figure 4.1, the core consists of a nucleus (often a verb) and its arguments.[1] The function of the nucleus is to give information about its argument or arguments.

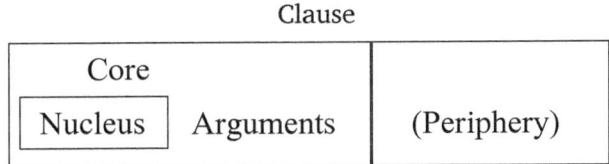

Figure 4.1. Components of the layered structure of the clause.

As noted in section 1.2 the constituents of a clause are diagrammed in RRG to show the layers of its structure in a "constituent projection." The nucleus is core-initial in Kankanaey; it expresses a predication (PRED) about its argument(s). Up to three arguments may follow a predicate. Arguments

---

[1] Van Valin and LaPolla (1997:26); Van Valin (2005:4).

in RRG are designated as reference phrases (RP) instead of using the more traditional "noun phrase" label, as explained in chapter 3. Other RPs that refer to non-argument entities such as time designations modify the core and occur in the core periphery. Figure 4.2 gives the maximal schema or template, using a ditransitive (three-argument) clause. The sample sentence is grammatical but pragmatically unlikely, due to the presence of lexical RPs in every position.

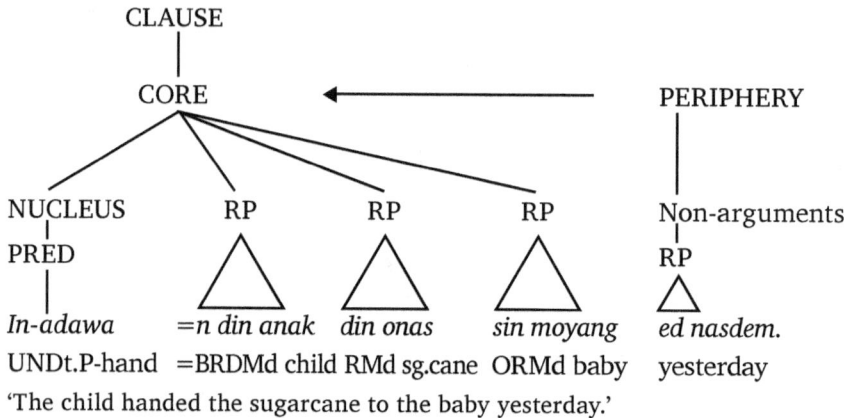

Figure 4.2. Kankanaey clause structure constituent projection.

4.1.1 The nucleus

A Kankanaey clause core may consist of only a nucleus, as in (4.1) with nature verbs that cannot take an overt argument. The lexical root expresses its own argument, something like 'The rain is raining.' (Verb morphology and the glosses for affixes are covered in chapter 2.)

(4.1)   *Man-?odan.*
         ACT-rain
         'It rains.'[2]

---

[2] The free translations use English simple present tense, and no habitual implication is present in the Kankanaey clause. In some contexts these could be translated better with progressive, future, or even past tense verbs in English.

Affixed predicates are not the only possible fillers of the clause nucleus. Unaffixed existentials and class roots can also function as predicates, as can a reference phrase. At this point the examples will all be affixed predicates; section 4.1.3 will explain the other types of clause nuclei.

4.1.2 Core arguments

With the exception of nature verbs, Kankanaey predicates take at least one argument. Based on the classification of the predicate, an argument can be identified as being like an Actor or more like an Undergoer— "macroroles" in RRG terms. If there is only one argument, this distinction does not affect the syntactic marking of a single argument, but when there are two or more arguments, the Actor-Undergoer distinction determines the order and marking of the arguments in the clause structure. Thus, transitive verbs identify their direct arguments by the order in which they occur (Actor precedes Undergoer) and by different RP markers. Third arguments are not direct but oblique, and are marked accordingly. This section will present the forms, positions, and functions of RPs in simple clauses, building on the presentation of RPs in chapter 3. (Chapter 6 will explain macrorole assignment and the details of grammatical relations, including case marking.)

Argument positions are generally filled by reference phrases in Kankanaey. Where other languages might use complement clauses, Kankanaey generally uses reference phrases with affixation on the nucleus. These RPs with affixed nuclei were presented in section 3.7. (See section 5.2 for complements as arguments.)

4.1.2.1 Direct arguments

4.1.2.1.1 Common reference phrases

The common RP can be identified by a Reference Marker (RM), which is the first word in the phrase. This marker identifies the syntactic relationship of the RP to the predicate. Table 4.1, repeated from table 3.1, shows that transitive Undergoer arguments pattern with single arguments in taking the RM, whereas transitive Actor arguments take the BRM. This clearly indicates an ergative pattern of RP marking.

The tags 'd' and 'i' refer to definite and indefinite, as explained in chapter 3. Because the transitive Actor referent in a clause is usually highly topical and identifiable, the definiteness operator is not an essential marker, and so it is often not used with the BRM.

Table 4.1. Kankanaey common RP markers

Relation to predicate:	Single argument	Transitive Undergoer	Transitive Actor
definite	*din* /=n (RMd)	*din*/=n (RMd)	=n *din* (BRMd)
indefinite	*di* /=y (RMi)	*di* /=y (RMi)	=n *di* (BRMi)

Example (4.2) shows a predicate with one common RP argument. Example (4.3) shows a predicate with two direct arguments. When there are two direct arguments, the first is always the Actor (the more agentive), followed by the Undergoer (the less agentive).

(4.2) *Man-ʔoga din anak.*
ACT-cry RMd child
'The child cries.'

(4.3) *I-tanga =n din anak din onas.*
UNDt-hold.in.mouth =BRMd child RMd sugarcane
'The child holds the sugarcane in his mouth.'

4.1.2.1.2 *Proper name reference phrases*

Table 4.2 displays the markers that precede proper names and kin terms. The tags for these markers include P for proper/personal. The clitic binding marker for transitive Actor arguments only appears after vowel-final words, otherwise there is no overt marker.

As with common nominals, the marking of the proper RP clearly follows an ergative pattern. Examples (4.4) and (4.5) show proper RPs as arguments in clauses.

4.1 Simple clause structure

Table 4.2. Kankanaey proper RP markers

	Single	Trans. Undergoer	Trans. Actor
proper and kin names singular	si / =s (PRM)	si / =s (PRM)	=n Ø (BPRM)
proper and kin names plural	da (PRM.pl)	da (PRM.pl)	=n da (BPRM.pl)

(4.4) Man-ʔoga si Langdew.
ACT-cry PRM Langdew
'Langdew cries.'

(4.5) Os-en Langdew din onas.
chew.cane-UND Langdew RMd sugarcane
'Langdew chews the sugarcane.'

4.1.2.1.3 Pronouns as reference phrases

An argument position may be filled by a pronoun, either demonstrative or personal. As explained in chapter 3, pronouns in Kankanaey are tagged by a person number (1–3 or combinations thereof), plural (tagged 's' and 'p') and a class number in Roman numerals. This section will show how the pronoun classes relate to argument positions in the clause structure.

Demonstrative pronouns (DEM) in Kankanaey follow an ergative pattern when used as reference phrases within a clause. Both a single argument and a transitive Undergoer argument are filled with DEM class I, while transitive Actors are expressed by DEM class II. Actor arguments always precede Undergoer arguments. Information in table 4.3 is repeated from chapter 3 for easy reference.

Table 4.3. Kankanaey demonstrative pronouns as direct arguments

TAG \ Class	Single/Trans. Undergoer I	Trans. Actor II
DEM1	na	nina
	da na (pl)	
DEM2	sa	nisa/nasa
	da sa (pl)	
DEM3	di	nidi/nadi
	da di (pl)	

Example (4.6) illustrates a demonstrative pronoun as the Undergoer argument of a transitive verb. The homophony of DEM3I with the indefinite RMi *di* is disambiguated by its position in the clause as well as prosodically.

(4.6)   *I-pigpig   din   anak   di.*
        UNDt-fling BRMd child   DEM3I
        'The child flings that.'

Chapter 3 showed that the Kankanaey personal pronouns present an interesting split pattern of marking the direct arguments in a clause. Table 4.4 repeats information from chapter 3. Note that classes I and II are enclitics, attaching with various degrees of morphophonemic change to the first element in the clause core.

4.1 Simple clause structure

Table 4.4. Kankanaey personal pronouns

pronoun class	I	II	III
	Single	Trans.Actor (and Possessor)	Trans. Undergoer (and Predicate)
1s	=ak	=ko/=k	(PRM +) sak?en
2s	=ka	=mo/=m	(PRM +) sik?a
1p	=kami	=mi	PRM + dakami
2p	=kayo	=yo	PRM + dakayo
3p	=da	=da	PRM + daida
1+2	=ta	=ta	PRM + daita
1+2p	=tako	=tako	PRM + datako
3s	Ø/sisya	=na	Ø/sisya
4(impersonal s/p)	Ø	=na	Ø/(siya/sa)
Blended:			
1sII + 2sIII	=naka		
3II + 2sIII	=daka		

Examples (4.7)–(4.9) illustrate clauses with pronoun arguments. In (4.7) the single argument is expressed by Class I. In (4.8) the Actor is a Class II pronoun while the Undergoer is expressed by Class III. Again, homophony of the forms, this time 3sII =na with DEM1I na, is not confusing when they are encountered in their position in the clause. In (4.9) a blended pronoun is exemplified.

(4.7) *Man-?oga=da.*
ACT-cry=3pI
'They cry.'

(4.8) *Liw?-an=na=s   dakami.*
forget-UND=3sII=PRM 1pIII
'He/she forgets us.'

(4.9) Asog-an=daka.
persuade-UND1=3II+2sIII
'He/They will persuade you.'

4.1.2.2 Oblique arguments

The preceding examples have shown direct arguments, those participants in a state of affairs that are required by the predicate and are judged most salient to the speaker's presentation. Other participants in the state of affairs, required or optional, appear as oblique-marked phrases. Oblique arguments may be common nominals, proper nominals, demonstratives, or personal pronouns. The Kankanaey forms of oblique marking are displayed in table 4.5.

Table 4.5. Oblique argument markers and pronouns

Type of RP	Marker and/or pronoun class	TAG
common nominal (definite)	sin	ORMd
(indefinite)	si (=s)	ORMi
place or time	ed	LOC
proper nominal (sg)	en	OPRM
(pl)	en da	
personal pronoun	en + III	

Although the ORMi *si* is homophonous with the PRM for proper RPs (cf. table 4.2), word order and the common vs. proper distinction disambiguate them, as in (4.10). Oblique arguments are bracketed in the following examples in this section.

(4.10) Man-sibo   si   Rony   [si   digo].
        ACT-sip   PRM   Rony   ORMi   broth
        'Rony sips (some) broth.'

4.1 Simple clause structure

Oblique arguments generally follow the direct arguments. A three-argument clause is repeated from figure 4.2 in (4.11), showing two direct arguments followed by an oblique argument.

(4.11)   *In-adawa*   *=n din anak din onas*   *[sin moyang].*
         UND.P-hand   BRMd child RMd cane   ORMd baby
         'The child handed the sugarcane to the baby.'

Example (4.12) demonstrates the null form of the 3s/4 pronoun and a lengthy oblique RP.

(4.12)   *Ibagak*   Ø   *[sin nay panteteeak sina].*
         tell=1sII   4III   ORMd DEM1V NOM.stay.1sII DEM1IV
         'I will tell it to these (people) I am staying with here.'

As table 4.5 shows, the OPRM *en* serves not only to mark proper nominals but also to identify personal pronouns as oblique arguments. Examples (4.13) and (4.14) show oblique arguments with *en*.

(4.13)   *Nan-solat=kayo*   *[en sisya].*
         ACT.P-write=2pII   OPRM 3sIII
         'You wrote to him.'

(4.14)   *In-paw?it=ko*   *di*   *[en Jerson].*
         UNDt.P-send=1sII   DEM3I   OPRM Jerson
         'I sent that [to Jerson].'

Oblique argument phrases include entities such as those bracketed in (4.15) to (4.18). Note that the indefinite ORMi marks phrases that are indefinite, even hypothetical. English glosses often use prepositions to identify the relationship of these oblique arguments to the predicate.

(4.15)   *Na-sawad=ak*   *[sin tolo ay pewek].*
         UNDs.P-block=1sI   ORMd three LK typhoon
         'I was hindered [by the three (back-to-back) typhoons].'

(4.16) Sokat-a(n)=k   din   pantalon=ko   [si   nalayak   ay
        change-UNDl=1sII   RMd   pants=1sII   ORMi   loose   LK

        bado].
        clothes
        'I changed my pants [for a loose garment].'

(4.17) Mai-arig=ak   [si   man-ayag]...
        UNDt-example=1sI   ORMi   ACT-invite
        'I may be compared [to someone who invites]...'

(4.18) Na~na-pno   din   beey=da   [si   mangili].
        UNDs.P-CV-full   RMd   house=3pII   ORMi   visitors
        'Their house was full [of visitors].'

Oblique arguments generally follow direct arguments, as in previous examples, but they may precede the second direct argument in certain contexts. In (4.19), for example, the single direct argument is lengthy and the bracketed oblique argument is a required participant.

(4.19) Enggay   na-i-polang   [en   sik?a]   din   nay
        already UNDs.P-Th-hand.over   OPRM   2sIII   RMd   this

        babai   ay   asawa=m.
        woman   LK   spouse=2sII
        'This woman, your wife, has now been handed over [to you] (i.e., become your responsibility.)'

In (4.20) the instrument of hitting is integral to the full meaning of the predication; this may license its preceding the Undergoer argument, or perhaps the information structure requires it (see chapter 7).

(4.20) Dosnog-e(n)=k   [si   bato]   din   logan.
        pound-UND=1sII   ORM   stone   RMd   vehicle
        'I pounded the vehicle [with a stone].'

4.1 Simple clause structure

4.1.3 Non-verbal predicates in the clause nucleus

The nucleus of the clause core to this point has been filled by predicates built from affixes and roots. Other predicates include class words, reference phrases and existentials.

4.1.3.1 Class roots and reference phrases as predicates

Class roots in the nucleus of a clause are not reference phrases, but classify the RP that stands as its argument. In (4.21), the predicate indicates that the single argument is a member of the designated class 'female'. In figure 4.3, no particular yams are referred to; rather, the class of food for his lunch is identified.

(4.21)   *Babai*   *di*   *oken=na.*
        female   RMi   puppy=3sII
        'His/her puppy is female.'

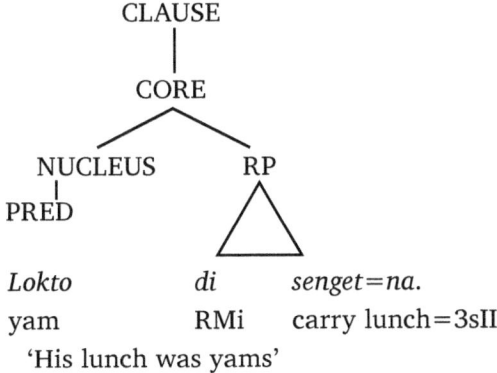

Figure 4.3 Clause with class-word predicate.

Reference phrases can also take the nucleus position, with another RP as the direct argument, forming a clause consisting of two juxtaposed RPs. This clause type was briefly introduced in chapter 3. Such clauses are equative, asserting a co-referential relationship between the two RPs. The first RP is in the clause nucleus, while the second RP is its argument. Predicate RPs are definite and referential; they may be pronouns or RM-marked RPs. Figure 4.4 exemplifies an equative clause construction.

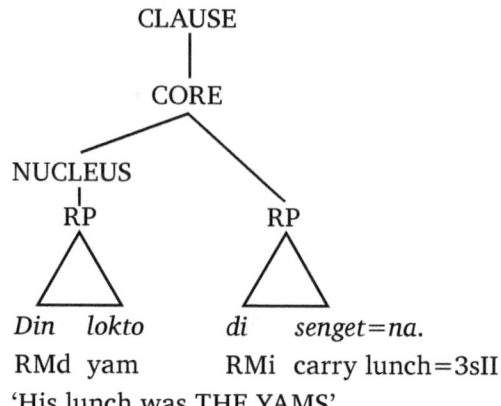

Figure 4.4. Focal equative clause.

Equative clauses may be used to contrast or identify a referent as the focus of the clause. Note that the nucleus holds a full RP with RM. Examples (4.22) and (4.23) show other RPs in the clause-nuclear position. Note that pronouns use class III. Chapter 7 on Information Structure examines the functions of focus clauses of this type.

(4.22) Sikʔa   di   kababasangan.
        2sIII   RMi   most.beautiful
        'You are the most beautiful one!'

(4.23) Si   Apo Diyos   di   kanayon   ay   gait=yo.
        PRM   Lord.God   RMi   constant   LK   companion=2pII
        'Lord God is your constant companion.'

4.1.3.2 Existential clauses

Existential predicates were introduced in chapter 2. Table 4.6 is repeated from that chapter, listing the existential predicates of Kankanaey.

4.1 Simple clause structure

Table 4.6. Kankanaey existentials

Positive	wada/wa
Negative	maga
	iwed

Existentials may occur in their root form or with various predicating or nominalizing affixes. Existentials predicate existence, possession, and physical presence as well as other functions. They take a single reference phrase as their argument.

4.1.3.2.1 Existence

Example (4.24) shows the simple existence meaning of *wada*.

(4.24) Man-kedaw=ak   en   Quinn   si   similya   mo   wada.
       ACT-request=1sI OPRM   Quinn   ORMi   seeds   if   EXIS
       'I'm going to ask Quinn for seeds if there are any.'

Existentials with an indefinite RP argument may introduce new participants. Example (4.25) is typical.

(4.25) Wada=y   si   Nabulay   ed   nabbaon   ed   Abas.
       EXIS=RMi   PRM   Nabulay   LOC   long-ago   LOC   Abas
       'There was a certain Nabulay long ago at Abas.'

Things that don't exist sometimes need to be pointed out, when a hearer might reasonably expect otherwise. These are instances of nonreferential RPs, and they use the indefinite RM. Often such information explains why events turn out the way they do, as in (4.26).

(4.26) Iwed   di   danan.
       NEGEXIS   RMi   path
       'There wasn't any path/road (and that created the following problem).'

4.1.3.2.2 Possession

If an indefinite argument of an existential has a direct argument of its own, the clause asserts general possession, as in (4.27), or other associative relationships, as in (4.28). To assert possession of a particular item, the existential cannot be used. A different root, *oka* 'belong to', is used, discussed in chapter 2.

(4.27) *Maga=y   sapatos=na.*
        NEGEXIS=RMi shoes=3sII
        'He doesn't have any shoes.'

(4.28) *Ay wada=y   pan-tee-a(n)=na=s sa?*
        Q   EXIS=RMi NOM-stay<=3sII=DEM2IV
        'Does she have a place to stay there?' i.e., 'Is she going to stay with you?'

4.1.3.2.3 Presence

When the argument of an existential is a definite RP, the meaning is physical presence as in (4.29). Use of the definite RM before a possessed entity indicates presence, not possession, as may be seen in (4.30).

(4.29) *Ay iwed   si   Langdew?*
        Q   NEGEXIS   PRM   Langdew
        'Is Langdew not in/not here?' (e.g., asking at the door)

(4.30) *Wada   din   anan?ak   di   natey.*
        EXIS   RMd   children   BRMi   dead
        'The children of the deceased were present.'

4.1.3.2.4 Location

Examples (4.31) to (4.34) demonstrate the existential as a locative predicate. The locative phrase itself cannot be used as a predicate, a restriction that is different from Tagalog.

4.1 Simple clause structure 153

(4.31)　Din　　　kitkitoy　ay　anak=ko,　　wada　Ø　　metlaeng
　　　　RMd　　small　　LK　child=1sII　　EXIS　3sI　PART

　　　　en　　　sak?en.
　　　　OPRM　1sIII
　　　　'My littlest child, she is still with me.'

(4.32)　Mo　　　　maga=ak　　　sina　　　wada=ak　　ed　　Baguio.
　　　　if/when　NEGEXIS=1sI　DEM1IV　EXIS=1sI　　LOC　Baguio
　　　　'When I'm not here, I'm in Baguio.'

(4.33)　Idi　　　wada　Ø　　　sin　　gawa=n di　　ginawang,
　　　　when　EXIS　3sI　　ORMd　middle=BRMi　river

　　　　pag=et　　　　na-tokang　　　Ø.
　　　　then=PART　ST.P-fall.over　3sI
　　　　'When he was in the middle of the river, he (suddenly) fell over.'

(4.34)　Wa=y　　　balat　　　sin　　apis　　gowab=da.
　　　　EXIS=RMi　banana　ORM　area　　below=3pII
　　　　'There are banana trees just below their place.'

4.1.3.2.5 Indefinite reference

Existentials are often used in Kankanaey where English would have an indefinite pronoun, such as 'someone'. The argument of the existential in such cases is an RP with an affixed root of some kind as its nucleus. Such a nucleus refers to an entity that fills the role associated with the agreement affix. In (4.35) an Actor is cross-referenced on the RP nucleus; in (4.36) the Undergoer cross-referenced is the CONTENT argument of 'do'. When an Undergoer role is cross-referenced, the bound argument on the RP root is understood as the Actor, not the possessor, although in the English gloss the possessive 'have' may also be a good translation, as in (4.37).

(4.35) Wada=y   \<om\>ali.
EXIS=RMi   ACTm-come
'There is someone coming.'

(4.36) Iwed   di   am~ʔamag-ena.
NEGEXIS   RMi   CVC-do-UND.3sII
'He's not doing anything (lit. the thing that he is doing does not exist).'

(4.37) Wa=y   i-baga=k.
EXIS=RMi   UNDt-say=1sII
'I have something to say (lit. what I will say exists).'

One function of this indefinite reference is to soften a statement by making it indirect for some pragmatic purpose, as in (4.38) to (4.39).

(4.38) Wada   di   \<inm\>ali-a(n)=k   ngem   iwed=kayo.
EXIS   RMi   NOM-come\<=1sII   but   NEGEXIS=2pI
'There was a time when I came but you weren't (here).'
This statement is less direct/accusing than 'I came but you weren't here.'

(4.39) Wa=y   b\<om\>aba.
EXIS=RMi   ACT-go.down
'There's someone to get down.'
This is less direct than 'Stop the car! I want to get out.'

4.1.3.2.6 Number

The existential with a quantified indefinite RP asserts the quantity, as in (4.40). A quantifying adjective, such as 'many' or 'few', does not co-occur with the existential, but replaces it in asserting the quantity, as in (4.41).

(4.40) Wada=y   20 ay Day Care children.
EXIS=RMi   20 LK Day Care children
'There are 20 day-care children.'

4.1 Simple clause structure 155

(4.41)   *Ad?ado=y   lalaeg   ed   niman.*
           many-RMi   flies   LOC   now
           'There are lots of flies nowadays.'

4.1.3.2.7 Affixed existentials

The existentials may take certain predicative affixes, as pointed out in chapter 2. With *ma-*, it indicates a changeable state of existence, as illustrated in (4.42). The presence or absence of the definite operator on the RP argument is key to interpreting the meaning of the existential.

(4.42)   *Koma   mo   ammo=k   ay   man-?obla   sina   ta*
           PART   if   know=1sII   LK   ACT-work   here   so-that

           adi   ma-pa-iwed   di   ammo=k.
           NEG   UNDs-CAUS-NEGEXIS   RMi   know=1sII
           'If only I knew how to work here so I wouldn't forget what I know (lit. so what I know won't be caused to cease to exist).'

In examples (4.43) and (4.44) the CVC reduplication indicates an ongoing (progressive) situation.

(4.43)   *Dowa   ay   agew   ya   dowa   ay   labi=mi   ay*
           two   LK   day   and   two   LK   night=1pII   LK

           nan-ob~obla   yan   iw-iwed   pay.laeng
           ACT.P-CVC-work   and   CVC-NEGEXIS   still

           di   d<in>teng mi.
           RMi   UND.P-arrive=1pII
           'For two days and two nights we were working and still there was (being) nothing that we found.'

(4.44) Adi=ak   man-isolo   ed   niman mon wad~wada
        NEG=1sI   ACT-teach   LOC   now   but CVC-EXIS

        din   obla=k   sin   opisina.
        RMd   work=1sII   ORMd   office
        'I am not teaching now but I always have my work at the office.
        (lit. there is (always) my work)'

4.1.4 Peripheries in the clause

The core periphery was introduced in figure 4.1 above. In more complex clauses, each level in the clause may have its own periphery for modifying information; thus there are clause, core, and nuclear peripheries. This section will introduce the use of modifying words and phrases that occur in the peripheries. Peripheral elements are bracketed. (Chapter 5 gives an analysis of entire clauses as constituents in the peripheries.)

4.1.4.1 Clause-level peripheries

Whole clauses may be modified by phrases that express reasons, parameters or conditions for the event presented. Deictics with non-spatial reference can also modify whole clauses.

4.1.4.1.1 Prepositional phrases

Where English requires various prepositional phrases, Kankanaey generally uses an oblique RM and depends on the semantics of the predicate root to suggest the appropriate semantic relationship between the core and the adjunct phrase. However, Kankanaey does have a few prepositions that precede oblique-marked phrases for specific meanings, such as 'regarding' and 'depending on', among others, as in examples (4.45) and (4.46). Any affixation on these prepositions is frozen, and does not carry aspect or inflection.

4.1 Simple clause structure   157

(4.45) Adi=kayo   pan-talk-an   da   am~ama=yo
        NEG=2pI   UNDl-trust<   PRM.pl   pl-father=2pII

        [maipanggep   sin   kasapolan].
        regarding   ORMd   needs
        'Don't depend on your parents [regarding the things that are needed].'

(4.46) ...si   mga   tolo=y   agew   [insigon   sin   kadalas
        ...ORM   about three=LK   day   depending   ORMd   speed

        di   sanglay   ay   komompitay].
        BRMi   root.crop   LK   become.soft
        '(They store it) for about three days, [depending on the speed of
        the roots to become soft].'

Prepositional phrases that give reasons are in the clause periphery, as seen in (4.47) with the preposition *gapo* 'due to'.

(4.47) Sinokat-a(n)=k   din   agas   [gapo   sin
        change-UNDl=1sII   RMd   medicine   due.to   ORMd

        kina-ngina=na].
        NOM-expensive=4II
        'I changed the medicine [because of its expensiveness].'

4.1.4.1.2 Clause-modifying deictics

Chapter 3 described the attributive class V demonstratives that modify RPs. The same demonstratives may precede a clause (often linked with *ay*) in the left clause periphery. They contribute to the flow of the discourse by indicating attitudinal or evidential distance. In (4.48) the writer owns her own statement with demonstrative-1, and in (4.49) the demonstrative-2 is not literal, but associates the information with the reader, in this case as the source of the writer's information.

(4.48) [Nay]   enggay   ad?ado   di   insolat=ko.
       DEM1V   already much   RMi   write.P=1sII
       '[Here] it's really a lot (too much?) that I've written.'

(4.49) Advance congratulations=ak   tan   [sana   ay]
       advance congratulations=1sI   because   DEM2V   LK

       man-graduate   Ø   sin   June.
       ACT-graduate   3sI   ORMd   June
       'I'll congratulate (your daughter) in advance because [there (i.e., as you said)] she is going to graduate in June.'

4.1.4.2 Core peripheries

The information in a core periphery modifies the entire core. One distinguishing feature of core peripheries is that they fall within the intonation curve of the clause. Kankanaey has a left core periphery as an optional position for certain time phrases. The right core periphery holds several types of oblique-marked phrases.

4.1.4.2.1 Left core periphery

Very few phrases are placed to the left of a Kankanaey core yet still within its intonational curve. Time phrases that are salient only to the event expressed by the core may occur in the left core periphery, proceeding without pause, as in (4.50). They are often linked with *ay*, as in (4.51) and (4.52) (time phrases bracketed).

(4.50) [Ed   niman]   i-tolong=ko   nan   kalloloya   ay   golis=ko
       LOC   now   UNDt-send=1sII   DRM   bad   LK   write=1sII
       '[Now] I send this awful handwriting of mine.'

4.1 Simple clause structure 159

(4.51)   [Dandani   inag?gew   ay]   wada=y   en   mang-ayag
        almost   daily   LK   EXIS=RMi   go   ANTI-invite

en sisya.
OPRM 3sIII
'[Almost every day] someone was calling for him.'

(4.52)   [Ed   niman   anggoy   ay]   man-solat=kami.
        LOC   now   only   LK   ACT-write=1pI
        '[Only now] are we (having a chance to) write.'

4.1.4.2.2 Right core periphery

The periphery to the right of the core holds several types of information: time and place designations, and adverbial phrases expressing temporal and manner modifications. With non-verbal predicates, a restriction on the range of the predicate is expressed by an oblique phrase in the core periphery as well.

4.1.4.2.2.1 Time and space designations

Time and space designations that modify the core of a clause usually follow the predicate and its arguments in the right core periphery. In Kankanaey, place names and time words referring to the past are marked by the definite locative *ed*, as in (4.53).

(4.53)   *Lawlawa   din   danan   ed   Kabasang   ed   idi.*
        bad   RMd   road   LOC   Kabasang   LOC   when
        'The roads were bad in Kabasang back then.'

Other time/space phrases take the Oblique Reference Marker *si* or its more definite variant *sin*, both shown in (4.54). They may be interpreted as required locative arguments or peripheral phrases based on the semantic representation of the predicate, but the distinctions can become fuzzy. For example the locative phrase 'at home' in (4.54) is probably a required argument of the predicate 'stay', but not of 'feed' in (4.55). Because the same oblique marker covers many relationships, there may be some ambiguity that the context would probably clear up, as in (4.56).

(4.54) *Man-tee=ka   sin   beey   si   bigat.*
        ACT-stay=2sI ORMd   house   ORMi   tomorrow
        'Stay at the house/home tomorrow.'

(4.55) *Man-megmeg=ka=s   manok   sin   beey.*
        ACT-feed=2sI=ORM   chicken   ORMd   house
        'Feed chickens at home/the house.'

(4.56) *S<inm>adot   Ø   sin   na-tey-an   ina=na.*
        ACT.discouraged   3sI   ORMd   UNDs.P-die-NOM   mother=3sII
        'She became discouraged when/because her mother died.'

4.1.4.2.2.2 Adverbial phrases

Adverbial phrases are also marked by the oblique marker *si*. The absence of the definite suffix *-n* (thus *si* not *sin*) helps to distinguish the phrases as nonreferential. Adverbial phrases may express a time duration or frequency, or they may express the manner of the predicating nuclear word.

Example (4.57) shows the salient time duration phrase (in brackets) modifying the nucleus.

(4.57) *S<in>akit=ko   [si   dowa   ay   agew]   din   tili=k.*
        UND.P-hurt=1sII   ORMi   two   LK   day   RMd   butt=1sII
        'My tailbone hurt [for two days] (lit. I pained my tailbone).'

Examples (4.58) and (4.59) show frequency phrases.

(4.58) *Nan-solat   si   Peds   [si   namindowa].*
        ACT.P-write   PRM   Peds   ORMi   twice
        'Peds wrote (a letter) [twice].'

4.1 Simple clause structure   161

(4.59) B<in>asa=k   [si   nasolok.mo   esa   ay   sinka-basa].
        read-UND.P=1sII ORMi   more.than   one   LK   UNIT-read
        'I read it [more than once (lit. more than one read-through)].'

Adverbial phrases that express manner are also oblique phrases, as in (4.60) to (4.62).

(4.60) *Maka-basa*   Ø   [si   *kosto]*.
        ACT.ABIL-read   3sI   ORMi   correct
        'She can read very well.'

(4.61) *Kana=na*   [si   *nakapsot*   ay   *kali]*...
        say.UND=3sII   ORMi   weak   LK   word/voice
        'She said in a weak voice....'

(4.62) *Gipgi~gipgip-en=da*   Ø   [si   *naingpis]*.
        CVCCV-slice-UND=3pII   4III   ORMi   thin
        'They slice them (the yams) thinly.'

4.1.4.2.2.3 Range restrictions

Many nonverbal predicates such as existentials and attributives may be restricted in their range by phrases in the core periphery. The indefinite oblique marker *si* does not give referential status to these phrases. In examples (4.63) and (4.64) the presence, possession or existence of the single argument of the existential predicate is restricted or described by the *si*-marked phrase (bracketed). Figure 4.5 shows the position of an oblique peripheral phrase.

(4.63) *Maga*   *da*   [=s   *ma-ila=na]*.
        NEGEXIS   3pI   ORMi   UND-see=3sII
        'They were not there [for him to see]' (i.e., they may have been there, but he didn't see them).

(4.64) Siyat   wa=y   pilak   [si   ni-libo].
        must   EXIS=RMi money   [ORMi UNDs-thousand]
        'There has to be money [in the thousands] (e.g., in order to go to America).'

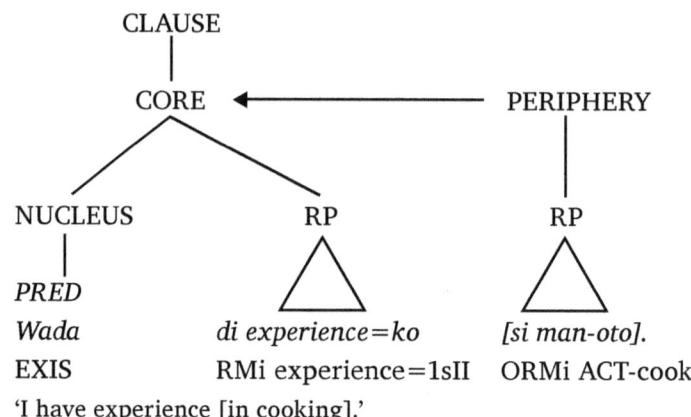

Figure 4.5. Existential clause with peripheral modifier.

In (4.65) to (4.67) the descriptive word in the predicate is restricted in its application to only the parameters or range indicated in the *si*-marked phrase. An English expansion might be "in terms of...."

(4.65) Enggay   na   [si   mai-baga=k].
        already DEM1I   ORMi   UNDts-say=1sII
        'This is enough [for me to say].'

(4.66) Siged   ka   [=s   ma-ong~ongngo-an].
        good   2sI   =ORMi   UNDls-CVC-kiss
        'You're nice [for kissing]!'

(4.67) Kitkitoy sa   [=s   bisaang].
        small   DEM2I   =ORMi   pig
        'That's a small pig (lit. small [for a pig]).'

4.1.4.2.2.4 Vocatives

Vocatives are not part of the clause core and may precede or follow it. In example (4.68) the two questions are taken from different paragraphs of the same narrative. In the first question, the vocative precedes the clause in a detached position (see chapter 5). In the second, the vocative follows the core with no intonational pause or marker, indicating its position in the core periphery.

(4.68)   "Ay   nanang,   ay   osto   adi   na?"
              VOC   mom   Q   correct   PART   DEM1I
              "'Mom, is this really right?"

              "Ay   osto   di   ay   nanang?"
              Q   correct   DEM3I   VOC   mom
              "Is that right Mom?'"

4.1.4.2.3 Differentiating oblique core arguments from core peripheral phrases

Oblique core arguments may be differentiated from peripheral phrases (bracketed) in that they are ordered prior to peripheral phrases, as in (4.69), where the location is an argument of the motion predicate, but the duration phrase is in the periphery. In (4.70) the two *sin*-marked phrases cannot be interchanged because the first is an oblique argument of the predicate *kom?ot* 'gulp down', while the second is a locative phrase in the periphery.

(4.69)   <Inm>ey=kami   sin   dontog   Kamanoboan   [si
              ACTm.P-go=1pI   ORMd   mountain   K.   ORMi

              piga   ay   agew].
              how.many   LK   day
              'We went to Kamanoboan Mountain for a few (lit. how many) days.'

(4.70) Kai-kom?ot　　　　　Ø　　sin　　babai　[sin
ACT.Th-gulp.down　3sI　ORMd　female　ORMd

gawan　di　　　danom].
middle　BRMi　water
'He (crocodile) swallowed down the woman [in the middle of the water (i.e., river)].'

RPs in the core periphery do not have ordering restrictions, although seldom would more than two be present in a given clause. Example (4.71) shows two peripheral RPs in optional order.

(4.71) Na-sigit-an=ak　　　　　　[sin　　seng?ew　di　　Baygon]
UNDls.P-allergic<=1sI　ORMd　fragrance　BRMi　Baygon

[sin　　kakitkitoy=ko].
ORMd　childhood=1sII
'I had an allergic reaction [to the smell of Baygon] [in my childhood].'

4.1.4.3 Nuclear peripheries

Nuclear peripheries hold adverbs that indicate aspectual information about the predicate, such as inchoativity, intensity, and completion. Aspect is normally expressed with affixation on the predicate (see section 4.2.1 for a full discussion of nuclear operators); these overt adverbs stress the particular aspect that they denote. For example, in (4.74) both the verbal prefix and the adverb express immediacy, and in (4.75) both the predicate's perfective affix and the adverb express completion.

Adverbs in the left periphery of the nucleus may immediately precede the predicate with no linker, as in (4.72). The linker *ay* is often used as well, as in (4.73) and in (4.74), where the adverb is linked from the right nuclear periphery.

(4.72) Dagos　　　　　man-biweng　din　　sailboat.
immediately　ACT-go.fast　　RMd　sailboat
'The sailboat immediately got going fast.'

4.1 Simple clause structure   165

(4.73) *Palalo   ay   inmopsat   di   mata=k.*
       overmuch   LK   became.pale   RMi   face/eye=1sII
       'My face became very pale.'

(4.74) *Ka-parti   abe   ay   dagos   din   akin-aso*
       IMM-butcher   PART   LK   immediately   RMd   owner-dog

   et   adi   na-observar-an   Ø.
   and   NEG   UNDl.P-watch<   4I
   'Furthermore, the owner of the dog butchered (it) immediately and it was not observed (for signs of rabies).'

For some adverbs the linker *ay* is optional, as seen in (4.75); these two clauses appeared together in a letter.

(4.75) *Enggay   ay   nakaro   di   sakit   Kili.   Enggay*
       already   LK   worsen.P   RMi   illness   Kili   already

   kinmapoy   Ø.
   became.weak   3sI
   'Kili's sickness has already gotten worse. He is already weak.'

4.1.5 A pre-core slot?

In RRG theory, there are possible pre- and post-core positions in which core NPs, PPs, and adverbs can occur without intonational pause. In many languages the PreCore Slot is the position for WH-question words and other narrow-focus constituents. In Kankanaey, this is not the case; instead, the equative clause structure introduced in section 4.1.3 is used. The WH-word or focal RP is placed in the clause-nuclear position, and all other constituents are nominalized by a preceding RM, and sometimes by nominalizing affixation as well. Note in the examples that the WH-word is an RP, and what follows is also an RP, marked with an indefinite RM. In (4.76) the predicate in the nucleus of the second RP is cross-referenced to the thing done—the referent of the WH-word. In (4.77) the nucleus of the second RP is nominalized for place/time/event (see chapter 3 for the discussion on nominalization). These examples include the ungrammatical results of an attempt to place the focal RP in a Pre-Core slot with no other changes. These ungrammatical versions are marked by asterisks.

(4.76) Sino=y   \<in\>am~ʔamag=mo?   *Sino   inamʔamag=mo?
        what=RMi   UND.P-CVC-do=2sII   what   were.doing=2sII
        'What you were doing (is) what?'   *"What were you doing?

(4.77) Pigʔan di   s\<om\>aa-an=da?   *Pigʔan   somaa=da?
        when   RMi   NOM-go.home\<=3pII   when   go.home=3pI
        'Their going home (is) when?'   *"When will they go home?"

Example (4.78) presents a basic clause with the RP in brackets, while (4.79) with bracketed RPs shows the RP-RP structure of the clause with a focused RP left-most in the clause. Note that in (4.79), the focus RP is in the nucleus of the core and the remainder of the core is comprised of an indefinite RP, with nominalizing affixation indicating the locus of 'dependence'.

(4.78) K\<in\>am~kamang-a(n)=k   [si   Diyos   anggoy]   si
        CVC.P-depend-UNDl=1sII   PRM   God   only   ORMi

        oway.
        always
        'I was always depending on God alone.'

(4.79) [Si   Diyos   anggoy]   [di   nan-kam~kamang-a(n)=k]
        PRM   God   only   RMi   NOM.P-CVC-depend\<=1sII

        si   oway.
        ORMi   always
        'Who I was depending on all the time (was) God alone.'

Kankanaey does use the pre-core slot in certain subordinate clauses (see chapter 5) and the post-core slot with a complex equative clause structure (see chapter 7).

4.1.6 Clitic pronoun displacement

As seen in table 4.4 above, class I (intransitive-argument) pronouns are clitics, as are class II (transitive Actor) pronouns. These clitic pronouns in Kankanaey follow the well-known Wackernagel's Law (Wackernagel 1892), by which they attach to the first word in the core, typically the nuclear predicate. When certain modifying words such as a modal or negative precede the nuclear predicate, any clitic pronoun is displaced to attach to it, thus preceding the predicate in the non-canonical RP-PRED-(RP) order. Often the displaced pronoun has a final =n, with no particular function discernable (thus tagged DISPlaced), and in some dialects or with some modifiers it is not required.

Examples (4.80) to (4.82) show clitics following a modal and a negative.

(4.80) *Siyat=ta=n   makiline   si   piga   ay   oras.*
       must=1+2I=DISP   join.line   ORMi how.many   LK   hours
       'We have to stand in line for hours.'

(4.81) *Adi=kayo   pantalkan   si   daida.*
       NEG=2pI   trust   PRM   3pIII
       'Don't depend on them (for support).'

(4.82) *Adi=da   gagaoden   din   danom.*
       NEG=3pI   paddle   RMd   water
       'They don't paddle the water (in a motorboat).'

Some sequential clause-linkage markers (conjunctions) can displace core pronouns as well, as in (4.83), where the linker consists of two words, and the pronoun comes between them (bracketed sequence).

(4.83) *Idolin=da   Ø   si   tolo   ay   agew   [asi=da   pag]*
       store=3pII   4III   ORMi   three   LK   day   then=3pII   then

       ipeey   Ø   sin   koli.
       put   4III   ORMd   jar
       'They set it aside for three days, and then they put it in the wine-jar.'

This accusative pattern (S and A pronouns displace, but not U) is different from many other Philippine languages that displace pronouns in other patterns.[3] The class assignment of the pronoun in its displaced position is not syntactically constrained, supporting Comrie's (1989:89) observation that the positioning rules governing clitic pronouns relate only loosely to their grammatical relation. With most modifiers that cause displacement, the class I pronoun is the preferred form of the clitic, especially with the group that have a tripartite split (see table 4.4 above). Example (4.84) shows the Actor pronoun =m '2s' as class II in the canonical clause order, but as class I when displaced by an adverb in (4.85).

(4.84) Ibaga=m   Ø   en   sak?en!
        tell=2sII 4III OPRM   1sIII
        'Tell it to me!'

(4.85) May, asi=ka   ibaga Ø   en   sak?en mo
        OK   and.then=2sI   tell   4III OPRM   1sIII   if

        mansolat=ka.
        write=2sI
        'OK, then tell it to me when you write.'

The displacement of clitic pronoun arguments to a pre-nuclear position in the clause core suggests a second constituent projection or template for the Kankanaey clause, shown in figure 4.6.

---

[3] See, for example, Quakenbush and Ruch (2006) for Kalamianic, and Kroeger (1993) for Tagalog.

4.2 Modifiers in the clause   169

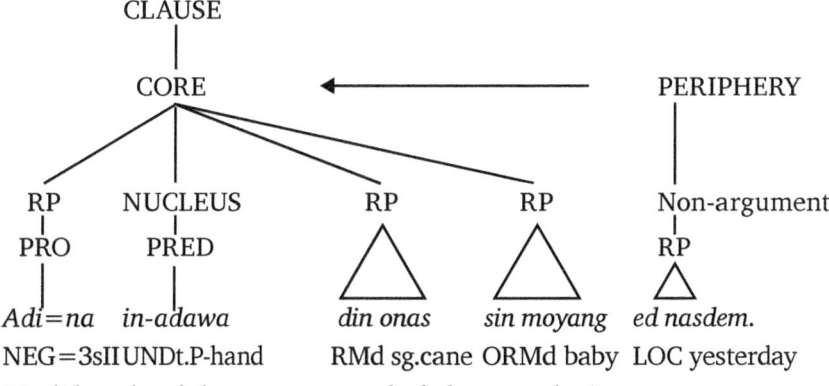

'He did not hand the sugarcane to the baby yesterday.'

Figure 4.6. Kankanaey clause structure constituent projection #2.

4.2 Modifiers in the clause

Modifiers, grammatical and adverbial, can occur at every constituent level: at the nuclear level, the core level, and the clause level. RRG represents the grammatical modifiers in an "Operator Projection" separate from the Constituent Projection. Adverbial modifiers and the plethora of higher-level modifying semantic particles that are typical of Philippine languages are covered in section 4.2.4.1. Table 4.7 (modified from Van Valin 2005:9) shows the operator categories relevant to Kankanaey, their relation to the layers of the Kankanaey clause, and the forms that they take in Kankanaey.

Operators maintain a linear order in the clause, with nuclear operators closest to the nucleus and clause level operators furthest from the nucleus. Among the affixes, nuclear affixation is closer to the root than the core-level modifying affixation, with the exception of perfective aspect.

Table 4.7. Layers of the clause with operators

Level	Operator	Form
Nuclear	Internal temporal aspect Perfective aspect Nuclear negation	Reduplicative affixes Affix *baken* negator
Core	Event quantification Deontic modality Core negation	Affix Core-internal modals *baken* and *adi* negators
Clause	Epistemic modality Propositional negation Evidentials Illocutionary force	Core-external modals *baken* negator Particles Particles

Figure 4.7 shows the display of both the constituent nodes and possible operators in a Kankanaey clause.

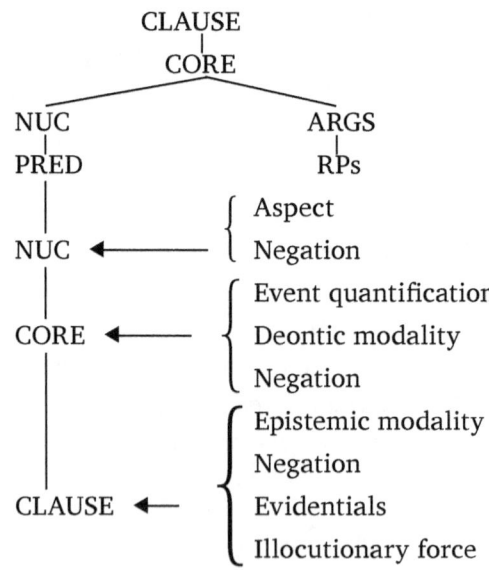

Figure 4.7. Constituent and operator projections for Kankanaey.

4.2.1 Nuclear operators

4.2.1.1 Internal temporal aspect

Internal temporal aspect refers to the internal temporal situations of a predicate, specifically whether the state of affairs has continuity over time. Internal aspect is marked on the root by means of reduplicative affixation. In general, CV reduplication indicates duration of a static situation, while CVC reduplication indicates progressive, repeated or ongoing dynamic situations and CVC(C)V reduplication indicates repetitive, vigorous or otherwise intensified continuation of a dynamic situation. Words that begin orthographically with a vowel have a glottal stop preceding the vowel, the first C of the reduplication. In the following examples the glottal stop is represented where relevant to the reduplication.

4.2.1.1.1 Durative aspect

Durative aspect specifies an unchanging, continuous duration of a static situation. Durative aspect is indicated by a reduplicated CV prefix on the root. With one-syllable or vowel-reduced roots, reduplication is applied after the predicative affixation (see appendix A). Durative aspect pairs naturally with State predicates, as in (4.86) and (4.87). Predicates built on physical motion/position roots may be Activities or States; with CV reduplication they are specifically States, as in 4.88).

(4.86) *ma-ʔi~ʔila* 'visible'
(4.87) *na-be~beteng* 'was drunk'

(4.88) T\<om\>okdo=ka.   T\<om\>o~tokdo   si   Dolika.
       ACTm-sit=2sI   ACTm-CV-sit   PRM   Dolika
       'Sit down!'   'Dolika is seated.'

CV reduplication of a result-state root specifies durative aspect with result-state predicates. Durative aspect precludes interpretation of the predicate as the achievement of the state, as seen in (4.89) and (4.90).

Morphophonemic vowel deletion in the root triggers the application of reduplication to the predicate-initial CV, as in (4.91).

(4.89) *Mo na-be~beteng   Ø   yan yamyama(n)=m   Ø...*
       If UNDs.P-CV-drunk 3sI and scold =2sII   3sIII
       'If he is (*gets) drunk and you scold him....'

(4.90) *Na-lo~lokaw-an   din   tobo.*
       UNDls.P-CV-hole<   RMd   pipe
       'The pipe is (*became) hollowed out.'

(4.91) *Nanapno(na~na-pono)   din   beey=da   si   mangili.*
       UNDs.P-CV-full   RMd   house=3pII   ORM   outsiders
       'Their house was full of visitors.'

When the logical structure of a word includes a change-of-state predicate, CV reduplication indicates duration of the changed state, which can yield a perfective sense of ongoing relevance of the change of state. Example (4.92) shows this use of CV reduplication, which is restricted to nominalized and relativized clauses.

(4.92) *Na-tenaw   Ø   et   owat   din   scarf   di*
       UNDs-melt   4I and   only   RMd   scarf   RMi

       na-i-wa~waglat   sin   baliwang.
       UNDs-Th-CV-discard   ORMd   yard
       'It (snowman) melted and only the scarf was (left) discarded in the yard.'

Reduplicative CV affixation with *man-* is not possible with most activity predicates, but with physical position roots or perception state roots, CV with *man-* indicates duration of the effect of the activity (similar to CV with achievement predicates noted above), or duration of the exhibited situation that was expressed as an activity. This may be seen in (4.93), where the position is taken and maintained by a volitional actor. In (4.94) the use of CV correlates with the time phrase to indicate the ongoing experience

4.2 Modifiers in the clause

expressed by the activity 'live'. Example (4.95) shows CV reduplication that indicates duration of the experience as a temporary or stage-level state. It is notable that each example observed of this particular word (*manlalayad* 'happy') is followed by a causing event, limiting the experience state to that context rather than a general life attitude. Example (4.96) is also a context-limited expressed-experience activity.

(4.93) *Nan-sa~sadag=ak   sin   esa=y   kaiw   et*
       ACT.P-CV-lean.on=1sI   ORMd   one=LK   tree   and

   boy~boya-e(n)=k   din   bapor.
   CVC-watch-UND=1sII   RMd   boat
   'I was leaning against a tree and watching the boats.'

(4.94) *Mabayag   ay   man-bi~biyag   da   nay   ay ili,   asi*
       long.time LK   ACT-CV-live   pl   DEM1V   LK town   then

   pay   man-taoli   san   siged   ay   kabibiyag=da.
   PART   ACT-return   DRM   good   LK   lifestyle=3pII
   'It will be a long time these towns must live before that pleasant lifestyle of theirs returns (after earthquake).'

(4.95) *Man-la~layad=kami   tan   laton   ay   dinmateng   baw.*
       ACT-CV-joy=1pI   because   OK   LK   arrived   EVID
   'We are happy because we found out she arrived OK.'

(4.96) *Man-a~agag=ak   ay   <om>ey.*
       ACT-CV-hurry=1sI   LK   ACTm-go
   'I am in a hurry to go.'

Both CV and CVC reduplication can occur with potential activity predicates. CV reduplication may modify the potentiality operator, indicating the continuing potentiality or lack thereof over time, as in (4.97). CVC reduplication, on the other hand, expresses an at-the-moment situation as in (4.98).

(4.97) Adi   maka-i~inat   si   Poltag.
        NEG   ABIL-CV-pull.away   PRM   Poltag
        'Poltag wasn't able to pull away (implied: he was stuck, he tried repeatedly)'

(4.98) Maka-ot~ota =ak.
        ABIL-CVC-vomit=1sI
        'I feel like I can/am going to vomit.'

CV reduplication indicates the continuing duration of a passive state. This reduplication is also seen in the second clause of (4.99) and in (4.100).

(4.99) Nan-ta~tangad   Ø   et   anggay   ma-i~ila=n
        ACT.P-CV-face.up   3sI   and   already   UNDs-CV-see=RMd

        ngalab=na.
        privates=3sII
        'She was facing upwards and her private parts were completely visible.' (woman turned to stone)

(4.100) Nay   etay   mai-li~ligat-an=ak.
        DEM1V   PART   UNDds-CV-hardship<=1sI
        'Oh my, here I am being given/having a very hard time.'

4.2.1.1.2 Progressive aspect

Progressive aspect specifies an ongoing atelic activity, or iterative punctual activity, depending on the root. Progressive aspect is indicated by CVC reduplication. Reduplicative CVC affixation on activity predicates indicates progressive aspect. In (4.101), the reduplication indicates progressive aspect, thus, 'I was listening...' Imperatives, as in (4.102), use the progressive as a softening device, thus more literally, 'Don't be listening to...'

4.2 Modifiers in the clause

(4.101) *Deng~dengek(denge-en=ko)*   *din*   *bogaw*   *di*
CVC-hear-UND=1sII   RMd   shout   BRMi

mang-an~ʔanap   *en*   *sakʔen.*
ANTI-CVC-search   OPRM   1sIII
'I was listening to the shouts of those searching for me (he was hiding).'

(4.102) *Adi=kayo*   *deng~dengngen*   *din*   *lawlawa*   *ay*
NEG=2pI   CVC-hear.UND   RMd   bad   LK

i-bag~baga   *=n di*   *odom.*
UNDt-CVC-say   =BRMi   other
'Don't listen to/pay attention to the bad things that others are saying!'

In (4.103), from the background section of a narrative, the speaker's ongoing activity is interrupted as the story unfolds. In (4.104) the progressive has a pragmatic overtone of present reality, which enhances the expression of the inner emotion.

(4.103) *Ed*   *agsapa=s sa*   *ay*   *man-ot~oto=ak*
past.time   morning=DEM2IV   LK   ACT-CVC-cook=1sI

yan   *aket...*
and   PART
'This morning there I was cooking, and to my surprise....'

(4.104) *Laylaydek(lay~layad-en=ko)*   *di*   *music.*
CVC-happy-UND=1sII   RMi   music
'I really enjoy music (so please send me a CD).'

CVC reduplication indicates continuation over time with Activity, Process, and all Causative predicates, as in (4.105) and (4.106). With Semelfactive and most Achievement predicates the progressive aspect gives an iterative or plural meaning, as in (4.107).

(4.105) *man-tay~tayaw*   'is flying'
(4.106) *tap~tapi-an*   'is adding to'
(4.107) *bom~b<om>tak*   'are exploding (plural)'

Reduplication of the initial CVC of the root of a process predicate indicates progressive aspect, an ongoing state of affairs. Example (4.108) includes a process predicate with progressive aspect.

(4.108) *Mantaoli=kami   yan   medyo   p<om>od~podot   yan*
        return=1pI   and   somewhat   CHANGE-CVC-hot   and

   natenaw   Ø.
   melted   4I
   'We returned and it was getting a little warmer and it (the snowman) had melted.'

Reduplication of the initial CVC of the root (or word, with morphophonemic changes) can occur with <om>-affixed achievement and accomplishment predicates. Predicates formed from roots that specify punctuality are achievements and take an iterative reading with CVC reduplication, as in (4.109), or repeated instances of the change of state with plural subjects, as in (4.110).

(4.109) *B<in>om~b<om>tak   din   bomba   ed   Camp John Hay.*
        P.CHANGE-PROG-burst   RMd   bomb   LOC   Camp John Hay
        'The bombs were exploding at Camp John Hay.'

(4.110) *B<om>al~bala   din   Japon   ed   Baguio City.*
        CHANGE-PROG-emerge   RMd   Japanese   LOC   Baguio City
        'The Japanese were coming out into Baguio City.'

With physical roots, the change of position is in progress, as in 4.111) and 4.112).

(4.111) *?<om>al~alagey   si   Mayor Ismit.*
        CHANGE-PROG-stand   PRM   Mayor Ismit
        'Mayor Ismit is getting to his feet.'

(4.112) B<om>ab~baba   sin   baliwang   di   iskowilaan
       CHANGE-PROG-descend   ORMd   yard   BRMi   school

       din   esa.
       RMd   one
       'The one (airplane) was coming in low over the school yard.'

With experience-stative roots that are not telic, CVC reduplication with the CHANGE operator indicates ongoing time and increase in the experience, as in (4.113). The presence of both PROCESS and INGRESSIVE operators in accomplishment predicates gives room for both telic interpretations and progressive modifications.

(4.113) S<om>ad~sadot   si   Meli.
       CHANGE-PROG-sad   PRM   Meli
       'Meli is getting steadily more depressed.'

As noted in chapter 2, some achievement predicates are formed by perfective affixation on result-states. When the approach of such an event is presented as perceptible and taking place over time, usually a relatively short time, CVC reduplication indicates progress toward the change of state creating accomplishment predicates, as in the second clause of (4.114) and in (4.115).

(4.114) Ilagalagaan=yo   Ø   yan   dooy   ay   anggay
       do.laga.ritual=2pII   3sIII   and   DEM3III   LK   already

       mat~ma-tey=et   Ø!
       PROG-UNDs-die=PART   3sI
       'You keep doing the ritual for him and there he's already dying!!'

(4.115) Mag~magʔas(ma-ʔegas)   di   pantalon=(n)a.
       PROG-UNDs-fall   RMi   pants=3sII
       'His pants are falling down (e.g., as he runs).'

CVC reduplication with an active accomplishment predicate is most often found in nominalized or relativized clauses. In such cases it can indicate plurality or repetition of habitual actions, as in (4.116) or progressive aspect as in (4.117).

(4.116) Ammo-a(n)=na   din   siged   ay   <in>am~amag   di
       know-UNDl=3sII   RMd   good   LK   UND.P-CVC-do   RMi

       ipogaw   ed   nabaon.
       people   LOC   long.ago
       'He'll learn the good (things) that people did long ago.'

(4.117) Ay ad?ado di   am~amag-en=yo?
        Q   much   RMi   CVC-do-UND=2pII
        'Do you have a lot to do? (lit. Is what you are doing much?)'

Note that in (4.118), when CVC reduplication is applied to the causative achievement predicate, the punctual nature of the change of state gives an iterative rather than progressive-aspect interpretation.

(4.118) Mo   wada   di   ma-bay?an   si   i-lako=yo,
        if/when   EXIS   RMi   UNDs-left   ORMi   UNDt-buy=2pII

        i-dol~dolin=yo   ∅   koma.
        UNDt-CVC-put.store=2pII   4III   PART
        'Whenever there is (money) left over from what you have for buying, you should put it in storage (save it).'

CVC reduplication with *ma-* passives indicates an on-going current situation, as in the bracketed word in (4.119).

(4.119) Dalon   b<inm>ab~baba   din   eroplano   et
        much   ACTm.P-CVC-descend   RMd   airplane   and

        [ma-il~ila]   din   Americano.
        UNDs-CVC-see   RMd   American
        'The airplane was coming down low and the American (soldier) was being seen.'

4.2.1.1.3 Comparative aspect

Attributes build their comparative form with CVC reduplication of the root, as in (4.120) and (4.121).

(4.120) *Dak~dakdake   din   oboan=yo   mo   din   kawwitan.*
        CVC-large   RMd   hen=2pII   than   RMd   rooster
        'Your hen is larger than the rooster.'

(4.121) *Ma-bik~bikas=ka   mo   si   Margit.*
        ATT-CVC-strong=2sI   than   PRM   Margit
        'You are stronger than Margit.'

Many different roots may be affixed with *ma-* and then reduplication applied *after* affixation to the first CVC of the resulting word; this process yields a derived attributive predicate indicating current or customary stage-level attributes. Examples (4.122) and (4.123) are formed from property and internal-experience roots, respectively.

(4.122) *Mal~ma-liteng   san   kapi;   ipaatong=yo   Ø.*
        PROG-ATT-cold   DRM2   coffee heat =2pII   4III
        "That coffee is cold; heat it up.'

(4.123) *Mab~ma-bain   si   Emy.*
        PROG-ATT-embarrassed   PRM   Emy
        'Emy's feeling shy.'

These derived attribute predicates are formed with a variety of roots—actions in examples (4.124) and (4.125), and a class root used metaphorically in (4.126).

(4.124) *mag~ma-geyek*
        CVC-ATT-tickle
        'ticklish'

(4.125) *mat~ma-tao*
　　　　CVC-ATT-bark
　　　　'characterized by loud and continuous barking'

(4.126) *mak~ma-keweng*
　　　　CVC-ATT-ear
　　　　'attentive'

4.2.1.1.4 Momentary aspect

Momentary or diminutive duration of an activity or state is expressed with the prefix *panga-*, as in (4.127).

(4.127) *Man-panga-ey=ak.*
　　　　ACT-momentary-go=1sI
　　　　'I will just go for a minute.'

4.2.1.1.5 Intensive aspect

CVC(C)V reduplication shows intensive aspect, indicating markedly repetitive or long-lasting actions or intensive quality, as in (4.128).

(4.128) *Layde~layd-e(n)=k   ay   <om>ey   issa.*
　　　　CVCCV-enjoy-UND=1sII   LK   ACTm-go   DEM2V
　　　　'I really want to go there.'

Root reduplication and time phrases are pragmatically incompatible with many experience-state predicates, as inner experiences are not often thought of in linear terms. Some examples, however, show that with these predicates a time phrase indicates duration, 'for *x* time,' as seen in (4.129) and (4.130). In the latter example, the intensive CVCV reduplication indicates repeated rather than extreme attacks of dizziness.

(4.129) *Na-olaw=ak   si   dowa   ay   agew.*
　　　　UNDs-dizzy=1sI   ORMi   two   LK   day
　　　　'I was dizzy for two days.'

4.2 Modifiers in the clause

(4.130) *Enggay maka-bowan ay ma-ola~olaw=ak.*
already ABIL-month LK UNDs-CVCV-dizzy=1sI
'It's been a month that I have been having dizzy spells.'

Reduplication of the initial CVC(C)V of a result-state root indicates intensive aspect, as in (4.131).

(4.131) *Na-gala~galabgab-an din takkay=ko sin sibit.*
UNDls.P-CVCCV-scratched< RMd hand=1sII ORMd thorn
'My hands were all scratched up from the thorns.'

When appropriate, activity predicates can express intensive or repetitive aspect by CVC(C)V reduplication. Example (4.132) is typical.

(4.132) *?<om>oga~oga din moyang.*
ACT-INTS-cry RMd baby
'The baby is bawling and bawling.'

4.2.1.2 Perfective aspect

The perfective affix in Kankanaey indicates whether a state of affairs is completed. In a narrative, time orientation in real-time past is generally set with a perfective-marked predicate on the event line, with subsequent events carrying the neutral imperfective form. Later perfective-marked predicates in a narrative are often states or negated situations off the main line of the action. Perfective aspect not only adds the temporal perspective of past time, it specifies realis—the success or effectiveness of an activity or change of state.

Predicates that are not marked for perfective aspect are neutral and are interpreted in relation to the context. Imperfective (neutral) may imply irrealis. With affixes that do not support intent (such as *ma-* and *maka-*), imperfective marking indicates possibility or potential for the information in the predicate.

The marking for perfective aspect is on the predicating affixes. Affixes that in their neutral form begin with *m-* or *p-* replace those phonemes with *n-* to specify perfective; all other predicating affixes use *in* as an infix or a prefix, as seen in (4.133) to (4.136). Attribute predicates cannot indicate perfective aspect. As noted in chapter 2, the attributive affixes are frozen forms.

(4.133) *ma-ek/na-ek*
'fall/fell asleep'

(4.134) *maki-inom/naki-inom*
'drink/drank with'

(4.135) *t<om>ayaw/t<in><om>ayaw*
'fly/flew away'

(4.136) *ponas-an/p<in>onas-an*
'wipe/wiped'

At times, in conversation or narrative, Kankanaey places an action in the immediate past using *ka-+CVC*, tagged 'RECENT', as in (4.137). This affix does not index an absolutive or Class I argument, but rather its single argument is a class II pronoun, or takes the bound marker.

(4.137) *Ka-bang~bangon=(n)a,   isonga   mas~ma-sadot*
RECENT-get.up=3sII   therefore   CVC~UNDs-sluggish

paylaeng.
still
'He just got up, so he's still feeling sluggish.'

Kankanaey also uses various particles to make explicit some finer distinctions of a clause's temporal setting. The clitics =*n* and =*nto* attach to vowel-final predicates or clitic pronouns to indicate 'already' and 'future', respectively. The 'future' particle is especially relevant with existentials or other non-verbal predicates that do not show aspect, as in (4.138) and (4.139).

4.2 Modifiers in the clause

(4.138) Wada=nto   di   ib?a=yo   ay   en=kayo
       EXIS=FUT   RMi   friend=2pII   LK   go=2pI

   tang~tangad-en   sin   Kapitolyo.
   CVC-look.up-UND   ORMd   capitol
   'You will have a friend to go look up to (for help) at the Capitol Building (if you vote for me).'

(4.139) Palalo=nto   di   lagsak   ading=ko.
       extreme=FUT   RMi   happiness   younger.sibling=1sII
   'My younger brother is going to be ever so happy (lit. his happiness will be extreme) (when he gets this gift).'

4.2.1.3 Nuclear negation

Kankanaey does not have a negative affix, such as the English forms *non-* or *un-*. Antonyms serve to indicate polar opposites. Existentials are lexical, *wada* as positive and *maga* or *iwed* (dialect difference) as negative.

When a reference phrase serves as the nucleus of an equative core, the stative negator *baken* is used as its negator, as in (4.140) and (4.141). This is nuclear negation, not core negation, as seen by the bracketing.

(4.140) [Baken   din   bol~bolsada=da]   di   nem~nemnem-en=da.
        NEG   RMd   pl-pocket=3pII   RMi   CVC-think-UND=3pII
   'It is not their pockets that they are thinking about. (good politicians)'

(4.141) [Baken sak?en]   di   nang-(g)asto~gastos   sin
        NEG   1sIII   RMi   ANTI.P-CVCCV-spend   ORMd

   pilak=yo.
   money=2pII
   'It wasn't me who kept spending all your money.'

Baken is also the negator for stative predicates of every type. It may be that state negation is nuclear negation, denying the truth of the state rather than the relation of the single argument to that state. It may also simply be that core negation is expressed differently for stative and dynamic situations; with this interpretation, stative negation is described with other core negation in section 4.2.2.3.3.

4.2.1.4 Action directionals

Kankanaey does not have many prepositions, and none that correspond to English locatives such as 'on', 'in', or 'toward'. Instead, many Kankanaey roots specify direction lexically, as may be seen in (4.142) and (4.143).

(4.142) *Man-song=ka   ay   gakki.*
       ACT-go.upstream=2sI   VOC   crab
       'Go upstream, crab.'

(4.143) *Osdong-an=(n)a   din   posong.*
       look.down-UNDl-3sII   RMd   pool
       'He looked down into the pool.'

4.2.2 Core-level operators

4.2.2.1 Participant directionals

As already mentioned, Kankanaey does not use particles or prepositions to indicate direction. When a predicate denotes movement or change of location of one of the participants, the predicating suffix *-an* or the circumfix *i-...-an* may index the static or directional locus. The indexed participant will be the entity toward or away from which the movement takes place. This can be physical or metaphorical direction, as may be seen in the sample predicates in (4.144).

(4.144) *togpa-an*   *i-layaw-an*   *i-gaga-an*
       saliva-UNDl   UNDd-flee<   UNDd-chew<
       'spit at/on'   'flee from'   'chew for (as for a baby)'

4.2 Modifiers in the clause 185

4.2.2.2 Event quantification

When an activity is performed by all members of a group of participants, and that fact is noteworthy, a collective prefix *ka-* or *an-* (COLL) is used, following an Actor-indexing predicate affix as in (4.145) and (4.146). CV reduplication also specifies plurality of actors with predicates that are inherently reciprocal, such as 'converse', 'separate', or 'meet', as in (4.147).

(4.145) *Man-ka-ma-maga=da   am?in.*
  ACT-COLL-CV-NEGEXIS=3pI   all
  'They will all disappear together.'

(4.146) *T<om>an-a-tai=da.*
  ACT-COLL-CV-defecate=3pI
  'They all defecated.' (animals leaving an enclosure)

(4.147) *Man-a~abat=tako   si   tapi   =n di   agew.*
  ACT-CV-meet=1+2pI   ORMi   add   BRMi   day
  'We'll all meet together another day.

4.2.2.3 Modals and negation

Most core operators in Kankanaey are monomorphemic words that precede the nucleus of the core. The core-level analysis is attested by their ability to displace core argument pronouns to a pre-predicate position, described in section 4.1.6. Modals and negation are core operators.

Modals in this section include words that indicate the ability, need or propensity of a participant to act. Section 4.2.2.3.1 looks at deontic notions of personal ability and obligation. Section 4.2.2.3.2 looks at intention and motivation. (The inherent ability to perform an action is also indicated by the prefix *maka-*, described in section 2.3.1.)

4.2.2.3.1 Deontic modals

Modals with a deontic reading modify the core and are linked with *ay*. These modals displace any clitic pronoun to the second position. The scope of possibility is within the participant, not the situation, as indicated by the asterisk in (4.148).

(4.148) *Mabalin=yo   ay ala-en   din   alikamen.*
       possible=2pII LK take-UND RMd tools
       'You'll be able to take the tools.'
   * 'It's possible that you will take the tools.'

Example (4.149) exemplifies an alternate possibility structure, *kaya* 'able' (a particle which may be borrowed from the Tagalog modal noun).

(4.149) *Ay kaya=m   ay mang-(g)awa?*
       Q   able=2sII LK ACT-judge (legal)
       'Are you able to decide the sentence?'

Deontic obligation also is expressed with two forms. *Siyat* displaces clitic pronouns, and indicates necessity or obligation, whether physical or social, as examples (4.150) and (4.151) demonstrate.

(4.150) *Siyat   man-yogton   Ø,   asi   t<om>ayaw   Ø.*
       must   ACT-crouch   4I   and.then   CHANGE-fly   4I
       'It has to crouch, in order to/then take off.'

(4.151) *Siyat=ka=n   man-tee   sin   beey.*
       must=2sI=DISP ACT-stay ORM house
       'You must stay at home/the house.' (due to the hearer's pregnancy)

Less commonly used is the word *masapol* 'necessary', but when it displaces the core pronoun, it can be seen to apply the necessity to a core argument rather than to the entire situation, as in (4.152).

4.2 Modifiers in the clause 187

(4.152) *Masapol=na   di   doktol   ay   mang~mang-set*
necessary=3sII   RMi   doctor   LK   ANTI-CVC-do.well

ya   mang-i-dawat   sin   agas.
and   ANTI-Th-give   ORMd   meds

'He needs the doctor to be taking care of him and to give him the medicines.'

4.2.2.3.2 Motivation

Motivation is another modifier of the actor's performance of the predicate. Motivation particles are taken to be modals based on their frozen form and their ability to displace core pronouns. Examples (4.153) and (4.154) illustrate presence and absence of motivation. In (4.153) there is self-motivation, a cognitive purpose in 'going' to do something. In (4.154) the actor is explicitly without motivation, as the experience just happens without intention.

(4.153) *En=(n)a   <in>abat   din   gayyem=na.*
go=3sII   UND.P-meet   RMd   friend=3sII
'She went to meet her friend.' (purpose)

(4.154) *Mo   eteng=ka=n   i-al~ʔalin   di*
If   unmotivated=2sI=DISP   UNDt-PROG-jealous   RMi

asawa=m...
spouse=2sII...
'If you just feel jealous about your spouse (for no reason)...'

4.2.2.3.3 Core-level negation

Negation is a modification that indicates things that are not true—events that do not happen, states that do not hold. What is negated in core-level negation is the connection between the predicate and its participant(s) in a particular situation. As a core operator, the negator displaces core clitic pronouns.

Baken negates all state predicates. Examples include identificational (class root) predicates, as in (4.155) and (4.156).

(4.155) *Baken anak si Marjane.*
 NEG child PRM Marjane
 'Marjane is not a child.'

(4.156) *Anggan mo baken=ka=n diadal...*
 even if NEG=2sI=DISP educated.person
 'Even though you are not an educated person....'

Negation of attribute predicates are seen in (4.157) through (4.159).

(4.157) *Baken na-dayetdet din bab?a=k.*
 NEG ATT-evenly.spaced RMd tooth=1sII
 'My teeth are not evenly spaced.'

(4.158) *Matekyeng din eges=tako et baken=tako*
 full RMd stomach=1+2plI and NEG=1+2pI

 man-dagaang.
 ATT-hungry
 'Our stomachs will be full (of water) and we won't feel hungry.'

(4.159) *Baken=ak ma-bikas ay mandan.*
 NEG=1sI ATT-strong LK walk
 'I'm not a good hiker.' (lit. strong to walk)

Negation of inadvertent experience-states is also expressed with *baken*, as in (4.160). In (4.161), from a text translated from English, the context gives a 'habitual' interpretation to the *ma-* affixed predicate.

(4.160) Baken=takon   ma-sdaaw   tan   say   iyat   di
        NEG=1+2p   UNDs-amazed   because that's way   BRMi

   ipogaw.
   person
   'We aren't surprised, since that's how people are.'

(4.161) Din   ogali=na   abe   et   masapol   ay   baken
        RMd   custom=3sII   PART   PART   necessary LK   NEG

   ma-bonget   Ø.
   UNDs-anger   3sI
   'As for his character, it is necessary that he not be short-tempered.'

The negator *baken* is also used to negate result-state predicates. This overlap with attribute negation indicates that the negated state is descriptive rather than indicating an achievement (change of state) that did not or will not happen. Admittedly, the fine line between a purely descriptive state and a resultant state is hard to document in many cases. In examples (4.162) and (4.163) an achievement reading is not possible.

(4.162) Baken   na-beteng   si   Sefin.
        NEG   UNDs.P-drunk   PRM   Sefin
        'Sefin isn't/*didn't get drunk.'

(4.163) Baken   na-pno   din   tangki.
        NEG   UNDs.P-full   RMd   tank
        'The tank is not/*didn't get full'.

Adi is the negator for non-stative predicates. Process predicates are negated with *adi*, as in (4.164).

(4.164) Adi   <inm>ad?ado   din   pilak=ko.
        NEG   CHANGE.P-much   RMd   money=1sII
        'My money didn't increase.'

The negator *adi* is also used with achievement and accomplishment predicates. Example (4.165) shows negation with an <om> accomplishment. It comes from instructions on how to prepare rice wine.

(4.165) *Siyat   ma-kotob   Ø   ay   pasya   ta   adi*
         must   UNDs-cover   4I   LK   well   so.that NEG

  l<om>eg~legsew   Ø.
  CHANGE-CVC-stink   4I
  'It must be tightly covered so that it is not getting stinky.'

Adi is the negator with *ma-/na-*affixed result-state roots that have formed achievement predicates, disambiguating the "fine line" between those result-states and achievements. Negation with a perfective-marked result-state predicate indicates an unambiguous achievement reading, as in (4.166), while (4.167) indicates a problem in a. such that the achievement of a 'full' state will not happen to the sack. As a descriptive state in b., the negator is *baken*. Example (4.168) compares the negated achievement predicate and the negated state predicate.

(4.166) *Adi   na-nged   si   Poltag.*
         NEG   UNDs.P-drown   PRM   Poltag.
         'Poltag didn't drown.' *Poltag wasn't dead from drowning.

(4.167) a. *Adi   ma-pno   din   sako.*
            NEG   UNDs-full   RMd   sack
            'The sack won't get full.'

       b. *Baken   na-pno   din   sako.*
           NEG   UNDs-full   RMd   sack
           'The sack is not full.'

4.2 Modifiers in the clause

(4.168) *Sapay.koma.ta adi=kayo ma-oma en sak?en.*
hopefully NEG=2pI UNDs-bored OPRM 1sIII
'I hope you won't get/*aren't tired of me.'

Laton, baken=ak na-oma.
OK NEG=1sI UNDs-bored
'It's OK, I'm not bored.'

A very common use of the negated achievement predicate is in a purpose clause with *ta* 'so that', as in (4.169). In (4.170) CVC reduplication indicates an accomplishment with internal time duration even though the experience did not happen. Again, the negator in this mid-river misadventure is *adi*.

(4.169) *Paalonsod-e(n)=m din agdan ta adi*
set.at.slant-UND=2sII RMd ladder so.that NEG

ma-tokang Ø.
UNDs-tip.over 4I
'Set the ladder at a slant so that it won't/can't tip over.'

(4.170) *Adi na-lit~litaw di nemnem=ko et*
NEG UNDs.P-CVC-lost RMi thought=1sII and

nan-pakod=ak si bato.
ACT-clutch=1sI ORMi stone
'My thoughts were not getting lost (i.e., I kept my wits) and I grabbed onto a large rock.'

The negator *adi* is used with activity predicates, as seen with the activities in (4.171) to (4.174).

(4.171) *Adi=kami man-apoy si kanen=mi.*
NEG=1pI ACT-fire ORMi food=1pII
'We didn't (burn a fire to) cook our food.'

(4.172) Adi=ak   man-i-solo   ed   niman.
         NEG=1sI   ACT.Th-teach   LOC   now
         'I am not teaching at this time.'

(4.173) Adi   man-sakit   din   eges=ko.
         NEG   ACT-sick/hurt   RMd   stomach=1sII
         'My stomach doesn't hurt.'

(4.174) Adi=da   bayo-en   Ø;   owat=da=n
         NEG=3pI   pound-UND   4III   only=3pI-DISP

         ka-i-oto   sin   banga.
         IMM-Th-cook   ORMd   pot
         'They don't pound it; they just cook it (whole) in the pot.'

Negation of semelfactives is also with *adi*, as in (4.175).

(4.175) Adi=ak   p<in>ikpik   Ø   yan   nay   na-ek
         NEG=1sI   UND.P-pat   3sIII   and   here   UNDs-sleep

         met.laeng.
         PART
         'I didn't pat her and here she fell asleep anyway.'

If potentiality is implied, the negation of that potentiality is with *adi*. Examples (4.176) and (4.177) show that when *ma-* is negated, the prefix *ka-* often substitutes for it to specifically indicate and perhaps intensify the impossibility.

(4.176) Adi   ka-bilang   di   badang=yo.
         NEG   UNDs.INTS-count   RMi   help=2pII
         'Your help can not be calculated (i.e., you were so very helpful).'

4.2 Modifiers in the clause

(4.177) Adi   ka-silaw-an   di   danan   tan
       NEG   UNDls.INTS-light<   RMi   way   because

       masde   di   liboo.
       thick   RMi   cloud
       'The way couldn't be lit up because the cloud/fog was so thick.'

As noted above regarding result-state predicates, passivized predicates may also show ambiguity as to whether they represent a situation as an event or a descriptive state. The negation of passivized states depends on this interpretation. Thus, in (4.178) the negator *baken* and the durative *CV-* gives the predicate a descriptive reading, while in (4.179) *adi* is used for an event that did not happen. There is some dialect shift toward greater use of *adi*, making this a somewhat fuzzy area between the clear use of *baken* with identificational and attributive states and the clear use of *adi* with activity predicates.

(4.178) <In>ammo-an=(n)a   am?in   dana,   tan   baken
        UNDl.P-know<=3sII   all   pl.DEM1I   because   NEG

        met   nai-ta~tabon   Ø.
        PART   UNDts.P-CV-hide   4I
        'He learned all these things, because they certainly weren't hidden.'

(4.179) Ka-parti   abe   ay   dagos   din   akin-aso
        IMM-butcher   PART   LK   immediately   RMd   owner-dog

        et   adi   na-observar-an   Ø.
        and   NEG   UNDls.P-observe<   4I
        'The owner of the dog killed (it) immediately and it (dog) was not observed (for rabies).'

Adi may co-occur with deontic modals. In this construction, the clitic pronoun is displaced to the first modifier, which is the negator. An example is diagrammed as figure 4.8.

194　　　　　　　　　　　　　　　　　　　　　　　　　　*Simple Clauses*

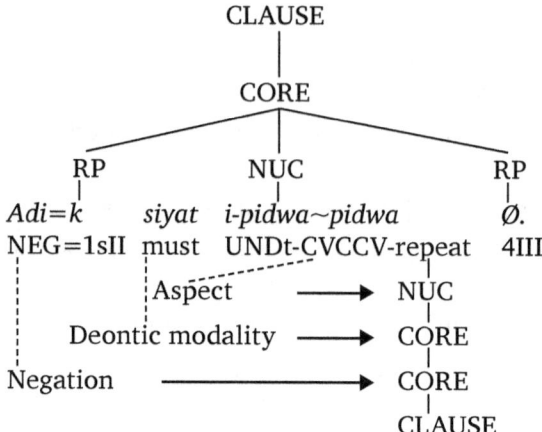

'I don't have to carry on about it (lit. repeatedly repeat).'

Figure 4.8. Aspect, modality, and negation operators in a Kankanaey clause.

4.2.3 Clause-level operators

Operators at the clause level include propositional negation, epistemic modality, illocutionary force and evidentials. Clause-level negation is indicated by *baken*. Epistemic modality uses linked modals that do not attract the core pronouns. Illocutionary force is shown by WH-words and particles, and evidentials appear as a diverse set of particles.

4.2.3.1 Clause-level negation

Baken negates a situation, especially the expected situation, i.e., 'it's not the case…'. Clitic pronouns are displaced by the clause-level negator, as with the core operators. The lexical form of the negator makes the level of modification clear. This use of *baken* to negate the proposition is exemplified in (4.180) to (4.183).

(4.180) *Baken=ak   nan-tet~tettee.*
　　　　NEG=1sI　 ACT.P-PROG-stay.home
　　　'It's not that I have been staying home (the reason for my inaction).'

4.2 Modifiers in the clause

(4.181) Baken=mi-n   owat   gaan   Ø.
       NEG=1pII=DISP   just   dislike 4III
       'It's not that we just didn't want to (after listing the reasons for not coming to an event).'

(4.182) Baken=kayo=n   masapol   ay i-baga   Ø.
       NEG=2pI=DISP   necessary LK UNDt-say   4III
       'It's not the case that you guys have to tell about it.'

(4.183) Baken=da=n   baw   na-na~ek.
       NEG=3pI=DISP   EVID   UNDs.P-DUR-sleep
       'They weren't sleeping after all.'

4.2.3.2 Epistemic modals

Epistemic modals express a possibility or necessity based on outside factors in regards to an action or situation. The modals are *mabalin* for possibility, as in example (4.184) and (4.185), and *masapol* for necessity. They are linked to the clause with *ay* but as clause-level operators they do not displace the clitic pronouns in the core. Epistemic modals are bracketed in (4.186) and (4.187). Note in (4.185) that *adi* negates the modal.

(4.184) Mo   i-saa=yo   si   Narding,   [mabalin
       if   UNDt-go.home=2pII   PRM   Narding   possible

       ay] maga=y   problima.
       LK   NEGEXIS=RMi   problem
       'If you take Narding back home, it's possible that there would be no problems.'

(4.185) [Adi   mabalin   ay]   ma-toloy=kami   ay
       NEG   possible LK   UNDs-continue=1pI   LK

       <om>ey   ed   Bangan.
       ACTm-go   LOC   Bangan
       'It's not possible that we will continue on our way to Bangan.'

(4.186) *[Masapol ay] man-lako=ka si baro ay gears.*
necessary LK ACT-buy=2sI ORMi new LK gears
'(Your car's condition makes it) necessary that you buy new gears.'

(4.187) *[Masapol ay] da din wada=d nowani di*
necessary LK pl RMd EXIS=LOC now RMi

ma-botos-an.
UNDl-vote<
'It has to be that the incumbants (those there now) be voted for.'

Figure 4.9 displays a clause with an epistemic modal.

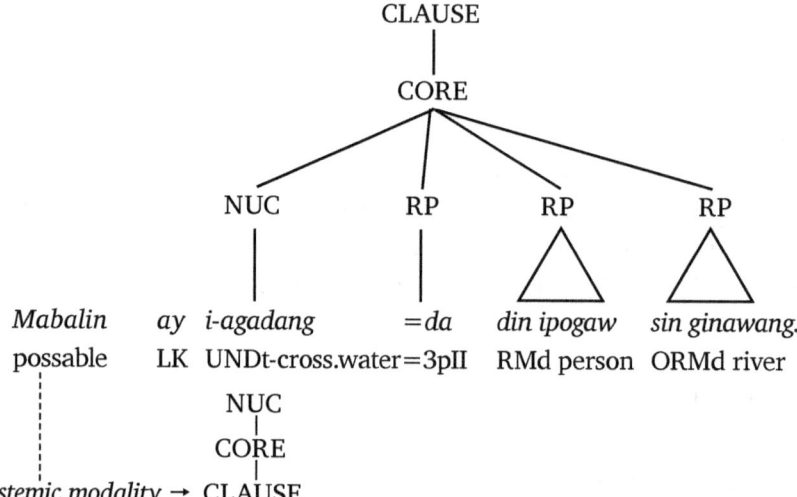

'It is possible (it worked) for them (crocodiles) to carry the people across the river.'

Figure 4.9. Clause with epistemic modality operator.

4.2.3.3 Illocutionary force

Several strategies are used in Kankanaey to express the illocutionary force of an utterance. The default indicative mood is unmarked.

Interrogative mood takes two forms—question morphemes and interrogative pronouns. The sentence-initial particle *ay* forms questions that ask for

4.2 Modifiers in the clause   197

a 'yes/no' answer. 'Why?' may be expressed informally with the discontinuous morpheme *Aket....mo?* bracketing the clause. Other content questions place a question word or phrase in the predicate position of an equative clause. Both types of questions are illustrated in (4.188).

(4.188) *Sino   pay   di   anak=mo?*
       what   PART   RMi   child=2sII
       'What then is your child?

       Ay   babai   ono   lalaki   kasin?
       Q   female   or   male   again
       Is it a girl, or another boy?'

Unmitigated imperatives use overt second-person pronouns and imperfective aspect. Mitigation is commonly expressed by the use of inclusive pronouns, or request particles. (See table 4.11 in section 4.2.4.2.) Another mitigation strategy is to use progressive aspect (CVC reduplication) as in (4.189).

(4.189) *Adi=ka   kan~kanan   en   lawa   din   <in>amag=da.*
       NEG=2sI   CVC-say   QT   bad   RMd   UND.P-do=3pII
       'Don't (be) say(ing) that what they did was wrong.'

Formulaic particles, such as the one in (4.190), fill the function of what is sometimes called 'optative mood' (wishes, blessings, etc.).

(4.190) *Kadimanet   b<om>aknang=ka.*
       prediction   UND.CHANGE-rich=2sI
       'You shall certainly become rich.'

4.2.3.4 Evidentials

A wide array of about fifty free-standing semantic particles encode the Kankanaey speaker's stance regarding his or her utterances. Particles cannot take affixation or participate in word formation, although some cliticize to other clause constituents. They can occur in many places in a clause, but most often follow the verb and any clitic pronoun and are subject to relative ordering among themselves. Wherever they occur, they modify the meaning at the level of clause or speech-act or perhaps a higher discourse level. See J. Allen (1978b) for an early discussion of the semantic particles including their co-occurrence and ordering. At the current stage of development, RRG does not have a framework to accommodate these modifying particles. The evidential particles, which are clearly clause-level modifiers, will be presented in this section; the rest of the particles are included in section 4.2.4.2.

Part of a speaker's responsibility for the factuality of his assertions is expressed by particles that indicate the source of his information. These are presented in table 4.8 and exemplified in (4.191) to (4.193).

Table 4.8. Evidential particles

EVIDENTIALS	baw	surprised realization
	kano	reported by third party (HSY)
	dedan	obviously, of course
	kayman	credit to hearer
	gayam	self-evident; surprised recollection
	adi.pay	tentative deduction

(4.191) *Adi pay mo <om>ey=kayo ed Filipinas et*
        EVID   if   ACTm-go=2pI   LOC Phils.   PART

   ma-taynan   Ø   issa?
   UNDs-leave.behind   3sI DEM2IV
   'Surely if you go to the Philippines she'll be left behind there (in Chicago)?'

(4.192) *Enggay   kano ay   adi=yo   en   man-oto=s*
        EXTENT   HSY   LK   NEG=2pII   go   ACT-cook=ORMi

   kan-en=yo.
   eat-UND=2pII
   'They say it's to the point where you guys don't even go cook food for yourselves.'

4.2 Modifiers in the clause

(4.193) *Man-tetek   din   dagem tan   bowan dedan di*
         ATT-cold   RMd   wind   because   month EVID   RMi

Diciembre.
December
'The wind was cold because (it was) the month obviously of December.'

4.2.4 Other modification

Previous sections showed the grammatical operators that modify each level of the clause. Other modifiers are a small set of adverbs discussed in section 4.2.4.1 that express timing, extent, and quasi-negative meanings. The other modifying semantic particles are presented in section 4.2.4.2.

4.2.4.1 Adverbs

Section 4.1.4.3 introduced the placement and linking of some adverbs in peripheral positions. This section will list them more fully, and show that they modify particular layers of the clause structure.

4.2.4.1.1 Timing and extent

A small set of adverbs can precede a predicate to add modifying information regarding the timing or extent of a state of affairs. Adverbial meanings of pace and manner, however, are achieved with affixed roots that denote these characteristics. Table 4.9 lists the timing and extent adverbs. Adverbs that modify the core will displace clitic pronouns.

Table 4.9. Timing and extent adverbs

Modification	Adverb	Gloss
temporal (core)	deda	still
	kasin	again
	asi	then, next
	dowan	at the same time
extent (core)	pag	all
	owat	only
	dadlon	thoroughly
extent (nuclear)	enggay	completely, to the extent that
	palalo	excessively

The temporal adverbs are exemplified in (4.194) and (4.195).

(4.194) *Deda=kayo   ay   maki-beb~beey   en   am~ama=yo.*
       still=2pI   LK   ACTa-CVC-house   OPRM   parents=2pII
       'You guys are still living in with your parents.'

(4.195) *Din   siping,   mabalin   ay   kasin=tako=n*
       RMd   money   possible   LK   again=1+2pII=DISP

       i-lagbo-an   Ø.
       UNDd-wage<   4III
       'The money, it's possible that we may earn it again.'

The extent to which a state of affairs holds true is indicated by extent adverbs. When *owat* puts a limit on a core, as in (4.174) above and in (4.196), it indicates that the participant only does the specified action. The word *pag* indicates the extent of participation (often co-occurring with 'all') while *dadlon* emphasizes the full extent of the effect, as in (4.197) and (4.198). Nuclear modifiers are linked with *ay* and do not affect the pronouns. Nuclear extent adverbs are shown in (4.199).

4.2 Modifiers in the clause

(4.196) Na-ataki   Ø   et   owat   b<om>a~baktad   Ø
      UNDs-attack   3sI   and   only   UNDm-CV-lie.down   3sI

      ed   bebeey=da.
      LOC   home=3pII
      'She had a heart attack and only lies down (i.e., is bed-ridden) at their home.'

(4.197) Tan   nabiteg=da   ngalod,   pag=da=n
      because   poor=3pI   PART   all=3pI=DISP

      ma-baa   nam?in.
      UNDs-send   all
      'Because they were poor (it follows that) all of them could be sent on errands.'

(4.198) Dadlon=da=n   tongpal-en   am?in   ay
      completely=3pII=DISP   fulfill-UND   all   LK

      in-bilin=ko.
      UNDt.P-instruct=1sII
      'They completely fulfilled all that I instructed.'

(4.199) Enggay   na-maga=y   bikas=ko   ya
      completely   UNDs-NEGEXIS=RMi   strength=1sII   and

      palalo   ay   <inm>opsat   di   mata=k.
      excessively   LK   CHANGE.P-pale   RMi   face=1sII
      'My strength was completely gone and my face became very pale.'

4.2.4.1.2 Quasi-negative adverbs

Another group of adverbs indicate a negative truth value for a clause core; *istay, daan,* and *kaman* each add implications regarding the state of affairs that is not real. In every case, clitic pronouns are displaced to attach to these adverbs that modify the core of the clause.

Istay indicates that something almost happened. In (4.200) it may be noted that what did not happen (irrealis) is expressed with the imperfective, while the true event *inmey* 'went' carries perfective (P) marking. *Daan* 'not yet' also negates a predicate, as in (4.201), where the predicate obligatorily takes imperfective aspect.

(4.200) *Istay=ak   <om>ey   sin   kad?an=yo   ngem*
almost=1sI   ACTm-go   ORMd   place=2pII   but

<inm>ey=ak   sin   clinic   yan...
ACTm.P-go=1s   ORMd   clinic   and
'I nearly went to your place but (instead) I went to the clinic and...'

(4.201) *Daan=da   paylaeng   i-taoli   Ø   sin*
not.yet=3pII   still   UNDt-return   4III   ORMd

<inm>ey-an=mi   ed   Bali.
ACT.P.NOM-go<=1pII   LOC   Bali.
'They still had not yet returned it when we left for Bali.'

The word *kaman* 'like, as if' does not exactly negate, but it indicates something short of truth or reality about the relationship between the predicate and its participants. When *kaman* modifies the core, it displaces the clitic pronoun. Examples (4.202) to (4.204) show this adverb at the core level with a variety of predicates.

(4.202) *Kaman=ak   baken   Kankanaey   ay   bolbolod-ek*
like=1sI   NEG   Kankanaey   LK   borrowing-UND.1sII

kali=yo.
word=2pII
'I'm like a non-Kankanaey (speaker), borrowing your (English) words.'

(4.203) *Kaman=kami=n   "busy"   ay   kanayon.*
like=1pI=DISP   busy   LK   always
'We seem to always be busy.'

4.2 Modifiers in the clause

(4.204) *Kaman=ka=n na-engit-an   si*
       like=2sI=DISP UNDsl-decorate<   ORMi

lawi=n di   kawwitan.
long.feather=BRMi   rooster
'You are like adorned with rooster-tail feathers.' (from a love poem)

The near truth of *kaman* 'like' can also apply to a whole proposition, as in (4.205) and (4.206). The core pronoun is not displaced by *kaman* when it serves as a clause modifier.

(4.205) *Kaman   nan-sa~sag?en=tako   basta*
        like   ACT.P-CV-near=1+2pI   provided

man-ngal~ngalat=tako=s   solat.
ACT-PROG-converse=1+2pI=ORMi   letter
'It is as if we are being near each other if we are conversing with each other by letter.'

(4.206) *Kaman   ad=ak   ka-bael-an.*
        like   NEG=1sI UNDls-able<
'It's as if I am absolutely unable.'

Truth value or realis is also overtly negated by the particle *koma*. The scope of the irrealis in (4.207) is the whole clause, since both cores are untrue.

(4.207) *P<in>ikpik=ko   Ø   koma   ta   na=ek   Ø   baw.*
        UND.P-pat=1sII   3sIII PART   so.that UNDs.P-sleep 3sI EVID
'I should have patted him so that he would have slept, I see.' (I didn't pat him and he didn't sleep.)

Koma translates as obligation in some clauses with imperfective aspect, as in (4.208). While it is difficult to translate every occurrence of this or any nuanced particle with any consistency, there is an element of speaker opinion in expressing obligation which may allow *koma* to join the other "attitude" particles in section 4.2.4.2.

(4.208) *I-toloy=ko   koma   ay   man-iskowila.*
       UNDt-continue=1sII   PART   LK   ACT-attend.school
       'I should (probably won't) keep going to school.'

4.2.4.2 Particles

The speaker-hearer dynamic in verbal interaction is encoded less by prosodic cues than by particles that give nuances of attitude to any utterance. Table 4.10 lists propositional modality particles that show a speaker's attitude toward the truth of his/her own utterance, apart from evidentials. The next four tables list particles that show a speaker's response to a situation or to another's utterance. Table 4.11 lists particles used with requests or commands, while table 4.12 lists particles used to indicate various degrees of surprise. Table 4.13 displays exclamations that indicate a speaker's general response; they may stand alone or precede a clause in the left-detached position. Table 4.14 covers particles used in explanation, concession, objection and emphasis. Table 4.15 lists a few other adverbial particles that do not fit the previous groupings. A few of the particles are duplicated between tables due to multiple semantic components. These tables represent the Kankanaey particles which have been observed; there may be others that the present author has not yet noticed! Examples (4.209) to (4.211) were specifically selected to illustrate the use of a variety and multiplicity of particles in just a few sentences.

(4.209) *Dooy   etay   ginminek   Ø   kasin   ya.   En   pinikpik*
        DEM3V   PART   quieted   3sI   PART   PART   go   patted
                 surprise   again   explanation

        ngin   Rosita   Ø.
        PART   Rosita   3sIII
        maybe
        'Oh, there he got quiet again. Rosita may have gone to pat him.'

(4.210) Ay   adi=ka   dedan   ammo   Ø?   Il~ilaem
         Q   NEG=2sI   PART   know   4III PROG-see.UND.2sII
                        obvious

         ngarod   ay   balat   ket!
         PART   LK   banana   PART
         confirm   certain
         'Don't you know that? (Surely you do!) You see that they are bananas surely!'

(4.211) Aw=et   adi   pay.dedan   sa!
         yes=PART   PART   PART   DEM2I
         immediacy   really settled
         'Yes, yes, of course (we already know) that!'

Table 4.10. Kankanaey confidence particles

CERTAINTY	adi	really, indeed
	od	certainly
	ket	positively
	ngalod	sincere certainty
	tet?ewan	truly
	sigurado	for sure
	mon	forceful affirmation
UNCERTAINTY	ngata	perhaps; conjecture
	baka	possibly
	siguro	possibly, probably
	ngin	maybe, with reservation
	=(n)samet	likely possibility

Table 4.11. Kankanaey request particles

kay	diminuative polite request
kod	polite request
man	strong request or command
paabe	pleading request

Table 4.12. Kankanaey surprise particles

aket	surprise
aya	surprise, request confirmation
baw kambaw 2	surprised realization
gayam 1	surprised recollection
etay	mild surprise

Table 4.13. Kankanaey exclamations

Positive/neutral	ana	surprise
	ado	protest
	aye	interest
	dake	admiration
	wey	surprise
	engngan	Look!
Negative	alla	warning
	ay.daetan	frustration
	ey	disappointment
	sis	disparagement, disgust
	wa, wo	disbelief
	ay.maney	exasperation
	ay (final)	emphatic, forceful

4.2 Modifiers in the clause

Table 4.14. Kankanaey interactive particles

EXPLANATION	gamin	reason, relevant thing
	gayam 2	self-evident reason
	ngalod	confirm; consequently
	ngay	defensive explanation
	(=n)tomet	pinpoints reason, often blaming
	ya	elicits sympathetic response
CONCESSION	kayman	agrees with, concedes to hearer
	iman	concedes to, sympathizes with third party
	od.baw	concedes to hearer after argument
OBJECTION	et.abe	disparagement
	etet	displeasure
	damdama	emphatic disapproval
	met	objection
	ngay	defensive objection
	pay.dedan	resist opposition, already settled
EMPHASIS	a (final)	polite, persuasive emphasis
	=et	suddenness or immediacy

Table 4.15. Miscellaneous particles

TEMPORAL	dagos	immediately
	enggay	already
	pay.laeng	still
MISCELLANEOUS	abe	also
	anggoy	only, just
	met.laeng	also, no other
	owat	only

5

Complex Clauses and Sentences

Sentences in Kankanaey have at least one clause which forms the central component of the sentence. A sentence may have detached positions, both pre- and post-central, that require a particle or intonational pause to mark them as detached. Peripheral positions modifying the central clause are located on both left and right, but there are no sentence-level peripheries. The constituent projection showing the basic structure of the sentence is given in figure 5.1.

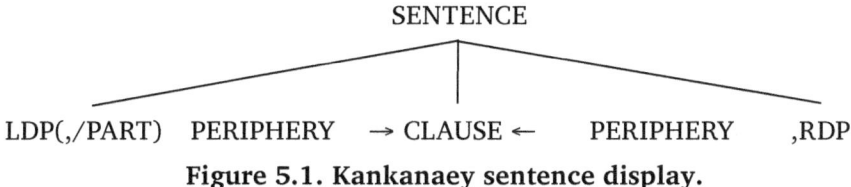

Figure 5.1. Kankanaey sentence display.

Basic clause structure with its constituents and layered representation was introduced in chapter 4. The current chapter explores how Kankanaey syntax handles complexity at various levels. Coordinate clauses can occur together in the central position of a sentence. The detached positions may hold words, phrases and clauses while the clause-level peripheries hold modifying clauses. Complexity may be found within a single clause, or in a sentence complex. Relative clauses are the final topic of this chapter. Since the influence of discourse pragmatics is greater at the sentence level than on the clause level, many of the following constructions can only be explained in terms of the pragmatic and semantic relationships between the constituents.

5.1 Clausal juncture in the sentence

A sentence may contain coordinate clauses, as indicated by the clause linkage marker (CLM) (underlined in examples (5.1) to (5.9)). Examples (5.1) to (5.3) show clausal conjunctions that bear a relation of simple temporal succession. Note that the coreferential pronouns are not deleted across these coordinate clause boundaries.

(5.1) D<om>ateng=da   <u>ya</u>   mang-(k)an=da.
       ACTm=arrive=3pI and   ACT=eat=3pI
       'They arrived and they ate.' (past time supplied by previous sentences)

(5.2) Mai-diplat=ak   <u>pag</u>   mai-beng   din   danom.
       UNDts-slip.fall=1sI   then   UNDts -spill.out RMd   water
       'I slipped and fell and then all the water spilled out.'

(5.3) Okis-an=da   Ø   <u>asi</u>=da   i-polkaw   Ø
       peel-UNDl=3pII   4III   and.then=3pII   UNDt-boil   4III

       sin   gambang.
       ORMd   large.pot
       'They peel them and then they boil them in the big pot.'

Another type of coordination expresses non-dependent logical succession, as in (5.4).

(5.4) Adi   maka-osok   din   posa,   *isonga*
       NEG   ACT.ABIL-squeeze.through RMd   cat   therefore

<in>ayag-a(n)=na   din   otot.
UNDl.P-call<=3sII RMd   rat
'The cat couldn't squeeze through, so therefore he called the rat.'

Other semantic relations in coordinate clauses include opposition 'but' and choice 'or'. Each clause is complete and independent, as can be seen in (5.5), where the first clause is declarative and the second interrogative.

(5.5) Nay   laton=ak   pay   *ngem*   into=y   mangi-saa
       DEM1V   OK=1sI   PART   but   where=RMi   NOM.Th-go.home

ngin   sin   dait=ko   ay   nay   mansakit?
PART   ORMd   friend=1sII   LK   DEM1V   ick
'I'm just fine but who (lit. where is one who) will take these sick friends of mine home?'

Three clausal temporal conjunctions—*pag, asi,* and *dowan*—displace clitic pronouns, as seen in (5.6) and (5.7). These three also function as temporal timing adverbs (covered in chapter 4) following other conjunctions, as in (5.8).

(5.6) G<om>ine~ginek   din   anak   *dowan*=da=n   mang-(k)an.
       UNDm.INTS-quiet   RMd   child   while=3pI=DISP   ACT-eat
       'The child became very still as they ate.'

(5.7) *Asi*=da   keb-en   Ø   *pag*=da=n   libot-an   Ø
       then=3pII   wet-UND   4III   then=3pII=DISP   wrap-UNDl   4III

sin   tobo=n di   balat.
ORMd   leaf=BRMi   banana
'Then they moisten it and then they wrap it up in banana leaves.'

(5.8) Man-a~abat=tako   si   tapi=n di   agew,   <u>ta</u>
       ACT-CV-meet=1+2pI   ORMi   add=BRMi day   so.that

<u>dowan</u>=tako=n   man-a   si   dait=tako.
while=1+2pI=DISP   ACT-get ORMi   companion=1+2pII
'We'll meet together another day, so that meanwhile we (can) get our other companions.' (guerilla fighters splitting up to go recruit others)

Coordinate clauses may also form a larger unit that is not necessarily in the sentence-central position. This is illustrated in (5.9), where two clauses share the left-detached position indicated by *mo* 'if'.

(5.9) Mo   s<om>aa=ak   ya   istolya-e(n)=k   di   iso
       if/when   ACTm-go.home=1sI   and   story-UND=1sII   RMi   same

=n di   ed   Manila   et   ma-ap~apos-an=da.
=BRMi   LOC   Manila   PART   UNDls-CVC-envy=3pI
'If/when I go home and tell what it's like in Manila, they will be so jealous!'

5.2 Detached positions

Constituents in the "left-detached position" (LDP) are marked in one of two ways: by an intonational pause, as in (5.10), or by a small group of particles,[1] including *yan* or *et* as in (5.11). Some of these particles are homophonous with coordinate clause linkage markers, but are distinguishable from them by their context and by their interchangeability with a pause or written comma. The "right-detached" position (RDP) is set off by an intonational pause, as in (5.12), which differentiates it from phrases in the post-core slot, as well as from peripheral phrases and clauses.

---

[1] Dooley and Levinsohn (2001:36) note that substituting a particle for a pause is common cross-linguistically.

5.2 Detached positions 213

(5.10) Ed   nabaon   kano,   wada=y   esa   ay   babai.
LOC   long.ago   HSY   EXIS=RMi   one   LK   woman
'Long ago, they say, there was a woman.'

(5.11) Mo   si   Delia   yan   sisya   di   presidente
as.for PRM   Delia   PART   3sIII   RMi   president

=n din   pupils government=da.
=BRMd   pupils government=3pII
'As for Delia, the president of their student government is she.'

(5.12) Medyo   maligligatan=ak,   kalkalo   ed   nowani.
somewhat   have.difficulty=1sI especially LOC   now
'I'm having a rather hard time, especially right now.'

5.2.1 Left-detached position

The LDP may have a single word, a full reference phrase, or a subordinate clause. The pragmatic function of the LDP is to orient the hearer in some way to the central clause that follows, whether time/space orientation, participant orientation, or logical orientation.

5.2.1.1 Time-space orientation in the Left-detached Position

A reference phrase (RP) may precede the central clause, giving the time or place orientation for either that particular clause or perhaps for an entire text. In (5.13), a simple demonstrative sets the place in contrast to other places. In (5.14) and (5.15), a time phrase gives the setting.

(5.13) Isna   et   iwed   di   am?amo=k   si
DEM1IV PART NEGEXIS RMi know=1sII   ORMi

ibadang=ko   tan   pag   electric.
help=1sII   because   all   electric
'Here, I don't know any (lit. there is nothing that I know) way to help because everything is electric.'

(5.14) Si   bigat   ay   agew   di   ponpon, adi=da
        ORMi   next.day   LK   day   BRMi   burial   NEG=3pI

  <inm>ali.
  ACTm.P-come
  'The next day, the day of the burial, they didn't come.'

(5.15) Mo   mamingsan   pay,   ilokano=y   pan-kal~kali=k.
        if/when   one.time   PART   Ilocano=RMi   NOM-CVC-talk=1sII
        'Sometimes, however, what I use for talking is Ilocano.'

Subordinate clauses expressing prior events as time orientation are often found in the LDP as well, as illustrated in (5.16) to (5.18). An orienting event may be nominalized for time/place, as in (5.19). Note that the RP nucleus can only take an ergative/possessive argument, even though it has predicating affixation as well as the nominalizing affixes.

(5.16) Idi   okmon-en=(n)a   Ø   yan   man-nalisnis   Ø.
        when   swallow-UND=3sII   4III   PART   ATT-delicious   4I
        'When he swallowed it, it was delicious.'

(5.17) Idi   naka-balkot=ak,   naek=ak.
        when   ACT.ABIL-pack.up=1sI   slept=1sI
        'When I had managed to pack up, I slept.'

(5.18) Domateng=da   pay,   kana-en   din   Major...
        arrive=3pI   PART   say-UND   BRMd   Major
        'When they arrived, the Major said...'

(5.19) Sin   daan=mi=n   <inm>ey-an   ed   Bambag
        ORMd   not.yet=1pII=DISP   NOM.P-go<   LOC   Bambag

  yan   man-sak~sakit   si   Manny.
  PART   ACT-CVC-sick   PRM   Manny
  '(At) our not yet having gone to Bambag, Manny was (already) being sick.'

5.2 Detached positions 215

The detached position of these time expressions that set the stage for the clause contrasts with restrictive time phrases found in the clause core periphery position seen in chapter 4.

5.2.1.2 Participant orientation in the Left-Detached Position

A phrase in the LDP identifying a particular participant may serve to alert the listener to a change or contrast in topic participants. Topic activation and topic contrast with simple clauses is described in the next two sections. (Topicalizing with equative clauses will be addressed in chapter 7.) The placement of vocatives in dialogue clauses is covered in section 5.2.1.2.3.

5.2.1.2.1 Topic activation with a simple clause

When a speaker wants to activate an entity from the context of a discourse s/he may mention it first in the LDP before making a comment about it. The purposes served by this preposing include changing the topic to another participant, as in (5.20) and (5.21), identifying one member of a group to be singled out for comment, as in (5.22), and giving explanations about an entity as part of the setting, as in (5.23). When preposed, this RP takes absolute case marking, and a resumptive pronoun (underlined in examples (5.20) to (5.23)) indicates its syntactic function in the clause. The 3s/4 absolutive pronoun in Kankanaey is a null form, but since the predicate cross-references the absolutive argument, there is no ambiguity when the resumptive pronoun has a null form.

(5.20) *Mo   din   si   nanang=na,   kambaw   iyat=na   en*
       as.for   RMd   PRM   mother=3sII   PART   say=3sII   QT

   man-sakit   din   toktok=na   ngem...
   ACT-hurt   RMd   head=3sII   but
   '(Meanwhile) as for her mother, well, she said she had a headache but....'

(5.21) *Mo   din   istolya   ay   in-solat=ko,   indawat=ko*
       as.for RMd   story   LK   UNDt.P-write=1sII   gave=1sII

   Ø   en   Jaime.
   4III   OPRM   Jaime
   'As for the story I wrote, I gave it to Jaime.'

(5.22) *Si   Dolika,   ab~aba-en=(n)a   si   Salmatin.*
       PRM   Dolika   CVC-carry.baby=3sII   PRM   Salmatin
       'Dolika, she was carrying baby Salmatin.'

(5.23) *Din   <ini>sʔek=da,   danggian   di   ngadan=na.*
       RMd   UNDt.P-plant=3pII   danggian   RMi   name=3sII
       'What they planted, its name is *danggian*.'

5.2.1.2.2 Topic contrast

When the purpose of topic activation is to indicate a contrast with other participants, *mo* 'as for' often precedes the RP as seen in some examples above and in (5.24) to (5.26).

(5.24) *Mo   din   bi~biteg   pay,   iwed   di   begas=da.*
       as.for RMd   pl-poor   PART   NEGEXIS   RMi   rice=3pII
       'As for the poor people, they didn't have rice.'

(5.25) *Mo   din   lagba,   owat   nai-sa~saig   Ø.*
       as.for RMd   basket   just   UNDts-CV-stack   4I
       'As for the basket, it was just stacked (with yams).'

(5.26) *Mo   din   pan-sawid=na   koma   yan*
       as.for RMd   NOM.use-ritual=3sII   IRR   PART

   <ini>wak=da=et   Ø.
   UNDt.P-drop=3pII=PART   4III
   'As for what they would have used for her ritual, they just dropped it (i.e., didn't use it).'

5.2 Detached positions

5.2.1.2.3 Vocatives

Naming an addressee is generally accomplished with the multifunctional *ay*, which in this context is understood as marking the name as a vocative. When the vocative precedes the clause in a dialogue, it is in the LDP. An intonational pause is only used when the vocative precedes the clause, as seen in example (5.27).

(5.27)   *Ay*   *nanang,*   *ay osto*   *na?...*   *Ay osto*   *adi*   *na*
         VOC   mom   Q   right   DEM1I   Q   right   PART   DEM1I

         ay   *nanang?*
         VOC   mom
         'Mom, is this right?...Is this really right Mom?'

5.2.1.3 Logical orientation in the Left-detached Position

Short comments can provide an orientation to the clause that follows them. Phrases and subordinate clauses that give a logical orientation, such as a condition or a reason, also appear before the pause or linking particle of the LDP. Lead-up events, such as perception or entering, which set the stage for the event in the main clause, may also be found in the LDP of a sentence.

5.2.1.3.1 Summarizing phrases

Certain single-word phrases or interjections, often augmented with semantic particles, summarize or comment on a situation from the speaker's point of view, as in (5.28) and (5.29).

(5.28)   *Olay*   *a,*   *into=y*   *iyat=tako?*
         Never.mind   PART   where=RMi   way=1+2pII
         'Well, never mind; what can we do?'

(5.29) *Esa   pay,   maga   abe   din   iskowila   ay   ka-tolong.*
       one   PART NEGEXIS also   RMd   student   LK   NOM-help
       'For another thing, the student helper isn't here either.'

Exclamations also serve as speaker comment, as in (5.30), where the narrator has just been informed of her friend's troublesome plan.

(5.30) *Wey,   soy (sino=y)   gapo=na   pay?*
       EXCL   what=RMi   reason=3sII   PART
       'Oh my! What's going on?'

The formulaic summary *idi siya di*[2] sums up a previous section of the discourse as the circumstances providing the context for the next paragraph or episode in a text, as in (5.31).

(5.31) *Idi siya=et di   yan   nan-a=et   din*
       when thus=PART DEM3I   PART   ACT-get=PART   RMd

   nakay   si   ando   ay   kaiw...
   old.man   ORMi   long   LK   wood
   'That being so (finding the animals gone, not having done the work) the old man grabbed a long stick....'

5.2.1.3.2 Reasons

The reason for something usually follows the main proposition in the right core periphery (see section 5.3.1), but with the phrase *gapo ta* 'since', a reason (often a previously-mentioned situation) can occur in a left-detached phrase, as in (5.32). Simple oblique RPs from the core periphery may also be preposed, as in (5.33), where it modifies the core 'I didn't tell'.

---

[2] See chapter 3 for more about the anaphoric *siya*.

5.2 Detached positions

(5.32) Gapo.ta   iwed   pilak=ko,   wada=y
       since   NEGEXIS   money=1sII   EXIS=RMi

<in>otang=ko   ay   at?atik.
UNDl.P-borrow=1sII   LK   few
'Because I didn't have any money, I incurred a little debt (lit. there was what I borrowed that was little.)'

(5.33) Si   bain=ko,   ad=ak   in-baga   ay   man-sakit
       ORMi   shame=1sII   NEG=1sI   UNDt.P-tell   LK   ACT-hurt

tili=k.
butt=1sII
'From embarrassment, I didn't tell that my tailbone was sore.'

5.2.1.3.3 Conditionals

The subordinating word *mo* may be translated 'if', as in (5.34), or 'when', concepts that are very close semantically, as seen in (5.9) above and also illustrated in (5.35). Either way, the clause in the LDP sets the hypothetical, irrealis orientation for understanding the matrix clause. Again, the comma is interchangeable with particles, as seen in (5.36), where the particle *et* separates the dependent clause from the central clause. Example (5.37) shows that the range of meaning of the conditional *mo* is actually broad enough to allow it to cover both participant preposing and hypothetical condition in a coordinate structure.

(5.34) Mo   sa=y   agawa-an=tako   di   adi=tako=n
       if   DEM2I=RMi   value-UNDl=1+2PII   RMi   NEG=1+2pII

ka-taktak-an   ya   ma-gasto-an,   i-saa=yo
NOM.delay<   and   UNDls-expense-NOM   UNDt-go.home=2pII

si   Narding.
PRM   Narding
'If what we value is our not being inconvenienced or having expenses, (then) take Narding home (from the hospital.)'

(5.35) Mo   kedng-e(n)=m   di   B.S. degree=m,
        if/when   finish-UND=2sII   RMi   B.S. degree=2sII

        into=y   obla-e(n)=m   ngin?
        where=RMi   work-UND=2sII   maybe
        'If/when you finish your bachelor's degree, where might you work?'

(5.36) Mo   ma-olas=ka   abe   et
        when   UNDs-time=2sI   PART   PART

        s<om>aa= ka,   a.
        ACTm-go.home=2sI   PART
        'Also when you are dismissed (from school), go home, eh?' (*olas* indicates 'dismissal-time')

(5.37) Mo   sik?a   ay   lalaki   ya   en=ka   maki-lagbo,
        as.for/if   2sII   LK   male   and   go=2sI   ASSOC-wage

        tayna(n)=m   si   asawa=m.
        leave-UND1-2sII   PRM   spouse=2sII
        'As for you, man, if you go take a paying job, leave your wife (at home).'

5.2.1.3.4 Lead-in events

Other types of clauses found in the LDP are events that are not mainline, but which give the necessary context for the thematic clause in the sentence. In (5.38), for example, the teacher had gotten chilled while finishing up her work at the school. The example sentence shows the shift from that scene to the next scene encoded as dependent clauses in the LDP, as reflected in the free translation.

5.2 Detached positions

(5.38)   S<om>aa=ak   sin   kotid=mi   et
        ACTm-go.home=1sI   ORMd   cottage=1pII   and

        s<om>gep=ak,   na-li~likod   da   din
        ACTm-enter=1sI   UNDs.P-CV-gather   pl   RMd

        gait=ko   sin   dap?o.
        companions=1sII   ORMd   fireplace
        'Going home to the teachers' cottage and entering, (I found) my companions were gathered around the fireplace.'

Perception verbs may be placed in the LDP as lead-in to the content of the perception, which is the central interesting information, as in (5.39), from a story about riding in an airplane. The particle *pay* 'furthermore' often occurs with dependent clauses in the LDP.

(5.39)   Pag   man-kilat   di   os~osdong-ak.   Tangad-ek
        all   ATT-white   RMi   look.down-UNDl.1sII   look.up-UND.1sII

        pay   ed   kayang   yan   man-ngisangis.
        PART   LOC   above   PART   sprinkle
        'Everything was white that I was looking down at. Looking up then, (I saw that) it was sprinkling.'

Arrival verbs are often required after movement verbs, and they are often placed in the LDP as background information, as in (5.40).

(5.40)   D<om>ateng=ak   pay,   kanan=da   en   man-taoli=ak
        ACTm-arrive=1sI   PART   say=3pII   QT   ACT-return=1sI

        ed   Trinidad.
        LOC   Trinidad
        'When I arrived, they told me to return to Trinidad.'

5.2.1.4 Ordering among constituents in the Left-detached Position

When more than one phrase or clause is placed in the LDP, the pragmatic scope of the orientation affects their order. Spatial orientation in (5.41) sets the stage for the logical orientation. Participant activation precedes the conditional clause in (5.37), but follows the formulaic summary *idi siya di* that signals the beginning of a new paragraph in (5.42).

(5.41)   Tan   mo   ed   Filipinas   pay   et   mo
Because   as.for   LOC   Phils.   PART   PART   if/when

wa=y   \<em\>ey-an   et   lagdeng=na
EXIS=RMi   NOM.go   PART   totally=3sII

din   siki   ay   man-dan.
RMd   leg   LK   walk
'Because (as for) in the Philippines, if there is somewhere to go, (one) has no other option than to go by foot (lit. perforce the foot that walks).'

(5.42)   Idi siya di,   kambaw   si   Doligen,   man-ot~oto
when thus DEM3I   PART   PRM   Doligen   ACT-PROG-cook

sin   beey=da.
ORMd   house=3pII
'That being so, (it turns out that) Doligen, he was cooking at their house.'

5.2.2 Right-detached position

Unlike the LDP, few sentence components can be found in a right-detached position. Tag questions and clarifying RPs are in the RDP, which is defined by its intonation break and the pragmatic function of either hearer-confirmation or explanation and clarification.

5.3 Clause peripheries 223

5.2.2.1 Tag questions

Tag questions request confirmation and follow an intonational pause, as in (5.43).

(5.43)   *Na-ragsak   pay.laeng,   siya   met?*
         ATT-happy   still   so   PART
         'Still happy, is that so?'

5.2.2.2 Clarifying Reference Phrases

Contrastive and clarifying constituents, as in (5.44) and (5.45), also follow an intonation break after the main clause. Constituents that are afterthoughts fit into this pattern as well.

(5.44)   *Sisya=y   nam-(p)arsua   ya   nang-ay~ayowan   en*
         3sIII=RMi   ANTI.P-create   and   ANTI.P-CVC. take.care OPRM

         datako,   baken   din   ap~apo=tako.
         1+2pIII   NEG   RMd   pl-ancestor=1+2pII
         'He is the one who created and has been taking care of us, not our ancestors.'

(5.45)   *Mo   si   Ana,   in-toloy=na   ay   man-iskowila,*
         as.for   PRM   Ana   UNDi-continue=3sII   LK   ACT-student

         daida   en   Ben   ay   sin-iyogtan.
         3sIII   OPRM   Ben   LK   unit-sibling
         'As for Ana, she continued to go to school, she and her brother Bennie.'

5.3 Clause peripheries

Like many verb-initial languages, the Kankanaey clause has both left and right peripheries, but uses the right periphery almost exclusively. Only deictics and epistemic adverbs have been observed modifying a clause in its left periphery. The right clause periphery may hold modifying clauses or clarifying restatements.

5.3.1 Clauses that modify in the right clause periphery

Modifying clauses that follow the clause are not right-detached, but in the right clause periphery. There is no intonational pause necessary at the margin of the periphery, although with longer constituents the breath-grouping tends to fall before the right peripheral element.

Among many others, Larson (1998:297–378) provides a thorough explanation of communication relations, as does Longacre (1996:51–97). This study does not attempt to give a detailed analysis of interclausal semantic relations, but rather points to the positions and marking that provide the syntactic framework for such an analysis. One of the difficulties in describing the complexity within Kankanaey sentences is that while there are many semantically distinguishable clause-linkage markers, many interclausal and intraclausal linkages are signaled by the ubiquitous neutral linker *ay*, for example, relative clauses, clausal complements, clarifying clauses, and linked cores in control constructions. It is left to the speaker and hearer to decipher, from the semantics of the predicates involved and the constituents of the construction, the correct interpretation of the relationship expressed by the linker *ay*.

Ad-clausal subordinate clauses are found in the right periphery, modify the whole clause, and are preceded by CLMs that express purpose, reason, and exclusive condition, as in (5.46) to (5.49). The CLMs are underlined in these examples.

(5.46) *En=kayo*   *ambos-en*   *din*   *Japs*   <u>*ta*</u>
      go=2pI   ambush-UND   RMd   J   so.that

      taoli-en=yo   *din*   *papilis.*
      return-UND=2pII   RMd   papers
      'Go ambush the Japanese (military) so that you bring back the papers.'

5.3 Clause peripheries

(5.47)   *I-pa-chekap=yo*   *agan?o*   Ø   *sin*   *shop*
         UNDi-CAUS-checkup =2pII   first   4III   ORMd   shop

         <u>*ta.say*</u>   *ma-pnek*   *di*   *bayer=yo.*
         so.that   UNDs-satisfied   RMi   buyer=2pII
         'Have it checked out first at the shop so that your buyer will be satisfied.'

(5.48)   *Anggay*   *ay*   *s<om>kaw*   <u>*tan*</u>   *man-dibidib.*
         already   LK   UNDm-cold   because   ACT-wind.blow
         'It was really getting cold because the wind was blowing.'

(5.49)   *<Om>ali=kami*   *sin*   *June 23*   <u>*mo*</u>   *ma-kdeng*   *din*
         ACTm-come=1pI   ORMd   June 23   if   UNDs-finish   RMd

         kasal.
         wedding
         'We will come on June 23 provided the wedding is finished.'

Embedded subordinate purpose and reason clauses may have their own topicalized phrases or conditional clauses in a pre-core position, sometimes with an intonational or particle-marked pause, as in (5.50). In an independent clause, these constituents would be placed in the left-detached position as sister to the main clause. Bickel (1993, cited in Van Valin 2005:193) found that in German a conditional clause may be fronted into the pre-core slot, and in Kankanaey the same position is open for phrases and clauses that modify a dependent clause. These elements are placed inside the clause as sister to the core in the only pre-core slot construction evidenced in Kankanaey. Figure 5.2 shows the constituent projection of a sentence that includes the pre-core slot.

(5.50)   *I-lipet=mi*   Ø   *tan*   *mo*   *dakami,*
         UNDt-report=1pII   4III   because   as.for   1+2III

         egyat-an=mi   *san*   *paltog.*
         fear-UNDl=1+2II   DRM   gun
         'We'll report them because as for us, we're afraid of those guns.'

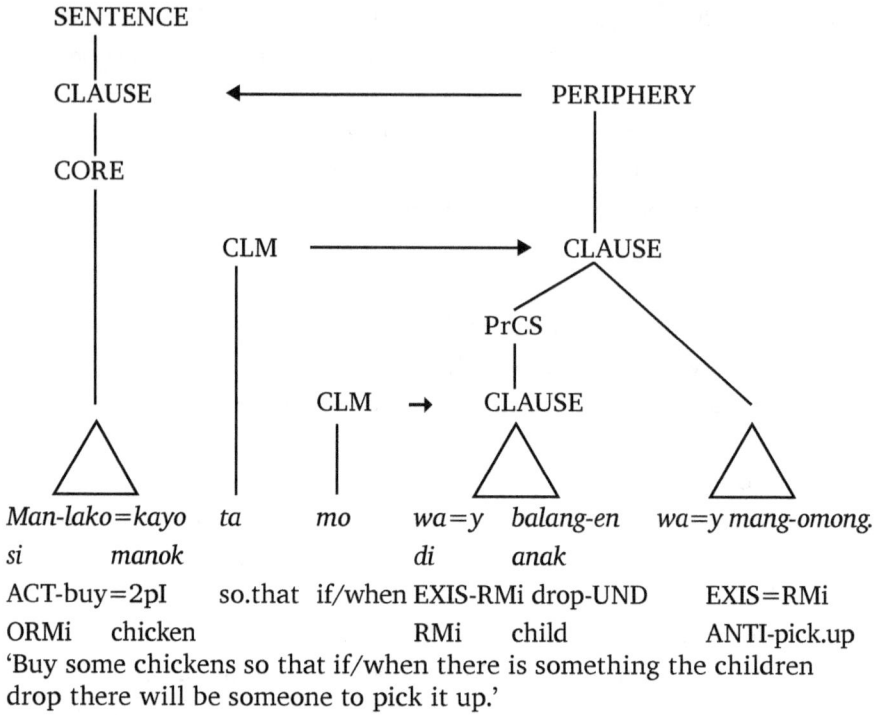

Figure 5.2. Pre-core slot in a subordinate clause.

Modifying clauses can precede the main clause in the LDP or follow the main clause in its periphery, depending on the clause linkage markers that are used. Table 5.1 shows the possible positions of clauses that express logical causative relationships in Kankanaey sentences, and the clause linkage markers that express them. This group of clause-linkage markers expresses the relationship of instigation and outcome (a little broader than cause and effect). The main clause presents one side of the relationship as the more salient situation, while the subordinate clause expresses the other side, either the instigating basis or the resultant event or state. The CLMs differentiate between hypothetical or future situations and actual situations.

5.3 Clause peripheries

Table 5.1. Reasons and results
(LDP= left-detached position, R-P$_{CL}$ = Right clause periphery)

	instigation	outcome	instigation	English approximation
irrealis	mo...LDP	main clause		'If X, then Y'
	main clause	ta... R-P$_{CL}$		'X, so that Y'
realis	gapo.ta...LDP	main clause		'Since X, Y'
		main clause	tan... R-P$_{CL}$	'X, because Y'

5.3.2 Clarifying restatement clauses

Clauses understood to be clarifying restatements or identifying clauses are not in the core, but are linked from the right clause periphery with the linker *ay* (here a CLM). The clauses may be complete, as seen in (5.51), where there is no coreferential argument between the two clauses.

(5.51) *Dooy   adi   ma-kaan   din   sakit=na*
        DEM3V   NEG   UNDs-remove   RMd   sick=3sII

       ay   anggay   mat~matey=et   Ø!
       LK   already   CVC-UNDs-die=PART   3sI
       'There, his sickness isn't being taken away, (he's) already dying!'

In example (5.52) the *ay*-linked clause (in brackets) modifies the nominalized clause *sin inmaliak* 'when I came'. The main clause is *baken kaman...* '(It) isn't like...'; the *ay*-linked clause adds clarifying information and is in the right periphery of the nominalized clause.

(5.52) *Baken   kaman   sin   <inm>ali-a(n)=k   [ay   man-liboo*
        NEG   like   ORMd   NOM.P-come<=1sII   LK   ACT-cloud

       yan   kana=k   en   snow].
       and   say=1sII   QT   snow
       '(It's) not like when I arrived, when there were clouds and I thought it was snow.'

In (5.53) the coreferential pronoun is omitted in the second clause, but not as core-level argument sharing, since a control/pivot relationship is not evidenced in these amplification clauses. The example in (5.54) is ambiguous, with one repeated pronoun and the absolutive either the null pronoun, or deleted. The position of these clarifying clauses within the matrix clause periphery allows (but does not require) coreferential pronoun deletion, a closer relationship to the matrix clause than coordinate clauses which virtually never share coreferential pronouns across the clause boundary (as noted in section 5.1).

(5.53) Ka-e~ey=ak   abe=d   Baguio   ay   adi
        IMM-CV-go=1sI   also=LOC   Baguio   LK   NEG

nan-pak~pakada.
ACT.P-CVC-say.farewell/permission
'I would also just go off to Baguio without letting anyone know.'

(5.54) Et   k<in>olang-an=da=et   din   soldado=n
        and   UNDl-lack<=3pII=PART   RMd   soldier=BRM

Lt. Polit   ay   p<in>altog-an=da.
Lt. Polit   LK   UNDl.gun<=3pII
'And they reduced the number of Lieutenant Polit's soldiers, shooting them.'

5.4 Complex clauses

Within a clause, regardless of its position in the sentence, there may be two or more cores joined together. The core juncture may be coordinate or subordinate. No evidence has been found for co-subordinate relations between clauses or clause cores. Section 5.4.1 covers "control" constructions with coordinate cores. Subordinate core junctures may be found where clauses are joined from the right core periphery with prepositional phrases, or when a matrix predicate takes a core as its complement. All core junctures are linked with *ay*.

5.4.1 Non-subordinate core junctures

In non-subordinate core junctures, the first core carries any perfective aspect marking as well as the illocutionary force while the second core has certain restrictions on affixation and argument omission. Single-argument control, Actor-control and Undergoer-control constructions are detailed in this section.

5.4.1.1 Single-argument control construction

In these constructions the first core has a single argument, often the EXPERIENCER of an inner state. The second core may also be intransitive, as in (5.55) with 'embarrassed to arrive', in which case the omitted pivot will be the single argument (S in examples below) of that predicate. If the second core is transitive and the actor is the coreferential argument, there are two possible affixations. The linked core may have an Undergoer-voice predicate with the actor (A_T) argument omitted, seen in (5.56). The second affixation possible for the linked core indexes transitive actors. This is the prefix *maN-* (*naN-* with perfective) as a "structural antipassive" (A_{ANTI}) (Cooreman 1994). This prefix creates a form, seen in (5.57), that cannot function predicatively by itself. The undergoer of a transitive predicate can only be the coreferential omitted argument if it is given detransitivizing passive morphology, as in (5.58).

(5.55)   *I-bado=m*   *na*   *ta*   *adi=ka*   *mab~ma-bain*
         UNDt-clothes=2sII   DEM1I   so.that   NEG=2sI   CVC-ATT-shame

         ay   *d<om>ateng*   *sin*   *iskowilaan.* $S_U=S_A$
         LK   ACTm-arrive   ORMd   school
         'Wear this so you won't feel embarrassed to arrive at the school.'

(5.56)   *Sa.pay.koma.ta*   *na-ragsak=kayo*   *ay*   *datng-an*   *nan*
         hopefully   UNDs.P-happy=2pI   LK   arrive-UNDl   DRM

         solat=ko. $S_U=A_T$
         letter=1sII
         'Hopefully you are happy to receive/come upon (this) my letter.'

(5.57) Ma-bain=ak   ay   manodsod (maN-sodsod). $S_U = A_{ANTI}$
        UNDs-shame=1sI   LK   ANTI-tell.negative
        'I'm embarrassed to give the bad news.'

(5.58) Mai-tapi=s   sisya   ay   mai-tayaw. $S_U = S_U$
        UNDts-add=PRM   3sIII   LK   UNDts-fly
        'He was included in being flown away.'

Verbs of motion can form core junctures with other verbs, as with the 'come to get' construction in (5.59), which has a preceding modal operator.

(5.59) Ay   mabalin   ay   <om>ali=kayo   ay   mang-a
        Q   possible   LK   ACTm-come=2pI   LK   ANTI-get

        en   sak?en   sina? $S_A = A_{ANTI}$
        OPRM   1sIII   DEM1IV
        'Would it be possible for you guys to come get me here?'

5.4.1.2 Actor-control constructions

In Actor-control constructions the first core has an ergative actor argument that controls the reference of the omitted argument of the second predicate. The omitted argument in the second core must be a direct core argument (S, A_T, U_T) but no other syntactic restrictions are placed on it. The second core may be intransitive, its single argument omitted. If the second core is transitive, there are the same two possible affixations that were noted above in section 5.4.1.1. It may use the marked antipassive *maN-* or it may use an Undergoer-voice affix. In the latter case, either its actor argument or its undergoer may be omitted as the pivot of the construction, depending on the co-reference with the actor of the first core.

Cores that modify a second core by indicating manner, phase[3] or other details are linked with *ay*, as in (5.60) to (5.62). In these examples the first core has an actor argument, and the omitted actor of the second core is

---

[3] As Perlmutter (1970) notes, phase predicates may modify at different levels. See section 5.4.4.1 example (5.88) for clause-level phase predicates.

5.4 Complex clauses 231

co-referential. This controller-pivot relationship is symbolized in the right column.

(5.60) *I-ginek=na* (Ø) *ay t<om>okdo sin*
UNDt-quiet=3sII (3sI) LK ACTm-sit ORMd

kad?ak. $A_T=S_A$
place.1sII
'She got (herself) quiet, sitting down beside me.'

(5.61) *Kana=k ay man-nem~nemnem, "Tet?ewa kayman*
say=1sII LK ACT-CVC-think true EVID

sa." $A_T=S_A$
DEM2I
'I said to myself (lit. I said thinking), "Yes, that's true."'

(5.62) *In-logi=mi ay mang-i-obla sin*
UND.P-begin=1pII LK ANTI-Th-work ORMd

papeles=ko. $A_T=A_{ANTI}$
papers=1sII
'We began to work on my papers.'

Transitive verbs of internal experience form complex clauses with two cores in those cases when the experiencer (Actor macrorole) is also an argument in the linked clause. The controller of this construction is the Actor of the first core; the pivot is only restricted to being a direct (i.e., not oblique) argument of the second core. Note that in both (5.63) and (5.64), the omitted argument in the second core is the Actor (A) argument; in (5.63) the transitive predicate takes the antipassive *maN-*, while in (5.64) the predicate indexes an Undergoer (U) (the CONTENT of the request).

(5.63) Laydelaydek   ay   mangila=d   Baguio. $A_T=A_{ANTI}$
       CVCCV~layad-en=ko   maN-ila=ed
       INTS-like-UND=1sII LK   ANTI.see=LOC   Baguio
       'I'd just love to see Baguio (City).'

(5.64) Layd-ek   ay   dop?et-en   mo   pig?an   di
       like-UND.1sII   LK   ask-UND   if   when   RMi

       <om>ey-an. $A_T=A_T$
       NOM-go<
       'I'd like to ask when the departure time is.'

In (5.65) the first Actor is coreferential with the absolutive argument of the associate-indexed predicate, in this case an Actor. In example (5.66) the co-reference is with the single Undergoer argument of a passive-voice predicate, showing that the pivot is not semantic. In (5.67a and b), two clauses from the same text show the second core argument as an Undergoer, again indexed with the (passive) stative affix *ma-i-* in a., which can only take one direct argument, and then with the unmarked theme-Undergoer-voice affix *i-* in b. The interpretation of the pivot in (5.67b) is pragmatic; in this text the referent is clearly 'the old man'; in another context it could be referring to a different deceased person, and a 3s pronoun (Ø) could be posited rather than an omitted argument.

(5.65) Awan, sigaa(n)=k   ay   maki-ey   en
       none   dislike.UND=1sII   LK   ASSOC-go   OPRM

       sik?a! $A_T=S_A$
       2sIII
       'No way! I don't want to go with you!'

(5.66) Sigaan=(d)a   abe   ay   ma-baa. $A_T=S_U$
       dislike.UND=3pII   also   LK   UNDs-send.on.errand
       'They didn't want to be sent on errands, either.'

5.4 Complex clauses

(5.67) a. *Ni-layad nina ay nakay ay*
UND.P-like DEM1II LK old.man LK

    mai-ponpon si kinakristiyano. $A_T=S_U$
    UNDts-bury ORMi Christianity
    'This old man wanted to be buried Christian-style.'

b. *Ni-layad=na ay i-ponpon=yo.* $A_T=U_T$
    UND.P-like=3sII LK UNDt-bury=2pII
    'He wanted you guys to bury him.'

Examples (5.68) to (5.72) use a variety of experience verbs of attitude and cognition. In (5.68) the second core uses the structural antipassive with the incorporated-theme prefix indicating the presence and definiteness of the Undergoer. Example (5.70) presents the pivot as the indexed Undergoer of the second core, while (5.71) has the ergative Actor as pivot. Example (5.72) has an embedded juncture, with both strategies for transitive second cores exemplified.

(5.68) *Anosam ay mangiayoan tan*
    anos-an=mo maN-i-ayoan
    patient-UNDl=2sII LK ANTI-Th-care.for because

    na-bay Ø. $A_T=A_{ANTI}$
    UNDs-tired 3sI
    'Put up with taking care of it for him because he's tired.'

(5.69) *Adi=na ammo ay maki-kadwa.* $A_T=S_A$
    NEG=3sII know.UND LK ASSOC-companion
    'He doesn't know how to get along with others.'

(5.70) *<Ini>tlok=na ay p<in>a-kan=ko.* $A_T=U_T$
    UNDt.P-allow=3sII LK UND.P-CAUS-eat=1sII
    'She allowed me to feed her (lit. allowed that I fed her).'

(5.71) Oonong-ek   ay   taltal-en   din
        persist-UND.1sII   LK   pry.open-UND   RMd

  tangeb. $A_T=A_T$
  door
  'I will persist in prying open the door.'

(5.72) Gaan=da   ay   mang-adal   ay   basa-en
        dislike=3pII   LK   ANTI-learn   LK   read-UND

  din   kali=tako. $A_T=A_{ANTI}=A_T$
  RMd   language=1+2p
  'They don't want to learn how to read our language.'

5.4.1.2 Undergoer-control constructions

Undergoer-control constructions are those in which the first core is transitive and its Undergoer is the controller of the shared argument (S) of the second core. The pivot in Undergoer-control constructions is restricted to the single argument of a (formally) intransitive predicate, indexed on the second predicate which is given voice marking to accommodate this restriction. Thus, in example (5.73), the Undergoer *dakami* '1p' is indexed as the intransitive Actor of the second clause. In (5.74), the Undergoer *sak?en* '1s' is indexed as the Undergoer of a state predicate, while in (5.75) passive morphology makes the Undergoer the single argument of the detransitivized predicate *tapi* 'to add or join'. In (5.76) the second clause has a semantically transitive predicate with a specific Undergoer; the antipassive predicate indexes the shared argument as the transitive Actor.

(5.73) Initdoan=da=s   dakami   ay
        <in>i-todo-an
        UNDl.P-teach<=3pII=PRM   1pIII   LK

  man-getad. $U_T=S_A$
  ACT-fell.tree
  'They taught us how to cut down trees.'

5.4 Complex clauses

(5.74) *Keddeng-an=da=s sak?en ay ma-tey.* $U_T=S_U$
sentence-UNDl=3pII=PRM 1sIII LK UNDs-die
'They will sentence me to die.'

(5.75) *<In>awis=na=s sak?en ay mai-tapi*
UND.P-persuade=3sII=PRM 1sIII LK UNDts-join

sin obla=da. $U_T=S_U$
ORMd work=3pII
'He persuaded me to join (lit. be joined) in their work.'

(5.76) *Tolong-a(n)=m kod sak?en ay en*
help-UNDl=2sII please 1sIII LK go

mang-anap sin antokos=ko. $U_T=A_{ANTI}$
ANTI-search ORM glasses=1sII
'Please help me go look for my glasses.'

5.4.2 Core subordination

Previous chapters have noted that Kankanaey makes extensive use of nominalized predicates that index an omitted absolutive argument. When such predicates have ergative arguments, these are included in the nominalized expression, creating nominalized cores. Oblique referents and phrases that modify the periphery of nominalized cores may be included, creating nominalized clauses. Complex RPs constructed from nominalized clauses are very common in Kankanaey.

In Kankanaey, clauses with temporal and locative functions are subordinated by nominalization and expressed as an oblique-marked reference phrase in the core periphery, as in (5.77). A few prepositions that express temporal functions, such as *inggana* 'until' in the bracketed subordinate clauses in (5.78) and (5.79), can take a linked clause rather than a nominalized phrase.

(5.77) Pagano   sisya   [sin   nan-tur~turay-an=(n)a   si
       pagan   3sI   ORMd   ACT.P.NOM-CVC-rule<=3sII   ORMi

   gobierno].
   government
   'He was following the traditional religion (lit. pagan) at/during the time that he was serving in the government.'

(5.78) Asi=kami   pay   b<om>alalong   [enggana   ay
       then=1pI   PART   ACTm-go.downhill   until   LK

   datng-en=mi   din   danan].
   arrive-UND=1pII   RMd   trail
   'Then we went downhill until we found the trail.'

(5.79) En=kami=et   nan-i~inom   [enggana   ay   l<om>abi].
       go=1pI=PART   ACT.P-CV-drink   until   LK   UNDm-night
   'We went out drinking until it was night.'

5.4.3 Quotation complement subordination

A direct quotation is the semantic complement of a speech or thought predicate. These complements may be whole sentences or paragraphs, and are considered as subordinate units that are extraposed as sister to the clause with the matrix (speech or thought) predicate. In Kankanaey, a direct quotation may precede or follow the matrix predicate. If it follows, it may be preceded by the clause linkage marker (CLM) *en* (tagged QuoTe), as in (5.80). If the matrix predicate follows, there is no CLM, as in (5.81). Figure 5.3 shows the extraposed position of direct quotation sentences.

(5.80) Anggay   yan   kana=na   en,   "Na-tey   baw
       already   PART   say.UND=3sII   QT   UNDs-die   EVID

   si   Nabulay."
   PRM   Nabulay
   'That being done, he said, "I realize Nabulay has died."'

5.4 Complex clauses

(5.81) Ma-kdeng   pay,   "May,   en=ka   i-gto   Ø,"
       UNDs-finish PART   OK   go=2sI   UNDt-store   4III

kana=na.
say.UND=3sII
'When that was finished, "OK, go put it away," he said.'

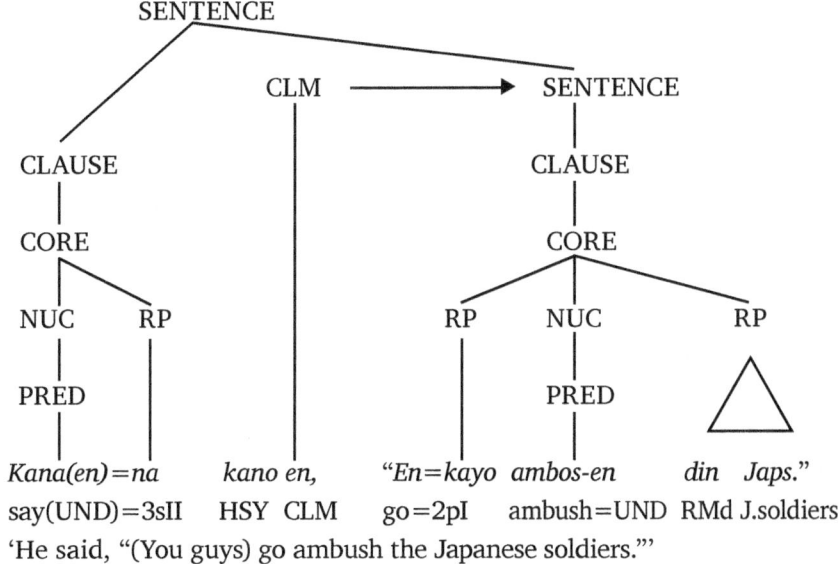

Kana(en)=na   kano en,   "En=kayo   ambos-en   din   Japs."
say(UND)=3sII HSY CLM   go=2pI   ambush=UND   RMd   J.soldiers
'He said, "(You guys) go ambush the Japanese soldiers."'

Figure 5.3. Direct quotation sentence.

Indirect quotation involves a clausal complement that indirectly expresses the content of verbs of expression or mental process. In Kankanaey these complement clauses are also extraposed; they are sisters to their matrix core. Like the direct-quotation complement, the CLM is *en*, as in (5.82) to (5.84). When the complement expresses uncertainty or a question, the CLM is *mo* 'if', as in (5.85).

(5.82) Nem~nemnem-e(n)=k   en   adi=ak   <om>ali=s
       CVC-think-UND=1sII   QT   NEG=1sI   ACTm-come=ORMi

bigat.
tomorrow
'I am thinking/considering that I won't come tomorrow.'

(5.83) Kana=na   en   <om>ey=ak   ed   Kabingan
      say.UND=3sII   QT   ACTm-go=1sI LOC   Kabingan

   sin   agsapa.
   ORMd   morning
   'She said that I was to go to Kabingan in the morning.'

(5.84) Iyat=na   en   man-sakit   din   toktok=na.
      say.thus=3sII   QT   ACT-hurt   RMd   head=3sII
      'She said that her head hurt.'

(5.85) Layd-ek   ay   dop?et-en   mo   pig?an   di
      like-UND.1sII   LK   ask-UND   if   when   RMi

   <om>ey-an.
   NOM-go<
   'I'd like to ask when (someone) is to go (i.e., departure time).'

Verbs of self-reporting speech often denote mental processes, as may be seen in (5.86) and (5.87). The implication with imperfective aspect is often negative, with an opposite outcome.

(5.86) Kana=k   en   man-solat=ak   si   lesson plan.
      say.UND=1sII   QT   ACT-write=1sI   ORM   lesson plan
      'I intended to write lesson plans (but didn't).'

(5.87) Kana=k   mo   na-laka   ay
      say.UND=1sII   if   ATT-easy   LK

   man-asi-il~ila=tako,   kambaw   na-ligat   Ø!
   ACT-RECIP-CVC-see=1+2pI   PART   ATT-hard   4I
   'I thought (mistakenly) it would be easy for us to get together, now I realize it is difficult!'

5.4 Complex clauses

Extraposition is attested by the presence of core-peripheral constituents preceding the complement, such as the time phrase *ed idi* 'previously' in the diagram of an indirect quotation sentence in figure 5.4.

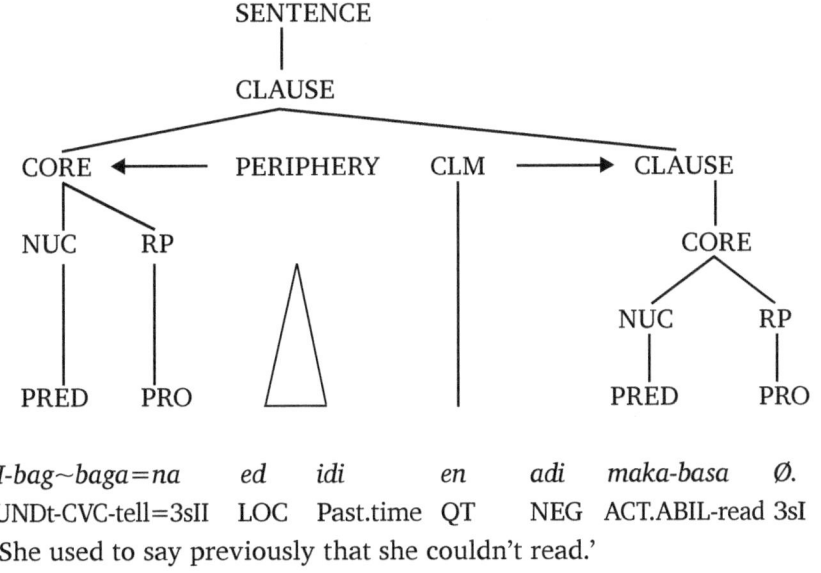

I-bag~baga=na   ed   idi   en   adi   maka-basa   Ø.
UNDt-CVC-tell=3sII LOC   Past.time   QT   NEG   ACT.ABIL-read 3sI
'She used to say previously that she couldn't read.'

Figure 5.4. Indirect quotation sentence.

5.4.4 Other clausal complements

When a clause serves as a complement (logical argument) of a Kankanaey predicate, it is preceded by *ay*, Kankanaey's ubiquitous linker. The following sections will consider predicates that can take clausal complements; these include temporal predicates, attributive predicates, nominal predicates, perception and performative predicates.

5.4.4.1 Temporal predicates

Temporal predicates may specify a point or phase (beginning, end, etc.), as in example (5.88). Other temporal predicates include *kanayon* 'all the time', *nabayag* 'for a long time', as in (5.89), or even specific time constructions, as in (5.90). These predicates take clausal complements which are subordinated, preceded by the linker *ay*.

(5.88) Nan-logi   ay   nan-sakit=ak   ed   Trinidad.
        ACT.P-begin   LK   ACT-sick=1sI   LOC   Trinidad
        'My being sick started in Trinidad (lit. It started that I was sick).'

(5.89) Na-bayag   ay   adi   nan-ngal~ngalat   din
        ATT-long.time LK   NEG   ACT-CVC-converse   RMd

        man-bonong.
        ACT-pray
        'The one who prays (i.e., traditional religious leader) didn't respond/ speak for a long time.'

(5.90) Enggay   maka-bowan   ay   ma-ola~olaw=ak.
        already ABIL.ACT-month   LK   UNDs-INTS-dizzy=1sI
        'It's already been a month that I've been having dizzy spells.'

5.4.4.2 Attributive predicates

Another type of predicate that takes complements is a small group of attributive words that express the speaker's evaluation of the state of affairs expressed in the entire clause. These propositional attitude predicates take the clause as complement, as in (5.91) to (5.93).

(5.91) Mayat ay   ma-iwed   di   disturbo   et
        good   LK   UNDs-NEGEXIS   RMi   disturbance   and

        na-olnos   di   ponpon.
        ATT-orderly   RMi   burial
        'It was good that there was no disturbance and the funeral went smoothly.'

5.4 Complex clauses

(5.92) | Sigurado | ay | adi=na | aboloy-an | san |
|---|---|---|---|---|
| for.sure | LK | NEG=3sII | agree-UND1 | DRM |

in-baga=yo	mo	baken	man-lig~ligat.
UNDt.P-say=2pII	if	NEG	ACT-CVC-suffer

'It's certain that he would not have agreed to what you said if it were not the case that he was under duress.'

(5.93) | Tet?ewa | ay | mo | <om>i-turay | din | aklong | et |
|---|---|---|---|---|---|---|
| true | LK | if | ACT(LH)-Th-rule | RMd | desire | PART |

sa=y	mang-i-turong	si	ka-dadael-an.
DEM2I=RMi	ANTI-Th-lead	ORMi	NOM-destroy<

'It's true that if desires rule a person, that will be what leads him/her to destruction.'

5.4.4.3 Nominal predicates

Kankanaey has several nonverbal predicates with an ergative/possessive argument that take a state of affairs as their second argument. Thus, in (5.94) the nominal predicate 'its sufficiency was...' takes the *ay*-linked clause as its complement. Similarly, in (5.95) in the second clause, beginning with *tan* 'because', the predicate 'its alternative is...' takes the following *ay*-linked clause as its argument. Example (5.96) may be seen as having a similar structure, with a full RP as the first argument and a clause as the second argument.

(5.94) | Eped=na | ay | s<in>akit=ko | si | dowa | ay |
|---|---|---|---|---|---|
| sufficiency=4II | LK | UND.P-hurt=1sII | ORMi | two | LK |

agew	din	tili=k.
day	RMd	butt=1sII

'It was enough to make my tailbone sore for two days.'

(5.95) Ten?e(n)=m   san   egen=mo   tan   kapya=na
        limit-UND=2sII DRM   load=2sII because   alternative=4II

   ay ma-yetyet-an=ka   sin   danan.
   LK UNDls-dented=2sI   ORMd   trail
   'Limit your load because otherwise on the trail you'll be dented
   (i.e., left with a dent mark in your skin) (from the head strap
   pressing on the forehead).'

(5.96) Gandat   di   d<om>atng-an   di   odan   ay
        characteristic BRMi   NOM-arrive<   BRMi   rain   LK

   ad?ado=y   ma-pannateng.
   many=RMi   UNDs-colds
   'It is a customary outcome of the arrival of rainy season that many
   have colds.'

5.4.4.4 Perception and internal experience predicates

Verbs of perception and internal experience may also take a clausal complement when there is no shared argument. Subordinated with *ay*, as in (5.97) to (5.100), there is no restriction on the affixation in the second clause. Figure 5.5 shows embedded complementation.

(5.97) Mo dengng-en   di   aag?i=na   ay   mai-ponpon   Ø...
        if hear-UND   RMi   relatives=3sII   LK   UNDts-bury   3sI
        'If his relatives hear that he is buried...'

(5.98) Na-ammo-an   ay   si   dakami   di   nan-basol.
        UNDls.P-know<   LK   PRM   1pIII   RMi   ACT-do.wrong
        'It became known that we were the ones at fault.'

(5.99) Sed~sed?-en=mi   kasin   ay   <om>ali   da   Marlyn.
        CVC-wait-UND=1pII   again   LK   ACTm-come   pl   Marlyn.
        'We are waiting again for Marlyn's group to come.'

5.4 Complex clauses

(5.100) *Layd-e(n)=k   ay   <om>aptik   din   labi.*
like-UND=1sII   LK   UNDm-short   RMd   night
'I want/ed the night to be cut short.'

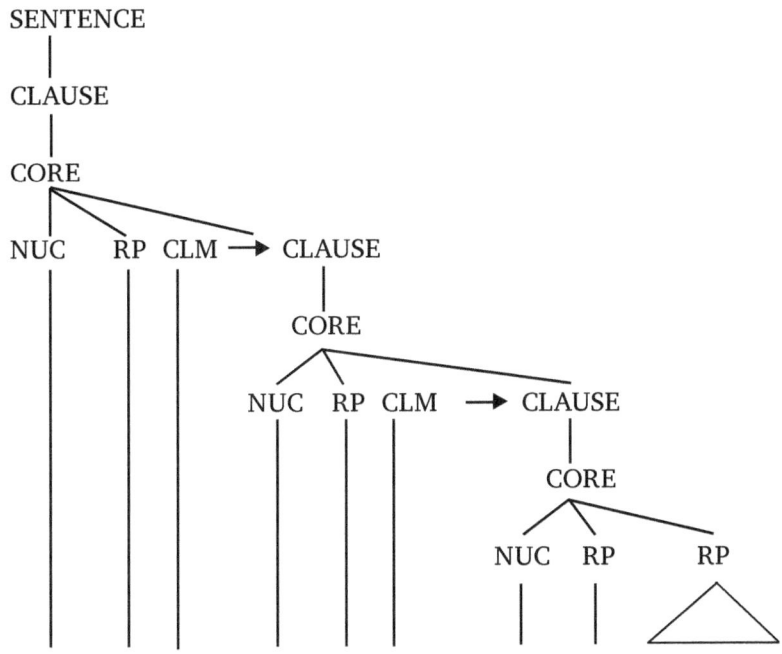

Layd-e-(n)=k   ay ammo-a(n)=m   ay lik~likna-e(n)=k   di tet?ewa ay ladsak.
like-UND=1sII   LK   know-UND1=2sII LK CVC-feel-UND=1sII RMI true LK happy.
'I want that you know that I am feeling true happiness.'

Figure 5.5. Recursive clausal complements.

5.4.4.5 Performative speech predicates

Performative speech verbs such as 'promise' take subordinate clauses as their complement and can not take a RECIPIENT argument. The complement does not share the co-referential Actor argument with the speech-predicate core, but rather the argument is overt in each core, as may be observed in (5.101) and (5.102). For these clauses the CLM is *ay*.

(5.101) *In-kali=n*   *Mayor   ay   lokat-an=(n)a   kasin*
        UNDt.P-promise=BPRM Mayor   LK   open-UNDl=3sII   again

   din   high school.
   RMd   high school
   'Mayor promised that he would open the high school again.'

(5.102) *Kolominto-a(n)=k   ay   maka-ammo=ak   sin*
        swear-UNDl=1sII   LK   ABIL.ACT-know=1sI   ORMd

   anak=yo.
   child=2pII
   'I solemnly swear that I will take responsibility (lit. able to know) for your child.'

5.5 The sentence complex

In oral and written texts, a type of sentence is often encountered that provides background information or recounts events that build or release tension toward or away from peak sections. This type of sentence consists of a running sequence of independent and dependent clauses loosely connected with a variety of CLMs. The sequence comprises a semantic unit in the story line or thematic development, and its highest node is labeled "sentence complex." "Reasoning sequences" tend to use explanatory CLMs, while "action sequences" use CLMs that loosely indicate temporal or logical succession. Because the participants carry over from one clause to the next, co-referential argument deletion can be examined in these contexts, revealing that 1s, 2p and personal 3p pronouns almost never are omitted, and therefore the 3s and 4 (impersonal) pronouns, although null, are not dropped. Pragmatics, especially the immediately preceding clause constituents, determines the referent of the null pronouns.

5.5 The sentence complex

5.5.1 Reasoning sequences

In the following three examples of "reasoning sequences," examples (5.103) to (5.105), the CLMs are bracketed giving reasons and results and extenuating circumstances, but not actions.

(5.103)   *Tamang-en=yo*   *amin*   *ed*   *demang*   *ay*
         look.far-UND=2pII   all   LOC   mid-distance   LK

         doy   *sin*   *kad?a=n di*   *bato,*
         DEM3V   ORMd   place=BRMi   stone
         'All of you look over there across the way where the stone is,'

         [ta]   *machinegun-an*   *din*   *soldados=ko*   Ø
         so.that   m.gun-UNDl   BRMd   soldiers=1sII   4III
         'so my soldiers will shoot at it with machine guns'

         [ta]   *ila-en=yo*   *di*   *ka-pigsa*   *=n di*
         so.that   see-UND=2pII   RMi   NOM-strong   =BRMi

         paltog   *di*   *Nipponggo,*
         gun   BRMi   Japanese
         'so you will see the strength of the guns of the Japanese,'

         [ta]   *adi=kayo*   *las~lasoy-en*   Ø,
         so.that   NEG=2pI   CVC-underestimate-UND   4III
         'so you won't underestimate them,'

         [tan]   *ed*   *niman*   *dakami*   *di*   *ap~apo=yo.*
         because   LOC   now   1pIII   RMi   CVC-lord=2pII
         'because now we are your rulers.'

(5.104) [Et mo]   panggep   abe   din   iskowila-e(n)=k,
       and if   regarding   also   RMd   student-UND=1sII
       'And then as regards my studies,'

       medyo   ma-lig~ligat-an=ak,
       somewhat   UNDls-CVC-difficult<=1sI
       'I'm having a rather hard time,'

       kalkalo   ed   nowani
       especially   LOC   now
       'especially nowadays'

       [ay]   na-ngina   amin   di   ma-lako-an
       LK   ATT-expensive   all   RMi   UNDls-buy<
       'when everything to be bought is expensive'

       [isonga]   s<om>aldeng=ak
       therefore   ACTm-stop=1sI
       'therefore I will stop (my education)'

       [ta]   man-anap=ak   kano=s   pan-obla-a(n)=k.
       so.that   ACT-seek=1sI   HSY=ORMi   NOM-work<=1sII
       'so I am to look (they say) for a place for me to work.'

(5.105) Siyat=da=n   ila-(e)n
       necessary=3pI=DISP   see-UND
       'They must watch out'

       [ta]   adi   kap~ka-pʔot-an   Ø
       so.that   NEG   UNDls-CVC-dew<   4I
       'so they (yams) don't get dewed on'

       [ono]   adi   ka-od~odan-an   Ø
       or   NEG   UNDls-CVC-rain<   4I
       'or don't get rained on'

5.5 The sentence complex

[tan   mo]   ma-p?ot-an   Ø,   ng\<om\>itit   Ø
because if   UNDls-dew\<   4I   UNDm-dark   4I
'because if they get dew on, they darken'

[yan]   man-pait   Ø   mo   kan-en   Ø
and   ATT-sour   4I   if   eat-UND   4III
'and they are sour if (one) eats them'

[yan]   adi   abe=n   kai-gto   Ø si   ma-bayag.
and   NEG   also=DISP   UNDts-store   4I ORMi UNDs-long.time
'and they also can't be stored for any length of time.'

5.5.2 Action sequences

"Action sequences" use the linkers *et* and *yan* which are almost as semantically bleached as *ay* but may indicate temporal or logical succession. Examples (5.106) to (5.108) show the types of relationships between clauses in action-sequence sentences. Again, the repetition of the personal pronouns—1s in (5.106) and 3p in (5.107)—justify the presence of the 3s and impersonal null pronouns.

Note that the first one or two clauses are marked as completive (P), setting the temporal framework for the rest of the clauses in the sequence, which are unmarked. This discourse-level temporal dependence is not restricted to action-sequence sentences, but may also cross syntactically unlinked sentence boundaries in Kankanaey.

(5.106) *Nan-sang?at=ak   sin   iskowilaan*
         ACT.P-climb=1sI   ORMd   school
         'I climbed uphill by the school'

         [yan]   man-posopos   abe
         and   ACT-turn   also
         'and turned back again'

[et] datng-e(n)=k   din   ketang
and   arrive-UND=1sII   RMd   creek
'and I found the creek'

[as(i)]=ak   pag   song-en   Ø
then=1sI   then   go.upstream-UND   4III
'and then I followed it upstream'

[et] d<om>ateng=ak   sin   danan   ed   na-ongdo
and   ACTm-arrive=1sI ORMd   trail   LOC   UNDs-above
'and I arrived at the upper trail'

[et] pag=ak   s<om>aa
and   then=1sI ACTm-go.home
'and then I went home'

[yan] man-sokat=ak
and   ACT-change=1sI
'and I changed clothes'

[et] pag=ak   ma~ma-ek.
and   then=1s   CV-UNDs-sleep
'and then I went to sleep.'

(5.107) Na-pno=da   sin   esa=y   kowarto
        UNDs-full=3pI   ORMd   one=LK   room
        'They filled one of the rooms'

[yan] en=ak=et   i-tining   Ø
and   go=1sI=PART   UNDt-peek   4III
'and I went to peek (at something)'

[et] kambaw   si   Nanny   ay   anggay   man-sak~sakit   Ø
and   EVID   PRM   N   LK   already   ACT-CVC-pain   3sI
'and (I saw that) it was Nanny, who was very sick'

5.5 The sentence complex 249

      [ay] kaman ma-tey Ø,
      LK   like   UNDs-die 3sI
      'like she was going to die,'

      [yan] pag=da=n   ayag-an   din
      and   then=3pI=DISP invite-UNDl RMd

      anak=da   ay wada=d   Baguio
      child=3pII LK EXIS=LOC Baguio
      'and then they called their son who was in Baguio'

      [yan] pag=da=n   <om>ali
      and   then=3pI=DISP ACTm-come
      'and then they came'

      [et] en=da   i-laga-an   Ø
      and   go=3pI UNDd-ritual 3sI
      'and they went to do rituals for her.'

(5.108) *Ad(i)=ak ammo   baw   Ø*
       NEG=1sI know(UND) EVID 4III
       'Well, I didn't know it'

      [yan] din   ka-tokmang=ko   ay   ka-dwa=k,
      and   RMd NOM-neighbor=1sII LK   NOM-two=1sII

      adi   dedan   t<inm>agtag   Ø
      NEG   EVID   ACTm.P-run   3sI
      '(but) my neighbor that was my companion, he didn't run away'

      [isonga]   na-pasobo   Ø
      therefore UNDs.P-endanger 3sI
      'so he got in a dangerous situation'

[et]   istay   todok-en   din   na-beteng   Ø
and   almost   stab-UND   BRMd   UNDs.P-drunk   3sI
'and the drunk guy almost stabbed him'

[ngem]   imbag.ta   wada=n   lagba   =s di
but   luckily   EXIS=RMd   back-basket   =DEM3IV
'but luckily there was the back-basket there'

[et]   sa=y   t<in>okang=na   ay   nang-tingga
and   DEM2I=RMi   UND.P-tip.over=3sII LK   ANTI-fend.off
'and he knocked that over to fend him off'

[et   asi   pag]   l<om>ayaw   Ø
and   then   then   ACTm-flee   3sI
'and then afterwards he ran away'

[yan]   <om>ali   Ø   baw   ed   beb~beey
and   ACTm-come   3sI   EVID   LOC   CVC-house
'and (evidently) he came to our home'

[ay]   man-og~oga   Ø
LK   ACT-CVC-cry   3sI
'he was crying'

[yan]   an~anap-en=(n)a   sak?en
and   CVC-seek-UND=3sII   1sIII
'and he was looking for me'

[tan]   in-pasobo=k   Ø   kano.
because   UNDt.P-endanger=1sII   3sI   HSY
'because he said I had endangered him.'

5.6 Relative clauses

Relative clauses (bracketed in these examples) are modifiers in reference phrases, as introduced in chapter 3. They are connected by the linker *ay* from

5.6 Relative clauses 251

the left periphery of the RP nucleus when descriptive and non-restrictive, as in (5.109) where the relative clause immediately precedes the nucleus, and generally from the right periphery when restrictive, as in (5.110).

(5.109) Di   ka-ado-an   ay   amag-en=da   si   tapey,
       RMi   NOM-many<   LK   make-UND=3pII   ORMi   ricewine

       din   [baken   d<in>eas-an   ay]   pagey.
       RMi   NEG   P-well.pounded-UND1 LK   rice
       'Mostly what they make into rice-wine, it's the under-pounded rice.'

(5.110) Si   naey   di   dad?at   di   ipogaw   [ay
       PRM   DEM1III   RMi   story   BRMi   person   LK

       na-tey   asi   b<om>angon   ed   na-baon.]
       UNDs.P-die   and.then   ACTm-get.up   LOC   ATT-long.ago
       'This is a story of a person who died and then revived long ago.'

The predicate in the relative clause is affixed to index the semantic role of an omitted argument that is coreferential with the head of the modified RP, as in the examples above and in (5.111). As with some other subordinated clauses, a gapped transitive actor role is indicated by the structural antipassive as in (5.112). Nominalizing affixes are used if the relative clause indicates the time or place of the predicate, as in (5.113).

(5.111) Din   istolya   [ay   in-solat   di   Amilikano]
       RMd   story   LK   UNDt.P-write   BRMi   American
       'The stories that the Americans wrote'

(5.112) Wada   di   an?anak   [ay   nang-i-pa-sgep   en
       EXIST   RMi   child   LK   ANTI.P-Th-CAUS-enter   OPRM

       dakami].
       1pIII
       'There was a child who invited us to come in.'

(5.113) Din   nay   ay   singbaan   [ay
         RMd   DEMIV   LK   church   LK

   pangi-mis~misa-an=da   en   sak?en]
   NOM.Th-CVC-services<=3pII   OPRM   1sIII
   'this church (where) they will be holding services for me' (e.g., mass for healing prayer)

The gap strategy cannot apply to possessors or arguments of already-nominalized predicates in the relative clause. In such cases, a resumptive pronoun is retained, using the minimally-specified impersonal (fourth person) class II pronoun, as in (5.114), where it is homophonous with third person singular, but in (5.115), it is clearly impersonal because the matrix co-referent is plural. The same pronoun indicates the actor of a nominalized Undergoer-indexed predicate, as in (5.116), where the coreferential matrix RP head is the first person pronoun. In the following examples the co-referential argument is underlined.

(5.114) Di   animal   [ay   na-tey   di   anak=<u>na</u>]
         RMi   animal   LK   UND.P-die   RMi   child=4II
         'An animal whose young has died'

(5.115) Dakayo   [ay   man-?es~?esa   di   poso=<u>na</u>]
         2pIII   LK   ACT-INTS-one   RMi   heart=4II
         'You whose hearts have become one'

(5.116) Am?amed   si   sak?en   [ay   iwed   di
         especially   PRM   1sIII   LK   NEGEXIS   RMi

   am~?ammo=<u>na</u>]
   CVC-know.UND=4II
   'Especially me, who knows nothing'

5.7 Conclusion

This chapter has gone beyond the simple clause to examine multiple-clause and multiple-core constructions. The RRG framework accommodated

5.7 Conclusion

coordinate junctures and subordinate junctures at both clause and core and nuclear levels, using peripheral, extra-core and detached positions. The next chapter takes a different approach to many of these structures, looking at the grammatical relations that they evidence.

6

Privileged Syntactic Arguments

The syntactic status of arguments in RRG is characterized in terms of the privileges given to one constituent, the Privileged Syntactic Argument (hereafter PSA) of a given construction. This chapter will first look in depth at the functions that are the province of the PSA of the clause. In section 6.2 the PSAs of several other key constructions are detailed. Section 6.3 explains the functions that are covered by non-PSA constituents.

6.1 The Privileged Syntactic Argument of the clause

In constructing a grammatical clause in Kankanaey, the first step is to determine the semantic representation—the "logical structure" (LS) of the predicate. This process is detailed in chapter 2, where it is seen that each *Aktionsart* classification has a unique logical structure that includes the salient argument positions.

The next step is to assign macrorole status to arguments in the logical structure, based on their position there. One of the arguments that has macrorole status is then chosen as the privileged syntactic argument of the clause. Section 6.1.1 will cover the process of macrorole assignment, PSA selection, and the coding and behavioral properties that the PSA of the Kankanaey clause exhibits.

6.1.1 Assigning macrorole status and the Privileged Syntactic Argument of the clause

In RRG, thematic roles such as PATIENT, LOCATION, EFFECTOR, etc. are correlated with their position in the LS of the predicate of the clause. There are five possible argument positions in the *Aktionsart* system; these are displayed in figure 6.1. These thematic relations between predicates and their arguments may be grouped into two semantic macroroles, Actor and Undergoer, which correspond to the syntactic arguments in a clause structure.

The possible assignment of macrorole status is represented by the Actor-Undergoer hierarchy, adapted for Kankanaey from Van Valin (2005:126). The arrows indicate the possible range of assignment. The principles that guide macrorole assignment are listed under the hierarchy diagram in figure 6.1.

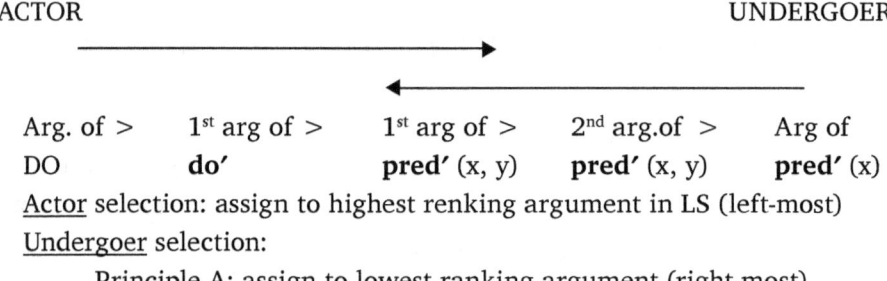

Arg. of >   1ˢᵗ arg of >   1ˢᵗ arg of >   2ⁿᵈ arg.of >   Arg of
DO   **do'**   **pred'** (x, y)   **pred'** (x, y)   **pred'** (x)

<u>Actor</u> selection: assign to highest renking argument in LS (left-most)
<u>Undergoer</u> selection:
      Principle A: assign to lowest ranking argument (right-most)
      -or-
      Principle B: assign to second lowest ranking argument

Figure 6.1. Actor-Undergoer hierarchy and assignment principles.

Macrorole status is assigned to the single argument of a predicate that takes at least one argument. (Nature predicates are an exception.) As the Actor-Undergoer hierarchy predicts, the Actor macrorole is given to single arguments of **do'** (x) and first arguments of **pred'** (x, y). The single argument of an intransitive state predicate, **pred'** (x), is assigned the Undergoer macrorole. In Kankanaey, as is seen in chapter 2, the predicate affix indicates whether the single argument is Actor or Undergoer, and thus indicates the type of predicate, i.e., *Aktionsart* classification.

When there is more than one argument in a predicate's logical structure, there is the possibility of a second macrorole. The selection principles are shown in figure 6.1. Assigning the Actor macrorole is a rather straightforward process, the Actor being the left-most in the LS. Some restrictions apply to the assignment of the Undergoer macrorole as the second argument—the argument must be referential and wholly included in any effect specified by the predicate. Thus, Activity predicates with non-referential arguments have only one macrorole; they are macrorole-intransitive.

With a complex predicate whose LS consists of a combination of logical structures, such as a causative predicate, there may be more than two argument positions shown in the LS. Figure 6.1 shows the two possible strategies for selecting one of the non-Actor arguments for Undergoer macrorole assignment. With Principle A the right-most argument in the LS is given Undergoer assignment. With Principle B the next-to-right-most argument is selected. The factors governing the choice between Principle A and Principle B are discourse-pragmatic.

Once the macrorole assignment is clear, one of the macrorole-assigned arguments is selected to bear the privileged relation to the predicate. This relation (PSA) is privileged syntactically in that it is signaled by coding properties and by behavioral properties, a distinction suggested by Keenan (1976). The PSA is coded by absolutive case marking and the indexing on the verb; the form of the predicating affixation indicates that argument's semantic function. Historically, this function has been called "focus" marking in Philippine linguistics.

6.1.2 Privileged Syntactic Argument case coding

The PSA of any clause is given absolutive case marking. For reference phrases this is expressed by the unbound reference phrase marker (RM) or the proper name reference marker (PRM). For pronouns, class I is used for single arguments and class III for the PSA of transitive clauses. Only one absolutive-marked participant is possible in a clause. (Section 6.3.2 will show that in a syntactically transitive clause, the Actor argument is given ergative case marking. All other arguments and adjuncts are given oblique marking.)

In basic two-argument Kankanaey clauses both the Actor and Undergoer may be topical and relevant, but an Undergoer is the default choice for PSA, an ergative pattern reflected in the absolutive marking on the PSA. In (6.1) the Undergoer argument takes the same RM as the single argument in (6.2).

(6.1)   *I-ali*   *=n din*   *babai*   *din*   *anak.*
       UNDt-come =BRMd woman RMd child
       'The woman brings the child.'

(6.2)   *<Om>ali*   *din*   *anak.*
       ACTm-come RMd child
       'The child comes.'

In examples (6.3) and (6.4) the same ergative pattern holds with proper names.

(6.3)   *I-agadang=na*   *si*   *Romy.*
       UNDt-cross.river=3sII PRM Romy
       'He takes Romy across the river.'

(6.4)   *Man-agadang*   *si*   *Romy.*
       ACT-cross.river PRM Romy
       'Romy crosses the river.'

Table 6.1 displays the personal pronouns of Kankanaey.

Table 6.1. Personal pronoun patterns

pronoun class	I	II	III
	Single	Trans.Actor	Trans.Undergoer
1s	=ak	=ko	(PRM +) sak?en
1p	=kami	=mi	PRM + dakami
2s	=ka	=mo	(PRM +) sik?a
2p	=kayo	=yo	PRM + dakayo
1+2		=ta	PRM + daita
1+2p		=tako	PRM + datako
3p		=da	PRM + daida
3s	Ø/sisya	=na	Ø/sisya
4 (impersonal s/p)	Ø	=na	Ø/siya

6.1 The Privileged Syntactic Argument of the clause

Except for third person singular and the impersonal fourth person, absolutive (PSA) pronouns have two different forms that indicate their relation as the single argument (class I) or as the transitive-Undergoer argument (class III). In example (6.5), two clauses have the same predicate *na-ila* and same participant ('you') selected as PSA. The first clause is transitive, with a Class III Undergoer PSA; the second clause is intransitive with a Class I Undergoer PSA. One could hypothesize that the conditioning factor for this split of pronoun form is phonological and posit bound vs. unbound allomorphs of the privileged pronoun, but example (6.6) disproves this hypothesis. In this example the process that displaces the Actor to a pre-predicate position has left the privileged Undergoer argument phonologically next to the predicate, yet it retains its Class III form.

(6.5)   Na-ila=k   sikʔa.   Na-ila=ka.
        UND.P-see=1sII   2sIII   UND.P-see=2sI
        'I chanced to see you.'   'You were seen.'

(6.6)   En=kami   i-ponpon   sikʔa   tan   na-tey=ka.
        go=1pI   UND-bury   2sIII   because   UND.P-die=2sI
        'We were going to bury you because you died.'

6.1.3 Ordering in basic clauses

Argument-ordering codes the syntactic functions of RPs within a clause. Single or Actor arguments occupy the first post-predicate position as in (6.7). This is an accusative pattern of semantic role neutralization. The only possible intervening elements are a small group of semantic particles. Rigid argument order serves to disambiguate ergative and absolutive reference phrases whose markers are homophonous following a consonant-final word. This is demonstrated in (6.8a), with the homophonous forms, and (6.8b) with the forms distinguished; in both cases the argument ordering is Actor-Undergoer.

(6.7)   Na-ek   din   moyang.
        UNDs-sleep   RMd   baby
        'The baby fell asleep.'

(6.8) a. *Kat-en   din   aso   din   posa.*
bite-UND   BRMd   dog   RMd   cat
'The dog bites the cat.'

b. *I-adawa=n din   anak   din   kawayan.*
UNDt-hand=BRMd   child   RMd   bamboo
'The child hands over the bamboo.'

Because the reference phrase markers distinguish a three-way ergative-absolutive-oblique distinction, the order of the absolutive Undergoer and any oblique argument may be pragmatically determined. Thus, in (6.9), the oblique argument 'stone' may precede the absolutive argument, because it is semantically needed to understand the precise meaning of *adosog* 'pound', or perhaps it is positioned as part of the predicate-focus structure, preceding the very topical 'vehicle' argument (see chapter 7 for more about topic and focus structure). In (6.10) the oblique recipient argument precedes the lengthy absolutive phrase (bracketed), avoiding the awkwardness that would result from placing 'to your care' after 'your spouse'.

(6.9) *Adosog-a(n)=k   si   bato   din   logan.*
pound-UNDl=1sII   ORMi   stone   RMd   vehicle
'I pounded on the vehicle with a stone.'

(6.10) *Enggay   in-polang=da   en   sik?a*
already   UNDts.P-hand.over=3pII   OPRM   2sIII

[nan   babai   ay   asawa=m].
DRM   female   LK   spouse=2sII
'They have now transferred to your care this woman who is your wife.'

Although oblique marking is the same for peripheral and core argument phrases, the order of the phrases differentiates them. Peripheral adjuncts such as time phrases must follow any oblique arguments, which belong to the core of the clause. Thus, in (6.11), the locative phrase required by the motion predicate must precede the peripheral time phrase.

6.1 The Privileged Syntactic Argument of the clause 261

(6.11) S<om>aa=ak ed Acop si bigat.
ACTm-go.home=1sI LOC Acop ORMi next.day
'I'm going home to Acop tomorrow.'

6.1.4 Privileged Syntactic Argument indexing on the predicate

The Kankanaey clause consists minimally of a predicate. Nature predicates have no overt argument and are macrorole atransitive. (The null fourth person absolutive 'it' cannot be posited here as a single argument because of its inability to be nominalized from such predicates.) Unaffixed and frozen form predicates take one absolutive argument, but there is no PSA indexing on the predicate.

6.1.4.1 Indexing with unaffixed and frozen form predicates

In clauses that identify a referent by class, or indicate attributes of a single participant, this single argument is semantically correlated with its predicate. Class roots take no indexing affixation, but the single argument is flagged as PSA (section 6.1.2) by the RM or a Class I pronoun. A small class of attribute predicates is formed with unaffixed property roots. Example (6.12) illustrates unaffixed identification and attribution predicates.

(6.12) *Doktor din anak=yo.*
doctor RMd child=2pII
'Your child is a doctor.

Ando=kayo ya ando din anak=yo.
tall=2pI and tall RMd child=2pII
You guys are tall and your child is tall.'

Most attribute predicates are formed with intransitive affixes as "frozen forms" (the affix does not carry any aspectual information), and the entity that is described (the attributant) is the privileged single argument, as in both clauses of (6.13). The indexing affixes are arbitrarily assigned to property roots to form attribute predicates.

(6.13) Man-kilat di   esa yan na-toling din odom.
       ATT-white RMi one and ATT-black RMd other
       'One is white and the others are black.'

6.1.4.2 Indexing with affixed predicates with one argument

Indexing affixes on all other roots indicate the generalized thematic relation and macrorole of the privileged argument. Regardless of role, the single argument is the PSA of the clause, signaled by the affix agreement of the predicate.

6.1.4.2.1 Single-argument state and state-change predicates

With predicates that have the LS **pred′** (x), the Undergoer macrorole is assigned to the single argument, as the Actor-Undergoer hierarchy predicts. As the PSA, the argument is indexed with the *ma-* prefix. In figure 6.2 the assignment of the macrorole and the subsequent indexing with the prefix are shown for the simple example (see example (6.14)). The logical structure indicates a thematic role of PATIENT as the single argument of the stative root and the affix *ma-* (tagged UND(ergoer-)s(tate)) indexes this role as a type of Undergoer. Macrorole assignment of the argument is shown with a solid line, while the indexing for the PSA is represented by a broken line.

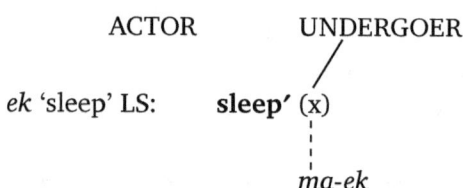

Figure 6.2. Macrorole assignment and affixation with a state predicate.

(6.14) Ma-ek   si   Kindi.
       UNDs-sleep PRM Kindi
       'Kindi is asleep.'

Single argument change-of-state predicates with the LS INGR **pred′** (x) or PROC **pred′** (x) are indexed with the infix <*om*> (tagged UNDm) on a

6.1 The Privileged Syntactic Argument of the clause 263

stative root, as in (6.15). The change may be punctual or not, depending on the meaning of the root.

(6.15) Ng<om>ato   din   *blood pressure=ko.*
       UNDm-high   RMd   blood pressure=1sII
       'My blood pressure is rising.'

6.1.4.2.2 Single-argument activity predicates

Single-argument predicates with the LS **do'** (x, [**pred'** (x)]) are indexed with one of the four Actor-indexing affixes in table 6.2, where it is seen that the Actor-indexing affixes in Kankanaey have distinctive semantic implications regarding agentivity.

Table 6.2. Actor-indexing affixation

Affix (and tag)	Agency implications
maN- (for a few roots) *man-* (ACT)	agency assumed but not required
maka- (ACT.ABIL)	abilitative, agency blocked
<om> (ACTm)	movement, no agency implicature

In (6.16), the single argument is an EFFECTOR and is indexed as a type of Actor with the prefix *man-* (ACT(or)) on the root.

(6.16) **do'** (x, [**hop'** (x)])
       Man-lakik?i   *si*   *Langdew.*
       ACT-hop.one.foot   PRM   Langdew
       'Langdew hops on one foot.'

Note in example (6.17) that although the two sets of predicates have the same affixes as in (6.13), the roots that take the affixes are very different. In (6.13) both are inherent color attributes. In (6.17) the first predicate indicates a dynamic situation (crying) and shows agreement with the privileged argument as an Actor while the second predicate describes a situation affecting the same entity (the children) but this time as Undergoers.

(6.17) Man-ʔoga   din   ananʔak   tan   na-kibtot=da.
       ACT-cry   RMd   children   because   UNDs.P-startle=3pI
       'The children cry because they were startled.'

The affixes *man-* and the less-common *maN-* are used to form intransitive predicates of agentive activity; the choice of affix is arbitrarily required by the root, as in (6.18).

(6.18) Man-golo   din   manbonong.
       ACT-create.disturbance   RMd   pray-er
       'The one who prays (traditional religious leader) will make a fuss.'

The abilitative Actor-indexing prefix *maka-* (*naka-* with perfective aspect) blocks agentivity in the Actor argument. Figure 6.3 shows two possible affixations for the Actor argument of the movement predicate *ali* 'come'. The abilitative indicates potential for action when imperfective. With perfective aspect it indicates fortuitous success in a situation. In (6.19) the writer politely implies that only inability would keep the reader from attending the next day's event, while in (6.20) the packing activity took some time or effort to complete.

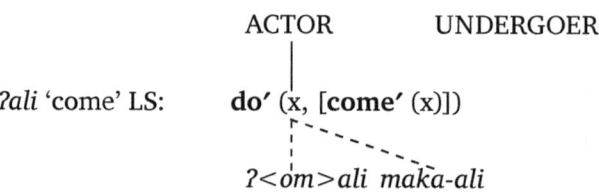

Figure 6.3. Macrorole assignment and affix indexing for two Actor roles.

(6.19) Sapay.koma.ta   maka-ali=kayo=s   bigat.
       hopefully   ACT.ABIL-come=2sI=ORMi   next.day
       'I hope you guys will be able to come tomorrow.'

(6.20) Idi   naka-balkot=ak,   na-ek=ak.
       when   ACT.ABIL.P-pack=1sI   UNDs-sleep=1sI
       'When I had managed to pack up, I slept.'

6.1 The Privileged Syntactic Argument of the clause 265

Predicates of physical movement are formed with movement or position roots and the infix <om>. These predicates may involve volition when the Actor is animate, as in (6.21), but also index inanimate self-affecting Actors (thus the added tag 'm(iddle)'), as in (6.22). (Section 6.1.4.6.3 presents a small class of movement roots that index the moving participant as Undergoer.)

(6.21)   *Ay*   *<om>ali=ka?*
       Q   ACTm-come=2sI
       'Are you coming?'

(6.22)   *L<inm>osop*   *din*   *lobid.*
       ACTm.P-untied   RMd   rope
       'The rope came untied.'

Physical movement predicates may take <om> when the action is natural, unmotivated or unintentional, such as pawing the ground as in (6.23). More intentional movements are affixed with *man-*, as in (6.24).

(6.23)   *K<om>od~kodkod*   *din*   *kabayo.*
       ACTm-PROG-paw.ground   RMd   horse
       'The horse is pawing the ground.'

(6.24)   *Peteg*   *di*   *layad=ko,*   *man-tal~talok=ak.*
       extreme   RMi   enjoy=1sII   ACT-CVC-jump=1sI
       'I was so happy, I was jumping up and down.'

6.1.4.2.3 Two-argument activity predicates

Many activity predicates have two arguments in the logical structure, which is represented as **do'** (x, [**pred'** (x,y)]). The second argument may be non-referential, or incompletely affected, or not specifically identified. In such a case the second argument cannot be linked to the Undergoer macrorole, and the clause has only one macrorole assigned, the Actor. In Kankanaey the Actor is assigned as PSA, and an Actor-referencing affix is used to form the predicate of an intransitive clause. The second argument is given oblique marking.

The linking between the Actor argument in the logical structure and the affixation used is shown in figure 6.4. The predicate 'eat' with the Actor-referencing affix does not require mention of the unspecified food that is eaten, but it is clearly implied, as the second clause proves. In (6.25), the second participant is non-referential and the clause is intransitive, with an oblique second argument.

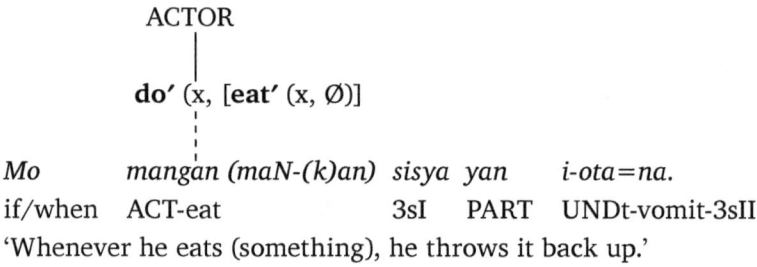

Mo	mangan (maN-(k)an)	sisya	yan	i-ota=na.
if/when	ACT-eat	3sI	PART	UNDt-vomit-3sII

'Whenever he eats (something), he throws it back up.'

Figure 6.4. Macrorole assignment and affix linking with a one-macrorole activity predicate.

(6.25) Man-lako=kayo abe si sin-asawa ay manok.
ACT-buy=2pI also ORMi unit-spouse LK chicken
'Also buy a pair of chickens.'

6.1.4.3 Indexing with multiple-argument clauses

If more than one participant is referential in the state of affairs, the Actor macrorole assignment is very straightforward—it is left-most in the Logical Structure, as seen in figure 6.1. More variable is the Undergoer assignment; it is available to many participants, as specifically licensed by each root. Selection may follow Principle A or Principle B in figure 6.1.

If there are both Actor and Undergoer macroroles assigned from the logical structure, the Undergoer participant is the required default choice for PSA. This is an ergative pattern, assigning to the Undergoer argument the same privilege as the single argument of an intransitive predicate. The predicate affix will index the non-Actor argument that has been given Undergoer macrorole assignment.

There are some exceptions to the Undergoer-as-PSA requirement. Section 6.1.4.6 looks at situations when a predicate meets the conditions for having both an Actor and an Undergoer, but because of specific semantic conditions the Undergoer is not selected as PSA. This is a PSA modulation

6.1 The Privileged Syntactic Argument of the clause

construction in that the Actor macrorole in such a situation is chosen as PSA, forming a marked antipassive-voice predicate.

In most situations, though, predicates with two macroroles will be formed with Undergoer-indexing affixes. Table 6.3 lists these affixes and suggests a common thematic role that an Undergoer so indexed would fill.[1]

6.1.4.3.1 Transitive Undergoer-indexing affixes

Table 6.3. Undergoer-indexing affixation

Affix (and tag)	Position of PSA(x) in LS	Likely thematic role
-en (UND)	do'......pred' (x)	PATIENT
i- (UNDt)	do'....be-LOC' (y, x) use' (y, x)	THEME INSTRUMENT
ma- (UNDs)	pred' (y, x)	STIMULUS (with nonagentive PERCEIVER)
-an (UNDl)	do'...be-LOC' (x, y)	STATIC LOCUS
i-...an (UNDd)	do'...be-LOC' (x, y)	DIRECTIONAL LOCUS

An Undergoer PSA will be indexed by a predicate affix from table 6.3, and that PSA will be marked with absolutive case, demonstrative class I or pronoun class III. Table 6.3 indicates for each indexing affix the likely argument position where the PSA so indexed would be found. Also included is a typical thematic role that an argument might have in that position.

Principle A for Undergoer macrorole assignment (see figure 6.1) yields predicates affixed with -en or i-. With most predicates -en indexes the most PATIENT-like argument. The affix i- generally indexes a THEME, the rightmost argument (y) in LSs that have locative predicates such as **be-at'** (x, y) or **be-with'** (x,y). The second (INSTRUMENT) argument of **use'** (x, y) is also indexed by i-. The prefix ma- usually occurs with intransitive predicates but is also allowed with transitive perception predicates. Principle B assigns Undergoer macrorole status to the first argument of locative predicates, a static LOCATION or GOAL indexed by -an, while RECIPIENTS and BENIFICIARIES

---

[1] Table 6.3 abbreviations for indexing affixes: ACTor, ACTor-m(iddle), Th(eme), UNDergoer-s(tate), UNDergoer(patient), UNDergoer-t(heme), UNDergoer-l(ocus), UNDergoer-d(irection), UNDergoer-m(iddle).

use *i...an* which indexes arguments toward which or away from which the activity moves.

The following examples show the possible linking of macroroles to the argument structure, and the affixation that results. The logical structures of these predicates are shown, with macrorole possibilities and the linking from PSA (x, y, z, or w) to affixation.

Figure 6.5 shows the two affixations possible with the stative root *layad* 'enjoy', as seen in example (6.26). With only the Actor macrorole assigned, the *man-* indexing shows that the PSA is the Actor and the predicate is intransitive. When both macroroles are assigned, the Undergoer macrorole is selected as PSA. The *-en* affixed predicate is macrorole-transitive and syntactically transitive.

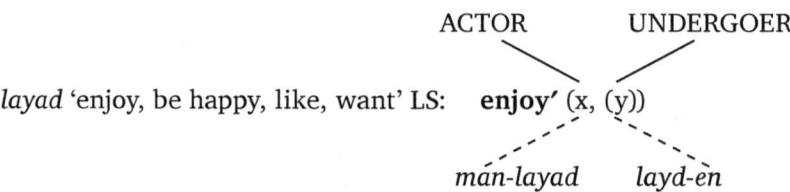

layad 'enjoy, be happy, like, want' LS: enjoy′ (x, (y))

Figure 6.5. Macrorole assignment and affix linking with a two-argument state predicate.

(6.26) *Man-layad   si   Bitmar.   Layd=ena   din   mangga.*
        ACT-enjoy   PRM   Bitmar   enjoy=UND.3sII   RMd   mango
        'Bitmar is happy. She likes/wants the mango.'

Perception-state predicates generally have arguments that indicate CONTENT of the perception by a conscious PERCEVER. Both arguments are given macrorole assignment, the Undergoer macrorole is the PSA, and the predicate is transitive. When the Actor of such predicates is consciously experiencing her perception, an Activity component **do′** could reasonably be posited in the logical structure. The first display in figure 6.6 for the predicate 'see' shows the Actor macrorole assigned to the left-most argument. If the right-most argument is not given macrorole status due to indefinite reference, the Actor is assigned as PSA with the affix *man-*, forming an intransitive Activity predicate 'look for', as in (6.27). If the Undergoer macrorole is assigned to the CONTENT argument, it must be assigned as PSA, indexed

6.1 The Privileged Syntactic Argument of the clause

by *-en*. The second display in figure 6.6 does not have the **do'** predicate. The PERCEVER is assigned the Actor macrorole, but such an Actor is specifically fortuitous, non-agentive, non-directive of the perception, as reflected in the free translation of (6.28). The PERCEVER maintains its canonical syntactic status as ergative Actor. This transitive use of *ma-* is only possible with perception predicates. If the Actor is not specified, it will not receive macrorole assignment and the *ma-* indexed predicate will be intransitive.

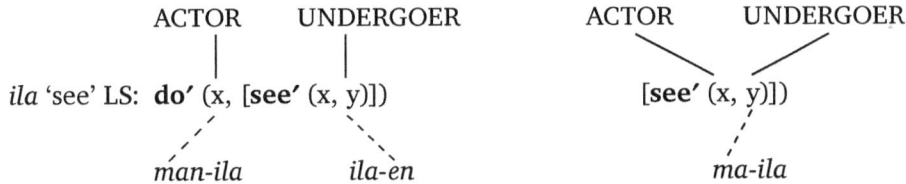

Figure 6.6. Macrorole assignment and affix linking with a perception-state predicate.

(6.27) Man-ila=ka=s   asawa=m.
       ACT-see=2sI=OPRM   spouse=2sII
       'Keep an eye out/Look for a wife (for yourself)!'

(6.28) Ed   England   na-ila=k   di   snow.
       LOC   England   UNDs.P-see=1sII RMi   snow
       'In England I had the chance to see snow.'

The diagram in figure 6.7 shows a complex causative logical structure and the various options for Undergoer assignment. Four affixations are possible with the action root *pespes* 'squeeze', as seen in (6.29) to (6.32). Note that *-en* is used for a more PATIENT-like Undergoer, one that is bodily affected. The Actor macrorole is only given PSA status and indexing affixation on the predicate when there is no specific, fully affected argument that qualifies for Undergoer assignment, as is the case in (6.29).

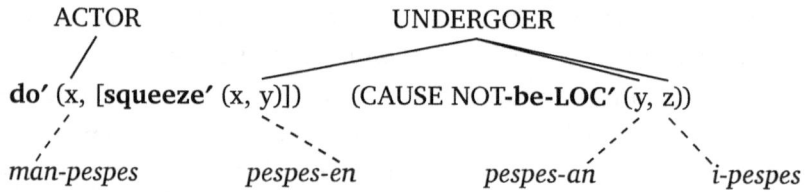

Figure 6.7. Macrorole assignment and affixation with a causative option.

(6.29) Man-pespes=ka   si   kalamansi.
        ACT-squeeze=2sI ORMi   calamansi
        'Squeeze some calamansi (citrus fruits).'

(6.30) Pespes-e(n)=naka.
        squeeze-UND=1sII+2sI
        'I'm going to give you a hug!'

(6.31) P<in>espes-an   Marta   din   kalamansi.
        UNDl.P-squeeze<   Marta   RMd   calamansi
        'Marta squeezed the calamansis.'

(6.32) I-pespes=mo   din   danom=na   sin   tasa.
        UNDt-squeeze=2sII   RMd   water=4II   ORMd   cup
        'Squeeze the juice into the cup.'

In figure 6.8 the display shows predicates formed with the action root *ponas* 'wipe' with a full range of participants. Note that in the absence of any PATIENT argument, the THEME indexing is *-en*. This action ('wipe') most typically is performed for the purpose expressed in the CAUSE part of the logical structure, but the **use'** predicate is a credible addition to the root meaning. Examples (6.33) and (6.34) show the indexing for each different PSA possibility.

6.1 *The Privileged Syntactic Argument of the clause*   271

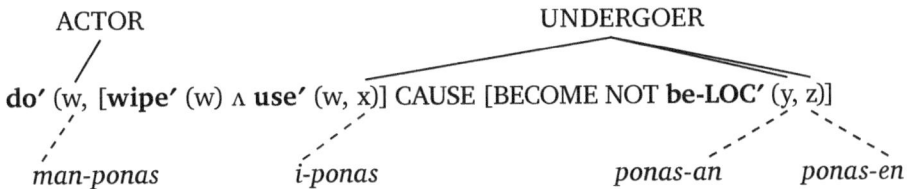

do' (w, [**wipe'** (w) ∧ **use'** (w, x)] CAUSE [BECOME NOT **be-LOC'** (y, z)]

man-ponas   i-ponas   ponas-an   ponas-en

Figure 6.8. Macrorole status and affixation with no PATIENT in the Logical Structure.

(6.33) *Man-pon~ponas   din   katolong.*
        ACT-CVC-wipe   RMd   helper
        'The helper is wiping.

        Ponas-a(n)=na   din   lamisaan.
        wipe-UNDl=3sII   RMd   table
        She's wiping the table.'

(6.34) *I-ponas=mo   nan   kalaley.*
        UNDt-wipe=2sII   DRM   rag
        'Wipe with this rag.

        Ponas-e(n)=m   din   kaloloya.
        wipe-UND=2sII   RMd   dirt
        Wipe away the dirt.'

Predicates that denote a change of location for a THEME Undergoer caused by an Actor have the logical structure:

[**do'** (x, [**root'** (x, (z))])] CAUSE [INGR/BECOME **be-LOC'** (y, z)].

All three arguments (x, y, z) are required by the predicate. The z-argument THEME PSA is typically indexed with *i-* . When such predicates index the Actor, the affixes *man-* and *i-* very often occur together for this function as *man?i-*, tagged ACT.Th, to indicate that the activity includes the movement of a THEME. Some examples of Actor-indexed location-change predicates are listed in (6.35), and two full clauses examples in (6.36).

(6.35) man?i-takin   'take along/ cause to go with'
man?i-baa   'send on errand/cause to go somewhere for a purpose'
man?i-dateng   'bring/cause to arrive with'
man?i-daton   'offer as a sacrifice/transfer ownership via sacrifice'
man?i-lako   'sell/transfer ownership to another'

(6.36) *Man?i-ali=ka=s   gayang.*
ACT.Th-come=2sI=ORMi   spear
'Bring a spear.'

Man?i-baa=ka   kod   si   odom.
ACT.Th-send=2sI   PART   ORMi   other
'Please send somebody else.'

Figure 6.9 shows the typical ditransitive root *todo* 'teach: cause someone to come to know something', a transfer of information. If there is no Undergoer-macrorole assignment, the Actor is indexed with *man-* or *man?i* and given PSA status, as in examples (6.37a) and b) following figure 6.9. With transfer predicates, *i-...-an* indexes a RECIPIENT, as in (6.37c), and *i-* indexes the THEME, as in d). Although either argument may be given macrorole assignment as being more salient, the THEME argument takes precedence over the RECIPIENT if both are specific entities. The reason for this is that the non-macrorole third argument is given oblique marking, and a THEME with definite oblique marking will be interpreted as partially affected. A RECIPIENT, which is likely to be a person, can maintain its specific reference using the oblique reference marker. Therefore if both RECIPIENT and THEME participants are specific and salient, the THEME will be the PSA. There is no evidence of ditransitivity on the syntactic level, i.e., there are no predicates that take three direct core arguments.

6.1 The Privileged Syntactic Argument of the clause 273

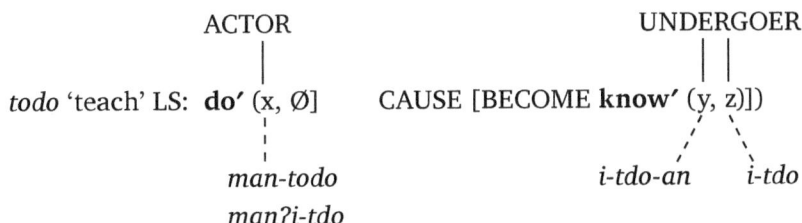

Figure 6.9. Macrorole assignment and affixation with a three-place predicate of transfer.

(6.37) a. Nan-todo=ak   si   Day Care children
          ACT.P- teach=1sI ORMi   Day Care children
          'I taught day-care children.'

     b. Man-it~i-tdo=ak   si   Sunday School.
        ACT-CVC-Th-teach=1sI   ORMi   Sunday School.
        'I am teaching Sunday School.'

     c. It~i-tdo-an=yo=s   sisya   sin   iyat=na
        CVC-UNDd-teach<=2pII=PRM   3sIII   ORMd   way=3sII

        ay   man-obla.
        LK   ACT-work
        '(You guys) be teaching her about how to work.'

     d. Ini-tdo=n   Todyak   din   danan
        UNDt.P-teach=BPRM   Todyak   RMd   path

        sin   pamilya=na.
        ORMd   family=3sII
        'Todyak showed/pointed out the path to his family.'

6.1.4.4 Indexing with valency-augmenting affixation

Three constructions in Kankanaey increase the options for macrorole assignment. The first is the presentation of a self-affecting motion as reflexive, having an Undergoer that is co-referential with the Actor. A second is the introduction of a second argument such as a comitative or instrument with intransitive roots. The third is the overt introduction of a causing AGENT to the logical structure of a predicate.

6.1.4.4.1 Self-affecting movements and activities

As seen in chapter 2, physical roots may form an activity predicate of self-movement or state predicates of position. Both may be formed with <om> indexing the single argument, as seen in figure 6.10, where the Actor macrorole is posited for movement, (see example (6.38a)), and Undergoer macrorole for position states. Physical-position roots may also present the single argument as a THEME Undergoer, using the prefix i-, as in (6.38b). The second form is less formal, and is often used for commands. The PSA linked to the Undergoer macrorole is co-referential with the overt Actor and cannot be given expression in the clause (thus the '?' gloss in example (6.38b).

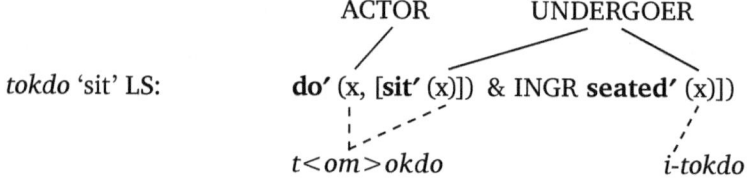

tokdo 'sit' LS: **do'** (x, [**sit'** (x)]) & INGR **seated'** (x)])

t<om>okdo   i-tokdo

Figure 6.10. Macrorole assignment and affixation with self-affecting movement.

(6.38) a. *T<om>okdo=ka!*   b. *I-tokdo=m*   Ø!
        ACTm-sit=2sI   UNDt-sit=2sII   ?
        'Sit up/down!'   'Sit (your body?) down!'

6.1.4.4.2 Applicative affixation

In Kankanaey, the variable assignment to the Undergoer macrorole, and thereby to PSA status, can be rather widely expanded using the Undergoer voice affix *i-* as an applicative to license the argument status of various participants that are not required or specified by the predicate. Additional predicates with their argument positions are added to the LS, creating more options for forming macrorole transitive predicates.

6.1 *The Privileged Syntactic Argument of the clause* 275

The logical structure in these cases has an extra element, perhaps a comitative or a **use'** predicate that takes the added argument. The added argument may be given macrorole status as the Undergoer, and the affix *i-* indexes that comitative or instrument as the PSA. Figure 6.11 and example (6.39) show the logical structures and affix indexing with two intransitive roots.

```
    ACTOR           UNDERGOER        ACTOR          UNDERGOER
      |                  \              |                \
do' (x, [[sleep' (x)]] ∧ be-with' (x, y)]   do' (x, [use.as.pillow' (x, y)])
```

Figure 6.11. Macrorole assignment and applicative affixation.

(6.39) *I-ek=na*   *din*   *daldali=na;*   *i-pongan=(n)a*
       UNDt-sleep=3sII   RMd   doll=3sII   UNDt-pillow=3sII

      din   *towalya.*
      RMd   towel

      'She takes her doll to sleep with her; she uses the towel as a pillow.'

The *i-...-an* (directional) circumfix indexes the SOURCE in (6.40) and creates a transitive predicate.

(6.40) *I-layaw-a(n)=m*   Ø   *mo*   *seppat-en=daka.*
       UNDd-run.away<=2sII   3sIII   if   beat-UND=3sII.2sI
      'Run away from him if he beats you.'

Conveyance predicates are regularly formed with the *i-* applicative affixed to motion roots, as in (6.41), but unusual possibilities are very wide-ranging. Example (6.42) shows how handily the *i-* applicative with a class root can express the situation. An argument that might be conceived as a metaphorical THEME may be available as PSA with *i-*, as in (6.43).

(6.41) *I-ey=mo*   *sa*   *en*   *ama=m.*
       UND-go=2sII   DEM2I   OPRM   father=2sII
      'Take that to your father.'

(6.42) *Owat=ak   in-loga~logan   din   odom   ay   pilak.*
        only=1sI   UNDt.P-INTENS-vehicle   RMd   other LK   money
        'I used (lit. vehicled) the rest of the money for my repeated vehicle rides.'

(6.43) *I-oga=m   Ø   ta   ma-kaan   din*
        UNDt-cry=2sII   4III   so   UNDs-remove   RMd

        sakit   di   nemnem=mo.
        hurt/sick   BRMi   thought=2sII
        'Cry them (feelings) out so your painful feelings/thoughts will be gone.'

6.1.4.4.3 *Affix-agreement linking with derived* pa- *causative predicates*

As noted in chapter 2, the causative *pa-* prefix adds a causer, an AGENT participant who causes a state of affairs; this AGENT must be assigned the Actor macrorole. Any of the other participants in the logical structure may be assigned to the Undergoer macrorole. This causative prefix combines with other predicative affixes to indicate which argument has been selected as PSA. Chapter 2 has many examples of this construction, so a short presentation here will suffice to illustrate the argument-affixation linking. Examples (6.44a-c) below figure 6.12 demonstrate the possibilities with the root *kan* 'eat', which takes a volitional AGENT as CAUSER.

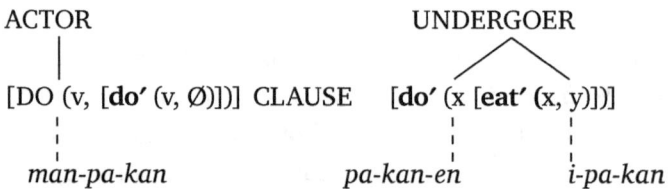

Figure 6.12. Macroroles and affixation with overt causative prefix.

(6.44) a. *Man-pa-kan=kami   si   koniho.*
            ACT-CAUS-eat=1pI   ORMi   rabbit
            'We feed (i.e., are raising) rabbits.'

b. *Pa-kan-en=yo   din   babai   agan?o.*
   CAUS-eat-UNDc=2pII RMd female first
   'Feed the female first.'

c. *Adi=kayo   i-pa-kan   din   nalogit.*
   NEG=2pII   UNDt-CAUS-eat   RMd   dirty
   'Don't feed (them) the dirty stuff.'

Manpa- is the affix that cross-references the AGENT or a reflexive AGENT-PATIENT, as in (6.45).

(6.45) *Man-pa-ila=ak   si   doktor.*
       ACT-CAUS-see=1sI ORMi doctor
       'I will have a doctor see me.'

In general, *pa...en* follows Principle B above (see figure 6.1), indexing the next-to-last argument in the LS, often a possible ACTOR—the Causee—thus the tag UNDc. Unlike an accusative language, which would tend to mark the Causee with a dative or a preposition (Van Valin 2005:235–236), Kankanaey easily assigns Undergoer macrorole status to the causee by *pa...en* affixation, as in (6.46).

(6.46) *En=ak   pa-lobwat-en   dakayo ed   Baguio.*
       go=1sI CAUS -depart-UNDc 2pIII   LOC Baguio
       'I am going to see you off (lit. cause to depart) in Baguio.'

With no other affixation, *pa-* indexes the second argument of **pred'** (x, y), which is usually the most-affected PATIENT participant, as seen in (6.47).

(6.47) *En=ak   pa-ripir   din   beey=ko.*
       go=1sI CAUS.UND-repair RMd house=1sII
       'I'm going to have my house repaired.'

The prefix *i-* with *pa-* is often used to index the content of communication or perception events, as in (6.48) and (6.49).

(6.48) I-pa-ila=k   din   litrato=yo   sin
        UNDt-CAUS-see=1sII RMd   picture=2pII   ORMd

   pamilya=k.
   family=1sII
   'I will show your picture to my family.'

(6.49) Asi=na   i-pa-dnge   Ø   sin   soldados=na.
        then=3sII UNDt-CAUS-hear   4III   ORMd   soldiers=3sII
        'Then he told (lit. caused to hear) it to his soldiers.'

With many roots, the THEME indexed by *i-pa-* is a participant that is moved in the process of the event. In example (6.50) the items to be laundered will be taken elsewhere; the affixation for laundering per se is shown in example (6.51). In (6.52) the root is 'edge' and the action of moving the vehicle to the edge is implied by *i-pa-*.

(6.50) Sokat-a(n)=m   san   bado=m   ta
        change-UNDl=2sII   DRM   clothes=2sII   so.that

   en=ak   i-laba   Ø.
   go=1s   UNDt-launder   4III
   'Change your clothes so I'll go launder them.'

(6.51) Ay   l<in>aba-a(n)=m   din   langpin   Dollika?
        Q   UNDl.P-launder<=2sII   RMd   diaper   Dollika
        'Did you launder Dollika's diapers?'

(6.52) Dalas-e(n)=k   ay   i-pa-igid   Ø   sin   danan.
        do.quickly-UND=1s   LK   UNDt-CAUS-edge   4III   ORMd   road
        'I quickly pulled over to the side of the road.'

6.1.4.5 Indexing with valency-reducing derived predicates

Several predicates have derivative affixation that reduces valency, namely recent-past, emotion-causing and reciprocal predicates.

6.1 The Privileged Syntactic Argument of the clause 279

6.1.4.5.1 Recent past clauses

The combination of CVC reduplication with the prefix *ka-* indicates recently completed activities or changes of state. This predicate is highly irregular in that it does not inflect for aspect (the CVC reduplication is part of the affix), nor does it mark its single argument with absolutive case. The single argument is an ergative pronoun or RP, as in example (6.53). If there is a definite second argument, this construction includes the indexing prefix *i-* and the Undergoer is the PSA, as in (6.54).

(6.53) Ka-dat~dateng=mi=d   labi   en   da   Pedring.
       RECENT-arrive=1pII=LOC   night   OPRM   pl   Pedring
       'We just arrived last night—Pedring and others and I.'

(6.54) Ka-i-paw~paw?it=ko   din   solat.
       RECENT-Th-send=1sII   RMd   letter
       'I just now sent off the letter.'

6.1.4.5.2 Emotion-causing predicates

When the ability to cause emotions or mental states can be attributed to something or someone, such a potential attributive predicate (introduced in section 2.3.1.3) is formed with *ka-* followed by CV reduplication of the emotion or mental-state root. Something in the nature (thus any nominal logical structure [...x...]) of the single argument has the potential to cause the mental state in necessarily unspecified EXPERIENCERS. The Logical Structure (compare to Van Valin and LaPolla 1997:402) shows that only one macrorole assignment is possible, the left-most argument as Actor. The PSA is assigned to that argument, as shown in figure 6.13 for example (6.56). The affix does not inflect for perfective marking, but the context determines the interpretation as either actual or potential, as seen in (6.55) and (6.56).

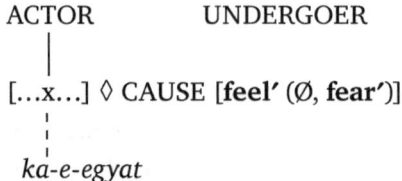

Figure 6.13. Macrorole assignment and *kaCV*-indexing for state-causing predicates.

(6.55) *Ka.si~siyek   di   in-yat=da   ay*
        CAUS.-amuse   RMi   UNDt.P-way=3pII   LK

naN-(s)ong~songbat   sin   questions.
ANTI-CVC-answer   ORMd   questions
'The way they were answering the questions was funny (caused amused feelings).'

(6.56) *Baken   koma   ka.e~egyat   di   pese.*
        NEG   IRR   CAUS.fear   RMi   death
'Death should not be scary (cause fear).'

6.1.4.5.3 Reciprocal activities and states

Adding the prefix *ʔasi-* to a root that inherently takes two participants creates a predicate in whose logical structure the x and y arguments are simultaneously reciprocal. The prefix *ʔasi-* allows both Actors to be merged into one macrorole, leaving the undergoers of the action implicit. The Actor-indexing affix *man-* indexes the plural argument, as in figure 6.14. Examples (6.57) and (6.58) also show this indexing.

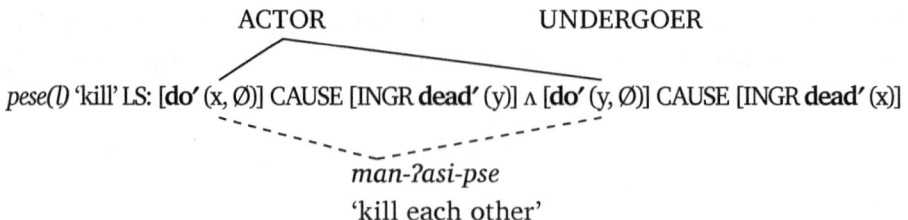

Figure 6.14. Reciprocal macrorole assignment and indexing.

6.1 The Privileged Syntactic Argument of the clause   281

(6.57) Man-ʔasi-dongpal=da   et   na-boong   din   ispiko
        ACT-RECIP-collide=3pI   and   UNDs.P-shatter   RMd   glass

        =n di   taxi.
        BRMi   taxi
        'They crashed into each other and the taxi's windshield was shattered.'

(6.58) Man-asi-ammo=kayo.
        ACT-RECIP-know=2pI
        'Get to know each other (e.g., introduce yourselves).'

The infix <in> with man- (incidentally homophonous with perfective aspect in Undergoer voices) indicates a type of reciprocal state with only one plural argument, as in (6.59) and (6.60).

(6.59) Man-k<in>awʔit   din   kawal.
        ACT-RECIP-link   RMd   chain
        'Chain (links) are linked to each other.'

(6.60) Man<in>ammo=kayo   baw.
        ACT-RECIP-knkow=2pI   EVID
        'You know each other (already) I see.'

6.1.4.6 Indexing with voice alternations that reduce syntactic transitivity

There are four voice alternations in Kankanaey that reduce the syntactic transitivity of a predicate that has two or more arguments in its logical structure. Antipassive voice selects the Actor as PSA in a transitive clause. Passive voice suppresses the Actor of a transitive predicate. Two other Actor-suppressing affixations are used in special situations.

6.1.4.6.1 Antipassive voice

As pointed out in section 6.1.4.2.3, some Kankanaey predicates may have more than one argument position in their logical structure, but due to the unavailability of a second argument for macrorole assignment they are syntactically intransitive. Undergoer voices are not appropriate when the goal or trajectory of the action has low identifiability or affectedness. Cooreman (1994:51) notes that the "degree of difficulty with which an effect stemming from an activity by A on an identifiable O can be recognized" influences the use of the "semantic/pragmatic antipassive." In such situations, Kankanaey selects the single Actor macrorole as PSA and the non-Actor argument is given oblique status. This modulation may qualify the Actor voice as a semantic/pragmatic antipassive, as has been suggested for Sama (Van Valin and LaPolla 1997:301), but in this study the macrorole assignment principles outlined in figure 6.1 provide for the Actor to be given default PSA status for Activity predicates in the *Aktionsart* classification with no marked status as an antipassive.

There are, however, situations where both the Actor and Undergoer macroroles are linked to identifiable and affected arguments in the logical structure, but other factors intervene, forcing the Actor to be selected as PSA. The Undergoer is given oblique argument marking, but maintains its definite and wholly-affected interpretation. This non-default choice of PSA, and the oblique marking of the Undergoer-assigned second argument creates a typical antipassive voice, both PSA-modulation and argument-modulation being evidenced.

Special antipassive affixation specifies semantic details regarding one of the arguments. Situations calling for the antipassive voice include precipitate Actors using *ka-*, abilitative (non-agentive) Actors using *maka-*, Actors who are lower in inherent lexical content than the Undergoer, and specific Undergoers that are only partially affected, both of these last two using <*om*>.

6.1.4.6.1.1 Precipitate Actors

When the Actor is presented as acting with haste, an action root is affixed with *ka-*, an indexing that gives the Actor PSA status. This affix is very important in stories, almost invariably marking at least one action at the peak of the narrative. Intransitive predicates may be formed with *ka-* 'IMM(ediate)' as in (6.61), but *ka-* can also be used for transitive predicates, creating an antipassive-voice predicate. The definite PATIENT argument is given definite but oblique marking, as in (6.62), with no loss of referentiality or affectedness. If a THEME argument that would normally be indexed with *i-* is the affected argument, that affix is retained to flag its role, but the Actor still takes the PSA assignment, as in (6.63).

(6.61) Et   doy   etay   ka-sigbo,   en=(n)a   pay
       and   DEM3V   PART   IMM-dive   go=3sII   PART

       kano=n   ila-(e)n   Ø.
       HSY=DISP   see.UND   4III
       'And there he just dove right in, he went to see (what had happened).'

(6.62) Ka-ladkiking=ak   sin   malita=k   yan   en=ak
       IMM-pick.up=1sI   ORMd   suitcase=1sII and   go=1sI

       mai-abat   en   daida.
       UNDts-meet   OPRM   3pIII
       'I snatched up my suitcase and went to be taken to meet up with them.'

(6.63) Ka-i-payag   Ø   sin   sokod=na   yan
       IMM-Th-set.down   3sI   ORMd   staff=3sII   and

       ka-dama   Ø   sin   sana   ay   banig   Nabulay.
       IMM-attack   3sI   ORM   DEM2V   LK   ghost   Nabulay
       'He just dropped his walking stick and attacked that ghost of Nabulay.'

6.1.4.6.1.2 Abilitative Actors

Sometimes an Actor argument is non-agentive in the sense that the situation is fortuitous rather than due to the intent of the Actor. Sometimes an Actor is presented as simply capable of doing something. Without an argument assigned as the Actor macrorole, the transitive Undergoer voices are not available. The Actor-indexing *maka-* (ACT.ABIL) prefix licenses a non-agentive Actor macrorole, and gives it PSA status.

This PSA may be the single direct argument, as in (6.64). If another participant is affected and specific, it has Undergoer macrorole status, but is given definite oblique marking to maintain its specificity. If the effect of the action involves a change of location, the THEME role index *i-* co-occurs with *maka-*. Thus, in the second clause of (6.65), the girl Maligtay is very clearly the Undergoer of the predicate *goyod* 'pull on, drag', but the negative antipassive presents the Actor as unfortuitous or incapable. In (6.66) the predicate *baga* 'tell' would take *i-* in the default Undergoer-voice, but in this instance of expressing inability, an antipassive is required and the content of the 'telling' is given definite oblique marking. Discourse pragmatics affects the choice to use this antipassive. Many instances of this construction are used with the negative, telling why something didn't happen.

(6.64) *Maka-dan=ak   si   at?atik.*
       ACT.ABIL-walk=1sI ORMi   few
       'I'm able to walk a little bit.' (after surgery)

(6.65) *Man-eset   si   Maligtay   et   adi*
       ACT-do.well   PRM   Maligtay   and   NEG

       maka?i-goyod   si   Mrs   Aglo.
       ACT.ABIL.Th-drag PRM   Mrs   Aglo
       'Maligtay (hung on) tight and Mrs. Aglo could not pull her away.'

(6.66) *Adi=ak   maka?i-baga   isnan   iyaman=ko*
       NEG=1sI   ACT.ABIL.Th-tell ODRM   thanks=1sII

       en   dakayo.
       OPRM   2pIII
       'I cannot express this my gratitude to you all.'

6.1.4.6.1.3 Actors and Undergoers in conflict with the lexical content hierarchy

Silverstein (1976:113) proposed an "inherent lexical content" hierarchy, in which participants or entities are ordered as follows:

1st Person > 2nd > 3rd > human > animate > inanimate

Sometimes there are situations where the trajectory of effect points in the opposite direction from this hierarchy, such that a lower-ranked participant has an effect on a higher-ranked entity. Kankanaey predicates prefer to code this inversion with the affix <om>, which creates an Actor-indexed predicate with its single argument the lower-ranked participant no matter what the state of affairs may be. An Undergoer participant with higher lexical content is obligatorily implied but omitted,[2] a different sort of argument-modulation than other antipassive constructions. Depending on the Actor's place in the hierarchy, the Undergoer may be an unidentified animate entity or the very specific first or second person. The affix is tagged 'ACT' because it cross-references the left-most participant in the logical structure of the predicate; the tag '(LH)' (for the influence of the lexical content hierarchy) identifies this use of <om>. As with other antipassive affixes, a THEME-role Undergoer is acknowledged with the i- prefix. This is seen in (6.67) where the action of 'governing' is predicated of an inanimate concept toward humans.

(6.67) Mo ?<om>i-turay din aklong si
if ACT(LH)-Th-govern RMd desire ORMi

kina-baknang...
NOM-rich
'When/If the desire for wealth drives a person/people....'

The only possible implied participant in (6.68) and (6.69) is first person, as reflected in the English translations. In (6.70) the dog's propensity is to bite people; cats or other animates are not in mind.

(6.68) Ay ?<om>ayag=ka?
Q ACT(LH)-call=2sI
'Are you calling me?'

---

[2] In Iloko, a different strategy (agent neutralization) is employed in these situations. The higher-agency participant pronoun is omitted in transitive constructions, e.g., "the first person singular ergative enclitic…cannot appear before the second person singular absolutive" (Rubino 2005:334).

(6.69) Sigolo   anggay   ay   l<om>iw?an   si   da   Dal
        probably   already LK   ACT(LH)-forget   PRM   pl   Dal

        en   Lindi   tan   ma-bayag   ay
        OPRM   Lindi   because   UNDs-long.time   LK

        adi=da   <om>il-ila.
        NEG=3pI   ACT(LH)-PROG-see
        'Dal and Lindi have probably already forgotten (me/us) because it's been a long time since they've been seeing (me/us).'

(6.70) K<om>at   din aso!
        ACT(LH)=bite RM   dog
        '(Careful!) The dog bites (people/you)!'

The potential causative state predicates shown in figure 6.13 may also be expressed with this use of <om> when inanimate entities affect animate entities just from their own inherent properties. These predicates differ from the *kaCV-* marked predicates in that the <om> marked predicates are generally built from physical-state roots while *kaCV-* marked predicates are generally built from emotion-state roots and are not sensitive to the lexical content hierarchy.

Examples (6.71)–(6.73) show this affix with physical state roots. Figure 6.15 illustrates the predicate in (6.72). This use of <om> cannot assert any particular event, but rather a potential effect.

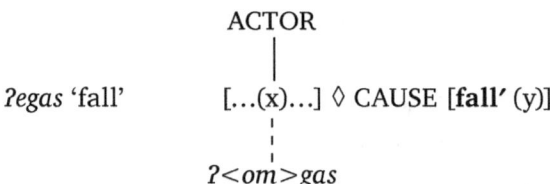

Figure 6.15. Macrorole assignment and affixation related to the Lexical Content Hierarchy.

6.1 *The Privileged Syntactic Argument of the clause* 287

(6.71) *?<om>olaw   di   samdak.*
ACT(LH)-dizzy RMi mushroom
'Mushrooms cause dizziness.'

(6.72) *?<om>gas   sa!*
ACT(LH)-fall DEM2I
'You'll fall there!! (It is slippery or steep and will cause you to fall.)'

(6.73) *B<om>eteng   san   San Miguel.*
ACT(LH)-drunk DRM San Miguel
'That San Miguel (beer) is intoxicating/can make one drunk.'

The antipassive *<om>* can also co-occur with the overt causative *i-pa-*, shown in (6.74), to index inanimate CAUSERS affecting unspecified animate entities.

(6.74) *Lawa   di   sobra   ay   kapi,*
bad RMi too.much LK coffee

<om>i-pa-ilas   Ø.
ACT(LH).Th-CAUS-insomnia 4I
'Too much coffee is bad, it causes insomnia.'

Pragmatic considerations underlie the choice of this affix, for example, as a softening device in hortatory discourse. Thus, in example (6.67) above, the construction allows an ambiguous implication for the participants who are unflatteringly accused of being driven by their economic desires. In (6.75) the speaker's son has quit school to help her to support the family; she presents his role as helper as more salient than her implied role as the person being helped.

(6.75) *ta   t<om>olong   Ø   ay   man-anap   si*
so.that ACT-help 3sI LK ACT-search ORMi

pan-biyag=mi
NOM-life=1pII
'so that he will help me make our living'

Inversion of the inherent lexical content hierarchy does not necessarily trigger the use of <om>. In example (6.76) the affected participant has a salient semantic role, a directional locus. In this case, the BENEFICIARY is given explicit reference rather than being implied; it has been assigned as the PSA with the unmarked Undergoer voice rather than with <om>. In (6.77) the blended pronoun *daka* (3sII.2sI) codes the same marked inversion instead of using <om>.

(6.76) *I-amag-a(n)=m   kod   sak?en   si   reference=ko.*
       UNDd. make=2sII   please   1sIII   ORM   reference=1sII
       'Please write (lit. make) (for) me a [character] reference.'

(6.77) *Bangon-en=daka   ay   masapa.*
       get.up-UND=3sII.2sI   LK   early
       'It (the rooster) will get you up early.'

As noted in chapter 2 (section 2.2.7.2), when an Undergoer is only partially affected, the Actor is cross-referenced with <om_2> and the Undergoer is given definite oblique marking, as in (6.78) (see also example (2.102) in chapter 2).

(6.78) *G<om>isgis   ka   sin   kawayan.*
       ANTI-split   2sI   ORMd   bamboo
       'Split some of the bamboo.'

6.1.4.6.2 *Passive voice with* ma-

Passive voice in Kankanaey does not change the choice of argument for PSA status; the Undergoer of a two-argument predicate is still chosen. Rather, it shows argument-modulation by blocking any agentive Actor. The passive voice creates an intransitive state predicate by adding the prefix *ma-* (tagged 's' (state)) to other Undergoer-voice affixation. Passive voice is often used on pragmatic grounds because it reflects marked semantic features—the interest of the speaker is only in the effect upon the Undergoer and the erstwhile Actor is suppressed.

The passive *ma-* co-occurs with the other basic Undergoer-indexing affixes, thus *ma-i, ma...an,* and *ma-i...an.* The PATIENT-marking suffix *-en* is deleted with *ma-*, however, creating some ambiguity between simple states and passive states. As with the Undergoer voices described above, any salient non-Actor participant in a state of affairs may be assigned the Undergoer macrorole in passive voice.

The co-occurrence of *ma-* with other Undergoer-voice affixes was introduced in chapter 2. The examples here may suffice to show the Actor as irrelevant, unknown, or non-specific, as in example (6.79), with the affix *na...an* indexing a static-locus Undergoer and the 'teacher' argument the THEME, not the EFFECTOR. In the situation denoted by example (6.80), the passive predicate presents the speaker as the source from which the 'crying' event occurred; her role as the Actor is not alluded to, and is much less relevant than her affectedness.

(6.79)   *Na-tapi-an=kami=s   esay   mistala   sin*
         UNDls-add<=1pI=ORMi   one   teacher   ORMd

   Central.
   Central
   'We've had another teacher added to our ranks at Central (lit. we were added-to with one teacher).'

(6.80)   *Ma?i-oga-an=ak   yan   mansakit   din   toktok=ko.*
         UNDds-cry<=1sI   and   hurt   RMd   head=1sII
   'I'm all cried out and now I have a headache.'

There is an exception to the strong exclusion of an Actor argument. A natural cause may be indicated as an oblique argument, as in examples (6.81) and (6.82), but no volition can be attributed to it.

(6.81)   *Na-sawad=ak   sin   tolo   ay   pewek.*
         UNDs-block=1sI   ORMd   three   LK   typhoons
   'I was blocked by the three (back-to-back) typhoons.'

(6.82) Na-baen-an=ka=s   gayang.
        UNDls-warn.omen>=2sI=ORMi crow
        'You were warned by a crow.'

6.1.4.6.3 ma- with movement roots

It was noted in section 6.1.4.2.2 that most movement predicates are formed with the moving entity as Actor. A small subclass of motion roots arbitrarily take *ma-* to cross-reference the participant as Undergoer (UNDm), as in examples (6.83) and (6.84). This construction uses the prefix normally used on passives, perhaps suggesting reflexive/self-affecting movement, because the single participant of motion predicates is both EFFECTOR and THEME. This small group of roots denies macrorole status to the single participant as Actor, and indexes the (co-referential) Undergoer with passive morphology. This may be structurally analogous to a passive version of the "false reflexives" (Van Valin and LaPolla, 393–394) on motion verbs observed in some Australian languages[3] in which valency reduction by affixation creates an intransitive predicate cross-referencing one or the other of two co-referential arguments.

(6.83) ...mo   <om>ingpis   ono   ma-labas   din   liboo.
        when   UNDm.thin   or   UNDm-pass.by   RMd   cloud
        '...when the cloud dissipates or passes by.'

(6.84) Kanan=(n)a   kano   =s di,   yan   dowan=et
        say=3sII   HSY   DEM3IV   and   while=PART

        ma-limos   Ø.
        UNDm-leave.home   3sI
        'He reportedly said that while departing.'

---

[3] Heath (1979:411) mentions an example that "involves *garugaja-* 'to pass by', here in the false Reflexive sense 'to go past'....The infrequent occurrence of the False Reflexive and its tendency to occur with a small set of stems closely fit the pattern set by similar False Reflexives in other Australian languages which I have examined."

6.1 The Privileged Syntactic Argument of the clause 291

6.1.4.6.4 Impersonal constructions

Another argument-modulating voice construction is formed with the default Undergoer-voice indexing, but the Actor macrorole is suppressed by omission, and interpreted as nonreferential and not salient. The predicate thus retains its dynamic force as expressing an action or event rather than a passive state. This construction is common in procedural and hortatory texts, as in (6.85), and may play a mitigating role presenting the Actors as self-evident and indirect, as in (6.86).

(6.85) *Sitsit-an   din   danom.*
  drain-UNDl   RMd   water
  'Drain out the water (general instructions regarding fishpond maintenance).'

(6.86) *Siyat   ikgot-an   di   i-lagbo-an.*
  must   store-UNDl   RMi   UNDd-salary<
  'Earnings should be stored up (advice to newlyweds).'

6.1.4.7 Indexing with valency-maintaining affixation

6.1.4.7.1 Applicative affixation to license variable Undergoer assignment

The circumfix *i-...-an* has been shown in earlier examples as the indexing affix for directional-locus required arguments such as RECIPIENTS. As an applicative *i-...-an* can cross-reference other directional-type arguments that are not required, such as the BENEFICIARIES in (6.87) and (6.88). The non-specific THEMES are given indefinite oblique marking.

(6.87) *I-anap-an=yo   kod   din   i~iyogtan=yo*
  UNDd-search<=2pII   please   RMd   pl-yng.sib=2pII

  si   pan-obla-an=da.
  ORMi   NOM-work<=3pII
  'Please look on behalf of your younger siblings for a place for them to work.'

(6.88) *I-lako-a(n)=m   kod   sak?en   si   arina   si*
       UNDd-buy<=2sII please   1sIII   ORMi   flour   ORMi

   bigat.
   next-day
   'Please buy me some flour tomorrow.'

6.1.4.7.2 Associative affixation

The prefix *maki-* agrees with a single participant who is joining other participants (thus tagged ASSOC). In example (6.89) the Actor is presented as joining or associating with others in the specified activity, often activities typically done as a group. In (6.90) the speaker and probably others are already planning a trip, so the hearer would be joining them. In (6.91) it is assumed that wage-earners work with others. Usually, it is Actors who join in with activities but Undergoers that join other entities may also be indexed with *maki-*, as in example (6.92).

(6.89) *Maki-mis~misa=ak   si   Domingo.*
       ASSOC-CVC-mass=1sI ORMi   Sunday
       'I am going to Mass on Sundays.'

(6.90) *Ay   maki-ali=ka?*
       Q   ASSOC-come=2sI
       'Are you coming along?'

(6.91) *Di   nemnem=na   yan   maki-lagbo   Ø   kano.*
       RMi   thought=3sII   PART   ASSOC-wage   3sI   HSY
       'His idea, he says he will get a job (lit. join-earn.wage).'

(6.92) *Adi=kayo   kamas-an   Ø   tan*
       NEG=2pI   weed.ricefield-UNDl   4III   because

   maki-gabot   din   pagey.
   ASSOC-pull.out   RMd   rice
   'Don't weed it (i.e., field) because the rice plants will (be) pulled out along with (the weeds).'

6.1 The Privileged Syntactic Argument of the clause 293

Oblique RPs in clauses with *maki-* affixed predicates may refer to the other participants in the shared activity, as in (6.93), or an Undergoer argument, as in (6.94) and (6.95), where the Actor-indexed predicate forms an antipassive-voice construction.

(6.93) *Deda=kayo ay maki-be?~be?ey en am~ama=yo.*
still=2pI LK ASSOC-CVC-house OPRM CVC-father=2pII
'You guys are still living in with your parents.'

(6.94) *Maki-tawid din anak di bag?en sin*
ASSOC-inherit RMd child BRMi slave ORMd

kinabaknang di among=na.
NOM-rich BRMi boss=3sII
'The slave's children will join (others) in inheriting his boss's wealth.'

(6.95) *Est-e(n)=m ay maki-ad~adal sin*
do.well-UND=2sII LK ASSOC-CVC-study ORMd

kali=n Diyos.
word=BPRM God
'Diligently study (in class) the words of God.'

With a few roots, such as *ngalat* 'converse' and *asawa* 'spouse', *maki-* does not indicate joining in an already-begun activity, but in a reciprocal activity, thus, 'chat with' and 'marry'. Example (6.96) shows a reciprocal interpretation of an associative cross-reference.

(6.96) *Mo maki-gobat=kayo sin Japon, pesl-en=daka.*
if ASSOC-war=2pI ORMd Japanese kill-UND=3II.2sI
'If you join in war with Japan, they will kill you.'

6.1.4.7.3 Reflexives

In sections 6.1.4.4.1 and 6.1.4.6.3 self-affecting movements were seen to form implied reflexive constructions. Other reflexive constructions require an overt RP referring to the Actor's *awak* 'body'. In (6.97) this phrase is indexed by the *i*-, and in (6.98) it is the oblique Undergoer argument of the antipassive *ka*-affixed predicate.

(6.97) *I-saad=na din awak=na ay pangolo.*
UNDt-establish=3sII RMd body=3sII LK leader
'He sets himself up as leader.'

(6.98) *Ka-pese Ø abe sin awak=na sin*
IMMED-kill 3sI PART ORMd body-3sII ORMd

bokod=na ay kampilan.
own=3sII LK sword
'He suddenly killed himself too with his own sword.'

6.2 Privileged Syntactic Arguments of other constructions

As noted above, the PSA of a clause may be signaled by various coding properties. Privileged syntactic arguments also exhibit privileged behaviors: a privileged argument may serve as the controller of other constructions such as reflexive antecedence or pivot interpretation. A privileged argument may also serve as a pivot, the missing argument in a construction. The following sections cover controllers and pivots in several constructions in Kankanaey, especially noting the use of a structural antipassive construction, the nonfinite predicate indexed with the prefix *maN-*.

6.2.1 Control of reflexive antecedence

Examples (6.99) and (6.100), repeated from (6.97) and (6.98) above, with co-reference marked, show that in overt reflexive clauses the possessive pronoun of the reflexive RP is co-referential with the Actor argument. The Actor is a semantic controller, as may be seen in (6.99), where the Actor is the ergative argument, and in (6.100) it is the absolutive argument in the clause.

6.2 Privileged Syntactic Arguments of other constructions 295

(6.99) *In-saad=na$_i$*   *din*   *awak=na$_i$*   *ay*   *pangolo.*
       UNDt-establish=3sII RMd   body=3sII   LK   leader
       'He set himself up as leader.'

(6.100) *Ka-pese*   *Ø$_i$*   *abe*   *sin*   *awak=na$_i$*   *sin*
        IMMED-kill   3sI   PART   ORMd   body-3sII   ORMd

bokod=na   *ay*   *kampilan.*
own=3sII   LK   sword
'He suddenly killed himself with his own sword.'

6.2.2 Pivot with left-displaced pronominal arguments

Some modals, adverbs, and conjunctions displace core argument personal pronouns to a pre-nuclear position, as was explained in chapter 3. The pivot for this displacing construction is syntactic, following an accusative pattern: S and A pronouns are displaced. Table 6.4 below repeats the personal pronouns chart from table 6.1 with the accusative pattern of displacement shown in the heading. 3sI and 4I are not included, because when 3s is explicit (*sisya*) it is not clitic, and the null forms of 3s and 4 cannot be proven to be clitic.

Table 6.4. Personal pronoun displacement patterns

pronoun class	Displace		Do not displace
	I (S)	II (A)	III (U)
1s	=ak	=ko	sak?en
1p	=kami	=mi	dakami
2s	=ka	=mo	sik?a
2p	=kayo	=yo	dakayo
1+2	=ta	=ta	PRM + daita
1+2p	=tako	=tako	PRM + datako
3p	=da	=da	PRM + daida
3s, 4		=na	
1sII.2sI	=naka		
3s/pII.2sI	=daka		

The blended pronouns also participate in displacement constructions, the only instance of an absolutive Undergoer argument in the pre-nuclear position, as seen in (6.101).

(6.101) Awni   ta   asi=naka   pa-bela-en   abe.
       wait.a.bit   so   then=1sII.2sI   CAUS-go.out-UND   also
       'Wait a bit and then I'll let you go out too.'

6.2.3 Controller and pivot interpretation in core junctures

Chapter 5 covered core junctures in detail; this section summarizes the evidence for the PSA functions in these constructions. The controller in coordinate core junctures controls the co-reference of the pivot (shared argument missing from the second core). This PSA is semantic as it may be the single argument, the transitive actor, or the transitive undergoer, depending on the matrix predicate. The controller is indicated as the first term in the controller-pivot equations, noted after examples (6.102) to (6.107).

6.2 Privileged Syntactic Arguments of other constructions 297

When the controller of co-reference in a coordinate core juncture is the single argument of an emotional state predicate, the pivot is either the single argument of the next clause or the transitive actor. Examples (6.102) and (6.103) demonstrate the possibilities for transitive actors, either as the ergative actor of an Undergoer-voice predicate or as the indexed transitive actor of a structural antipassive predicate, as introduced in chapter 5.

(6.102) *Sa.pay.koma.ta na-ragsak=kayo ay datng-an*
hopefully UNDs.P-happy=2pI LK arrive-UND1

nan solat=ko. $S=A_T$
DRM letter=1sII
'Hopefully you are happy to receive/come upon (this) my letter.'

(6.103) *Ma-bain=ak ay manodsod (maN-sodsod).* $S=A_{ANTI}$
UNDs-shame=1sI LK ANTI-tell.negative
'I'm embarrassed to give the bad news.'

When the controller is the transitive actor of the matrix core, the pivot is only restricted to being a direct argument of the second core, as seen in the second term in the notation of co-referential equations. (The fuller list of examples is in chapter 5.) Examples (6.104) and (6.105) repeated from chapter 5 are typical.

(6.104) *Laydelaydek ay mangila=d*
CVCCV~layad-en=ko maN-ila=ed
INTENS-like-UND=1sII LK ANTI.see=LOC

Baguio. $A_T=A_{ANTI}$
Baguio
'I'd just love to see Baguio (City).'

(6.105) *Ni-layad   nina   ay   nakay   ay   mai-ponpon*
　　　　UND.P-want   DEM1II   LK   old.man   LK   UNDts-bury

　　　　si   kinakristiyano.　　　　　　　　　　　　　$A_T = S_U$
　　　　ORMi   Christianity
　　　　'This old man wanted to be buried Christian-style.'

The free variation between the two possible affixations for transitive actor pivots (either the structural antipassive or an Undergoer voice) raises the question of which was the previous syntactic norm. It may be that allowing the Undergoer voice is a newer innovation still in process, an incomplete adoption (or "co-opting" in Cooreman's (1994) term). On the other hand, perhaps the antipassive is the construction growing in favor.

Undergoer-control constructions are those in which the first core is transitive and its Undergoer is the argument that is shared with the second core. In 6.106), 1sIII is the Undergoer of the verb 'persuade', and is coreferent with the single argument of 'be joined' in the second core. Note that there is no overt 1s pronoun in the second core; it is the omitted pivot in this construction. Unlike Actor-control constructions, the pivot in Undergoer-control constructions is restricted to the argument indexed on the second predicate, and any transitive Actor pivot is required to be marked by the antipassive *maN-*, as the ungrammaticality of (6.107b) attests.

(6.106)　*<In>awis=na=s   sak?en   ay   mai-tapi*
　　　　UND.P-persuade=3sII=PRM   1sIII   LK   UNDts-join

　　　　sin   obla=da.　　　　　　　　　　　　　　　$U_T = S_U$
　　　　ORMd   work=3pII
　　　　'He persuaded me to join (lit. be joined) in their work.'

(6.107) a.　*Tolong-a(n)=m sak?en   ay   en   mang-anap*
　　　　　 help-UND1=2sII   1sIII   LK   go   ANTI-search

　　　　　 sin   antokos=ko.　　　　　　　　　　　$U_T = A_{ANTI}$
　　　　　 ORMd   glasses=1sII
　　　　　 'Please help me go look for my glasses.'

b. *Tolong-a(n)=m   sak?en   ay en   anap-en
   help-UND1=2sII   1sIII   LK go   UND-search

   din   antokos=ko. $U_T \neq A_T$
   RMd   glasses=1sII

6.2.4 Pivot in nominalization

6.2.4.1 Absolutive-pivot nominalization

Any predicate can be nominalized by placing it in a reference phrase nucleus, preceded by an RM. The pivot of nominalization is the absolutive argument of the predicate, whether there is indexing affixation or not. This argument is omitted and is the entity to which the construction refers. Examples (6.108) to (6.112) show the nominalization (in brackets) of intransitive and transitive predicates. The free translations indicate the semantic role of the pivot as suggested by the affixation on the nominalized predicate.

(6.108) *Man-ayag   [da din   man-ot~oto]   ay   mang-(k)an.*
        ACT-invite   pl RMd   ACT-CVC-cook   LK   ACT-eat
        'The ones (EFFECTORS) cooking called (for people) to eat.'

(6.109) *Mo   [din   ma-lames]   yan   ma-sait   Ø.*
        as.for   RMd   ATT-fat   PART   ATT-tasty 4I
        'As for the fat ones (ATTRIBUTANTs), they are tasty.'

(6.110) *Est-en=da   [din   ma-kan].*
        do.well-UND=3pII   RMd   UNDs-eat
        'They take care with the stuff (PATIENTS) to be eaten (i.e., the food).'

(6.111) Nan-otang=ak   [si   in-dawat=ko   sin
       ACT.P-debt=1sI   ORMi   UNDt.P-give=1sII   ORMd

   odom   ay   man-a~agag].
   other   LK   ACT-CV-hurry
   'I went into debt for something (THEME) I gave to the others who were in a hurry.'

(6.112) Adi   in-taoli   da   Amyan   [din
       NEG   UNDt.P-give   pl   Amyan   RMd

   in-pa-lako=k   en   daida].
   UNDt.P-CAUS-buy=1sII   OPRM   3pIII
   'Amyan's group did not return the thing (THEME) I had asked/given them to sell (e.g., books).'

6.2.4.2 Non-absolutive nominalization

A different situation arises when a predicate is nominalized to refer to a participant that is not indexed by the voice affix. Transitive actors are not indexed on the predicate in Undergoer voices, nor are adjunct phrases. Nominalizing a transitive actor requires the structural antipassive affix *maN-*. A time or place is indexed by adding the suffix *-an* to other affixation, creating nominalizing affixation.

6.2.4.2.1 Nominalizing transitive actors

A nominalized predicate uses the affix *maN-* to refer to the actor argument of a transitive predicate in the nucleus of a reference phrase. Example (6.113) compares the nominalization of the (a) Undergoer and (b) Actor from a basic clause. Examples (6.114) and (6.115) show other nominalized transitive actors. As with antipassive-voice predicates, if the second participant is a THEME, it is also indexed on the predicate with the prefix *i-*, acknowledging its erstwhile macrorole availability. Examples (6.116) and (6.117) have this prefix. The free translation of some of these examples uses a relative pronoun in English to avoid excessive awkwardness.

6.2 Privileged Syntactic Arguments of other constructions

(6.113) K<in>at   di   aso   din   anak=ko.
       bite-UND.P   BRMi   dog   RMd   child=1sII
       'A dog bit my kid.'

   a. din   k<in>at   di   aso
       RMd   bite-UND.P   BRMi   dog
       'the one (PATIENT) the dog bit'

   b. din   nang-(k)at   sin   anak=ko
       RMd   ANTI-bite   ORMd   child=1sII
       'the one (EFFECTOR that) bit my kid'

(6.114) Sisya   [din   mang-ay~ayoan   sin   mansakit].
        3sIII   RMd   ANTI-CVC-care.for   ORMd   sick.one
        'He is the one (EFFECTOR) caring for the sick one.'

(6.115) <Om>ad?ado   koma   [di   mang-onod   sin   siged
        UNDm-many   PART   RMi   ANTI-follow   ORMd   good

        ay danan].
        LK path
        'The ones (who) follow the good way will hopefully become many.'

(6.116) [din   nang-i-la~lamsit   en   sak?en]
        RMd   ACT-Th-CV-deceive   OPRM   1sIII
        'the ones (EFFECTORs who) had deceived me'

(6.117) Pag=na=n   dad?at-en   Ø   [sin
        then=3sII=DISP   relate-UND   4I   ORMd

        nang-i-baa   en   sisya].
        ANTI-Th-send.on.errand   OPRM   3sIII
        'Then he related it to the one (EFFECTOR who) had sent him on the errand.'

Antipassive nominalization in equative clauses (with RP-RP structure) often specifies the role of a particular person. This is a very common construction in prayers and wishes—"Would you please be the one to do such-and-such"—rather than the more direct "Please do such-and-such," as in (6.118). This construction is also fairly common in plot development as participants are identified to fill particular topical roles. Example (6.119) shows this antipassive nominalization on the last word. Note that the class III pronoun is in the nucleus of this narrow-focus equative clause.

(6.118) *Sapay.koma.ta* si   *Apo Diyos*   di   *mamindisyon*
                                                        maN-bindisyon
         wish   PRM   Lord God   RMi   ANTI-bless

        sin   *obla=tako.*
        ORMd   work=1+2pII
        'May the Lord God bless (lit. be the one to bless) our work.'

(6.119) "*En=ka*   *i-tining*   *mo*   *na-pas?od-an*   *din*
         go=2sI   UNDt-peek.at   if   UNDls-take.in<   RMd

        teytey   *di*   *beey=mi,"*   *kana-(e)n=da*   *et*
        ladder   BRMi   house=1pII   say-UND=3pII   and

        si   *sak?en*   *di*   *en*   *nang-i-tining.*
        PRM   1sIII   RMi   go   NTI-Th-peek.at
        '"Go peek (and see) whether the ladder to our house has been taken in (i.e., they have left)," they said, and the one who went to peek at it was me.'

6.2.4.2.2 Nominalizing places and times

When a predicate is in the nucleus of a reference phrase, it can refer to its time or location or the nature of its activity by means of nominalizing affixation. The affix is usually the suffix *-an* in conjunction with the nominalizing *pan-/nan-* or *paN-/naN-* with perception and action roots (bracketed) in (6.120) to (6.122). Note that with perfective aspect this nominalizing prefix

6.2 Privileged Syntactic Arguments of other constructions 303

is homophonous with the perfective structural antipassive. With state roots, *ma-/na* co-occurs with the suffix *-an*, as in (6.123). This affixation is analyzed as a circumfix, with (P) marking perfective aspect when applicable; the tag NOM with 's' indicates the state-related nominalizing affix.

(6.120) *Mabalin   ay   solat-a(n)=m   si   kadwa=m*
       possible   LK   write-UNDl=2sII   PRM   spouse=2sII

      [sin   pan-ob-obla-an=(n)a].
      ORMd   NOM-CVC-work<=3sII
      'It's possible for you to write to your husband at his place of working.'

(6.121) *Nan-ko~koyog=da   inganas   [si*
       ACT-CV-accompany=3pI   until   ORMi

      nan-soko-an   din   Japon].
      NOM.P-surrender<   BRMd   Japanese
      'They all stayed together until the (time of) surrender of the Japanese.'

(6.122) *Ed   Burnham   [di   tolag-an   ay*
       LOC   Burnham   RMi   agree-UNDl   LK

      pan-asi-ila-an=mi].
      NOM-RECIP-see<=1pII
      'At Burnham (Park) was where it was agreed that we'd meet each other.'

(6.123) *S<inm>adot   Ø   [sin   na-tey-an   tatang=na].*
       UNDm-sad   3sI   ORMd   NOMs.P.-die<   father=3sII
      'He got depressed when his dad died (time/event of his father's death).'

6.2.4.2.3 Nominalizing the broad concept

The time/place affixation can index a generalized conception of the predicate as a state or event, as in (6.124), or as the means of its coming about, as in (6.125). The widespread use of nominalized forms, especially in written texts, is exemplified in 6.126).

(6.124) *Ad~ad?ado [di na-abak-a(n)=k] mo [din*
CVC-many RMi NOMs.P-defeat<=1sII than RMd

nang-abak-a(n)=k].
NOM.P-defeat<=1sII
'I had more events of losing than of winning.' (Note: *abak* as a state indicates losing while *abak* as an activity indicates winning.)

(6.125) *Sa [=y nang-ammo-a(n)=k sin address=yo].*
DEM2I=RMi NOM.P-know<=1sII ORMd address=2pII
'That's how I found out your address.'

(6.126) *Iwed [di ma-dteng-a(n)=k [si*
NEGEXIS RMi NOMs-arrive<=1sII ORMi

nan-kolang-an] [din nai-olog-an=(n)a]].
NOM.P-lack< BRMd NOMs.Th-meaning<=4sII
'I didn't find any problems with the translation (lit. there was nothing I came across that was a lack of its translation).'

6.2.4.2.4 Nominalization in WH-question formation

WH-questions are NP-NP equative clauses in Kankanaey. The first NP is the interrogative pronoun, the second may have a nominalized predicate with agreement to the questioned NP. Thus, the absolutive argument is the pivot in forming questions on arguments of a predicate. Example (6.127) shows three nominalized predicates with predicating affixation indexing the pivot that is co-referential with the question word.

6.2 *Privileged Syntactic Arguments of other constructions* 305

(6.127) *Sino   di   ma-tey?*   *Sino   di   i-dawat=na?*
        who   RMi   UNDs-die   what   RMi   UNDt-give=3sII
        'Who will die?'   'What will he give?'

        Sino   di   man-ʔoto?
        who   RMi   ACT-cook
        'Who will cook?'
        lit.: 'The (one) will die is who?' 'The (thing) he will give is what?'
        'The (one) will cook is who?'

Questioning a transitive actor must use the marked antipassive nominalization, a constraint similar to the PSA-only extraction restriction in Sama question formations (Van Valin and LaPolla, 332). This is exemplified in example (6.128). Questioning an adjunct also requires that the affixation signal its role with the *-an* nominalizing suffix, as seen in (6.129) and (6.130).

(6.128) *Sino   di   mang-i-ʔoto   sin   digo?*
        who   RMi   ANTI-Th-cook   ORMd   broth
        'Who will cook the broth? (lit. the (one) will cook the broth is who?)'

(6.129) *Pigʔan   di   <om>ali-an=da?*
        when   RMi   NOM-come<=3pII
        'When is (the time of) their coming? (lit. their coming/-time is when?)'

(6.130) *Into=y   <om>ey-an=tako?*
        where=RMi   NOM-go<=1+2pII
        'Where are we going? (lit. our going/-place is where?)'

6.2.5 Pivot interpretation in relativization

As detailed in section 5.6, a relative clause is linked to its nominal head with *ay*, and one referent in the clause is the pivot of the construction. The pivot is the omitted argument indexed by affixation, either predicating or nominalizing affixes including the structural antipassive, as in example (6.131). In cases when the head nominal is co-referential with a possessor or ergative argument in a nominalized complement, the co-referent is given the impersonal pronoun (4II=*na*) as a minimally-specified resumptive pronoun, as in example (6.132).

(6.131) din   ngad~ngadan   di   Americano   ya   Pilipino [ay
        RMd   CVC-name   RMi   American   and   Filipino LK

nang-amag   sin   organization].
ANTI.P-make   ORMd   organization
'...the names of the Americans and Filipinos who had created the organization.'

(6.132) Am?amed   si   sak?en   [ay   iwed   di
        especially   PRM   1sIII   LK   NEGEXIS   RMi

am~ammo=na]
CVC-know.UND=4II
'Especially me, who knows nothing.'

6.2.6 Summary of Privileged Syntactic Argument codings and behaviors in Kankanaey

Table 6.5 summarizes what this chapter has explained regarding the properties of the privileged syntactic argument of several grammatical constructions in Kankanaey.

6.2 Privileged Syntactic Arguments of other constructions

Table 6.5. PSA properties for Kankanaey constructions

PSA	Properties	Form
S or U	flagging in the clause	absolutive case
S or A	ordering in the clause	first argument position
S or U derived-S (A)	indexing on the predicate	voice affix indicating thematic role marked antipassive voice
A	control reflexive antecedence	co-referential with possessor of reflexive word
S or A	pivot in left-displacement	clitic displacement
S / A / U in different constructions	control pivot interpretation in core junctures	depending on matrix predicate
S, A, U, d-S	serve as pivot in core junctures	restrictions depending on controller in matrix clause
S, U, d-S	serve as pivot in nominalization for RPs including WH-question formation	nominalizing affixation required for obliques
S, U, d-S	serve as pivot in relativization	nominalizing affixation required for obliques

Some common constructions that are often addressed in studies of grammatical relations were not addressed specifically in this examination of Kankanaey PSAs for the following reasons:

1. Quantifiers do not "float" in Kankanaey; they were examined in chapter 3 as they relate to RPs.

2. No predicates that could "raise" an argument from a dependent complement clause have been observed in Kankanaey.

3. Topicalized possessor phrases do not exhibit "possessor ascension," but leave a resumptive pronoun, as chapter 5 noted when covering topicalization.

6.3 Non-Privileged Syntactic Argument functions

6.3.1 Co-reference across clause boundaries

Many languages employ a strategy of omitting a co-referential nominal across clause boundaries. In Kankanaey, however, as Himmelman (1999) also noted in Tagalog, the transitive actor pronoun is not freely omissible in contexts in which zero anaphora could be expected pragmatically. A topical absolutive argument (PSA), on the other hand, does not always have a pronominal reference in a clause and a pronoun-deletion strategy might be a very useful hypothesis to explain the apparent absence of many PSA RPs in connected and even contiguous clauses. Looking at the entire spectrum of participant tracking strategies, however, has led to a null-pronoun analysis instead of an absent-argument (pivot) interpretation for Kankanaey.

It should be noted that Kankanaey does not depend on voice alternations for participant tracking. Voice alternation serves to indicate the semantic role in relation to each predicate while pronouns track topical referents. The topic is maintained whether it is the possessor (POSS) of an object, the ergative Actor (A_T) of transitive predicates, the absolutive Undergoer (U_T) of a transitive predicate, or the single argument of intransitive predicates (S_A, S_U, S_{ANTI}). Example (6.133) shows the presence of the co-referential pronoun in every clause when the participant is 3p (subscript j) with argument function as noted.

(6.133) Ngem   adi=da_j ammo   di   kad?a=k   isonga
        but   NEG=3pII   know   RMi   place=1sII   therefore
                     A_T

        nan-taoli=da_j tan   maga=y
        ACT-return=3pI   because   NEGEXIS=RMi
               S_A

6.3 Non-Privileged Syntactic Argument functions

    ma-dnge=da$_j$=s   man-kanipas.
    UNDs-hear=3pII=ORMi   ACT-rustle
           A$_T$

'But they didn't know where I was so they went back because they didn't hear anything rustling (lit. there was nothing they could hear that was rustling).'

Example (6.134) shows a 3s participant (subscript i) also tracked pronominally.

(6.134) T<in>apan-an   Poltag$_i$ di   tolo=y   kenggit,
       UNDl.P-bait<   Poltag   RMi   three=LK trap
                   A$_T$

    ma-pika=et   Ø$_i$ et   e(n)=na$_i$
    UNDm-stand=PART   3sI and go=3sII
                       S$_U$ A$_T$

    osdong-an   din   posong.   En=na$_i$ pay
    look.down-UNDl   RMd pool   go=3sII   PART
                                     A$_T$

    ila-(e)n,   na-kga=et   Ø$_i$ sin   ad?ado   ay
    see-UND   UNDs-attract=PART 3sI   ORMd many   LK
                                     S$_U$

    wadingan. Ka-taoli   Ø$_i$ sin   kad?an   Il?ilit
    w-fish   IMM-return 3sI   ORMd place   Il-ilit
                              S$_A$

    yan kana=na$_i$,   "Tap~tapan- a(n)=m   din   odom..."
    and say=3sII   CVC-bait-UNDl=2sII RMd other
           A$_T$

Ka-la~labos	Ø$_i$	ay	ka-kaan	Ø$_i$	sin
IMM-CV-naked	3sI	LK	IMM-remove	3sI	ORMd
S$_A$				S$_{ANTI}$	

wanes=na$_p$,	ka-pidit	Ø$_i$	sin	tolo=y
loincloth=3sII	IMM-pick.up	3sI	ORMd	three=LK
POSS		S$_{ANTI}$		

kenggit	yan	\<om\>ey	Ø$_i$	et	i-si~sin?eng
trap	and	ACTm-go	3sI	and	UNDt-CV-watch
			S$_A$		

Il?ilit	Ø$_i$.
Il-ilit	3sI
	U$_T$

'Poltag baited three traps, got up and went to look at the pool. Seeing it, he was attracted by the many *wadingan* fish. He went right back to where Il-ilit was and said, "Keep baiting the others..." He stripped naked, removing his loincloth, snatched up the three traps and went and Il-ilit was watching him.'

6.3.2 Flagging non-Privileged Syntactic Arguments in a clause

6.3.2.1 *Non-privileged syntactic argument Actors in transitive clauses*

Actor arguments in syntactically transitive clauses are not chosen as the PSA, but they are equally topical with the privileged Undergoer, in the sense of being fully referential, expressing known, accessible information. They are required, even when co-referential between adjoining clauses. These non-PSA Actor arguments are flagged with class II if pronominal, or marked by the bound RM. Because Actors are highly topical, the definiteness operator on the BRM is often implied but not specified. Many previous examples have shown the non-PSA Actor arguments with their unique marking.

6.3 Non-Privileged Syntactic Argument functions 311

In the impersonal Undergoer-voice construction introduced in section 6.1.4.6.4, it was shown that Actors were omitted in some contexts such as procedural instructions, also as in (6.135).

(6.135) *Est-en   ay pitay-en   din   makan.*
         do.well-UND   LK mash-UND   RMd   food
         'Thoroughly mash the food.'

6.3.2.2 Non-PSA Actors in passive clauses

Agentive ACTORS of passive constructions are completely suppressed as may be seen in the ungrammaticality of example (6.136). If the EFFECTOR is a natural event such as an earthquake or landslide, however, it may be specified with the oblique RM, as shown in (6.137), repeated from (6.81) above.

(6.136) **Nai-ali*   din   agas   sin   nars.*
         UNDts.come   RMd   medicine   ORMd   nurse
         * for 'The medicine was brought by the nurse.'

(6.137) *Na-sawad=ak   sin   tolo   ay   pewek.*
         UNDs-block=1sI   ORMd   three   LK   typhoons
         'I was blocked by the three (back-to-back) typhoons.'

6.3.2.3 Non-PSA, non-Actor core arguments

The semantic representation of a predicate may include arguments that are not given macrorole status. These are oblique core arguments, whether common RP, name or pronoun. Oblique arguments are definite when they are pronouns or proper names. Common oblique RPs can be marked with indefinite *si* or definite *sin*. Oblique arguments are bracketed in the following examples.

Activity predicates often cannot assign the Undergoer role because the second argument is undifferentiated or only partially affected. Examples (6.138) and (6.139) show a predicate with only an Actor macrorole; the second arguments are oblique because they are not fully affected.

(6.138) *Nan-sibo   din   anak   [si   digo].*
ACT.P-sip   RMd   child   ORMi   broth
'The child sipped (some) broth.'

(6.139) *Nan-sibo   din   anak   [sin   digo].*
ACT.P-sip   RMd   child   ORMd   broth
'The child sipped from/some of the broth.'

When a locative predicate is part of the logical structure, the LOCUS argument may be oblique but specific, and marked for definiteness. For example, figure 6.9 showed that the predicate 'teach' has three core arguments—an EFFECTOR teacher, a RECIPIENT learner, and THEME information that becomes known. In (6.140) the RECIPIENT was not given macrorole assignment, and is marked with the definite oblique ORMd.

(6.140) *Ini-tdo=n   Todyak   din   danan   [sin*
UNDt.P-teach=BPRM   Todyak   RMd   path   ORMd

pamilya=na].
family=3sII
'Todyak showed/pointed out the path to his family.'

To give more examples, in (6.141) the oblique argument is nonreferential, especially in light of the imperfective marking suggesting that such a tape has yet to be recorded. In (6.142) the oblique THEME argument is referential but non-identifiable. In (6.143) the oblique argument 'what is in the cup' is only partially affected, as specified by this use of the affix $<om_2>$ (see section 2.2.7.2).

(6.141) *Mo   mabalin   koma,   man-i-paw?it =kayo   [si*
if   possible   PART   ACT-Th-send=2sI   ORMi

mai-tape   ay   violin   Roby].
UNDts-tape   LK   violin   Roby
'If possible, (please) send what will be taped of Roby's violin.'

(6.142) Pag   nan-i-baa   si   Dulay   [si   en
       then ACT.P-Th-send   PRM   Dulay   ORMi   go

       mang-ayag   en   Lina].
       ANTI-invite   OPRM   Lina
       'Then Dulay sent someone to go call for Lina.'

(6.143) <Om₂>i-asin=ka   [sin   wada   sin   malakong].
        ACT-Th-salt=2sI   ORMd   EXIS   ORMd   bowl
        'Use some of what is in the bowl for salting.'

With the antipassive voice, the Undergoer has macrorole status, but is not selected for PSA assignment. In (6.144), shortened from (6.63), there are two antipassive-voice predicates with oblique Undergoers. Non-canonical coding for the Undergoers is shown both by THEME-indexing in the first clause, and by the interpretation of the definite oblique core arguments as exhibiting full affectedness.

(6.144) Ka-i-payag   Ø   [sin   sokod=na]   yan
        IMM-Th-set.down   3sI   ORMd   staff=3sII   and

        ka-dama   Ø   [sin   banig].
        IMM-wrestle   3sI   ORM   ghost
        'He dropped/threw down his walking-stick and attacked the ghost.'

6.4 Conclusion

This chapter has shown that the privileged syntactic argument in various constructions will exhibit certain coding properties and/or behavioral properties. The PSA of the clause is coded by case marking, indexing by the predicate affixes, and word order. Controllers and pivots in core junctures show certain properties depending on the predicates. Reflexives have a semantic Actor controller. Clitic displacement follows an accusative pattern. Nominalization, question formation, and relative clause formation work by a broad range of affixation that indexes the pivot. Topic chains do not show any restricted neutralization of semantic roles or PSA, while a null-form pronoun functions where other languages would use zero anaphora or equi-noun-phrase deletion.

7

Information Structure

7.1 Information structure

This chapter explores the interaction of discourse functions and syntactic structures to describe the process of information flow.[1] The discourse function of most utterances is to communicate information in a context of differing states of knowledge between a speaker and a hearer. Information may be classified as identifiable or unidentifiable in terms of the prior knowledge that the speaker assumes that the hearer has. Lambrecht (1994:109) suggests that an unidentifiable reference is totally new, but may be anchored by association with an identifiable entity. Identifiable referents may have been already mentioned in the immediate discourse, predictable from the discourse or accessible from general knowledge. The speaker presupposes some shared knowledge, and asserts information that is presumed to be new.

Information structure studies use the terms "focus" and "topic." Focus is taken to mean "the semantic component...whereby the assertion differs from the presupposition" (Lambrecht 1994:213). The "focus" of a sentence

---

[1] This chapter draws heavily on the research published as Allen 2007 in the *Philippine Journal of Linguistics* 38.

is that added information or changed information that is in contrast to what is already in the hearer's mind, while "topical" information is presupposed to be shared already by the speaker and hearer.

Within a clause there are two functions, corresponding in figure 7.1 to Nucleus and Arguments. The function of the nucleus is to predicate (assert, question, command, etc.) while the function of arguments is to refer to entities. Predicates as well as referents can be either new or predictable information.

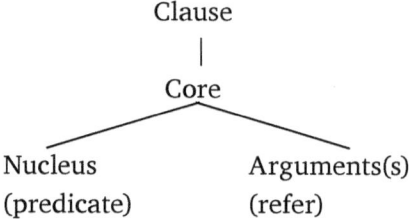

Figure 7.1. Clause structure with basic functions.

The syntactic structure of Kankanaey sentences comprises left- and right-detached positions and a central clause component, as seen in chapter 5. The potential domain of new information is defined by the scope of the illocutionary force operator of the central clause (Van Valin 2005:214). The actual focus domain for a particular clause may include the entire clause (the potential focus domain) or only part of it. Phrases and clauses in detached positions are not in a "daughter" relationship to the central clause, and thus do not fall within the focus domain. Independent coordinate clauses in a sentence each have their own potential focus domain. Thus, the highest potential level of focus domain is the independent clause.

7.1.1 Morphosyntactic variables in marking information

Kankanaey speakers manipulate several constructions and variables in order to enable the hearer to identify information as new, given, or accessible; to relate it to existing knowledge, and to follow the flow of thought. Although Kankanaey follows the assumption of Dooley and Levinsohn (2001:57) that information is presented in intonational units involving pitch, intensity,

7.1 Information structure

and pause, speakers do not use special prosodic intensity to highlight focus elements. Efforts to use this method for contrastive information have met with amusement.[2] Some languages, e.g., Huallaga Quechua (Weber 1989, discussed in Van Valin 2005:74), use evidential clitics or focus particles to indicate the focus of a sentence. Kankanaey has several evidential particles, most notably *kano* 'hearsay', but their placement does not correlate with either focus or topical information.

A variable that is important for information structure is definiteness. Personal/proper referring markers are always definite, as are personal pronouns. As noted in chapter 3, a Kankanaey RM (reference phrase marker) is the defining constituent of an expression whose function is to refer. The RMs (*di* and *si*) may take a suffix *-n* (thus *din* and *sin*) indicating 'definiteness'. This is probably an unfortunate designation, as there are several parameters that affect the presence of the suffix and they differ between the bound and free forms, but in general the 'definite' markers signal that the phrase is referring to an entity that the hearer can expect to identify. The unmarked RMs are less constrained.

Another important variable for information structure is voice affixation in nominalization. The affixes that create verbs and adjectives index one semantic role involved in the resulting predicate. Therefore, when an affixed root is preceded by an RM, the resulting reference phrase refers to an entity that fills the role indicated by the affix. This elegant system will be exemplified repeatedly in the following description.

The third variable directly related to information flow is the syntactic structure of sentences. Detached positions and the clause nuclear position are both important, especially with the variability of nuclear components in Kankanaey clauses.

7.1.2 Clauses with no focus domain

In the course of a text such as a narrative, there are recapitulations, summaries, and highly predictable outcomes that do not share any new information. In Kankanaey texts, there are many such clauses, whose

---

[2] Wari' (Turner 2006) and Karitiâna (C. Everett 2008) are two languages in Brazil that have also been shown to depend much more on morphosyntax than prosody to highligh a narrow-focus element.

function on the discourse level is to indicate boundaries or satisfy predictable expectations, such as arrival after a journey.

In letters, where participants automatically include the writer and speaker, formalities such as inquiring and informing about health frequently have no focus structure. Their pragmatic function is to prepare the way for the new information that is the point of the letter. Kankanaey writers tend to give a short heads-up just before such new information, as seen in the overt expressions bracketed in examples (7.1) to (7.4) as well as the general preface of example (7.5).

(7.1)   [Manang,   layd-e(n)=k   ay   ammo-a(n)=m   ay
        sister   like-UND=1sII   LK   know-UNDl=2sII   LK

        osto   ay]...
        correct   LK
        'Sister, I want you to really know that...'

(7.2)   [Wada   baw   di   damag-e(n)=k   mo]   siya   ay
        EXIS   EVID   RMi   news-UND=1sII   if   thus   LK

        tet?ewa...
        true
        'Oh yeah, I have something to ask whether it is true that...'

(7.3)   [I-pa-damag=ko   abe   en   dakayo   ay]...
        UNDt-CAUS-news=1sII   also   OPRM   2pIII   LK
        'I report also to you that...'

(7.4)   [Isonga   nan-solat=ak   en   dakayo]   ta
        therefore   ACT-write=1sI   OPRM   2pIII   so.that

        <om>ali=kayo...
        ACTm-come=2pII
        'So I am writing to you so that you will come...'

(7.5)   *Palalo=y*   *gasat=ko*   *ed*   *niman*   *ay*   *timpo.*
        excessive=RMi luck=1sII   LOC   nowadays LK   time
        'I have had a lot of bad luck recently.'

7.2 New information—the focus domain

Most clauses do share new information, however, and of these there are three general types. A predicate may make a totally new assertion about new referents, or predicate a new assertion about a given or accessible referent. Van Valin and LaPolla (1997:202), crediting Lambrecht (1994), uses the labels "sentence-focus" and "predicate-focus" for these, noting that "focus" is the part of an sentence "that is unpredictable or unrecoverable from the context." Because the potential focus domain is not the sentence but rather the independent clause, the term "clause-focus" will be used instead of "sentence-focus." Sections 7.2.1 and 7.2.2 will examine clause- and predicate-focus constructions in Kankanaey.

Lambrecht's "narrow-focus" clause has only one constituent in the actual focus domain. It asserts that an identifiable referent is the same as some other given or accessible referent. In such a clause, the new information is the identification of the first as co-referent with the second. Section 7.2.3 will explore the contexts in which equative clauses function as narrow-focus constructions in Kankanaey.

Speakers of Kankanaey generally introduce important participants with clause-focus constructions, move narratives forward with predicate focus constructions, and use narrow focus to identify or contrast individual participants. They use detachment of various entities to change discourse topic or to indicate contrasting subtopics. In all these constructions they manipulate the variables of voice, constituent position, RP markers, and pronouns to reflect the degree to which they believe their hearers can identify and process the information. Exceptions to the rules of general usage can be found, of course, indicating that the correlation of structure to function may be adjusted as a speaker assesses the interest, need, or ability of the hearer to identify each referent.

The potential focus domain (dotted lines) and one possible actual focus domain (triangle) are illustrated in figure 7.2.

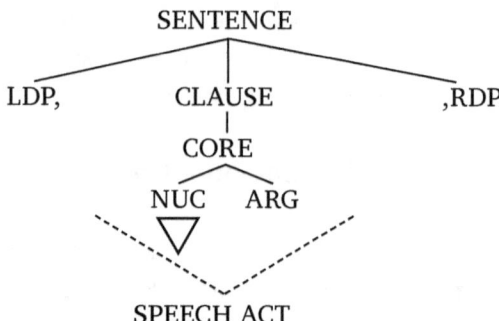

Figure 7.2. Kankanaey sentence with potential and one actual focus domain.

7.2.1 Clause focus

Clause focus is commonly used in presentational constructions where new participants or situations are introduced. In Kankanaey this may be expressed by an existential or verbal predicate in the nucleus with its absolutive argument marked as indefinite. Existential predicates often open a narrative or introduce participants, as in (7.6), using the indefinite RM=y. The place-name *Bakun* is assumed to be known to the hearers, who live in the next municipal district. Example (7.7) follows (7.6) in the story, and brings in the main entities (gods and people) as indefinite entities using *di* and *si*. Except for the district name and the demonstrative pronoun, all the information in these two examples is new to the hearers.

(7.6)   *Wada=y   na-kayang   ay   dontog   ed   Bakun.*
       EXIS=RMi ATT-high   LK   mountain LOC   Bakun
       'There is a high mountain in Bakun.'

(7.7)   *Man-beey   kano   di   kabonyan   sidi   ay*
       ACT-house   HSY   RMi   god   DEM3IV   LK

       man-pa-kan   si   man-illeng   isdi.
       ACT-CAUS-eat   ORMi   ACT-rest   DEM3IV
       'Gods live there, they say, who feed those who rest there.'

7.2 New information—the focus domain

Even when an existential introduces a new participant by name, the indefinite RM precedes the personal marker, as in (7.8), indicating that the name is new to the hearer. In example (7.9) this opening sentence of a story plunges into the tale using the indefinite RM *di* for the first mention of these participants. The use of the indefinite RM instructs the hearer to create a 'slot' for these participants, whose relevance will become clearer as the story progresses. A more formal story introduction is exemplified in (7.10), where several indefinite markers are used but translated in English as definite 'the'.

(7.8) *Wada=y   si   Nabulay   ed   na-baon   ed   Abas.*
      EXIS.RMi   PRM   Nabulay   LOC   ATT-long.ago   LOC   Abas
      'There was a certain Nabulay long ago in Abas.'

(7.9) *Na-sinop   di   nankakay   ay   man-to~tolag   mo   into*
      UNDs-gather   RMi   elders   LK   ACT-CV-agree   if   how

   di   ma-iyat...
   RMi   UNDs-do
   'Some elders were gathered discussing about how to....'

(7.10) *Na-solok   si   tolonpo   ay   tawen   di*
       ATT-more.than   ORMi   thirty   LK   year   RMi

   <inm>ey   ay   b<inom>tak-an   di   gobat   ay
   ACTm.P-go   LK   NOM.P-burst<   RMi   war   LK

   kanan=da   en   World War II.
   say.UND=3pII   QT   World War II
   'More than thirty years (are what) have gone (since) the outbreak of the war that they call WWII.'

7.2.2 Predicate focus

Lambrecht's (2000) definition of predicate focus structure as quoted in Van Valin (2005:70) applies to clause structures in Kankanaey in which the nucleus of the clause core is an affixed root or a class or attribute root. Such a predicate "expresses new information about [a] topic. The focus domain is the predicate phrase (or part of it)." The unmarked clause structure of Kankanaey is a predicate followed by one or two direct arguments and possibly one or two oblique referring phrases. Predicate focus (the unmarked focus type in Kankanaey) always presents the predicate as new information; one of the arguments or obliques may also be new. The following discussion subdivides predicate focus according to which part of the clause is new information. Focal constituents are bracketed.

A description of Kankanaey in terms of "topic" and "comment" on the clause level is not attempted here because of the mismatch in Kankanaey of syntax with identifiability. While the single argument of an intransitive predicate patterns with the Actor argument of a transitive predicate as generally the most identifiable, continuous, and important referent (i.e., topic), it patterns with the Undergoer argument of transitive predicates syntactically as to predicate indexing and case marking. Actors are syntactically and phonologically bound to their predicates, and Kankanaey maintains an obligatory VAU word order, making a simple topic-comment division very awkward.

7.2.2.1 Predicate only is new

Predicate-only focus is very common in Kankanaey narratives and letters, as the story line about the participants goes forward, expectations are met or revised, or news about topics of common interest is shared.

Example (7.11), from a narrative, follows the introductions of the main character and also Nabulay's ghost and then gives the surprising information that the main character (Ø 'he') attacked it. In example (7.12) only the actions of the characters present new information. Note that the verbal affix *ka-* in both examples indicates precipitous action with prominence on the activity rather than its effect.

(7.11) ...yan [ka-dama]   Ø   sin   sana   ay   banig   Nabulay.
       ...and IMM-attack 3sI ORMd   DEM2IV LK   ghost   Nabulay
       '...and he suddenly attacked that ghost of Nabulay.'

7.2 New information—the focus domain

(7.12) [Apayaw-en]=da=s   sak?en   tan   ka-on?ona=ak.
chase-UND=3pII=PRM   1sIII   because   IMM-precede=1sI
'They chased after me because I had rushed ahead.'

Class or attribute roots as the non-verbal predicate may hold the new information in a clause. Class-root predicates are not to be confused with RP predicates, covered in section 7.2.3. Although in English an indefinite noun phrase can form an equative clause, for example, "John is a good friend," in Kankanaey such a predicate cannot be an RP, as seen in (7.13).

(7.13) *Di   siged   ay   gayyem   si   Juan.
       [Siged   ay   gayyem]   si   Juan.
       RMi   good   LK   friend   PRM   Juan
'John is a good friend.'

7.2.2.2 Undergoer is new

In many cases, an unidentifiable undergoer is introduced as an indefinite oblique referent. Cooreman (1983) found that in Chamorro the voice of the verb indicated the relative topicality (givenness) of the affected participants. In Kankanaey, when the actor is known but the undergoer is new information, the verb tends to have actor voice, which allows only the Actor as direct argument, and undergoers must be oblique.

In example (7.14) the speaker has been invited to go help dig for treasure. Taking a lunch and some tools is not surprising information in the context, but at this first mention, they are given oblique status and the contracted indefinite ORM =s.

(7.14) ...et   nan-a=kami[=s   baon   ya   laminta].
       ...and   ACT.P-get=1pI=ORMi   lunch   and   tool
'...and we got a lunch and some tools.'

New participants can enter a narrative as direct Undergoer arguments of a verb if they are 'accessible' from the context, as in (7.15), where the speaker tells of seeing an accident. Vehicles are an accessible part of a shopping trip context. Note the indefinite =y on the

Undergoer argument, even though it is the argument indexed on the verb, and more new information occurs as a subordinated predicate in the relative clause.

(7.15) Ed   agsapa,   en=kami   man-markit   yan
       LOC   morning   go=1pI   ACT-market   and

          <in>ila=mi[=y   taxi ya   jeep   ay man-asi-dongpal=da].
          UND.P-see=1pII-.RMi   taxi and jeep   LK ACT-RECIP-bump=3pI
          'This morning, we went shopping and we saw a taxi and a jeep that collided.'

7.2.2.3 Predicate and Actor are new

DuBois (1987:839) noted several universal tendencies regarding the way transitive Actors and Objects function in a discourse. Of interest here is that themes and topics tend to be expressed more as Actors than as Objects, and that new participants tend to be introduced through an Object function much more than as Actors. In Kankanaey, it is not frequent that a new participant is introduced as the Actor of a transitive verb. Actors are not often expressed with a full RP, but tend to be pronouns, which presupposes anaphoric reference. Even when an Actor is expressed with a common RP, it is generally assumed to be definite and the case marker may not have the overt -*n* marking, as has been mentioned. Violating this constraint can only be done under special circumstances.

When the Actor is a recoverable entity, and his role is not central to the storyline, the Kankanaey speaker may presume upon the hearer's shared knowledge and bring such Actors temporarily on stage as direct RPs without preamble. In (7.16), the writer is explaining why he did not arrive when planned. Casilo and Minda are known to the reader, and their minor roles in this drama are only mentioned this once. In (7.17) the specific identity of the new actor argument is irrelevant.

7.2 New information—the focus domain

(7.16) [Kanan   kano=n   Casilo]   en   wada   koma=y
       say.UND   HSY=BPRM   Casilo   QT   EXIS   IRR=RMi

       mai-dawat   en   sak?en   ay   gastos-e(n)=k]
       UNDts-give   OPRM   1sIII   LK   spend.UND=1sII

       ngem   [na-ladaw   ay   in-pa-ammo=n   Minda]   Ø.
       but   UND.P-late   LK   UNDT.P-CAUS-know   Minda   4III

       'Casilo had reportedly said that there would be something to be given to me for the fare, but Minda was late in letting (me) know it.'

(7.17) K<in>at   di   aso   din   anak=ko.
       UND.P-bite   BRMi   dog   RMd   child=1sII
       'A dog bit my child.'

At narrative peaks, new information can be introduced in unconventional ways. In a story of a man who failed to come up after diving into a river, a very new and surprising participant is brought on stage in the Actor role, preceded by surprise particles that alert the listener, as in (7.18).

(7.18) Kambaw   etay   in-pe-peteng-an   di   dalit   Ø!
       SURP   SURP   UNDd.P-CV-restrain<   BRMi   eel   3sIII
       'Imagine! An eel was restraining him!'

7.2.2.4 Emphasis on key pieces of information

This chapter cannot cover all the devices used by Kankanaey speakers to manage information flow by marking certain constituents as pivotal or of extra importance. Chapter 4 introduced discourse-level semantic particles, one group of which is used for emphasis. Another emphasizing strategy will be presented here.

The stark clarity of the existentials—either existence or not, either present or totally absent—lends itself to emphatic uses in a discourse.[3] In (7.19) the information being presented is that the character Poltag did not come

---

[3] A similar use of the existential has also been attested in Belait (Clynes 2005:439) and in Karo Batak (Woolams 2005:544).

up after his dive. The narrator could have used the core negator *adi* to express this meaning. The construction using the negative existential as the predicating nucleus intensifies the knot in the narrative in this dramatic moment at the center of this underwater-rescue story. Similarly in (7.20), the child's failure to cooperate is the turning point for the mother in a cautionary folk tale.

(7.19) *Maga=y   t<om>emwa   en   Poltag.*
        NEGEXIS=RMi ACTm-emerge.upwards OPRM   Poltag
        'There was no emerging by Poltag (i.e., Poltag didn't emerge)!'

(7.20) *Maga=y   en   nan-ʔoto   sin   anak=na.*
        NEGEXIS=RMi go   ACT-cook   ORMd   child=3sII
        'There was no going to cook by her child (i.e., her child didn't go cook).'

The existential *wada* is sometimes used to emphasize the reality of the assertion, nuances of which may be seen in (7.21) and (7.22).

(7.21) *Wada   ay   ilan=da   din   galey   ay   mankeykey.*
        EXIS   LK   see=3pII   RMd   blanket   LK   move
        'They actually saw the (shroud) blanket move.'

(7.22) *Kaman=kayo   ngay   wada   ay   domateng.*
        like=2pI   PART   EXIS   LK   arrive
        'It's as if you are truly arriving' (the particle adds wistfulness to the wishful assertion).

7.2.3 Narrow focus

When only one RP constituent of a clause is in the actual focus domain, the focus is narrow. The classic example of narrow focus in many languages is the fronted WH-question in the pre-core slot. Other strategies in English are the various cleft constructions, as well as intonation signals such as pitch and intensity, which indicate a focal constituent *in situ*.

Kankanaey cannot use any of the strategies mentioned above. It is possible for focal corrective contrast on predicates to be flagged by semantic particles

7.2 New information—the focus domain 327

of contrast or opposition. Negating the wrong presupposition is also a syntactic option and is often strengthened by an objection particle, as in (7.23).

(7.23) I-bag~baga=da   en   man-pa-ila=ak   si
       UNDt-CVC-say=3pII   QT   ACT-CAUS-see=1sI   ORMi

doktol   ngem   iwed   met   di   pilak=ko.
doctor   but   NEGEXIS   PART   RMi   money=1sII
'They keep telling me to consult a doctor (for which I would need to pay) but I don't have any MONEY/don't HAVE any money.'

The default construction, however, for narrow focus in Kankanaey is the equative clause, which consists of two juxtaposed RPs. This construction was briefly introduced in chapters 3 and 4. Equative clauses, like all others in Kankanaey, are nucleus-initial; therefore, the first RP is in the nuclear position, and the second RP is its argument, as diagrammed in figure 7.3. In this construction the first RP is the focus domain.

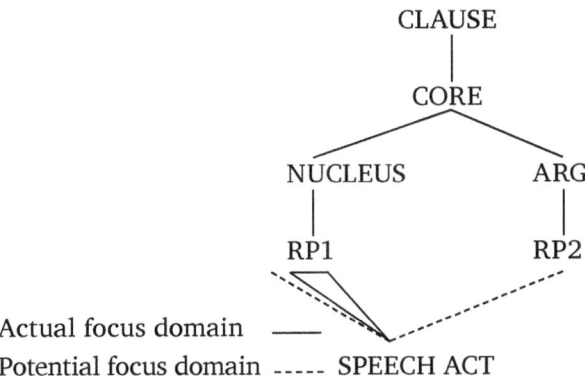

Figure 7.3. Equative clause structure in Kankanaey with focus domains.

For Kankanaey it is useful to distinguish between completive and contrastive narrow focus, suggested by Dik's (1981:42) analysis involving contrastive and corrective parameters.

In this section, completive narrow-focus constructions are examined, including content questions and answers, and identifying (specificational) statements. Contrastive narrow-focus constructions are also discussed, including corrective statements and statements that emphasize the uniqueness of the co-referential relationship.

7.2.3.1 Content questions and answers

A content question uses one of the interrogative pronouns listed in (7.24) as the first RP in a completive equative clause.

(7.24) *sino*   'who, what, which'
        into   'where'
        pig?an 'when'

The question 'how?' is formed with *into=y iyat* 'where (is) the way', and 'why?' is formed with *sino=y gapo* 'what (is) the reason'. Example (7.25) shows both the interrogative pronoun and the answer pronoun in the initial position of equative clauses. These are narrow-focus clauses in which the existence of "your/my son" is clearly presupposed and the first RP questions or asserts a co-referential relationship.

(7.25) *Sino*   *din*   *anak=mo?*   *Sisya*   *din*   *anak =ko.*
        who   RMd   child=2sII   3sIII   RMd   child=1sII
        'Q: Who/which is your son? A: He is my son. (lit. Your son is which? My son is he.)'

In (7.26) the question 'when?' uses a predicate nominalized for time/place.

(7.26) *Pig?an*   *di*   *pang-i-dawt-a(n)=m*   *en*   *sisya?*
        when   RMi   NOM-Th-give<=2sII   OPRM   3sIII
        'When are you going to give it to him? (lit. your time of giving it to him is when?)'

7.2.3.2 Specificational clauses

An RP that has an affixed root in the nucleus refers to the entity that fills the semantic role indicated by the affixation. The second RP of equative

7.2 New information—the focus domain

clauses often has an indefinite RM and an affixed nucleus, creating an underspecified identity. When an equative clause functions to provide the identity for an underspecified referent, it is a specificational construction, in which one RP is a "variable," and the other RP provides the "value" for that variable (terms from Pavey 2008:305, citing DeClerck 1988). The Kankanaey construction places the value RP first (in the nucleus), while the variable RP is its argument. The second RP holds information that the speaker assumes the hearer is already aware of, while the first RP adds more information to specify the identity of the second RP. This most closely resembles the English pseudocleft, which has the variable RP in the subject position and the value RP as part of the predicate with the copular verb.[4] Example (7.27) shows a specifying clause and uses the English pseudocleft for the translation.

(7.27) Din   opisyalis=mi   di   nang-i-dalom.
        RMd   officials=1pII   RMi   ANTI-Th-file.charges
        'The (ones who) filed the charge were our officials.'

Example (7.28) also shows that the first RP in the specificational clause is the entity that fills the role marked on the second RP. The first RP is definite, the second underspecified and thus indefinite.

(7.28) [Din   address=yo   ay   wada   en   da   Ben]$_{PRED}$
        RMd   address=2pII   LK   EXIS   OPRM   pl   Ben

        [di   <in>osal=ko].$_{ARG}$
        RMi   UND.P-use=1sII
        'What I used was your address that was at Ben's (home) (pseudocleft in English).

Because the referent of the first RP is an easily identifiable participant, the 'new' information of the specificational clause is the assertion of co-referentiality, a relatively weak focus force.

When a speaker presents new information, s/he generally builds on the topic at hand, filling in gaps in the addressee's knowledge. A direct and simple clause is not always the most effective strategy. Kankanaey

---
[4] See Pavey 2004 for a full discussion of *it*-clefts and other cleft constructions.

speakers often use instead this specificational clause, the form of answers to questions that are unasked but assumed to be relevant to the addressee. Example (7.29) comes in the context of wedding advice mentioning possible difficulties, and the presupposed question might be something like: "What is a good thing to avoid saying in such situations?"

(7.29) Baken   din   pag   sia~sian   di   i-bag~baga.
        neg   RM   always CVCC.separate   RMi   UNDt-CVC-say
        'It's not always divorce! divorce! that (one) is to be saying.' (i.e., 'Don't continually threaten divorce.')

In (7.30) the narrow-focus clause is at the very end. Note that the idea of 'go peek' is introduced, and all the participants, especially the narrator herself, are "given" information. In the last clause (bracketed) the pairing of the participant (1s) with her role is an example of completive narrow focus, answering the implied question or interest in who actually performed the 'peeking' action. This construction further serves a discourse-level function of taking the action off the main storyline.

(7.30) "En=ka   i-tining   mo   na-pas?od-an   din   teytey
        go=2sI   UNDt-peek.at   if   UNDl-take.in<   RMd   ladder

        di   beey=mi,"   kanan=da   et   [si
        BRMi   house=1pII   say.UND=3pII   and   PRM

        sak?en   di   en   nang-i-tining].
        1sIII   RMi   go   ANTI-Th-peek.at
        '"Go peek (and see) whether the ladder to our house has been taken in," they said, and the (one who) went to peek at it was me.'

Example (7.31) identifies a location in terms of the activity that gives its importance; having introduced a prospective customer for a shady deal, the storyteller sets the stage for the adventure (seeing the customer, i.e., meeting him) in the well-known Burnham Park. Note that the nominalizing affixes are on the root 'see' rather than 'agree' since the park was the place to see someone, not the place where the agreement was made.

(7.31) Ed   Burnham   di   tolag-an   ay
        LOC   Burnham   RMi   agree-UNDl   LK

pan-asi-ila-an=mi.
NOM-RECIP-see<=1pII
'At Burnham (Park) was where it was agreed that we'd meet (lit. see) each other.'

The discourse context must always be taken into account in order to interpret the pragmatic function of an equative clause that identifies a participant by its role. The purpose seen above is specificational. A second purpose is to contrast a participant with other possible participants, a relatively stronger focus force.

7.2.3.3 Contrastive focus clauses

Equative clauses can contrast new information with possible alternatives. The strongest contrast is most clearly expressed when correcting a presupposition. When the context for an equative clause calls for a corrective, contrastive function, both the RPs are marked as definite, as in (7.32) b.

(7.32) a: In-takin=mo   si   Biktorya.
            UNDt.P-take.with=2s   PRM   Biktorya

        b: Aga, si   Bangilay din nang-a~kadwa   en   sak?en.
            No   PRM   Bangilay RMd ANTI.P-CV-be.with   OPRM 1sIII

        a: 'You took Biktorya along.'
        b: 'No, the (one who) was with me was BANGILAY.'

Example (7.33) comes from advice to a newly-married couple; the speaker has just admonished them to stop leaning on their parents for support. His corrective admonition uses narrow focus on the pronoun *dakayo* '2pIII' to contrast the couple with the parents for the role of provider.

(7.33) *Dakayo   di   mang-i-ligat   si   ka-tago-an=yo.*
       2pIII   RMi   ANTI-Th-difficult   ORMi   NOM-live<=2pII
       'The (ones to) struggle (lit. undergo hardship) for your (own) livelihood are YOU.'

7.2.3.4 Emphatic narrow focus

A second function of contrastive narrow focus is to emphasize the exclusive uniqueness of the co-referential relationship. As can be seen from example (7.33) above, assigning someone to a role often signals responsibility; sometimes the force is that of blame. In (7.34) the recipient of the scolding letter mentioned earlier learns that he has been overextending his parents' generosity. Both parties know the facts; the equative construction serves to stress his role in this case.

(7.34) *Sik?a   di   nang-(g)asto~gastos   sin   pilak=mi.*
       2sIII   RMi   ANTI.P-CVCCV-spend   ORMd   money=1pI
       'The (one who) kept spending all our money is you.'

When the information in both RPs of an equative clause is highly identifiable, as in the case of focal (class III) pronouns and previously-mentioned predicates, the impact of the narrow focus is to emphasize the assertion that the participant in fact fills the role, as in (7.35), with a corroborating emphatic particle.

(7.35) *Si   naey   man   di   <in>ila=k.*
       PRM   DEM1III   PART   RMi   UND.P-see=1sII
       '(I insist) what I saw is really this.'

7.2.3.5 The demonstrative as referent in equative clauses

The class I demonstrative pronoun *sa* 'that' (near-hearer) can take the role of a general focal pronoun with anaphoric reference functions, as in example (7.36). This example comes from a story in which some parents send their child back and forth between them rather than stop their work to peel his sugarcane for him. The narrow focus is used to contrast or uniquely assign

7.2 New information—the focus domain 333

the role to one participant, who is identified by a demonstrative pronoun. In the context of repeated refusals to peel the sugarcane, the construction is clearly indicating narrow focus.

(7.36) I-ey=mo   Ø   en   ina=m   ta
        UNDt-go=2sII   4III   OPNM   mother=2sII   so.that

        sa=y   mang-(g)el?ad.
        DEM2I=RMi   ANTI-peel
        'Take it to your mother so that the (one who) will peel it is that one (i.e., so THAT ONE (she, not me) will peel it).'

In (7.37) the immediate antecedent, 'Aug. 22', controls the reference of the demonstrative that begins the second clause. Brackets indicate the constituent positions.

(7.37) S<om>aa=ka   sin   Aug. 22   tan
        ACTm-go.home=2sI   ORMd   Aug. 22   because

        [sa]_PRED   [=y   <om>ali-an   da   Ben]._ARG
        DEM2I   =RMi   NOM-come<   pl   Ben
        'Come home on August 22, because the coming-time of Ben and family is that.'

Sometimes the demonstrative *sa* has no anaphoric referent, but rather has cataphoric reference to a definite RP which is placed to the right in the post-core slot. The phrase that is co-referential with the predicate RP follows without intonational pause in the post-core position (unlike the English translation, which must insert a pause). The resulting clause delays the identification of the 'value' RP until after the 'variable' indexed role has been activated. This is a common construction in Kankanaey, a method of managing the information flow so that the hearer is easily able to follow and comprehend. Example (7.38) is a wry comment after a description of someone's independent behaviour. The speaker activates the idea of what might be the reason for the behaviour, and then suggests the answer.

(7.38) [Sa]_PRED [=y layden=(n)a]_ARG [din
       DEM2I   =RMi like.UND=3sII   RMd

ang?anggoy=na]._PRED CO-REFERENT
alone=3sII
'What he likes is that, (the) being on his own.'

The clause in figure 7.4 comes from a similar point in a story of an eel, where the speaker acknowledges the possible question of how it (the eel) could have held down a man, and then gives the answer. The figure shows the post-core slot with the 'value' RP as the co-referent of the demonstrative that is in the clause nucleus. This is the only type of clause that uses the post-core position in Kankanaey. Its closest comparable form in English would be a right-dislocated reverse pseudocleft![5]

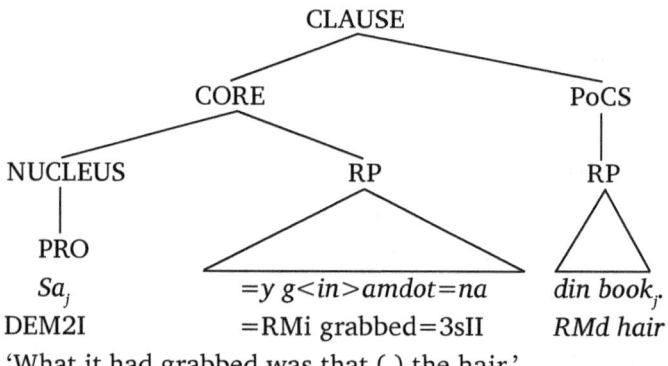

Figure 7.4. Kankanaey clause structure
with focal RP in post-core slot.

The near-hearer demonstrative *sa,* or the general-anaphoric pronoun *siya,* or the two in combination *(siya sa)* may be used in a generalized sense to refer to information that the hearer holds as activated from the immediate context. Equative clauses with the general pronoun *siya* as the first RP do not always identify or stress an entity to fill a role, but may give emphasis to important concepts on a paragraph level, especially as they relate to causal relationships between clauses, giving a general

---
[5] Compare to "right-dislocated pseudocleft" (Pavey 2004:56).

7.3 Outside the focus domain 335

anaphoric sense of 'thus, like, so'. This use of the pro-form *siya* was noted in chapter 3.

An equative clause with a general deictic that refers to a large amount of information serves as a summarizing or closing device at the end of some unit at a higher level than the clause. In (7.39) and (7.40) the clause is summarizing the preceding paragraph, while (7.41) closes an entire discourse.

(7.39) *Isonga   mo   mamingsan   yan   sa=y*
       therefore   if/when   one.time   PART   DEM2I=RMi

   adi=mi   pan-solat-an.
   NEG=1pII   NOM-write<
   'So sometimes, (the reason for) our not writing (to you) is that.'
   (i.e., 'Sometimes that's why we don't write (you).')

(7.40) *Baken   siya   sa=y   pan-balin-a(n)=m   si*
       NEG   thus   DEM2I=RMi   NOM-change<<=2sII   ORMi

   kaag.
   monkey
   '(The reason for) becoming a monkey is not that.' (i.e., 'That's no reason to turn into a monkey.')

(7.41) *Siya   anggoy   sa   di   i-baga=k   en   dakayo*
       thus   only   DEM2I   RMi   UNDt-say=1s   OPNM   2pIII

   ay   sin-asawa.
   LK   UNIT-spouse
   'What I will say to you who are a (newlywed) husband-and-wife is only that (the entire preceding discourse).' (closing sentence)

7.3 Outside the focus domain

Information in a clause that is outside the actual focus domain is topical. Chapter 6 discussed topic continuity by means of pronoun reference across clauses. Other topical information in Kankanaey sentences is expressed by deictics, proper names, and definite RPs in any function of the clause. Both of the RPs in equative clauses hold topical reference; it is the relationship of the first RP to the second RP that is the new information in the actual focus domain.

As noted above in figure 7.2, the Kankanaey sentence has detached positions preceding and following the central clause. Material in the left-detached position is always topical (Van Valin and LaPolla 1997:228), and falls outside the potential focus domain. The detachment is indicated by an intonational pause (shown by a comma) or by one of four particles—*ket, et, yan,* or *pay*.[6] These detachment strategies will be illustrated in the examples that follow. Chapter 5 has already covered the types of information presented by full clauses in the LDP. The rest of this chapter will explore topical RPs in the LDP.

7.3.1 Detached Reference Phrases with basic clauses

In introductory sentences that open narratives, a detached RP may soften the impact of the barrage of new information by mentioning a new constituent in general (accessible) terms, which then becomes the topic of the ensuing clause, as in (7.42) and (7.43). In (7.44), an activated Undergoer clears the way for the brand new but minor participant, the indefinite 'dog' as Actor.

(7.42) | Din | ili | ay | Binggo | et | kitkittoy | ay | ili | Ø |
|---|---|---|---|---|---|---|---|---|
| RMd | town | LK | Binggo | PART | small | LK | town | 4I |

sin	Municipio	=n di	Dupax del Martes.
ORMd	Municipality	BRMi	Dupax del Martes

'The town that is Binggo, it is a small town in the municipal district of Dupax del Martes.'

---

[6]These particles are fairly interchangeable, but *pay* is often used to show contrast or temporal relation, and if the RP is rather lengthy, *yan* is the preferred particle.

7.3 *Outside the focus domain*

(7.43) Din   istorya   ay   nay   et   na-pasamak   Ø
RMd   story   LK   DEM1V   PART   UNDs-happen   4I

sin   1982.
ORMd 1982
'This story, it happened in 1982.'

(7.44) Din   esa=y   anak=ko   abe=d   Tabay   yan
RMd   one=LK   child=1sII   also=LOC   Tabay   PART

k<in>at   di   aso   Ø.
UND.P-bit   BRMi   dog   3sI
'My other (lit. one…also) child at Tabay, a dog bit him.'

In a discourse, there are referents that may not be highly accessible to the hearer. They may not have been individuated from a given group, or may have gone unmentioned for long enough that specific re-activation or identification is needed for the hearer to process additional information. This is achieved by left-detachment of the RP, which may also be accompanied by the detaching marker *mo*, glossed as 'as for'.

Left-detachment is appropriate when a previously introduced participant first begins to function in the discourse, as in (7.45), or when the narrative reverts back to a previous participant, as in (7.46). Such a participant may begin to operate as the discourse topic, taking the most identifiable form (pronominal argument). In (7.45) the background has been set, introducing the family members. The left-detachment sets the mother as the discourse topic and makes her the referent of the pronouns. The story then goes on to detail her misadventures.

(7.45) Din   nay   ay   esa=y   ina,   man-gapo   di
RMd   DEM1V   LK   one=LK   mother   ACT-reason   RMi

beteng=na,   lay~layd-e(n)=na   ay   en   maki-sida.
drunk=3sII   CVC-enjoy-UND=3sII   LK   go   ASSOC-feast
'Now this particular mother, because of her drunkenness, she loved to go to feasts.'

Prior to the sentence in example (7.46), the story has been about a child working in the field; it now switches back to the mother at home. Once the left-detached phrase has made the mother the discourse topic, she becomes the Actor and referent of the pronouns.

(7.46) | Mo | din | si | nanang=na, | kambaw | iyat=na | en |
|---|---|---|---|---|---|---|
| as.for | RMd | PRM | mother=3sII | PART | say=3sII | QT |

man-sakit	din	toktok=na	ngem...
ACT-pain	RMd	head=3sII	but

'(Meanwhile) as for her mother, well, she said her head ached but....'

A second purpose for left-detachment is to differentiate one entity from others in a set, as contrasting information is given about each. For example, in (7.47) the discourse is about funding for a project, and this particular referent stands in isolation from the others who were participants in previous clauses. Example (7.48) was uttered in the context of assigning duties to various members of a set.

(7.47) | ngem | din | odom | ay | nan-kari | en | t<om>olong |
|---|---|---|---|---|---|---|
| but | RMd | other | LK | ACT.P-promise | QT | ACT-help |

yan	iwed	di	sobalit=da.
PART	NEGEXIS	RMi	repay=3pII

'but the others who had promised to help, there wasn't any payment from them.'

(7.48) | et | mo | si | sik?a | pay, | en=ka | man-oto. |
|---|---|---|---|---|---|---|
| and | as-for | PRM | 2sIII | PART | go=2sI | ACT-cook |

'...and as for you, you go cook.'

Example (7.49) further shows the individuation function of detached phrases from a longer section of a text of wedding advice. The detached phrases (in brackets in this example) are not necessarily the explicit topic of their clauses but serve as subtopics of the larger category introduced in the first clause.

7.3 *Outside the focus domain* 339

(7.49) *Man-lako=kayo abe si sin-asawa ay manok.*
ACT-buy=2pI PART ORMi UNIT-spouse LK chicken

[*Di silbi =n di manok,] mo wa=y*
RMi purpose BRMi chicken if EXIS=RMi

balang-en di anak si makan ya
drop-UND BRMi child ORMi food PART

wa=y mang-omong. [*Din kawwitan,] man-tan?o*
EXIS=RMi ANTI-peck RMd rooster ACT-crow

Ø *sin g<om>abis-a(n)=na.*
4I ORMd NOM-dawn<=4II

'Also buy a pair of chickens. The purpose of chickens, if there is food that a child drops, there is something to peck it up. The rooster, it will crow at (its) dawn.'

7.3.2 Detached Reference Phrases with equative clauses

The first RP in an equative clause can be detached to activate or contrast it with other entities in the broader context. The resumptive pronoun must be a free-standing pronoun III in the clause nucleus, as in (7.50). The speaker has been reporting on her various children, so the detachment serves to set the referent in contrast. The equative clause can only be interpreted as expressing completive, identificational focus. If the referent had contrastive focus, it could not simultaneously take discourse-level contrast by detachment.

(7.50) *Mo si Delia yan sisya di presidente*
as.for PRM Delia PART 3sIII RMi president

=n din pupils government=da.
=BRMd pupils government=3pII

'As for Delia, the president of their student government is she.'

Prior to the sentence in (7.51), the narrator has been describing five wartime aircraft, three of which dropped supplies for ground forces. In (7.51) he contrasts the function or identity of the two remaining aircraft.

(7.51) Mo   din dowa pay, daida di   guardia.
       as.for RM   two yet   3pIII RM   guard
       'As for the other two, the guards were they.'

The second RP in an equative clause, the RP in the argument position, can be left-detached to activate a participant role, which the nuclear RP then identifies, as in (7.52). The resumptive pronoun is the null (Ø) 4I, leaving the clause looking like two RPs separated by a pause. The intonational pause and the indefinite RM on the first RP are the clues that it is a left-detached narrow-focus structure.

(7.52) Di   nabay?an,   din   esa ay   anak   ya   din   si
       RMi left.behind   RMd   one LK   child and   RMd   PRM

       ina=na   Ø.
       mother=3sII   4I
       'The (ones who) were left, (they were) the one child and its mother.'(after death of the man)

When the argument (second) RP of an equative clause has an affixed-root nucleus, any entity in that non-focal RP can be left-detached as a contrastive topic, and a resumptive pronoun will indicate its role. As described above, this detachment indicates contrast within the larger context. Example (7.53) shows the ergative argument (bracketed) of the affixed nucleus detached to contrast with others in a list.

(7.53) Mo   si   Nard, owat pay   din   man-sin~sinit
       as.for PRM   Nard   only PART   RMd   ACT-CVC-offend

       di   am~amag-e(n)[=na].
       RMi   UND-CVC-do=3sII
       'As for Nard (a toddler), what he's doing is just bothersome things.'

7.4 Conclusion

Recursive left-detachment is possible, as in figure 7.5, where contextual participants are activated, and then their funerals (topical in the context of mentioning their simultaneous deaths) detached as topics in an equative clause.

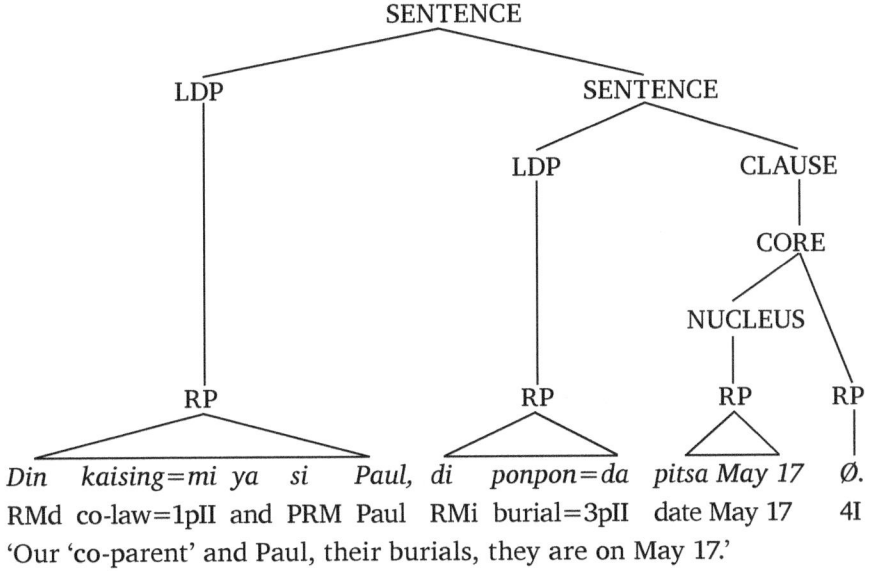

Din	kaising=mi	ya	si	Paul,	di	ponpon=da	pitsa May 17	Ø.
RMd	co-law=1pII	and	PRM	Paul	RMi	burial=3pII	date May 17	4I

'Our 'co-parent' and Paul, their burials, they are on May 17.'

Figure 7.5. Recursive left-detachment.

7.4 Conclusion

This chapter has explored the ways in which Kankanaey speakers control information flow to their hearers, introducing new information and acknowledging shared information. The following display, examples (7.54)–(7.63), traces the interaction of information structure and Kankanaey syntax through the various possible forms of one clause. The examples in the display illustrate the variety of options available to Kankanaey speakers for successful communication.

Comparative configurations of one clause with bracketed constituent positions:

Clause focus:

(7.54) [Wada]$_{PRED}$ [=y   dalit ay   nang-(g)amdot   sin
        EXIS   =RMi eel   LK   ANTI-grasp   ORMd

        book   Poltag.]$_{ARG}$
        hair   Poltag
        'There was an eel that grasped Poltag's hair.'

Predicate focus:

(7.55) [G<in>amdot]$_{PRED}$ [=na]$_{ARG}$ [din   book.]$_{ARG}$
        grasp-UND.P   =3sII   RMd   hair
        'He grasped the hair.'

Predicate focus with topical argument:

(7.56) [Din   book$_i$ yan]$_{LDP}$ [g<in>amdot]$_{PRED}$ [=na]$_{ARG}$ [Ø$_i$.]$_{ARG}$
        RMd   hair/eel   PART   grasp-UND.P   =3sII   4III
        'The hair$_i$, he grasped it$_i$.'

(7.57) [Din   dalit$_i$ yan]$_{LDP}$ [g<in>amdot]$_{PRED}$ [=na$_i$]$_{ARG}$ [Ø.]$_{ARG}$
        RMd   eel   PART   grasp-UND.P   =3sII   4III
        'The eel$_i$, he$_i$ grasped it.'

Predicate focus with topical possessor:

(7.58) [Si   Poltag$_i$ pay,]$_{LDP}$ [g<in>amdot]$_{PRED}$ [din   dalit]$_{ARG}$
        PRM   Poltag   PART   grasp-UND.P   BRMd   eel

        [din   book=na$_i$.]$_{ARG}$
        RMd   hair=3sII
        'As for Poltag$_i$, the eel grasped his$_i$ hair.'

7.4 Conclusion

Completive narrow-focus:

(7.59) [Din   book]$_{PRED}$ [di   g<in>amdot=na.]$_{ARG}$
       RMd   hair   RMi grasp-UND.P=3SII
       'The hair was what he grasped.' (e.g., answers 'What did he grasp?')

Contrastive narrow-focus:

(7.60) [Din   book]$_{PRED}$ [din   g<in>amdot=na.]$_{ARG}$
       RMd   hair   RMd grasp-UND.P=3sII
       'What he grasped was the hair.' (e.g., corrects 'He grasped the shirt')

Completive narrow-focus with topicalized argument RP:

(7.61) [Di   g<in>amdot=na,]$_{LDP}$ [din   book]$_{PRED}$ [Ø.]$_{ARG}$
       RMi grasp-UND.P=3sII   RMd   hair   4I
       'What he grasped, it was the hair.'

Left-detached predicate RP in completive narrow-focus clause:

(7.62) [Din   book,]$_{LDP}$ [sa]$_{PRED}$ [=y g<in>amdot=na.]$_{ARG}$
       RMd   hair   DEM2I RMi grasp-UND.P=3sII
       'The hair, that was what he grasped.'

Completive narrow-focus clause with co-referential RP in post-core slot:

(7.63) [Sa]$_{PRED}$ [=y g<in>amdot=na]$_{ARG}$ [din   book.]$_{POST\text{-}CORE}$
       DEM2I RMi grasp-UND.P=3sII   RMd   hair
       'That was what he grasped (,) the hair.'

8

Conclusion

This study has taken an in-depth look at the Kankanaey language. It began with its morphology, went through the basic clause and reference phrase structures, and then looked at more complex structures. It finished by analyzing information flow, noting how the structures at every level contribute to clear communication in Kankanaey. The phonology and morphophonology are described in appendix A.

The model that provided the framework for this analysis is Role and Reference Grammar. RRG has an inventory of structural positions that served this study very well. Especially helpful was the idea of a layered structure for both clauses and reference phrases with its concept of 'core' as a separate level. This concept provided insight for the analysis of core-level modification and core-level juncture, especially when considering complex clause constructions. A second very helpful part of the model was the interface between semantics and syntax as conceived in RRG. This was especially informative in understanding the Kankanaey predicate affixation system.

An important area for further Kankanaey studies is the topic of discourse analysis, suggested by the study of information structure. This area of further research awaits description.

Appendix A

Phonology and Morphophonology of Kankanaey

This description of Kankanaey (ISO: kne) phonology is based on the dialect of approximately 10,000 people living in Kibungan, Benguet Province. Data upon which this study is based was gathered in Kibungan between October 1974 and March 1975, under the auspices of SIL Philippines.

Kankanaey phonology, as presented here, describes the basic phonological components of the language as well as the complicated rules of interaction in the phonology and morphophonemics. A final section details the phonological repercussions of reduplication.

A.1 Basic phonology

A.1.1 Phonological word

The phonological word consists of one to eight syllables, and is generally coterminous with a grammatical word. Phonological and grammatical words differ when the phonological word consists of two or more grammatical words, as when enclitic pronouns form part of the phonological word, e.g., ʔa'sawa=m (wife=2s) 'your wife', pi'nadas=ko (tried=1s) 'I tried'.

In the phonological word one syllable bears primary stress, the other syllables a lesser degree of stress. Stress always falls on one of the last two syllables, beyond that it is unpredictable. In some cases its position is the minimal difference between a pair of words, exemplified in the following pairs.

'ʔotot	'rat'	ʔo'tot	'flatulence'
'saʔoŋ	'adze'	sa'ʔoŋ	'canine tooth'
man'balin	'to travel'	manba'lin	'to become'

The phonological constituents of stress tend to include prolongation of the syllable peak, increase in volume, and rise in pitch.

A.1.2 Syllables

A syllable consists of an obligatory onset and peak with an optional coda. The onset and coda are filled by consonants, and the peak is filled by a vowel. There are two syllable patterns, CV and CVC. Examples of CV syllables are *mo* 'if, when'; *ta* 'so that'; *di* 'that'. Examples of CVC syllables are *mon* 'but', *tan* 'because', *met* 'opposition particle'.

There is no restriction on the distribution of the two syllable types, CV and CVC, within the phonological word, e.g., *'bogat* 'rumen', *tip'kan* 'mosquito', *dit'ʔa* 'floor', *ka'li* 'language'.

Distribution of segments within the syllable has the following restrictions: in unaffixed roots, the glottal stop never occurs syllable-final; neither do the glides *j* and *w* when preceded by the vowels *i* and *o*, respectively.

A.1.3 Phonemes

A.1.3.1 Consonants

Table A1. Kankanaey consonants

	Bilabial	Alveolar	Palatal	Velar	Glottal
Plosive	p b	t d		k g	ʔ
Nasal	m	n		ŋ	
Fricative		s			
Approximant			j	w	
Lateral		l			

The following list shows examples of contrasting phonemes.

b	[tɨˈbɨk]	'sharp stick'	[ˈkoba]	'g-string'
p	[tɨˈpɨk]	'mouth'	[ˈkopa]	'backpack carrier'
d	[daˈlit]	'eel'	[digˈwaj]	'mangosteen'
t	[taˈliliŋ]	'chisel'	[tigˈwi]	'bird'
g	[ˈpɨwɨg]	'knee'	[ˈsogod]	'comb'
k	[ˈpɨwɨk]	'typhoon'	[ˈsokod]	'cane'
ʔ	[ˈʔagɨw]	'sun'	[laˈʔɨm]	'inside'
m	[ʔoˈdom]	'other'		
n	[ʔoˈdan]	'rain'		
ŋ	[ʔoˈdaŋ]	'lobster'		
s	[ˈsawa]	'unit of 10'		
l	[ˈlaja]	'ginger'		
w	[ˈʔagɨw]	'sun'	[ˈtawa]	'window'
j	[ˈʔatɨj]	'liver'	[ˈdaja]	'sky'

A.1.3.2 Vowels

The four vowels of Kankanaey are shown in figure A1.

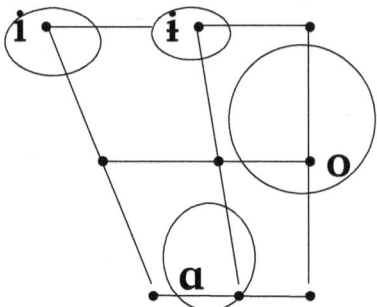

Figure A1. The vowels of Kankanaey.

The four vowels form a not-quite-symmetrical system; the back vowel has a wider range of pronunciation than the other vowels (see section 1.3.4). Vowels are distinguished from each other, as exemplified in the list that follows.

i	['sigid]	'broom'				
ɨ	['sigɨd]	'good'	[pak'dɨ]	'warning sign'	['ʔitɨk]	'lie'
a	['sagad]	'broom'	[pak'da]	'bridge'		
o	['sigod]	'original'	['ʔotɨk]	'brain'		

A.1.3.3 Interpretation of ambivalent segments and sequences

The close vocoids *i* and *o* are interpreted as their corresponding approximants *j* and *w* when they occur as syllable onset or coda, e.g., *ja'ʔod* 'back of knee', *wa'nis* 'g-string', *ʔi'wij* 'rattan'.

Ambivalent sequences of two vocoids in which both vocoids occur as syllable peaks (*oa, oi, ia, io, iɨ*) are interpreted as having an approximant as onset of the second syllable that corresponds with the preceding vocoid, thus *owa, owi, ija, ijo, ijɨ*, e.g., *bo'waja* 'crocodile', *ko'wako* 'pipe', *manto'wili* 'to

A.1 Basic phonology

look back', *ʔija'dojad* 'to rock in arms', *si'jam* 'nine', *nabi'jogan* 'dirty', *ma'sijɨk* 'to laugh'. This interpretation is corroborated by morphophonemic evidence indicating the presence of a semivowel. In some roots, an unstressed vowel is deleted when certain affixes are added, but the semivowel is retained, e.g., <in> + *ʔi'jat* becomes *in'jat*; *ka-* + *do'wa* becomes *kad'wa*.

Ambivalent consonant clusters and lengthened consonants are interpreted as sequences of two consonants, since they occur only word medially between two syllable peaks, forming the coda of one syllable and the onset of the next syllable, e.g., *ʔit'sa* 'tea', *ʔin'to* 'where', *tig'wi* 'species of bird', *kom'paj* 'sickle', *mankɨd'jat* 'to raise eyebrows', *kaw'witan* 'rooster'.

A.1.3.4 Phoneme variants

Stops are never aspirated; they are unreleased when they occur syllable final. The palatal approximant /j/ is phonetically rounded [ɥ] when it follows /o/ in the syllable coda position, e.g., *'laboj* ['labɑɥ] 'variety of moss', *taŋ'soj* [taŋ'sɑɥ] 'water cress'.

The close front vowel /i/ has two allophones, [i] and a slightly laxed [ɪ] preceding a velar nasal, word-final, or in a closed syllable. The open central vowel is most commonly realized as [ɜ], the more open variant only occurring in stressed open syllables. Examples include:

i	*pit'pitan* [pɪt'pitɜn]	'grasshopper'	*'giŋa* ['gɪŋɜ]	'snail'
	'sobil ['sobɪl]	'lips'	*la'bɪ* [lɜ'bɪ]	'night'
a	*'ʔawak* ['ʔawɜk]	'body'	*si'libam* [si'libɜm]	'be careful'

The close central vowel /ɨ/ exhibits slight variations: it tends to be slightly more open in closed syllables, and tends to move back when the coda is a velar stop.

The phoneme /o/ has two close variants, [u] and [ʊ] and one mid variant [o]. The [ʊ] variant occurs only in unstressed closed nonfinal syllables, except when contiguous to [ʔ] or [k], and in final syllables when the coda is [j] and the onset is not [ʔ]. The variants [u] and [o] fluctuate elsewhere with the restriction that [u] never occurs following [k] or at the end of a word. The following examples show the distribution.

motꞌjok [mʊtꞌjok]	'summit'	*ꞌlobok* [ꞌlobok]	'grave'
laꞌmot [lɜꞌmot]	'root'	*ʔogꞌsa* [ʔogꞌsɑ]	'deer'
donꞌtog [dʊnꞌtog]	'mountain'	*lokꞌto* [lokꞌto]	'yam'
laꞌboj [laꞌbʊɥ]	'variety of moss'	*ꞌiko* [ꞌiko]	'tail'
ʔoꞌgali [ʔoꞌgɑli] ~ [ʔuꞌgɑli]	'custom'		
ꞌlogan [ꞌlogɜn] ~ [ꞌlugɜn]	'ride'		

A.1.3.5 Distribution

The oral stops occur without restriction in both onset and coda slots of the syllable. [ʔ] occurs only in syllable onset. In word-medial consonant clusters, the oral consonants can occur in almost any combination with any of the consonants. The only cluster combinations that are not attested are *bp, pb, gŋ, jw* and *pw*. There are no consonant clusters word initially or finally.

Vowels occur only in the peak of the syllable, and may occur contiguous to any consonant. There are no vowel clusters.

A.1.4 Orthography

The orthography for Kankanaey makes several departures from the phonemic transcription in order to conform more closely to the orthography of the national language, Pilipino. This orthography was developed with community input and testing and is now widely used in the Kankanaey language community. It is based on the following correspondences between a phonemic transcription and conventional symbols.

/ɨ/ is represented by the symbol *e*. For example, *abe* 'also', *eweg* 'snake'.

/j/ is represented by the symbol *y*. For example, *motyok* 'summit', *laboy* 'moss'.

/ʔ/ is not written word initially and intervocallically. Word medially, contiguous to a preceding consonant, it is represented by a hyphen. The following words illustrate the representation of the glottal stop.

kaiw	'wood, tree'	*abe*	'also'
man-ani	'to harvest'	*nad-ep*	'extinguished'

/ŋ/ is represented by the digraph *ng*, thus *tangsoy* 'water cress', and *nadnge* 'heard'. Hyphen is used to distinguish the velar nasal from a sequence of *n* and *g*, thus *man-gen* 'to carry', but *mangan* 'to eat'.

It was noted in section 1.1 that stress is contrastive in some word pairs, and is not predictable. Nevertheless, it is omitted from the orthography for three reasons: (1) very few word pairs are distinguished by stress alone; (2) stress is not marked in Pilipino; and (3) in reading tests, the readers had no difficulty in placing stress properly even though it was not indicated in the written text. Consonant gemination influenced by secondary stress is not indicated orthographically.

A.2 Morphophonemics of Kankanaey

This section covers the interaction of phonology with morphological processes in Kankanaey. The Kankanaey lexicon is built with root morphemes, many of which allow extensive affixation. Prefixes, suffixes, infixes, and combinations thereof combine with root morphemes to create words that can function in the Kankanaey syntax. Affixation can create a wide range of phonological effects, which are covered in this section. Examples are given in phonemic (not orthographic) transcription.

A.2.1 Stress shift

Inherent root stress shifts one syllable to the right upon suffixation of roots whose canonical form is other than 'CV(C) or CVC'CV. With roots of canonical form CVC'CVC, such stress shift occurs only when the final vowel of the root is *i*. The first three examples below illustrate the syllable patterns in which stress shift does not occur. The remaining examples show a few of the wide range of syllable structures in which it does occur.

Root	+ -in or -an	Gloss[1]
ˈdan	ˈdanin	'walk'
pokˈʔi	pokˈʔiʔan	'push apart'
kibˈtot	kibˈtotin	'startle'
padˈsik	padsiˈkan	'insert in the ground'
ˈsilpo	silˈpoʔan	'connect'
kalosˈkos	kaloskoˈsin	'wash downhill'

A.2.2 Glottal epenthesis

Upon suffixation of vowel-final roots, a glottal stop is inserted between the final vowel of the root and the suffix vowel, blocking the formation of vowel clusters in conformity to syllable structure conditions. The following examples show glottal epenthesis with -*en* or -*an* suffixation.

pokˈʔa	pokˈʔaʔin	'remove from near surface'
komˈto	komˈtoʔan	'cut off top of bush'
saliwˈʔa	saliwʔaˈʔin	'divert'

A.2.3 Nasal assimilation

When a prefix ending in a velar nasal is affixed to a root with initial nonglottal stop or sibilant, the velar nasal assimilates in place of articulation to the initial consonant of the root. When the initial root consonant is a sonorant, the prefix nasal assimilates to the alveolar point of articulation. If the initial consonant of the root is glottal, no assimilation occurs.

The somewhat unusual assimilation of a velar nasal to the alveolar point of articulation preceding sonorants might lead to a question whether the final nasal of the prefix could be underlyingly alveolar, or whether the prefix has velar and alveolar allomorphs. A comparison with a nearby related language (Sagada Kankanay) reveals that the same velar nasal-final prefix does not assimilate with initial sonorant consonants in that language,

A.2 Morphophonemics of Kankanaey

suggesting that the analysis of the prefix as having an underlying velar nasal is correct. Although a separate rule could be posited applying only to sonorant-initial roots, Philippine languages with similar assimilation rules have most often been described as using a single process, and this approach is taken here.

A.2.4 Initial consonant deletion

The initial nonsonorant consonant of a root is deleted when preceded by a prefix with a final velar nasal or derived nonvelar nasal. This rule clearly operates on the output of the nasal assimilation rule above, as that rule is the only one which derives nonvelar nasals. It is necessary to specify that these nasals are derived, because initial consonants do not delete in roots prefixed by affixes *man-* or *pan-*, whose final nasal is underlyingly alveolar.

Table A2 displays derivations that exemplify the application of nasal assimilation and consonant deletion when *maŋ-* is prefixed to various roots.

Table A2. Examples of nasal assimilation and consonant deletion

Root	ʔobad	kan	bidkiŋ	sadoŋ	wanes	ŋalat
+maŋ-	maŋ ʔobad	maŋkan	maŋbidkiŋ	maŋsadoŋ	maŋwanes	maŋŋalat
Nasal assimilation	---	---	mambidkiŋ	mansadoŋ	manwanes	maŋŋalat
Consonant deletion	maŋobad	maŋan	mamidkiŋ	manadoŋ	---	---
	'untie'	'eat'	'pick up'	'dance'	'wear loincloth'	'converse'

A.2.5 Vowel syncope

The root-initial vowel, with infixed or prefixed CV'CV(C) roots in which no consonant cluster precedes the initial root vowel (V1),[1] syncopates

---

[1] According to this condition on consonant clusters, syncope occurs with VC-prefixes only in the case of *maŋ-* and then only after the initial consonant deletion role has applied. If it were to occur with other CVC- prefixes, an unallowable three-consonant cluster would result.

(deletes) as follows: close central vowels syncopate before any vowel; close noncentral vowels syncopate only before noncentral vowels.

Root-final vowels: with suffixed CV'CV(C) roots (and subsequent stress shift), the final vowel (V2) of the root syncopates as follows: close central vowels syncopate following any vowel, front vowels syncopate following front vowels, and back vowels syncopate following noncentral vowels. This rule could almost be stated as the mirror image of the root-initial-vowel syncope rule, except that a final close front vowel *i* does not syncopate when preceded by the close back vowel *o*.

Four derivations involving the roots *'pisit* and *pi'sit* are displayed as follows, demonstrating that stress is pivotal in the operation of vowel syncope.

Root		+*maŋ*-	+-*in*
		(V1 syncope)	(V2 syncope)
'pisit	'pick up between thumb and forefinger'	*ma'misit*	*pi'sitin*
pi'sit	'squash'	*mam'sit*	*pis'tin*

Examples in table A3 follow four types of affixation with various roots, and show the application of the vowel syncope rules.

Table A3. Examples of vowel syncope

Affixation Root	Prefixed (ma-, ʔi-)	Infixed (<om>,<in>)	Suffixed (-in, -an)	Combination (ka...an, <in>...an, paŋ...an, ma...an, pan...an)
kɨ'diŋ 'finish'	mak'diŋ	kom'diŋ	kɨd'ŋin	kakdi'ŋan
ʔi'das 'attain'	ʔid' ʔas	ʔom'das	ʔidda'san	ʔinda'san
ta'lik 'trust'	ʔitta'lik	tomma'lik	tal'kin	panal' kan
li'ŋib 'hide'	ʔilli'ŋib	lommi'ŋib	liŋ'ban	maliŋ'ban
to'pig 'throw'	it'pig	tom'pig	toppi'gin	panpi'gan
po'no 'fill'	map'no	pom'no	pon'ʔin	---

A.2.6 Vowel harmony

In the infix <om> (a verbal affix), the vowel of the affix harmonizes with a following close central vowel. This harmony is optional if syncope has created a CV(C) syllable to precede the stressed syllable. The following examples show vowel harmony applied to two <om>-affixed roots.

'ʔij+<om> → ʔi'mij 'go'
kɨ'diŋ +<om> → kom'diŋ ~kɨm'diŋ 'finish'

A.2.7 Gemination

Upon affixation (including reduplicative affixation), the initial consonant of the pre-stress syllable geminates if the stressed syllable is preceded by at least two open syllables.

$\emptyset \rightarrow C_X$ / #Y...VC_X___V'C...Z# where #Y...Z# is a word consisting of two or more morphemes.

asi'kaso + -in	→ asikka'soʔin	'take care of'
ta'lik + <om>	→ tomma'lik	'trust'
CV reduplication + 'sijik + -an	→ sissi'jikan	'amused by'

A.2.8 Glottal metathesis

Glottal stop metathesizes with a following nonglottal consonant. Such a sequence never occurs underlyingly, but is derived from the operation of the V1 syncope rule, as seen in the examples that follow.

	Root	ʔi'dip	ʔi'mis
Affixation	ma-	+ʔi'dip	ʔi- + ʔi'mis
V1 syncope		maʔ'dip	ʔiʔ'mis
Glottal metathesis		mad'ʔip	ʔim'ʔis
		'extinguished'	'use for bathing'

A.2.9 Morphophonemic rule interaction

Generally speaking, the ordering relationship between the preceding rules is fairly transparent, so a brief summary will suffice.

Stress assignment must precede gemination and syncope of V2, because both the latter rules are affected by stress movement. In the case of gemination, its interaction with stress shift varies, depending on the nature of the syllables preceding the stressed syllable. In a form such as ʔasi'kaso+-en, in which two open syllables precede the stressed syllable both before and after stress shift occurs, the two rules are neutral with respect to feeding and bleeding. Stress shift must precede, however, because the reverse order would result in an incorrect form *ʔassika'soʔen. With roots having a syllable structure similar to ʔali'goŋgoŋ, stress shift and gemination have a bleeding relationship, because the stress shift rule results in there being a closed syllable in the pre-stress position. Finally, in roots of the form konta'la, stress shift feeds gemination. Stress shift feeds syncope of V2, because the syncope rule operates only on unstressed vowels, and stress shift acts to destress the vowels in question.

Nasal assimilation is ordered before initial consonant deletion, because the nasal assimilation rule derives the [-back] nasal needed to meet the structural description of the consonant deletion rule.

Initial consonant deletion precedes V1 syncope and gemination, standing in a feeding relationship to both these rules. It reduces consonant clusters which would otherwise block V1 syncope, and creates the open syllable

A.3 Morphophonemics of reduplicated forms 359

needed for the operation of the gemination rule. Glottal epenthesis precedes V2 syncope. V1 syncope precedes V2 syncope and gemination, standing in a bleeding relationship to both these rules. V1 syncope precedes glottal metathesis, because it feeds it, creating the ʔC cluster upon which the metathesis rule operates. V2 syncope also bleeds gemination.

The derivations in table A4 show the ordered rules providing the correct output with affixed forms.

Table A4. Examples of the ordered application of rules

Underlying forms: →	maŋ-+di'ɲi → maŋdi'ɲi	di'ɲi+ \<om\> → domi'ɲi	ta'lik+-in → ta'likin	ma-+ta'lik → mata'lik	po'no+-in → po'noin
Ordered rules: ↓					
Assimilation	mandi'ɲi	--		--	--
C1 deletion	mani'ɲi	--		--	--
ʔ epenthesis	--	--		--	po'noʔin
Stress shift	--	--	tali'kin	--	pono'ʔin
V1 syncope	man'ɲi	--	--	--	--
V2 syncope	--	dom'ɲi	tal'kin	--	pon'ʔin
ʔ metathesis	--	--	--	--	--
Gemination	--	--	--	matta'lik	--
Vowel harmony	--	dim'ɲi ~dom'ɲi	--	--	--
	'hear'	'listen to me'	'trust'	'trustworthy'	'fill'

A.3 Morphophonemics of reduplicated forms

A.3.1 Kankanaey reduplicative affixes

Reduplication as affixation is discussed in chapters 2 and 4 of this volume. Beard (1998:48) defines reduplication as "a process which copies all or part of the phonological representation of a stem as an affix." McCarthy and Prince (1998:285) note that in reduplication "the prosodically fixed material stands as a kind of affix, copying segments of the base to which it is adjoined." Blust (2009:403) shows that much reduplication in Austronesian languages may be satisfactorily analyzed as suffixal foot reduplication (base plus reduplicant). In Kankanaey, reduplication is best analyzed as *pre-fixal* foot reduplication, repeating an initial part of a stem or word. This is clearly seen with CV reduplication as in the following examples.

man-to-tokdo   'to be seated'
man-la-lanib   'to be exuding oil'

Although many languages with productive partial reduplication will also make use of full reduplication (Moravscik 1978:328), this is not true of Kankanaey. The three Kankanaey reduplication patterns have the following syllable shapes: C_1V_1, $C_1V_1C_2$, and $C_1V_1C_2(C_3)V_2$. (The third pattern, CVC(C)V, indicates intensive aspect and will not figure in this analysis.) Reduplication is a type of affixation, serving an array of semantic and syntactic functions that have been noted in the main body of this work.

For example, CV reduplication pluralizes nouns and kin terms, adjectivalizes numerals, adjectivalizes verb roots prefixed with *ka-*, forms the superlative with adjectives affixed with *ka-...-an,* and with affixed verbs, indicates continuity in a state or activity already begun, sometimes implying repetition, plurality of subject, permanence, or irrevocability. CVC reduplication has a similar number of functions. This, coupled with the fact that many verb roots are semantically incompatible with one or more types of reduplication, creating a number of incomplete paradigms, makes it imperative to limit the present discussion to avoid becoming bogged down with irrelevant details.

This description is limited to CV and CVC reduplication of inflectionally affixed verbs, noting that evidence from other functions of reduplication has contributed no significant effect on the conclusions. Two types of CVC reduplication will be distinguished, one which indicates progressive action, and one which indicates intensive, comparative, potential, repeated, or customary action, depending on the semantic components inherent in the root. These two types of CVC reduplication will henceforth be designated CVC(1) and CVC(2), respectively.

A.3 Morphophonemics of reduplicated forms

A few forms exhibiting a third type of CVC reduplication are also considered, exemplified in table A5. In these forms, CVC reduplication is combined with the infixation of a glottal stop after the second consonant of the root to diminutivize a noun or to indicate that the action of a verb is done in pretense or play. As the glottal infix never occurs without accompanying CVC reduplication, this is considered a discontinuous affix.

Table A5. Paradigm with CVC + <?>

	Root	CVC + <?>	Gloss
1	wa'ʔo	wawwaʔ'ʔo	'only eight'
2	ka'pi	kapkap'ʔi	'few old coffee beans'
3	ka'bajo	man-kabkab'ʔajo	'pretend to ride horseback'
4	ʔak'lat	ʔakʔak'lat	'tattered old jacket'
5	kan'tina	man-kankan'tina	'play at keeping store'
6	ki'jap	kikkiʔ'ʔap	'toy chicks'
7	bo'waja	bobboʔ'ʔa ja	'toy crocodile'

A.3.2 Glottal metathesis or assimilation

With reduplicated forms, the glottal metathesis rule in 2.8 must be modified to account for cases where the glottal assimilates to rather than metathesizes with the following consonant. Compared with the examples given in 2.5 for the vowel syncope rules, it is apparent that the factor conditioning assimilation rather than metathesis is the presence of a root-medial glottal. The following two rules replace the metathesis rule given in section 2.8. Glottal stop metathesizes with the following consonant if the consonant following the next vowel is not a glottal. Glottal stop assimilates to the following consonant if the consonant following the next vowel is also a glottal stop.

The following examples provide evidence for the revised glottal metathesis and assimilation rules:

CVC + <ʔ>+waˈʔo	*wawʔaʔ''ʔo	wawwaʔˈʔo	'only eight'
CVC(1) +mantaˈʔoli	*mantatʔaʔoli	mantattaˈʔoli	'returning'
CVC(1) +ʔi ˈbaʔon	*ʔibabˈʔaʔon	ʔibabˈbaʔon	'taking a lunch'

A.3.3 Semivowel replacement

The sequences *ij* and *ow* never occur preceding syllable boundaries in unreduplicated forms, but CVC reduplication may create these sequences. A semivowel is replaced by glottal stop when it occurs syllable-final following its corresponding vowel (*i* with *j* and *o* with *w*) and when the initial consonant of the syllable does not belong to the progressive reduplication morpheme.

This rule specifies that semivowel replacement does not apply in syllables with initial glottal stop because of forms such as *ʔijʔiˈjogtan* (CVC(2) +ʔiˈjogtan) 'younger sibling', where the semivowel is retained. The rule also excludes CVC(1) reduplication while allowing for application to CVC(2) reduplication, as seen in the following pair.

mantowtoˈwili   'is turning the head'
mantotʔoˈwili   'repeatedly turns the head'

Semivowel replacement is ordered before the glottal metathesis or assimilation (see 3.2), because it stands in a feeding relationship to it, creating the *ʔC* cluster upon which the latter rule operates. This relationship is illustrated by the following derivation:

CVC+<ʔ>+ kiˈjap → kijkiˈjʔap
semivowel replacement → kiʔkiʔˈʔap
glottal assimilation → kikkiʔˈʔap 'toy chicks'

A.3.4 Consonant cluster simplification

A consonant is deleted when it occurs between consonants. The motivation for this rule is the syllable structure rules of Kankanaey with a maximal syllable template of CVC. This rule accounts for the absence of the infixed glottal following the second consonant of the root in forms such as the following example.

CVC<*ʔ*>+*kan'tina* 'store' → **mankankanʔ'tina* *mankankan'tina* 'to play store'

A.3.5 Postphonological reduplication

Generative linguists have maintained the distinction between syntax and phonology, regarding syntactic rules as providing the input to phonological rules and therefore necessarily preceding them. The role of morphological rules, including reduplication, is not so clear, but they have been regarded as applying to the output of syntactic rules in order to spell out the exact underlying representation upon which the phonological rules will operate.

There is evidence, however, that some morphological processes can apply following phonological rules. Aronoff (1976), for example, distinguishes reduplication rules from other word formation rules in that they can apply either before the phonology, before word-level rules, or after the phonology. He is careful to point out, however, that reduplication rules do not interact with the rules of the phonology in the same sense as ordinary phonological rules, but occur only at the clearly defined breaks in the phonology. Carrier (1979) also notes that in Tagalog some reduplicative affixation takes place after the application of phonological rules, interspersing morphology with phonology. French (1988) analyzed reduplication in Tagalog as an ordered step of the verb formation schema, ordering prefixation and suffixation first, followed by reduplication, followed by infixation.

In more recent years, Spencer (1998:130) speaks of reduplication as "a morphological operation which...has been fruitfully analyzed as a species of affixation of a prosodic template to a stem." This definition acknowledges that an affixed root (a stem) may be considered as the base to which the reduplication template applies. He notes that reduplication in Tagalog "can affect a root which has already been prefixed" (ibid.).

The reduplicated forms in Kankanaey considered thus far can all be accounted for under the theory that morphological processes such as reduplication precede all phonological rules. Reduplication in the previous examples has applied before phonological rules and created sequences to which the phonological rules then apply. Reduplication in most cases is applied independently of other affixes and copies from the initial segments of the root.[2]

A small ad hoc class of words, however, applies CVC(1) reduplication *after* other affixes and phonological rules have applied. The affixed word is taken as the base upon which the reduplicative affix is built. Table A6 gives several examples of postphonological CVC(1) reduplication contrasted with CVC(2) reduplication with the same root.

Table A6. Examples of postphonological CVC(1) reduplication

	CVC(1)	CVC(2)	
ma-+'sijik	masma'sijik	masis'ʔijik	'laugh, be amused'
ma-+kɨd'sɨ	makmakɨd'sɨ	makɨdkɨd'sɨ	'be naughty'
ma-+sa'dot	masmasa'dot	masadsa'dot	'be lazy, sad'
ma-+ʔi'gas (mag'ʔas)	magmag'ʔas	maʔigʔi'gas	'fall'
ma-+ʔi'dɨp (mad'ʔɨp)	madmad'ʔɨp	maʔidʔi'dɨp	'be extinguished'
man-+'dan	manman'dan		'walk'
sɨ'gip+<om> (sim'gip)	simsim'gip		'enter'

Inkelas and Zoll (2005:25) propose the Thesis of Morphological Targets, namely that "a reduplication construction calls for morphological constituents (affix, root, stem or word), not phonological constituents (mora, syllable, or foot)." They contrast that thesis with McCarthy and Prince's (1995) Base-Reduplicant Correspondence Theory that specifies the target of reduplication as phonological. As shown above, Kankanaey post-phonological reduplication shows the template to be clearly phonological, ignoring morphological boundaries.

---

[2] Inkelas and Zoll (2005:183) suggest an infixing analysis for reduplicative morphemes within an affixed word. The present study would define infixes as morphemes that are placed only inside a root, and reduplication as a prefix that usually is based on a root, but in these few cases covered in this section, is based on a stem.

Appendix B

Reference Phrase Markers, Pronouns, and Affixes

Reference Phrase Markers

	Single	Trans. Actor	Trans. Undergoer	Oblique
common nominals (definite)	*din/=n*	*(=n) din*	*din/=n*	*sin* *ed* (LOC)
Tag:	RMd	BRMd	RMd	ORMd
common nominals (indefinite)	*di/=y*	*(=n) di*	*di/=y*	*si/=s*
Tag:	RMi	BRMi	RMi	ORMi
personal names, kin (sing.)	*si/=s*	*(=n) Ø*	*si/=s*	*en*
Tag:	PRM	BPRM	PRM	OPRM
personal names, kin (plur.)	*da*	*(=n) da*	*da*	*en da*
Tag:	PRM.pl	BPRM.pl	PRM.pl	OPRM pl
DEM-related RM	*nan* (1) *san* (2)			*sinan/is-nan* (1) *issan* (2)
Tag:	DRM			ODRM

Demonstrative Pronouns

	Single/trans. Undergoer	Trans. Actor and possessor	Focal (may take PRM)	Oblique	Attributive
TAG:	I	II	III	IV	V
1	na	nina	naey	sina/isna/=s na	nay
2	sa	nisa	sana	issa/=s sa	sana
3	di	nidi	dooy	sidi/isdi/=s di	doy

Personal Pronouns

pronoun class	I	II	III	OPRM + III
	Single	Trans. Actor and possessor	Focal and trans. Undergoer	Oblique
Tripartite split:				
1s	=ak	=ko	(PRM +) sak?en	
2s	=ka	=mo	(PRM +) sik?a	
1p	=kami	=mi	PRM + dakami	en III
2p	=kayo	=yo	PRM + dakayo	
Accusative split:				
3p	=da	=da	PRM + daida	
1+2	=ta	=ta	PRM + daita	
1+2p	=tako	=tako	PRM + datako	
Ergative split:				
3s	Ø/sisya	=na	Ø/(PRM +) sisya	
4(impersonal)	Ø	=na	Ø	(use DEM)
Blended: 1sII.2sI	=naka	---		
Blended: 3sII.2sI	=daka			

Predicating Affixes

Voice	imperfective form	perfective form
Actor-indexing	man-	nan-
	maN-	naN-
	maka-	naka-
	maki-	naki-
	ka-	--
	<om>	<in(o)m>
Undergoer-indexing	ma-	na-
	i-	in-
	-en	<in>
	-an	<in>...-an
	i-...-an	in-...-an (ni- before l)

Nominalizing Affixes

Affix	Root or predicate type	Semantic denotation	Examples
akin-	nominal	refers to the possessor	*akinʔaso* 'dog's owner'
ka-	activity or state	refers to a companion	*katolong* 'helper' *katokdo* 'seat-mate' *kaising* 'co-in-law'
	attribute	refers to an attribute something has or to a related time span	*kabalom* 'your youth' *kapigsa* 'strength'
ka-CVC	state	refers to time span	*katagtago* 'lifetime'
ka-ma-	state	refers to time of the state	*kamatago* 'lifetime'
ka-...-an	activity	refers to the activity itself as an event	*kapolagan di bato* 'falling of rocks' *kaiologan* 'translation'
	state or attribute	refers to time, place, other related concepts or entities	*kaekan* 'what one sleeps on' *kaadʔadoan* 'majority, most' *kabigatan* 'next day' *kasapolan* 'what is needed'
kina-	attribute	refers to the attribute itself	*kinatetʔewa* 'truth'
maN-, mangi-	activity	refers to the Actor argument of transitive roots	*nangelay sin lokto* 'one who peeled the yams' *mangibaga* 'one who tells something'

Nominalizing affixes, cont.

-an	<om> and ma-affixed predicates	refers to the time or place of the state or activity	*emeyan* 'time/place of going' *gomabisana* 'time of becoming dawn' *naitapian* 'what something was added/joined to'
p-...-an (substitute p- for m-, n- is perfective)	predicates with man-, maN- or maki-	refers to the activity itself or the associated time or place of the activity	*panliplipilan* 'repair shop' *nakiasawaanmi* 'time we wed' *panobtobtoban* 'act of adding something to something' *nangananmi* 'place we ate'
pangi-...-an (nangi-...-an is perfective)	predicates with i-	refers to the location where the activity is directed	*pangidawtan* 'who to give it to' *pangitangadan* 'who to look up to' *nangipay-an da* 'where they put it'
pan-...-an	nominal	refers to something used to bring about the nominal	*pan-gapoan* 'used for reason/excuse' *panpolian* 'for purposes of breeding/descendants'
ipaN-	activity root	refers to something nonspecific used for the activity	*ipangan* 'food to eat with rice'
paN-, pan-	any	instrument used	*panlogan* 'use for riding a vehicle'

Appendix C

Sample Kankanaey Texts[1]

C.1 Narrative

(1) *Istolya =n di owat paki-lag~lagbo ay*
 story BRMi just ASSOC.NOM-PROG-wage LK

 iwed di pamosposana
 NEGEXIS RMi purpose.3sII

 'A story of just working a job without a purpose'

(2) *Kaman sin ed idi ay*
 like ORMd LOC then LK

 naki-lag~lagbo-ak si talak ay pala
 ASSOC.P.NOM-PROG-wage-<.1sII ORMi truck LK for

---

[1] Names and specific details have been changed in these texts to protect the authors' identities.

man-kal~kalga	*si*	*nateng*	*ed*	*Mountain*		
ACT-PROG-cargo	ORMi	vegetables	LOC	M		

Trail	*ya*	*man?i~i-ey*	*ed*	*Manila.*
T	and	ACT.Th-PROG-go	LOC	Manila

'(What I could tell about is) like back when I was working on a truck that loaded up vegetables on Mountain Trail (road) and took them to Manila.'

(3)   *Di*   *apo=k*   *Ibwo.*
       RMi   boss=1sII   (pseudonym)

'My boss was an Ibwo (ethnic group).'

(4)   *Na-tken*   *di*   *ogali*   *=n di*   *Ibwo.*
       ATT-different   RMi   custom   BRMi   (pseudonym)

'Ibwos' customs are strange.'

(5)   *Palalo=y*   *kina-iket*   *da.*
       excessive=RMi   NOM-stingy   3pII

'They have a lot of stinginess.'

(6)   *Di*   *ka-ad?ado-an*   *mo*   *man-biahi*   *kami*   *sin*   *sapyol*
       RMi   NOM-much<   if   ACT-trip   1pI   ORMd   driver

ko   *yan*   *at-atik*   *di*   *i-dawat*
1sII   PART   little   RMi   UNDt-give

da=s   *pala*   *kan-en*   *mi*   *sin*   *danan.*
3pII=ORMi   for   eat-UND   1pII   ORMd   path

'Generally when my driver and I made a run, what they gave us for food on the way was only a little bit.'

C.1 Narrative

(7) *Mo wada pay di ma-dadael sin amag di*
if EXIS PART RMi UNDs-destroy ORMd make BRMi

talak yan dakami di maka-ammo ay
truck PART 1pIII RMi ABIL-know LK

mang-amag sin talak.
ANTI-make ORMd truck

'Furthermore, when something broke on the truck, we were the ones responsible to fix the truck.'

(8) *Tan mo kanan mi en i-ey mi sin*
because if say.UND 1pII QT UNDt-go 1pII ORMd

pan-lip~lipil-an yan kanan din apo mi
NOM-PROG-repair< PART say.UND BRMd boss 1pII

ay man-seg~seg?ang en asi na i-dawt-an
LK ACT-PROG-pity QT then 3sII UNDd-give<

dakami si pala kan-en onno kaman
1pIII ORMi for eat-UND or like

pinaka-lagbo mi ay nan-lipil sin talak
NOM-wage 1pII LK ANTI.P-repair ORMd truck

yan kambaw=et et?etek na.
and EVID1=PART lie 3sII

'Because when we said that we would take it to a repair shop, our boss said pleadingly that he would give us something for our food or for like a wage for having fixed the truck, and then it turned out to be a lie.'

(9) *Idi*   *<inm>ey*   *onno*   *na-labas*   *di*   *tolo*   *ay*
when   ACTm.P-go   or   UNDs.P-pass   RMi   three   LK

tawen   *ko*   *ay*   *<inm>on~onod*   *si*   *talak,*
year   1sII   LK   ACTm.P-PROG-follow   ORMi   truck

ma-iwed   *di*   *kanan*   *din*   *apo=k*
UNDs-NEGEXIS   RMi   say.UND   BRMd   boss=1sII

en   *tap~tapi-ana*   *di*   *lagbo=k.*
QT   PROG-add-UNDl.3sII   RMi   wage=1sII

'When three years of my working on a truck had gone, or passed by, there was (still) no promise from my boss to add to my wage.'

(10) *Siyaet*   *di,*   *na-kaan*   *onno*   *na-abos*
thus=PART   DEM3I   UNDs.P-remove   or   UNDs.P-use.up

di   *anos*   *ko,*   *k<inm>aan=ak.*
RMi   patience   1sII   ACTm.P-remove=1sI

'That being the case, my patience went away or got used up, I quit.'

(11) *Tan*   *nemne~nemnem-ek,*   *owat=ak*   *anggoy*
because   INTS-think-UND.1sII   just=1sI   only

ma-kay,   *dowan*   *maga=y*
UNDs-old(male)   while   NEGEXIS=RMi

i-lag~lagbo-ak.
UNDd-PROG-wage<.1sII

'Because I was constantly thinking, I'm just only getting older while there is no one that I am earning wages for.'

C.1 Narrative   375

(12) S<inm>aa=ak=et   ed   bebbeey,   en=ak=et
     ACTm.P-go.home=1sI=PART   LOC   home   go=1sI=PART

     nan-ob~obla=s   payew   ya   nem?a.
     ACT.P-PROG-work=ORMi   field   and   garden
     'I just went back home, I went to just work in fields and gardens.'

(13) Idi   d<inem>teng   di   gasat   ko,   naki-asawa=ak
     when   ACTm.P-arrive   RMi   luck   1sII assoc.p-spouse=1sI

     si   ka-illi-an   mi.
     ORMi   NOM-town<   1pII
     'When I got lucky, I married with a (girl) from our town.'

(14) Inggana=d   nowani   es?esa   di   anak   ko
     until=LOC   now   two   RMi   child   1sII

     ay   ng<in>adan-an   mi=s   Cory.
     LK   P-name-UNDl   1pII=PRMI   C
     'As of now, I have just one child that we have named Cory.'

(15) Siya   anggoy   na=s   mabalin   ay
     thus   only   DEM1I=ORMi   possible   LK

     ma-istolya=k.
     UNDs-story=1sII
     'This is all I can tell a story about.'

C.2 Procedural

(1) *Iyat   di   binobodan   ay   ma-amag*
    method BRMi 'binobodan'   LK   UNDs-make
    'How Binobodan is made'

(2) *Di   mola   ay   am~amag-en   da=s   binobodan,*
    RMi   plant   LK   PROG-make-UND   3pII=ORMi   binobodan

    din   sanglay   ono   din   kanan   da   en
    RMd   sanglay   or   RMd   say.UND   3pII   QT

    kakkiw,   telay,   katimoro,   balongoy   ono   din
    kakkiw   telay   katimoro   balongoy   or   RMd

    kanan   da   en   cassava.
    say.UND   3pII   QT   cassava

    'The plants that they make into *binobodan*, these are the root crops or what they call *kakkiw, telay, katimoro, balongoy* or what they call *cassava*.'

(3) *Di   iyat   da   ay   mang-amag   isna,   kelay-an   da*
    RMi   way   3pII   LK   ANTI-make   DEM1IV   peel-UND1   3pII

    Ø   ono   okis-an   da   Ø   asi   da
    4I   or   strip-UND1   3pII   4I   then   3pII

    i-polkaw   Ø   sin   gambang.
    UNDt-boil.whole   4I   ORMd   pot

    'The way they make this, they peel them or strip the skins off them and then they boil them whole in the pot.'

C.2 *Procedural* 377

(4) Mo   na-oto   Ø   okat-en   da   Ø   sin
    if   UNDs.P-cook   4I   dish.out-UND   3pII 4I   ORMd

   segyap   *ono*   *ligao*   *mo*   *na-baew*   Ø
   flat.basket   or   winnower   if   UNDs.P-cooled   4I

   bobod-an   *da*   Ø   *ay*   *kaman*   *din*   *iyat*   *di*   *tapey.*
   yeast-UNDl   3pII   4I   LK   like   RMd   way   BRMi   wine

   'When it's cooked they spread them out on the woven tray or winnower; when it's cooled off they put yeast in it like the wine method.'

(5) *I-peey*   *da*   Ø   *sin*   *lagba*   *ay*   *na-ap?ap-an*
    UNDt-put   3pII   4I   ORMd   basket   LK   UNDs.P-cover<

   si   *tobo*   =n di   *balat.*
   ORMi   leaf   BRMi   banana

   'They put it in a basket that's covered in banana leaves.'

(6) *I-dolin*   *da*   Ø   *si*   *mga*   *tolo=y*   *agew*   *ono*
    UNDt-store   3pII   4I   ORMi   about   three=LK   day   or

   na-solok   *insigon*   *sin*   *ka-dalas*   *di*
   ATT-more   depending   ORMd   NOM-speed   BRMi

   sanglay   *ay*   *k<om>ompitay.*
   root.crop   LK   UND-soften

   'They store it for about three days or more depending on how quickly the roots get soft.'

C.3 Letter—Expository

(1) *July 4 Mangi-bil~bilang   ay   Allens,*
    July 4 ANTI.Th-PROG-count LK   Allens
    'July 4 Dear Allens, (lit. who are including)'

(2) *Kadat-dateng   mi=d   labi   en   da   Mayor ya*
    RECENT-arrive 1pII=LOC   night   OPRM   pl   Mayor and

   si   Patricia.
   PRM   Patricia
   'We just arrived last night, Mayor's group and Patricia and I.'

(3) *Tan   ey=ak   in-amag   papel   ko   sin*
    because go=1sI   UNDt.P-fix   paper   1sII ORMd

   resignation   ko   ta.say   ma-libri=ak   ay
   resignation   1sII   so.that   UNDs-free=1sI   LK

   komplito   ed   opisina   isonga
   completely   LOC   office   therefore

   na-po=ak   ed   gov.   office.
   UNDs.P-be.from=1sI   LOC   government   office
   'Because I went to fix my papers regarding my resignation so that I would be completely free from the office, therefore I came from the government offices.'

(4) *Din   <in>awat   ko   ay   <inm>ona   ay   solat,*
    RMd   UND.P-receive   1sII LK   ACTm.P-precede   LK   letter

C.3 *Letter—Expository* 379

July 6–7 di miting ed Baliling et sa=y
July 6–7 RMi meeting LOC Baliling and DEM2I=RMi

ammo-k ay ey-an tako.
know-UND.1sII LK NOM-go< 1+2p

'The first letter that I received, (it said that) July 6–7 was the meeting at Baliling and that's what I knew as our time to go.'

(5) *Adi=ak naka-sagana, mabalin mo ma-ag~agew*
NEG=1sI ABIL.P-ready possible if UNDs-PROG-day

ta dowan=ak man-sagana=s bado=k.
so.that while=1sI ACT-ready=ORMi clothes=1sII

'I was not able to get ready, it would be possible if it's later in the day so I have time to get my clothes ready.'

(6) *Ay mabalin ay <om>ali kayo ay mang-a en*
Q possible LK ACTm-come 2pI LK ANTI-get OPRM

sak?en sina sin alas 7:00 tapno
1sIII DEM1IV ORMd time 7 so.that

maka-pirmiso=ak pay en Mayor Caspian?
ABIL-permission=1sI PART OPRM Mayor Caspian

'Is it possible for you to come and get me here at 7:00 so I can (have time to) get permission from Mayor Caspian?'

(7) *Man-lobwat tako=s na=s 7:10.*
ACT-depart 1+2pI> DEM1IV=ORMi 7:10

'We (would) leave here at 7:10.'

(8) Man-seed=ak,   Manang   Angelina
    ACT-wait=1sI1 older.sister Angelina
    'I am waiting, (your) sister Angelina.'

C.4 Letter—Expository

(1) Dear   Allens, Hi! Komosta kayo amin issa?
    dear   Allens   hi   greeting 2pI   all   DEM2IV
    'Dear Allens, Hi! How are you all there?'

(2) Iso   na   abe=n   dakami sina.
    thus   4II also=OPRM   1pIII   DEM1IV
    'It's the same also with us here.'

(3) Kanak   mo   na-laka   ay   man-asi-il~ila
    say.UND.1sII   if   ATT-easy   LK   ACT-RECIP-PROG-see

    tako   kambaw   na-ligat   nan   ili
    1+2p   EVID1   ATT-difficult   DRM   country

    yo   ay   ed   USA.
    2pII   LK   LOC   USA
    'I expected (wrongly) that it would be easy to visit each other but come to find out this country of yours, the USA, is difficult.'

(4) Ma-litaw   ta   mo   iwed   di   mapa   si
    UNDs-lost   1+2   if   NEGEXIS   RMi   map   ORMi

    e~egen-an   baw   adi,   baken   kaman   ed
    DUR-hold-UND1   EVID1   PART   NEG   like   LOC

C.4 Letter—Expository 381

    Filipinas   Ø   *ta*   *ma-ila*   *di*   *ey-an.*
    Philippines   4I   so.that   UNDs-see   RMi   NOM-go<

'A person will really get lost if there's not a map to be holding, I find, not like in the Philippines where (you can) see where (you're) going.'

(5) *Isna*   *et*   *iwed*   *di*   *am~ammo-k*   *si*
    DEM1IV   PART   NEGEXIS   RMi   PROG-know-UND.1sII   RMi

    i-badang   *ko*   *sin*   *nay*   *beey*   *di*
    UNDt-help   1sII   ORMd   DEM1V   house   BRM

    anak   *ko*   *tan*   *pag*   *baw*   *electric*   *di*   *ma-osal,*
    child   1sII   because   all   EVID1   electric   RMi   UNDs-use

    para   *laba*   *yan*   *machine washer and dryer,*   *dishes*
    for   laundry   PART   machine washer and dryer   dishes

    yan   *machine,*   *det?a*   *yan*   *baken*   *lampaso*   *ay*
    PART   machine   floor   PART   NEG   husk   LK

    shampooer, baliwang di   *beey*   *sin*   *gabgab yan*   *lawnmower.*
    shampooer yard   BRMi house ORMd grass   PART lawnmower

'Here, I don't know how to help in this house of my son's because I find everything to be used is electric—for laundry a machine washer and dryer, for dishes a machine, for floors not a coconut-husk (but) a shampooer, outside of the house for the grass a lawnmower.'

(6) *En*   *ta*   *man-markit*   *yan*   *baken*   *ta=n*   *man-dad?an*
    go   1+2I   ACT-market   PART   NEG   1+2I=DISP   ACT-hike

    ay   *logan*   *isonga*   *kaman*   *baw*   *kosto=s*   *nan*
    LK   vehicle   therefore   like   EVID1   right>   ODRM1

kad?an	yo	mo	wada=y	am~ammo		et
location	2pII	if	EXIS=RMi	PROG- know.UND		PART

ma-tago	ta,	ay	siya.
UNDs-live	1+2I	Q	thus

'If you go shopping, you don't walk (but) vehicle therefore it's like this place of yours is just right, if you know things you'll live, isn't that right?'

(7)
Tan	mo	ed	Filipinas	pay	et	mo	wa=y
because	if	LOC	Philippines	PART	PART	if	EXIS=RMi

ey-an	et	lagdeng	na	din	siki	ay
NOM-go<	PART	nothing.else	4II	RMd	foot	LK

man-dan	mo	lako	abe	yan	na-ngina	Ø.
ACT-walk,	if	purchase	also	PART	ATT-expensive	4I

'Because in the Philippines, if there's somewhere to go to you have no choice but to walk, as for purchases, they are expensive.'

(8)
Siya	ngin	di	tan	baken	da=n	man-eset
thus	perhaps	DEM3I	because	NEG	3pI=DISP	ACT-do.well

ay	man-obla	din	ipogaw	ay	owat	din	beteng
LK	ACT-work	RMd	people	LK	only	RMd	drunkenness

da	di	ammo	da.
3pII	RMi	know.UND	3pII

'Maybe it's like that because the people don't work well, they only know how to get drunk.'

(9)
Kosto	sa	si	ngalat	ko=n	dakayo	ay
right	DEM2I	ORMi	chat	1sII=OPRM	2pIII	LK

   pang-annak-ek.
   NOM-child<.1sII
   'That's enough for my chat with you my niece and nephew.'

(10) *Your auntie, Clara*

C.5 Letter—Hortatory

(1) *Lay~layd-ek ay Leo, Leticia,*
   PROG-joy-UND.1sII LK Leo Leticia
   'Dear Leo (and) Leticia (lit. whom I love),'

(2) *Man-layad din poso=k si dakdake ay nang-awat*
   ACT-joy RMd heart=1sII ORMi large LK ANTI-receive

   sin solat yo.
   ORMd letter 2pII
   'My heart was extremely happy to receive your letter.'

(3) *Tan ammo-k ay i-bilang yo pay.laeng si*
   because know-UND.1sII LK UNDt-count 2pII still PRM

   sak?en ay ama ay pan-dawat-an si siged ay
   1sIII LK father LK NOM-receive< ORMi good LK

   balakad ta wada di pan-onod-an kayman si
   advice so.that EXIS RMi NOM-follow< EVID2 ORMi

   siged ay danan di iyat ay ma-tago.
   good LK path BRMi way LK UNDs-live
   'Because I know that you still consider me as a father from whom to receive good advice so that (as requested) there will be a good path to follow regarding how to live.'

(4) *Mayat din ogali yo.*
    good RMd custom 2pII
    'Your attitude (lit. custom, characteristic) is good.'

(5) *Leo, Leticia, mo na-awat-ak din solat si iwed*
    Leo, Leticia, if UNDs.P-receive<.1sII RMd letter ORMi NEGEXIS

    di kolang=na, es?esa di problema ay adi kayo
    RMi lack=3sII only.one RMi problem LK NEG 2pI

    man-asi-awat-an.
    NOM-RECIP-receive<
    'Leo, Leticia, if I understood the letter perfectly (lit. without any lack), there is just one problem that you are having a misunderstanding about.'

(6) *Din nanka-po-an yo, layd-en da amin din ka-sapol-an*
    RMd NOM-be.from< 2pII joy-UND 3pII all RMd NOM-need<

    yo si kasal.
    2pII ORMi wedding
    'Your family, they want (to provide) everything that you need for the wedding.'

(7) *Dakayo anggoy di kad?an din problima, man-gapo din*
    2pIII only RMi location BRMd problem ACT-reason RMd

    ogali ay pagano.
    custom LK pagan
    'The problem is only with you, because of the pagan customs.'

(8) *Ammo-k ay mo adi kayo layd-en din bonong ya*
    know-UND.1saII LK if NEG 2pII joy-UND RMd prayers and

C.5 Letter—Hortatory 385

>
> tayaw ay kanan   da, da am?a   yo   en   da
> dance LK say.UND 3pII pl male.relative 2pII OPRM pl
>
> in?a   yo   adi da=n   man-lay~layad ay
> female.relative 2pII NEG 3pI=DISP   ACT-PROG-joy   LK
>
> mang-il~ila   en   dakayo sin   kasal.
> ANTI-PROG-see   OPRM 2pIII ORMd   wedding
>
> 'I know that if you don't want the prayers and dancing as they call it, your relatives (lit. male and female older relatives) will not be happy seeing you at the wedding.'

(9) Man-golo   da din   man-bonong et   kalkallo ay lawa din
    ACT-disturb   pl RMd   ACT-pray   and   more   LK bad   RMd

    kasal   yo.
    wedding   2pII

    'The pagan priests will make a fuss and your wedding will be even worse.'

(10) Siya   na   di   i-baga=k   en   dakayo mo mabalin ay
     thus   DEM1I RMi   UNDt-say=1sII   OPRM 2pIII if possible LK

     pati-en   yo,   ta   pan-sigd-an   yo   ay   dowa.
     obey-UND   2pII so.that NOM-good<   2pII LK   two

     'What I say to you is this, if it's possible for you to obey it, so that you two are better off.'

(11) Anggan i-bolos   yo   ta   amag-en din   man-bonong
     even.if UNDt-release   2pII so.that do-UND RMd   ACT-pray

din   layd-ena   ta.say   man-lagsak da   iman   abe.
RMd joy-UND.4II so.that ACT-happy 3pI PART also

'Just allow the priests to do what they like so that they will be happy, too.'

(12) *Basta   baken dakayo di   mang-i-bonong ya   man-ayaw,*
provided NEG 2pIII RMi ANTI-Th-pray and ANTI-dance

mayat met.laeng.
good still

'So long as you aren't the ones to say the prayers and dance, it will be good just the same.'

(13) *Sa=y   onod-en   yo   pay   abe, din   kina-kristiano*
DEM2I=RMi follow-UND 2pII PART also RMd NOM-Christian

ay layd-en yo   ta   adi   kayo man-basol.
LK joy-UND 2pII so.that NEG 2pI ACT-sin

'What you follow for your part also, the Christianity that you want so that you don't sin.'

(14) *I-lol~lowalo=k   di   siged ay kasal   yo   ya   siged*
UNDt-PROG-pray=1sII RMi good LK wedding 2pII and good

ay biyag yo.
LK life 2pII

'I am praying for a nice wedding for you and a good life for you.'

(15) *Din   i-bil~bilang   yo   ay   ama, Ramon Ginso*
RMd UNDt-PROG-count 2pII LK father R G

'The one you are considering as a father, Ramon Ginso'

References

Adelaar, Alexander. 2005. The Austronesian languages of Asia and Madagascar: A historical perspective. In A. Adelaar and N. Himmelmann, 1–42.

Adelaar, Alexander, and N. Himmelman, eds. 2005. *The Austronesian languages of Asia and Madagascar.* London and New York: Routledge.

Allen, Janet L. 1978a. Kankanaey adjuncts. *Studies in Philippine Linguistics* 2(1):82–102.

Allen, Janet L. 1978b. The limiting glottal infix in Kankanaey. *Studies in Philippine Linguistics* 2(1):73–76.

Allen, Janet L. 1989. Definiteness as it affects participant introduction. *Philippine Journal of Linguistics* 20(1):29–43.

Allen, Janet L. 2006. The ubiquitous, anomalous -*om*- infix in Kankanaey. *Tenth International Conference on Austronesian Linguistics, 17–20 January 2006, Palawan, Philippines.* Linguistic Society of the Philippines and SIL International. Online: http://www.sil.org/asia/philippines/ical/papers.html.

Allen, Janet L. 2007. Focus and activation in Kankanaey. *Philippine Journal of Linguistics* 38:116–134.

Allen, Janet L. 2008. Between actor and undergoer: The -*om*- predicates in Kankanaey. *Studies in Philippine Languages and Cultures* 19:92–101.

Allen, Lawrence P. 1975. Distinctive features in Kankanaey. *Philippine Journal of Linguistics* 6(2):23–30.
Allen, Lawrence P. 1977. Reduplication and cyclical rule ordering in Kankanaey morphophonemics. *Studies in Philippine Linguistics* 1(2):280–295. Online: http://www.sil.org/asia/philippines/sipl/SIPL_1-2_280-295.pdf.
Allen, Lawrence P. 1980. The interaction of reduplication and phonology in Kankanaey. *Philippine Journal of Linguistics* 11(2):27–43.
Allen, Lawrence P. 2011. Kankanaey-English dictionary. Unpublished ms.
Allen, Lawrence P., ed. 1975. *Dad-at di nankakay ed nabbaon: Tales of the old folks from long ago.* Manila: Summer Institute of Linguistics, Philippines, Inc.
Anderson, Stephen R. 1993. Wackernagel's revenge: Clitics, morphology, and the syntax of second position. *Language* 69:68–98.
Anderson, Stephen R. 2008 [written 2002]. Second position clitics in Tagalog. In S. Inkelas and K. Hanson (eds.), *The nature of the word*, 549–566. Cambridge, Mass.: MIT Press.
Andrews, Avery. 2007. Relative clauses. In Shopen, 2nd ed., (1), 132–222.
Arce-Arenales, Manuel, Melissa Axelrod, and Barbara A. Fox. 1994. Active voice and middle diathesis: A cross-linguistic perspective. In B. Fox and P. Hopper, 1–22.
Arka, I. Wayan, and Malcolm Ross, eds. 2005. *The many faces of Austronesian voice systems: Some new empirical studies.* Pacific Linguistics 571. Canberra: Research School of Pacific and Asian Studies, The Australian National University.
Aronoff, Mark. 1976. Word formation in generative grammar. *Linguistic Inquiry Monographs I.* Cambridge, Mass.: MIT Press.
Atayoc, Jovita; Rafael Guerzon; and Julio Tatpiec. 1976a. *Pasigeden di biyag.* Manila: Summer Institute of Linguistics Philippines, Inc.
Atayoc, Jovita; Rafael Guerzon; and Julio Tatpiec. 1976b. *Man-esek ya manpakan.* Manila: Summer Institute of Linguistics Philippines, Inc.
Beard, Robert. 1998. Derivation. In Spencer and Zwicky, 44–65.
Blust, Robert. 1999. Subgrouping, circularity and extinction: Some issues in Austronesian comparative linguistics. In E. Zeitoun and P. J. K Li (eds.), *Selected papers from the Eighth International Conference on Austronesian Linguistics*, 31–94. Taipei: Academia Sinica.

Blust, Robert. 2009. *The Austronesian languages.* Canberra: Pacific Linguistics, Research School of Pacific and Asian Studies, Australian National University.
Brainard, Sherri, and Ena VanderMolen. 2006. Word order inverse in Obo Manobo. In Lawrence A. Reid, Hsiu-chuan Lioa, and Carl R. Galvex Rubino (eds.), *Current issues in Philippine linguistics and anthropology,* 364–418. Manila, Philippines: Linguistic Society of the Philippines and SIL Philippines. Online: http://www.sil.org/asia/philippines/ical/papers.html.
Brown, Lea. 2005. Nias. In A. Adelaar and N. Himmelmann, 562–589.
Burgess, Eunice. 1986. Focus and topic in Xavante. In J. Grimes, 27–41.
Bybee, Joan, John Haiman, and Sandra A. Thompson, eds. 1997. *Essays on language function and language type.* Amsterdam and Philadelphia: John Benjamins.
Carrier, Jill Louise. 1979. The interaction of morphological and phonological rules in Tagalog: A study in the relationship between rule components in grammar. Ph.D. dissertation. Cambridge, Mass.: MIT.
Chafe, Wallace. 1994. *Discourse, consciousness and time: The flow and displacement of conscious experience in speaking and writing.* Chicago: University of Chicago Press.
Clynes, Adrian. 2005. Belait. In A. Adelaar and N. Himmelman, 429–455.
Comrie, Bernard. 1989. *Language universals and linguistic typology.* Second edition. Chicago: The University of Chicago Press.
Cooreman, Ann. 1983. Topic continuity and the voicing system of an ergative language: Chamorro. In T. Givón (3), 425–489.
Cooreman, Ann. 1994. A functional typology of antipassives. In B. Fox and P. Hopper, 49–88.
Cooreman, Ann, Barbara Fox, and Talmy Givón. 1984. The discourse definition of ergativity. *Studies in Language* 8(1):1–34.
Crystal, David. 1997. *A dictionary of linguistics and phonetics.* Fourth edition. Oxford: Wiley-Blackwell.
Declerck, Renaat. 1988. *Studies on copular sentences, clefts and pseudoclefts.* Dordrecht: Foris.
Dik, Simon C. 1989. *The theory of functional grammar.* Part 1. Dordrecht: Foris.
Dik, Simon C., Maria E. Hoffmann, Jan R. deLong, Sie Ing Djiang, Harry Stromer and Lourens Devries. 1981. On the typology of focus phenomena. In Hoekstra et al., 41–74.

Dixon, R. M. W. 1994. *Ergativity*. Cambridge Studies in Linguistics. Cambridge University Press.

Dixon, R. M. W., and Alexandra Y Aikchenvald. 1997. A typology of argument-determined constructions. In J. Bybee et al., 71–113.

Dooley, Robert A., and Stephen H. Levinsohn. 2001. *Analyzing discourse: A manual of basic concepts*. Dallas: SIL International.

Dowty, David R. 1979. *Word meaning and Montague grammar*. Dordrecht: Reidel.

DuBois, John W. 1987. The discourse basis of ergativity. *Language* 63:805–855.

Everett, C. 2008. Constituent focus in Karitiâna. Unpublished ms. Online: [http://wings.buffalo.edu/linguistics/people/faculty/vanvalin/infostructure/Site/Papers.html].

Ewing, Michael C. 2005. Colloquial Indonesian. In A. Adelaar and N. Himmelmann, 227–258.

Fischer, Kerstin. 2006. Towards an understanding of the spectrum of approaches to discourse particles: Introduction to the volume. In K. Fischer (ed.), *Approaches to discourse particles,* 1–20. Oxford: Elsevier Ltd.

Foley, William A., and Robert D. Van Valin, Jr. 1984. *Functional syntax and universal grammar*. Cambridge Studies in Linguistics. Cambridge University Press.

Fox, Barbara A., and Paul J. Hopper, eds. 1994. *Voice: form and function*. Typological Studies in Language 27. Amsterdam and Philadelphia: John Benjamins.

French, Koleen M. 1988. *Insights into Tagalog: Reduplication, infixation, and stress from nonlinear phonology*. Publications in Linguistics 84. Dallas: Summer Institute of Linguistics and The University of Texas at Arlington.

Geladé, George P. 1993. *Ilokano-English dictionary*. Quezon City, Philippines: CICM Missionaries, Inc.

Givón, Talmy, ed. 1983a. *Topic continuity in discourse: A quantitative cross-language study*. 3 vols. Amsterdam and Philadelphia: John Benjamins.

Givón, Talmy. 1983b. Topic continuity in discourse: An introduction. In T. Givón (1), 1–42.

Givón, Talmy, ed. 1994a. *Voice and inversion*. Amsterdam and Philadelphia: John Benjamins.

Givón, Talmy. 1994b. The pragmatics of de-transitive voice: Functional and typological aspects of inversion. In T. Givon (ed.), 3–46.

Gonzalez, Andrew B., ed. 1973. *Parangal kay Cecilio Lopez. Essays in honor of Cecilio Lopez on his seventy-fifth birthday. Philippine Journal of Linguistics.* Special monograph issue no. 4. Quezon City: Linguistic Society of the Philippines.

Greenberg, J.H., Charles A. Ferguson and Edith A. Moravcsik, eds. 1978. *Universals of human language.* Volume 3: *Word structure.* Palo Alto: Stanford University Press.

Grimes, Joseph E., ed. 1986. *Sentence initial devices.* Dallas: SIL International and The University of Texas at Arlington.

Guerrero Valenzuela, Lilián, and Robert D. Van Valin, Jr. 2004. Yaqui and the analysis of primary object languages. *International Journal of American Linguistics* 70:290–319.

Halpern, Aaron L. 1998. Clitics. In A. Spencer and A. Zwicky, 101–122.

Haspelmath, Martin. 1999. On the cross-linguistic distribution of same-subject and different-subject complement clauses: Economic vs. iconic motivation. International Cognitive Linguistics Conference, Stockholm, 11 July 1999.

Haspelmath, Martin, Ekkehard König, Wulf Oesterreicher, and Wolfgang Raible, eds. 2001. *Language typology and language universals.* Berlin: Walter de Gruyter.

Heath, Jeffrey. 1979. Is Dyirbal ergative? *Linguistics* 17:401–463.

Himmelman, Nikolaus P. 1999. The lack of zero anaphora and incipient person marking in Tagalog. *Oceanic Linguistics* 38(2):231–269.

Himmelman, Nikolaus P. 2002. Voice in Western Austronesian: An update. In F. Wouk and M. Ross, 7–16.

Himmelman, Nikolaus P. 2005a. The Austronesian languages of Asia and Madagascar: Typological characteristics. In A. Adelaar and N. Himmelman, 110–181.

Himmelman, Nikolaus P. 2005b. Tagalog. In A. Adelaar and N. Himmelman, 350–376.

Hoekstra, Teun. 1988. Small clause results. *Lingua* 74:101–139.

Hoekstra, Teun, Harry van der Hulst, and Michael Moortgat, eds. 1981. *Perspectives on Functional Grammar.* Dordrecht: Foris.

Hohulin, Richard M., and E. Lou Hohulin. 2012. *A communicative grammar of Tuwali Ifugao.* Online: http://www.sil.org/asia/philippines/works-ifk.html.

Holisky, Dee A. 1981. On derived inceptives in Georgian. In Bernard Comrie (ed.), *Studies of the languages of the USSR*, 148–171. Edmonton: Linguistic Research.

Huang, Xuanfan, and Michael Tanangkingsing. 2005. Reference to motion events in six Western Austronesian languages: Toward a semantic typology. *Oceanic Linguistics* 44(2):307–340.

Husband, E. M. 2006. Stage-level/individual-level predicates and aspect. Talk given at the First Midwest Workshop on Semantics, Chicago, Ill.

Inkelas, Sharon and Cheryl Zoll. 2005. *Reduplication: Doubling in morphology.* Cambridge Studies in Linguistics 106. Cambridge: Cambridge University Press.

International Phonetic Association. 1999. *Handbook of the International Phonetic Association.* Cambridge: Cambridge University Press.

Johnson, Heidi Anna. 2000. *A grammar of San Miguel Chimalapa Zoque.* Austin: The University of Texas at Austin.

Jukes, Anthony. 2005. Makassar. In A. Adelaar and N. Himmelmann, 649–682.

Kaufman, Daniel. 2005. Aspects of pragmatic focus in Tagalog. In I. Arka and M. Ross, 175–196.

Keenan, Edward L. 1976. Towards a universal definition of 'subject'. In C. Li, 305–333.

Keenan, Edward L. 2009. Existential sentences in Tagalog: Commentary on the paper by Joseph Sabbagh. *Natural Language and Linguistic Theory* 27:721–735.

Kemmer, Suzanne. 1993. *The middle voice.* Amsterdam and Philadelphia: John Benjamins.

Kemmer, Suzanne. 1994. Middle voice, transitivity, and the elaboration of events. In B. Fox and P. Hopper, 179–230.

Kibungan Rural Health Unit. 1985. *Pasigeden di pamilya: Family health book in Kankanaey.* Manila: Summer Institute of Linguistics.

Klamer, Marian. 2005. Kambera. In A. Adelaar and N. Himmelman, 709–734.

Kroeger, Paul. 1993. *Phrase structure and grammatical relations in Tagalog.* Stanford, Calif.: CSLI Publications.

Kroeger, Paul. 2005. Kimaragang. In A. Adelaar and N. Himmelman, 397–428.

Kroeger, Paul. 2009. Malagasy clefts from a Western Malayo-Polynesian perspective: Commentary on the paper by Hans-Martin Gärtner. *Natural Language and Linguistic Theory* 27:817–838.

Lambrecht, Knud. 1994. *Information structure and sentence form*. Cambridge: Cambridge University Press.
Lambrecht, Knud. 2000. When subjects behave like objects. *Studies in Language* 24:611–682.
Larson, Mildred L. 1998. *Meaning-based translation: A guide to cross-language equivalence*. 2nd ed. Lanham, Maryland: University Press of America.
Latrouite, Anja. 2011. Voice and case in Tagalog. Ph.D. dissertation. Düsseldorf: Heinrich-Heine-Universität.
Lewis, M. Paul, ed. 2009. *Ethnologue: Languages of the world*. 16th ed. Dallas: SIL International. Maps from Online: http://www.ethnologue.com/show_map.asp?name=PH&seq=30.
Li, Charles N., ed. 1976. *Subject and topic*. New York: Academic Press.
Liao, Hsiu-chuan, and Carl R. Galvez Rubino, eds. 2005. *Current issues in Philippine linguistics and anthropology*. Manila: The Linguistic Society of the Philippines.
LinguaLinks.Online:http://www.sil.org/linguistics/GlossaryOfLinguisticTerms.
Longacre, Robert E. 1996. *The grammar of discourse*. Second edition. New York: Plenum Press.
Lowe, Ivan. 1986. Topicalization in Nambiquara. In J. Grimes, 131–147.
Matthews, Peter. 1997. *The Concise Oxford Dictionary of Linguistics*. Oxford: Oxford University Press.
McCarthy, John and Alan S. Prince. 1995. Faithfulness and reduplicative identity. In Jill Beckman, Laura Dickey, and Suzanne Urbanczyk (eds.), *University of Massachusetts Occasional Papers in Linguistics 18: Papers in Optimality Theory*. Amherst, Mass.: GLSA, 249–384.
McCarthy, John and Alan S. Prince. 1998. Prosodic morphology. In A. Spencer and A. Zwicky, 283–305.
Mercado, Raphael. 2004. Focus constructions and WH-questions in Tagalog: A unified analysis. *Toronto Working Papers in Linguistics* 23(1):95–118.
Palmer, Frank Robert. 2001. *Mood and modality*. Cambridge: Cambridge University Press.
Patterson III, Hugh. 2007. Distributed reduplication: A case study in Kankanaey, a language of the northern Philippines. Unpublished ms.
Pavey, Emma. 2004. The English IT-cleft construction: A Role and Reference Grammar analysis. D.Phil. dissertation. University of Sussex.

Pavey, Emma. 2008. Predication and reference in specificational sentences. In R. Van Valin, Jr., 305–317.

Payne, Thomas E. 1994. The pragmatics of voice in a Philippine language: Actor-focus and goal-focus in Cebuano narrative. In T. Givón, 317–364.

Payne, Thomas E. 1997. *Describing morphosyntax*. Cambridge: Cambridge University Press.

Perlmutter, David M. 1968. Deep and surface structure constraints in syntax. New York: Holt.

Perlmutter, David M.1970. The two verbs begin. In R. Jacobs and P. Rosenbaum (eds.), *Readings in English transformational grammar*, 107–119. Walthem, MA: Blaisdell.

Quakenbush, J. Stephen, and Edward Ruch. 2006. Pronoun ordering in Kalamianic. *Tenth International Conference on Austronesian Linguistics, 17–20 January 2006, Palawan, Philippines*. Linguistic Society of the Philippines and SIL International. Online: http://www.sil.org/asia/philippines/ical/papers.html.

Reid, Lawrence A. 1974. The Central Cordilleran subgroup of Philippine languages. *Oceanic Linguistics* 13(1–2):511–560.

Reid, Lawrence A. 2002. Determiners, nouns or what? Problems in the analysis of some commonly occurring forms in Philippine languages. *Oceanic Linguistics* 41(2):295–309.

Reid, Lawrence A., and Hsiu-chuan Liao. 2004. A brief syntactic typology of Philippine languages. *Language and Linguistics* 5(2):433–490.

Ross, John. 2002. Final words: Research themes in the history and typology of Western Austronesian languages. In F. Wouk and M. Ross, 451–474.

Ross, Malcolm. 2002. History and transitivity of Western Austronesian voice and voice-marking. In F. Wouk and M. Ross, 17–62.

Rothmayr, Antonia. 2009. *The structure of stative verbs*. Amsterdam and Philadelphia: John Benjamins.

Rubino, Carl. 2000. *Ilocano dictionary and grammar: Ilocano-English, English-Ilocano*. Honolulu: University of Hawaii Press.

Rubino, Carl. 2005. Iloko. In A. Adelaar and N. Himmelman, 326–349.

Sabbagh, Joseph. 2009. Existential sentences in Tagalog. *Natural Language and Linguistic Theory* 27:675–719.

Schachter, Paul. 1973. Constraints on clitic order in Tagalog. In A. Gonzalez, 214–231.

Schachter, Paul, and Fe T. Otanes. 1972. *Tagalog reference grammar*. Berkeley and Los Angeles: University of California Press.
Shopen, Timothy, ed. 1985. (2nd ed. 2007). *Language typology and syntactic description*. 3 vols. Cambridge: Cambridge University Press.
Siewierska, Anna. 2004. *Person*. Cambridge Textbooks in Linguistics. Cambridge: Cambridge University Press.
Silverstein, Michael. 1976. Hierarchy of features and ergativity. In R. M. W. Dixon (ed.), *Grammatical categories in Australian languages*, 112–171. Canberra: Australian Institute for Aboriginal Studies.
Silverstein, Michael. 1981. Case marking and the nature of language. *Australian Journal of Linguistics* 1:227–246.
Smith, Carlotta. 1997. *The parameter of aspect*. Second edition. Dordrecht: Reidel.
Spencer, Andrew. 1998. Morphophonological operations. In Spencer and Zwicky, 123–143.
Spencer, Andrew, and Arnold M. Zwicky, eds. 1998. *The handbook of morphology*. Oxford: Blackwell Publishers Ltd.
Spitz, Walter L. 2001. *Hiligaynon/Ilonggo*. Muenchen: Lincom Europa.
Talmy, Leonard. 1985. Lexicalization patterns: Semantic structure in lexical forms. In T. Shopen (3), 57–149.
Talmy, Leonard. 1991. Path to realization—via aspect and result. *BLS* 17:480–519.
Talmy, Leonard. 2000. *Toward a cognitive semantics*. Cambridge, Mass.: MIT Press.
Thompson, Sandra A., Robert E. Longacre, and Shin Ja J. Hwang. 2007. Adverbial clauses. In T. Shopen (2), 237–300.
Turner, Ingrid. 2006. Intonation and information structure in Wari'. M.A. Thesis. University of Manchester. Online: http://wings.buffalo.edu/linguistics/people/faculty/vanvalin/infostructure/Site/Papers.html].
Van Valin, Robert D., Jr. 1990. Semantic parameters of split intransitivity. *Language* 66:221–260.
Van Valin, Robert D., Jr., ed. 1993a. *Advances in role and reference grammar*. Amsterdam and Philadelphia: John Benjamins.
Van Valin, Robert D., Jr. 1993b. A synopsis of role and reference grammar. In R. Van Valin, 1–164.
Van Valin, Robert D., Jr. 2005. *Exploring the syntax-semantics interface*.

Cambridge: Cambridge University Press.

Van Valin, Robert D., Jr., ed. 2008. *Investigations of the syntax-semantics-pragmatics interface.* Amsterdam and Philadelphia: John Benjamins.

Van Valin, Robert D., Jr. 2010. Role and reference grammar as a framework for linguistic analysis. In Bernd Heine and Heiko Narrog (eds.), *The Oxford handbook of linguistic analysis*, 703–738. Oxford: Oxford University Press.

Van Valin, Robert D., Jr., and William A. Foley. 1980. Role and reference grammar. In E. A. Moravcsik and J. R. Wirth (eds.), *Current approaches to syntax*, 329–352. Syntax and Semantics 13. New York: Academic Press.

Van Valin, Robert D., Jr., and Randy J. LaPolla. 1997. *Syntax: Structure, meaning and function.* Cambridge: Cambridge University Press.

Vendler, Zeno. 1967. *Linguistics in philosophy.* Ithaca: Cornell University Press.

Wackernagel, Jacob. 1892. Über ein Gesetz der indogermanischen Wortstellung. *Indogermanische Forschungen* 1:333–436.

Wolff, John U. 2002. Final words: The development of the focus system. In F. Wouk and M. Ross, 437–450.

Woollams, Geoff. 2005. Karo Batak. In A. Adelaar and N. Himmelmann, 534–561.

Wouk, Fay, and Malcolm Ross, eds. 2002. *The history and typology of Western Austronesian voice systems.* Pacific Linguistics 518. Canberra: Research School of Pacific and Asian Studies, The Australian National University.

Zeitoun, Elizabeth. 2005. Tsou. In A. Adelaar and N. Himmelmann, 259–290.

Index

A

abilitative *see* potential predicates
accomplishment predicates 49
accusative pattern 259, 295
achievement predicates 49, 52
active accomplishment predicates 62–65
activity predicates 53–61
  experience predicates 58
  motion predicates 54
  perception predicates 58–59
  physical interactions 58
Actor 'focus' *see* privileged syntactic argument
adjectives *see* attributives
adverbial phrases 159–161
adverbs 164, 199
adversative *see* states, adversative

affected participants 46, 47, 49, 56, 58, 61, 65, 288, 311
affixes 34, 353
  circumfix 35
  infix 34
  nominalizing 126ff., 368–369
  predicating 41, 367
agency hierarchy *see* lexical content hierarchy
agentivity implications 263, 283, 311
Aktionsart classes 37
  tests 38–40
anaphor *siya see* pronouns
animacy hierarchy *see* lexical content hierarchy
antipassive *see* voice
  nominalized 300, 305
  structural 229, 251
applicative 74–75, 274–275, 291

aspect *see* operators, nuclear
associative predicates 76, 292
attribute states 42
attributive modifiers 109

B

Bontok 13

C

causative predicates 65–66
  overtly marked with *pa-* 65, 76–80, 276
class predicates 81
clause 139ff.
  constituent projection 139
clause linkage markers 210, 224, 226, 236–237, 247
cleft constructions 326, 329
clitic pronoun displacement *see* Wackernagel position
comitative 274
comparative aspect *see* operators, nuclear
complement clauses 239, 242–243
conditional 219
conjunctions *see* clause linkage markers
contact predicates *see* activity predicates, physical interactions
contrastive focus *see* focus, narrow
control constructions, *see* juncture, core
controllers and pivots 294
coordinate constructions 122, 124, 210, 228, 296

D

definiteness (*also see* indefinite) 113–114, 142, 310, 317
deictics 112, 157
deontic modals *see* operators, core
detached position
  left 213–222, 336–341
  right 222
determiner *see* reference-phrase marker
ditransitive *see* three-argument predicates

E

emphasis 207, 325, 332
epistemic modals *see* operators, clause
equative clauses 7, 132, 149, 302, 327
ergative pattern 6, 23, 141–143, 257, 266
evidentials *see* operators, clause
existential predicates 5, 8, 87–88, 128, 150, 321, 325
extraposition 236–239

F

focus (also *see* Philippine-type 'focus') 25, 315
  clause 320–321
  narrow 326–332
  predicate 321–326
focus domain 15, 316, 319, 326

Index 399

fronted position *see* pre-core slot *and* Wackernagel position

G

grammatical relations *see* privileged syntactic argument

I

Iloko 10–12, 285
immediacy, temporal 71
indefinite 114, 142, 147, 153
  nonreferential 151, 161, 312
instrument 274
intensive aspect *see* operators, nuclear
intransitive predicates *see* activity predicates *and* state predicates
split intransitivity 5

J

juncture
  clausal 210ff.
  core 228–236, 296, 298

L

lexical content hierarchy 284
locative predicates 87

M

macroroles 15, 256
  Actor assignment 256, 266

Undergoer assignment 257, 266, 269, 291
middle (self-affecting) 48, 55, 274, 290
modal (also *see* operators) 9
modifiers *see* operators
morphophonemics 3, 353–359
motion predicates *see* achievement predicates *and* activity predicates

N

negator 4, 8, 40
  core 188–189
  nuclear 183
  propositional 194
nominal marker *see* reference phrase marker
nominalized predicates 126ff., 299–300, 302
  (also *see* reference phrase, affixed roots in)
nonreferential *see* indefinite
non-verbal predicates 149, 241, 323
noun phrase, *see* reference phrase
noun *see* roots
numbers 118
numbers predicates 83–86

O

object 'focus' *see* privileged syntactic argument
oblique(s) 146, 160, 311
  differentiating arguments from peripheral phrases 159, 163, 260

operator projection 15
operators (also *see* negator) 23, 169–207
  clause
    epistemic modals 195
    evidentials 197, 317
    illocutionary force 196
  core
    deontic modals 185
    motivation 187
  in reference phrases 110–122
  nuclear
    aspects 171–180
    comparative 179
    directionals 184
    perfective aspect *see* perfective aspect
orthography 352

P

participant introduction 320–324
particles 4, 197, 204
passive *see* voice
peak-marking features 282, 325
perfective aspect 181
  imperfective as potential 73
  indicating achievements 51–52
peripheries
  clause 224, 156
  core 17, 140, 158
  in reference phrases 19, 106–110
  nuclear 16, 164
Philippine-type "focus" 257
  see predicate indexing and privileged syntactic argument

phonology 347–353
pivot *see* controllers and pivots
plural 116–118
possession predicates 81, 87
possessive 103
post-core slot 333–334, 343
potential predicates 68–71
  agentivity blocked in 68
  from imperfective passives 73
pre-core slot 165, 225
predicate affixes *see* predicate indexing
predicate indexing 261–294
prepositions 4, 156, 235
privileged syntactic argument
  in other constructions 294–306
  in the clause 255–294
process predicates 48
progressive aspect *see* operators, nuclear
pronouns 96–100, 143, 259, 306
  anaphor *siya* 134, 334
  demonstratives 96, 112, 157, 366
  focal 332
  impersonal 98–99, 134, 244, 247, 252
  personal 98, 366
  possessive 103
  with oblique argument 104
prosody 204, 317
PSA *see* privileged syntactic argument

Q

quantifiers 119
quotation 236–237

Index

R

reason 218
reciprocal 280
reduplication 3, 12, 33–34, 38, 117
  CV 171
  CVC 155, 173–180
  CVC(C)V 180
  interpretation with semelfactive 61
  morphophonemics of 359–363
  ordering 34
  postphonological 363
reference phrase 19, 91ff
  adjunct 110
  affixed roots in 126–132
  as clause nucleus *see* equative clause
  attributive modifiers 109
  coordinate 122, 124
  operators 110–122
  peripheries 19, 106–110
reference-phrase marker(s) 3, 9, 92, 365
  combinations 95
  common 92
  proper-name 94
reflexive 273, 277, 290, 293–294
relative clauses 108, 250–252, 305
roots 29
  action 32
  class 30, 100
  perception-stative 31
  physical 32, 50
  property 30
  stative 31

S

salience 272
semelfactive predicates 61
sentence articulations *see* focus
sentence type 244
state predicates 41–48
  adversative 48
  experience 43
  identificational 41
  individual 42
  perception 45
  result 46
  result-state 46
  stage-level 43, 46
  tests for 38, 40
stative modifiers 73
subject *see* privileged syntactic argument 7, 22

T

Tagalog 7–10, 57, 152, 308, 363
tense, *see* perfective aspect
thematic roles 267, 270–273
three-argument predicates 67
topic 215–216, 310, 315, 322, 324, 335
transitive predicates *see* voice, Undergoer
Tuwali Ifugao 13

U

Undergoer *see* macroroles

V

valency increasing 273
valency reducing 278, 281, 290
vocative 163, 217
voice (*also see* predicate
   indexing)
  Actor 53, 323
  antipassive 281–288, 313
  passive 72, 229, 288
  symmetrical 4
  Undergoer 267

W

Wackernagel position 6, 11, 167–168, 211
WH-question(s) 304, 326, 328

SIL International Publications
Additional Releases in the Publications in Linguistics Series

151. **Understanding biblical Hebrew verb forms: Distribution and function across genres,** by Robert E. Longacre and Andrew C. Bowling, 2014, ISBN 978-1-55671-278-4, *coming in 2014*
150. **Sudanese Arabic – English, English – Sudanese Arabic: A concise dictionary,** by Rianne Tamis and Janet L. Persson, 2013, 415 pp., ISBN: 978-1-55671-272-2
149 **A Grammar of Digo: A Bantu language of Kenya and Tanzania,** by Steve Nicolle. 213, 462 pp., ISBN: 978-1-55671-281-4
148. **A grammar of Bora with special attention to tone,** by Wesley Thiesin and David Wuber. 2012, 555 pp., ISBN 978-1-55671-301-9
147. **The Kifuliiru Language, Volume 2: A descriptive grammar,** by Roger Van Otterloo, 2011, 612 pp., ISBN 978-1-55671-270-8
146. **The Kifuliiru language, Volume 1: Phonology, tone, and morphological derivation,** by Karen Van Otterloo, 2011, 512 pp., ISBN 978-1-55671-261-6
145. **Language death in Mesmes,** by Michael B. Ahland, 2010, 155 pp., ISBN 978-1-55671-227-2
144. **The phonology of two central Chadic languages,** by Tony Smith and Richard Gravina, 2010, 267 pp., ISBN 978-155671-231-9
143. **A grammar of Akoose: A northwest Bantu language,** by Robert Hedinger, 2008, 318 pp., ISBN 978-1-55671-222-7
142. **Word order in Toposa: An aspect of multiple feature-checking,** by Helga Schröder, 2008, 213 pp., ISBN 978-1-55671-181-7
141. **Aspects of the morphology and phonology of Kɔnni,** by Michael C. Cahill, 2007, 537 pp., ISBN 978-1-55671-184-8

SIL International Publications
7500 W. Camp Wisdom Road
Dallas, TX 75236-5629

Voice: 972-708-7404
Fax: 972-708-7363
publications_intl@sil.org
www.ethnologue.com/bookstore.asp